# Architecting Enterprise Blockchain Solutions

# Architecting Enterprise Blockchain Solutions

Joseph Holbrook

SYBEX®
A Wiley Brand

Copyright © 2020 by John Wiley & Sons, Inc., Indianapolis, Indiana
Published simultaneously in Canada

ISBN: 978-1-119-55769-2
ISBN: 978-1-119-55768-5 (ebk)
ISBN: 978-1-119-55773-9 (ebk)

Manufactured in the United States of America

For general information on our other products and services please contact our Customer Care Department within the United States at (877) 762-2974, outside the United States at (317) 572-3993 or fax (317) 572-4002.

Wiley publishes in a variety of print and electronic formats and by print-on-demand. Some material included with standard print versions of this book may not be included in e-books or in print-on-demand. If this book refers to media such as a CD or DVD that is not included in the version you purchased, you may download this material at http://booksupport.wiley.com. For more information about Wiley products, visit www.wiley.com.

**Library of Congress Control Number:** 2019946697

V10017448_020820

This book is dedicated to my soulmate and wife, Frida, my daughter Destiny, and my stepson Lenin for their full support. The effort required for the writing and completion of this book, of course, took hours away from them.

# About the Author

**Joe Holbrook** has been in the IT field since 1993, when he was exposed to several HPUX systems onboard USS John F. Kennedy (CV-67). He migrated from the UNIX networking world to storage area networking (SAN) and then on to enterprise cloud/virtualization and blockchain architectures. He has worked for numerous companies such as HDS, 3PAR Data, Brocade, Dimension Data, EMC, Northrup Grumman, ViON, Ibasis.net, Chematch.com, SAIC, and Siemens Nixdorf.

Joe has also been a contract technical trainer for HPE (3PAR), Hitachi Data Systems, Training Associates, ITPrenuers, and Global Knowledge. Joe is a widely published course author on outlets such as LinkedIn Learning, Pearson Safari, INE.com, and Udemy.com. He has been a subject-matter expert for the CompTIA Cloud Essentials and Cloud Plus exams and a 2018 CompTIA Partner Conference trainer for the Cloud Plus TTT. Currently Joe is the owner of a new upstart learning platform called MyBlockChainExperts and is based in Jacksonville, Florida.

Joe is also a Certified Bitcoin Professional (CBP), Certified Blockchain Solutions Architect, and avid blockchain and cryptocurrency geek. He holds industry-leading certifications from Amazon Web Services, Google Cloud, Brocade, Hitachi Data Systems, EMC, VMware, CompTIA, HP 3PAR ASE, Cloud Credential Council, Palo Alto Networks, and numerous other organizations.

While in the Navy and attending Central Texas University, Joe received an AA degree. He received a certificate in total quality management from the United States International University (USIU) in San Diego. He received several certificates in information systems, project management, intranet development, and a BSIS from the University of Massachusetts – Lowell.

In 2007, Joe was given the AFCEA NOVA SuperNOVA award for outstanding event leadership and was awarded the Brocade Excellence Award in 2008 for his Brocade Services Partner Training Program implementation.

## About the Technical Editor

**Greg Phillips** is an On-prem Datacenter and Cloud Native Infrastructure Architect with over 25 years of experience in distributed systems and high-volume, multi-platform environments. Environments worked in have spanned DOD, commercial satellite communications, federal government, financial, manufacturing, transportation, service provider and other commercial sector Fortune 500 firms. He became interested in and got involved with BTC and Blockchain technology in 2013 and is currently researching Blockchain/DLT use cases for cable MSOs and content providers in the media/entertainment sector. Greg is also the founder of Think IT Data Solutions, which, in addition to providing managed IT services, provides technology-led business transformation solutions enabling fully autonomous closed-loop operations for enterprise clients.

## About the Technical Proofreader

Kunal Mittal is an Entrepreneur and serves on the Board of Advisors for multiple technology startups. Advisory roles and CTO positions is what he aspires to continue to do at early stage startups."?

He is a Technologist with over 20 years of experience working at all size companies, from early stage startups to large Enterprises. His strengths are product strategy, technology strategy, and execution. He enjoys building high performing teams to create a capacity to Innovate. Having lead small teams to large teams of more than 400 people, he has spearheaded all technology functions — Product Management, UX, Development, Quality Assurance, Architecture, Data Science, Cyber Security, Infrastructure, and Corporate IT.

Kunal's main experience lies in B2B SaaS, B2C, and building platforms that foster growth by creating a network effect between the business and customer.

Along with his wife, Neeta, he started a winery in Paso Robles (Central California) named LXV Wine, which won an award for being the 7th best Tasting Experience in the U.S. by *USA Today*.

He is also an instrument rated private pilot with 500+ hours of flying time under my belt.

# Acknowledgments

Thank you to Greg Phillips, Chief Technical Office (CTO) of ThinkIt Data Solutions for his advice and significant level of technical review of the subject matter. Greg has been my partner on numerous projects since our time together in the U.S. Navy.

Thank you to George Levy, Chief Learning Officer (CLO) at Blockchain Institute of Technology for his advice in making this book as focused as possible. George is a true blockchain visionary and is one of the top voices in the marketplace.

Thank you to Kenyon Brown, Pete Gaughan, John Sleeva, Athiyappan Lalith Kumar and Evelyn Wellborn.

# Contents at a Glance

# Contents

# Foreword

I remember how excited I was the moment I first found out that Joseph Holbrook would be writing a book called *Architecting Enterprise Blockchain Solutions*.

As chief learning officer at Blockchain Institute of Technology, I have had the opportunity to work and collaborate with Joseph over the years in numerous blockchain-related opportunities, and I have always found him to be a truly professional master on the topic, with an encyclopedia-like mind on the subject.

Beyond that, Joseph is a talented instructor who not only cares about delivering a clear message whenever he is sharing his knowledge, but he always focuses on delivering valuable lessons and actionable steps that will benefit the people he is sharing with.

So, knowing that Joseph was writing a book capturing his expertise on the important subject of architecting enterprise blockchain solutions, I knew I simply had to get it ASAP and add it to my library of indispensable blockchain-focused books.

During the time that I have known Joseph, I have learned much from our exchanges, and I highly admire his level of expertise. I have seen his passion and commitment to understanding and implementing enterprise-level blockchain technology projects, and as a result, he has become one of the most esteemed and authoritative expert contacts I reach out to when it comes to the topic of enterprise blockchain solutions. In this book, Joseph has delivered the most efficient and straightforward way to learn the knowledge he has acquired and applied in enterprise blockchain solutions.

As you work your way through the book, Joseph masterfully leads you through a clear learning path. He begins with an introduction into blockchain technologies, followed by an analysis of leading enterprise blockchains. He then continues by progressively adding new layers of knowledge, with each new chapter building on the previous one in a highly coherent and valuable guide. The book is filled with detailed explanations of many other essential topics including blockchain programming basics, as well as how blockchain can be implemented in multiple different enterprise-level scenarios. He has even included a truly visionary chapter with his insights on where the future of blockchain is headed.

Studying the book contents and seeing how Joseph has been able to both capture and explain what can otherwise be the complex topic of architecting enterprise blockchain solutions, I am pleased to say that this is by far the best guide I have found on the subject. It is an important and necessary book that should be required reading and on every bookshelf of anyone working with blockchain technology.

I feel honored to have the opportunity to write the foreword to this much-needed book by Joseph Holbrook, which I know will help open many eyes and minds around the world to all the opportunities that are possible through the use of blockchain in enterprise-level projects. Beyond that, I know it can help you gain the knowledge you will need to successfully implement blockchain in your own projects.

There is a wealth of knowledge about blockchain technology waiting for you in this book, and I wish you ever-growing success learning and applying it.

George Levy, CSBCP, CBP
Chief Learning Officer
Blockchain Institute of Technology
https://BlockchainInstitute.com
Miami, Florida, 2019

# Introduction

Blockchain is really about providing value to the enterprise. *Architecting Enterprise Blockchain Solutions* provides expert insight into enterprise blockchain understanding and direction for enterprise-focused sales team members who are both technical and nontechnical, systems engineers, application developers, and IT executives.

The competitive nature of the IT industry is constantly providing paths for enterprises, some of which provide value while others are mere distractions. This book aims to not only address the differences between technology distractions around blockchain technology but provide insight into why the technology is so disruptive to the "status quo" in sectors such as financial, government, and logistics.

As enterprise-focused professionals, we should focus on the opportunities that the disruptive nature of blockchain can provide, which entails everything from providing your customers direct value through cost savings to ensuring compliance requirements are met to providing a competitive edge. Blockchains are driving new business models in some sectors faster than others.

This book is not about cryptocurrency and how you can become rich trading Bitcoin or Dash. It is an enterprise-focused book on blockchain technology. The main focus of the book is on Hyperledger, R3 Corda, Quorum, Ripple, and Ethereum. A secondary focus is on other technologies that provide value as well such as off-chains like Blockstream or smaller blockchain projects such as Lisk or NEO that enterprises may be considering. The reality is that blockchains that utilize smart contracts provide immense value to enterprises when properly developed, planned, and implemented. I also cover in detail how to use IBM Blockchain Platform As A Service and AWS Blockchain Templates to drive your customers' proof of concepts (PoCs) and production blockchains.

The topics covered will give you a solid grasp of blockchain technology, blockchain architecture, blockchain development, blockchain security, blockchain roles, and demand for blockchain expertise.

So, whether you're just learning about what blockchain technology is or you're deeply involved in a PoC for a Fortune 500 enterprise, learning about the disruptive nature of blockchain technology is the right move. Not only should you understand that blockchain technology is so disruptive, but that it is also becoming a competitive necessity. Your competitors are likely investing in blockchain training, blockchain professional services practices, blockchain PoCs, and even enterprise implementations.

To wrap up, blockchain is the locomotive going down the tracks; either you can jump in front of the train or you can jump on board. The question is, do you want to be enabled in blockchain or do you prefer to let your competition deal with this? The competitive nature of business is clearly driving the hundreds of millions in investments in the blockchain space, and this is showing no sign of slowing down. Contrary to what the bank CEOs say, blockchain is here to stay and will continue to disrupt their businesses.

## Why You Should Read This Book

This book aims to be a reference as well as an inspiration to all IT-focused presales architects, systems engineers, application developers, sales executives, and even IT executives who are trying to understand where blockchain fits into their customer base or their own enterprises. Sales and professional services are all about driving revenue and providing value to your customer base. Blockchain technology, when correctly positioned, can do just this.

Application developers who are focused on understanding blockchain and how the technology translates into an application will benefit.

IT executives or IT analysts will certainly benefit from this book because they will understand how both the technical aspects and the business aspects of blockchain can drive value in their enterprises.

As a former presales engineer who has been involved in well over $100 million in documented transactions for companies such as 3PAR Data, HDS Federal (ViON), and Brocade Communications, I feel that this target group really needs to understand blockchain. The presales audience in some market segments needs to start envisioning where their customer base will go around this disruptive technology.

This book was written to address both the technical aspects of blockchain such as how to design and implement a blockchain and also the business aspects that the target audience needs to know such as competitive analysis, ROI/TCO, proof of concepts, and providing value to your customer base or your enterprise.

## How This Book Is Structured

*Architecting Enterprise Blockchain Solutions* comprises the following chapters:

**Chapter 1, "Introduction to Blockchain Technologies,"** covers the basics of blockchain technology, the history of the blockchain, how blockchain compares to other technology platforms, how blockchains are deployed for enterprises, blockchain transactions and how they provide value, and why the blockchain is considered revolutionary.

**Chapter 2, "Enterprise Blockchains: Hyperledger, R3 Corda, Quorum, and Ethereum,"** covers enterprise blockchain specifically focused on the technical merits of the enterprise blockchain. The chapter also covers where the blockchain fits into the enterprise. Areas of focus will be around defining enterprise blockchains on Hyperledger, R3 Corda, Quorum, and Ethereum.

**Chapter 3, "Architecting Your Enterprise Blockchain,"** covers the use cases, best practices, integration, scalability, and security design considerations for each of the enterprise blockchains. The chapter focuses on architecting Hyperledger Fabric, R3 Corda, Quorum, and Ethereum blockchains and will provide several use cases for deploying the enterprise blockchains.

**Chapter 4, "Understanding Enterprise Blockchain Consensus,"** covers the most common consensus methods used for blockchains and distributed ledgers. The main focus of the chapter will be on enterprise blockchains such in the Hyperledger Framework, R3 Corda, Quorum, and Ethereum. We will also compare and contrast Bitcoin and Ethereum. From a historical perspective, it is important to understand how Bitcoin works and how the Bitcoin blockchain compares to other blockchains such as enterprise blockchains.

**Chapter 5, "Enterprise Blockchain Sales and Solutions Engineering,"** details selling blockchain solutions and services and dives into requirements gathering and identifying use cases for enterprise blockchains. The chapter provides a technical presales perspective on how to sell blockchain services and hardware. The chapter also covers conceptual and nonconceptual patterns and will cover the routine presales tasks such as RFPs, demos, whiteboards, readiness assessments, and proof of concepts. We will also review requirements gathering and establishing a use case for blockchain solutions.

**Chapter 6, "Enterprise Blockchain Economics,"** covers the opportunities around blockchains and distributed ledgers. The chapter provides significant insight into opportunities around cost control, cost reduction, and cost avoidance around customer use cases. We will discuss how blockchains and distributed ledgers can facilitate impressive total cost of ownership (TCO) scenarios and clearly improve return on investment (ROI). The chapter is focused on the economics around blockchains.

**Chapter 7, "Deploying Your Blockchain on BaaS,"** covers blockchain as a service from both a use case and implementation perspective. The first part of the chapter gives an overview of blockchain as a service market and serves as a concise guide of current BaaS platforms with the main benefits, features, and use cases they provide. I will also discuss how to use a BaaS for proof of concepts and demos, especially for presales-focused readers. Then the second part of the chapter is more technical and covers actually deploying your blockchain on a BaaS. I will walk you through deploying a blockchain on Amazon Web Services (AWS) and IBM Cloud.

**Chapter 8, "Enterprise Blockchain Use Cases,"** covers some of the potential focus areas of enterprise blockchain use cases that can provide value to not only the organization but also their suppliers, customers, and partners. The chapter covers a few of the use cases that have been announced, along with their merits.

**Chapter 9, "Blockchain Governance, Risk, and Compliance ( GRC ), Privacy, and Legal Concerns.,"** covers the various challenges around blockchain adoption that focus on the compliance, regulatory, and legal concerns. The chapter covers the more common focus areas and also discusses how blockchains can be an ideal platform for regulatory compliance because they establish a historically trusted audit trail that can be verified in real time.

**Chapter 10, "Blockchain Development,"** covers an overview of blockchain development to provide insight into the most common development languages, the best practices, and the blockchains they are used for. The chapter will focus mainly on the aspects of development around Ethereum, Hyperledger, Corda, and Quorum blockchains as well as the development languages they are built on such as Solidity, Go, and Jotlin. There will be some examples provided and, of course, resources to learn more.

**Chapter 11, "Blockchain Security and Threat Landscape,"** covers many of the vulnerabilities that blockchain can be exposed to. The main focus will be on Ethereum, Corda, Hyperledger, and Quorum and their security concerns. The chapter will also cover what hashing is and how it plays into your blockchain security as well as what encryption and decryption are with blockchains. Compliance best practices, risk assessments, and risk mitigation will also be covered in detail. The chapter will also cover what vulnerabilities are common in blockchain technologies, discuss fundamental IT best practices as well as smart contracts security concerns, and discuss issues such as smart contract legal enforcement and legal prose. Lastly, the chapter covers critical concerns over Ethereum, Corda, Hyperledger, and Quorum that can affect aspects of the blockchains such as security, privacy, and availability.

**Chapter 12, "Blockchain Marketplace Outlook,"** covers the growing demand that has been clearly documented by the increased use cases around blockchain technologies and the consistent documented hiring around blockchain expertise. We also look at how blockchain got its start and where we are now in the technological evolution. We will review a timeline to gain an understanding of newer technologies that enhance the blockchain marketplace. I will also cover aspects of how a sales organization can get enabled and the determined demand for blockchain requirements. Lastly, I will cover the most common certification and training opportunities to help grow your business, knowledge base, and enablement toward blockchain.

## How to Contact the Author

If you have questions or comments or would like to find out more about Myblockchainexperts, please reach out to me on LinkedIn or feel free to email jholbrook2019@myblockchainexperts.net. I will respond promptly to all reasonable requests. Thank you.

# Chapter 1

# Introduction to Blockchain Technologies

Experts in the technology and financial sectors consider blockchain technology to be revolutionary. Your role, as a solutions engineer, presales engineer, or customer-facing sales professional, may require knowledge now or later in your career to sell blockchain technology solutions. It is important to appreciate how the blockchain is changing the world and how you as a value-added reseller (VAR)/vendor/integrator or even a professional services organization can participate in the blockchain revolution.

Blockchains are not a product to sell, such as a server, a data storage array, or a network router. Blockchains are an "exercise in development" to essentially sell, service, and develop a blockchain-focused solution. Blockchains can certainly "enable" products and, as a result it can be complex to design, implement, and develop applications around. Sometimes legacy applications can be extended, which is a common design and integration approach that enterprises should consider. Essentially, the technology behind blockchains is simple, but the implementation of the technology is where it gets more complex. The goal of this chapter is to break down blockchain technology for a sales-driven and technically focused audience.

This chapter discusses the technical merits of blockchain technology in a simple manner with direct correlations to how it applies to business.

**IN THIS CHAPTER, YOU WILL LEARN THE FOLLOWING ABOUT BLOCKCHAINS:**

- ◆ What a blockchain is and how to define a blockchain
- ◆ The history of the blockchain and why the history is important to appreciate
- ◆ How blockchains compare to other enterprise technology platforms
- ◆ What blockchain transactions are and how they provide value to the enterprise
- ◆ What a trustless model is compared to a trust model
- ◆ Why the blockchain is considered revolutionary
- ◆ Types of blockchain platforms

# What Is a Blockchain?

Blockchains have been considered a disruptive technology and the start of what has been coined the Web 3.0 generation. Web 3.0 is the next technology front on the Web where many devices are interconnected (called the Internet of Things) and used with technologies such as automated intelligence. Blockchain technology has significant ramifications for specific industries that perform fiduciary or intermediary duties, as you will see in this chapter and throughout the book.

To be clear, there is a significant amount of confusion about what a blockchain really is, how it creates value, and whether it's a cryptocurrency. Another issue is that blockchains have very different use cases; some blockchains are only for cryptocurrencies, while others do not support cryptocurrencies.

To gather an understanding of where blockchains and cryptocurrencies came from, it is important to appreciate Bitcoin. Bitcoin was the real start of blockchain technology because it provided a use case to society. Satoshi Nakamoto, in his 2008 paper "Bitcoin: A Peer-to-Peer Electronic Cash System," created the concept of the blockchain.

Nakamoto's paper had some detailed approaches to how a blockchain should be purposed for the benefit of the masses.

◆ A blockchain should be a trustless online payment network that is based on peer-to-peer (P2P) versions of electronic cash. The network is a robust node structure that works together with little coordination.

◆ A blockchain should alleviate the challenge of double spending, where funds can be over drafted and therefore lost to the wallet holder.

◆ A blockchain should implement the proof-of-work consensus method that rewards nodes that participate in the creation blocks (miners). The miners are rewarded for participation through an incentive approach, and this encourages miners to be honest.

◆ A blockchain should simplify privacy through a trustless system that removes intermediaries and introduces the use of anonymous public keys.

If you read Nakamoto's paper, you will likely conclude that enterprise permissioned blockchains were not in Nakamoto's vision at the time. The realization of this requirement for enterprises was not introduced for years after Bitcoin became mainstream.

One of the main challenges in the blockchain arena is how to answer the question, "What is a blockchain?" If you ask 10 different blockchain experts, you will get 10 different answers. The following are just some of the definitions of what a blockchain is:

◆ A blockchain is a shared distributed ledger or data structure.

◆ A blockchain is a distributed root of trust on a distributed ledger.

◆ A blockchain is a digital ledger in which transactions made in Bitcoin or another cryptocurrency are recorded chronologically and publicly.

◆ A blockchain is a type of distributed ledger for maintaining a permanent and tamper-proof record of transactional data.

◆ Blockchain technology is a distributed ledger technology that uses a distributed, decentralized, shared, and reciprocal ledger, and it may be public or private, permissioned or permissionless, and driven by tokenized crypto economics or token-less.

These definitions all focus on a ledger—specifically, a distributed ledger. A *ledger* is essentially a written or computerized record of all the transactions a business has completed. A *distributed ledger* is a database that is consensually shared and synchronized across networks that are spread across multiple sites, institutions, or geographies.

## My Approach to the Definition

My approach to defining blockchains is somewhat varied from what other blockchain evangelists will provide. I believe that there is no one correct definition that will provide a realistic understanding of the blockchain technology to everyone. This book presents several blockchain definitions that will vary depending on the audience.

My experience as a presales engineer has taught me that different types of audiences have different levels of interest in how technology works. For example, one would not expect an attorney to understand information technology the same way a SQL developer would. Both a developer and an attorney have different training and for that matter think differently.

My definitions of a blockchain focus on the following audiences:

◆ Technical, which includes IT staff, developers, and other technical stakeholders.

◆ Business, which are generally IT directors, C-level suite members, and stakeholders of financial organizations.

◆ Legal, which is generally any compliance-related auditors, corporate counsel, or other types of attorneys. Legal would entail government regulators, as well, depending on your use case.

### Technical Audience

Figure 1.1 shows the first definition of a blockchain from Nakamoto's 2008 paper. This is a definition for a technical audience. Satoshi's blockchain definition is somewhat complex, but in simple terms he is describing the chaining of blocks. From a historical and technical perspective, reviewing Nakamoto's definition should provide insight into his thinking when creating Bitcoin.

**FIGURE 1.1**

Nakamoto's original blockchain definition

```
1001    //
1002    // The block chain is a tree shaped structure starting with the
1003    // genesis block at the root, with each block potentially having multiple
1004    // candidates to be the next block.  pprev and pnext link a path through the
1005    // main/longest chain.  A blockindex may have multiple pprev pointing back
1006    // to it, but pnext will only point forward to the longest branch, or will
1007    // be null if the block is not part of the longest chain.
```

Comparing the definition in Figure 1.1 to the other widely used definitions listed earlier, you can see that there are significant differences. My point here is that if you're confused about what a blockchain is, you are not alone. The IT industry has done a poor job of providing a standard definition.

### Business Audience

During discussions with customers (or students), I like to compare blockchains to a hard-copy notebook. In essence, a blockchain is a ledger, albeit a distributed data structure and immutable ledger. When you write in a notebook, each entry will take up one line. Think of a blockchain as a notebook where entries will be written but cannot be erased.

Figure 1.2 compares the properties of a blockchain ledger to a notebook. Comparing a blockchain to a notebook is a simplistic approach, of course. A page is compared to a block on a blockchain and a page entry is actually a blockchain transaction. Blockchains are about implementing trust.

**FIGURE 1.2**
Comparing a blockchain
to a notebook

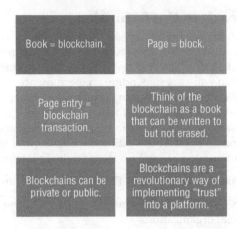

When it comes to comparing a blockchain to a notebook, it would be accurate to assume that not all blockchains are created equal, just as not all notebooks are created equal. For example, Ethereum handles transactions somewhat differently from Hyperledger Fabric when ordering and validation are considered. When you consider a notebook, you know that some notebooks have lines, some do not have lines, and perhaps some have boxes.

Blockchains are all about trust in the technology and removing third parties or intermediaries. A blockchain is a globally shared data structure, with a transactional backend database that is cryptographically secure. Everyone can read entries in the database just by participating in the network. If you want to change something in the database, you have to create a so-called *transaction*, which has to be accepted by all the others in the blockchain. The word *transaction* implies that the change you want to make (assume you want to change two values at the same time) is either not done at all or completely applied.

Blockchains are not built from any new transformative technology but are built from a unique syncing of three existing technologies: peer-to-peer networks, cryptography, and programs (known as *smart contracts* in the world of blockchains).

Another factor to consider is the cost. Even the cost of implementing these technologies is near zero when you consider there are numerous open source projects available. Blockchains are not complex technology when viewed holistically, but the complexity can be introduced when integrating these systems into the enterprise.

Let's compare Bitcoin to a blockchain and understand how these terms come together. Bitcoin is an unregulated digital currency that uses the blockchain technology as its transaction ledger. A blockchain is the platform for most cryptocurrencies and is the "enabler" for Bitcoin; Bitcoin is the application (cryptocurrency) that is being "enabled." Think of it like the blockchain is the train track, and Bitcoin is the train. Or, the blockchain is the telephone network, and Bitcoin is the phone.

At a high level, Bitcoin transactions work as follows. A sender wants to transfer funds to a recipient. The transaction is represented online as a block. The block is broadcast to every network participant. The network participants review the block, and if approved, it is added to the blockchain. Finally, the money moves from the sender to the recipient.

## Legal Audience

Lawmakers have even gotten into the arena of defining the term *blockchain*. A pair of U.S. representatives, California Democrat Doris Matsui and Kentucky Republican Brett Guthrie, introduced H.R. 6913, "Blockchain Promotion Act of 2018," to bring stakeholders together to develop a common definition of *blockchain*. The bill also recommends opportunities to promote new innovations. See https://www.congress.gov/bill/115th-congress/house-bill/6913.

In addition, the State of California recently defined what a blockchain and smart contract are. See http://leginfo.legislature.ca.gov/faces/billTextClient.xhtml?bill_id=201720180AB2658.

## Three Definitions of Blockchain

The blockchain technology has clearly been transformational in the financial, logistics, and government sectors. The following definitions are aligned to the specific audiences of technical, business, and legal that I'll be mentioning throughout this book:

- **Technical definition**—A globally shared and secured data structure that maintains a transactional backend database that is immutable.

- **Business definition**—A business network that is used between peers to exchange value. Value can be currencies, tracking information, or anything that interested parties require to be maintained on the blockchain ledger.

- **Legal definition**—A corruption-resistant string of ledger entries shared over a network by multiple parties not requiring a centralized intermediary to present and validate transactions.

As a customer-facing professional, you must define the right blockchain jargon to the right audience. Not everyone is going to be technical nor is everyone just concerned about the business aspects. When you're discussing blockchain with your customers, try to appreciate the role that they are in and cater the definition to them. This will likely facilitate understanding around the blockchain technology.

# History of Blockchains

As previously mentioned, the first known blockchain solution was Bitcoin. Bitcoin's main innovation was bringing cryptocurrency to the world. *Cryptocurrency* allows people to transfer value without the centralized high costs and improves on the slow transfer times and other challenges associated with legacy banking systems, such as SWIFT. SWIFT is a proprietary global financial network for its membership of banking institutions.

Bitcoin was essentially an experiment that started a march toward a decentralized payment approach that left banks out of the transaction. Bitcoin was devised during the great financial recession of 2007 and 2008. Removing the banks provides benefits such as decentralization, faster transfer, and lower risk because one controller is not performing payment processing centrally. Decentralization, P2P, and cryptography are at the core of Bitcoin's success around the world. In addition, its effects will certainly change the payment and remittance market for the better by lowering remittance costs for consumers.

Besides bringing cryptocurrency to the masses, Bitcoin's second innovation was the platform it runs on, which is the blockchain or distributed ledger. For enterprises, the blockchain disruption will take place because it provides one or more capabilities around compliance, cost efficiencies, or even transparent transactions for the customer base. The benefits for the enterprise in some industry verticals could be multifold such as what we are witnessing in the logistics sector around blockchain acceptance. I believe blockchain is the next great technology that will enable more financial engineering for companies just as cloud computing or offshoring has historically.

Cloud computing is a centralized form of data center management that is totally dependent on cloud providers performing accordingly. Trust is clearly expected for this relationship to work around data security, availability, and support. In Chapter 7, "Blockchain as a Service," I discuss more about cloud computing and how to deploy a blockchain on various providers.

Cloud computing has significant benefits to the user and has leveled the playing field between large Fortune 100 companies and small startups. Smaller companies can utilize cloud services at the same cost that a large company can. The cloud has also allowed companies to reduce overhead, reduce investments in infrastructure, and indirectly increase executive compensation along with corporate earnings.

In fact, a company's most important asset is sometimes not its employees but rather its data. Therefore, if companies are going to let another company control access to their data to save money, then those cloud companies, in my experience, will get into blockchain because of the ability to utilize a consortium and share costs. Blockchain as a service (BaaS) has already made significant headlines and has major backing by all the major cloud providers. The business model for many organizations follows the monetization of the collection, mining, and distribution of data. It's really all about the data and creating revenue from that data at the lowest cost historically.

This business model could also be enhanced through the use of consortiums. *Consortiums* are agreements that are made between organizations to work together and collaborate. Consortiums are communities of people or organizations with the same use case for a service.

Generally, these consortiums provide some benefits such as increased cooperation, standardization, integration ease, and even financial efficiency.

The consortium approach that is currently used in some of the most successful blockchain implementations can provide significant ROI, TCO, and other financial benefits to the member companies. If your customer has, for example, numerous points of overhead, then consider talking about blockchain use cases that they can relate to. Customers who have intermediaries such as transfer agents, customs inspectors, attorneys, and accountants are all spectacular potential targets for blockchain technology. In Chapter 6, "Enterprise Blockchain Economics," I cover the many benefits of blockchain economics such as consortiums.

The reality is that companies that have been immensely successful are investing millions and even hundreds of millions into blockchain technology. They are not doing it for "goodwill" but as a means of survival. It's all about the changing business environment, which is becoming globally centralized as a result of economics.

The list of companies that are investing in blockchain technology is a "who's who" of the Fortune 500, and I would not bet against them based on my experience. They see potential in the technology from several angles such as security, privacy, financial, and even legal requirements.

**NOTE**   "I think this is the beginning of the point where now these technologies are becoming mainstream enough, people understand it enough, that they can begin to deploy it. I expect this to grow pretty rapidly in the next couple of years." —Mark Russinovich, CTO MS Azure (`https://www.investors.com/news/blockchain-mainstream-industry-applications-microsoft-azure-cto/`)

Historically, some consistent factors of blockchains that have had a major impact on the enterprise acceptance of blockchain technology are as follows:

◆ Autonomous innovations such as smart contracts and decentralized applications (dapps) have contributed to the impact that enterprises can have through the efficiencies that can be attained.

◆ Cost-effective solutions have reduced intermediary costs or overhead costs such as reducing the number of intermediaries or all intermediaries for an enterprise.

◆ Transactions costs for payment remittance, such as on interbank transfers or settlements, have greatly affected profitability in companies, especially in the financial sector.

◆ Providing transparency in supply chains has enabled consumers to understand the sourcing of their buying choices and the chain of custody from source to market.

◆ Permissioned blockchains can scale and provide enterprise-level security.

◆ Perhaps the most important innovation is the smart contract. A *smart contract* is essentially computer code that executes a specific task and when properly developed as part of a distributed application can provide significant efficiencies, compliance, and performance. (During the course of the book, I will discuss smart contracts from both a business perspective and a technical perspective.)

It is important to understand how a technology has evolved, how it has changed over time and in structure, or how it provides value to organizations. I will now give you an idea of how blockchain really got started from an even older historical perspective.

The Byzantine Generals Problem (BGP) is considered a classic problem of computing. To explain the military metaphor, BGP can occur when a number of generals (from the same army or even allies) have surrounded a walled castle or a city on all its sides. The balance of power is such that all generals must attack at the same time in order to take the city.

In computer science, this is referred to as a *distributed node network*. It is critical to understand how a centralized system compares to a decentralized system to understand why Bitcoin came about. For example, what happens when a distributed system gets out of sync? How does the system handle an out-of-sync status?

In a centralized network, there is one central authority or server. The other participating nodes on the network act like clients or entities that accept messages and perform tasks.

In a decentralized network, there can be multiple servers that receive messages from one centralized server. The individual nodes are connected to the secondary servers. In another form of a decentralized network, all servers are of "equal" responsibility in the network, with no centralized server or master/slave relationship. In many cases, a decentralized network is considered a subset of a distributed network in many cases.

In distributed systems, there is no server with a centralized authority. Each node on the network is connected to every other node and has the same authority and processing capacity, which is shared. This is similar to a blockchain.

Figure 1.3 compares centralized systems, decentralized systems, and distributed systems with highlighted node connections.

**FIGURE 1.3**
Comparing networked systems

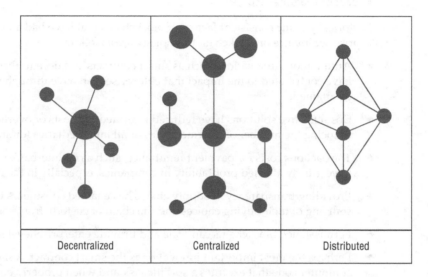

| Decentralized | Centralized | Distributed |

Blockchains by definition are not centralized systems, although some blockchains have centralized properties over decentralized or distributed properties. In Nakamoto's 2008 paper detailing Bitcoin, he outlined a solution to the nature of distributed nodes. (You can compare nodes to generals in our Byzantine Generals Problem.)

The industry really started after Nakamoto came out with Bitcoin in 2009. However, the enterprise environment did not really get started until 2015 with permissioned blockchains. (Permissioned blockchains are generally referred to as *enterprise blockchains*.) So, the blockchain technology is no more than 10 years old at the time of this writing, and enterprise blockchains such as Hyperledger (covered in Chapter 2, "Enterprise Blockchains: Hyperledger, R3 Corda, and Ethereum, Quorum") are less than 5 years old!

**NOTE**   The following are the release dates for popular blockchains:

◆   2009—Bitcoin

◆   2015—Ethereum

◆   2015—Hyperledger

◆   2017—R3 Corda

# Blockchain vs. Traditional Database

It is important to understand how the distributed blockchain ledger differs from a traditional database. A distributed ledger is a database that is stored and updated independently by each node in the blockchain. Every node essentially maintains a copy of the blockchain. For example, in the Ethereum blockchain network, there were more than 16,000 nodes at the time of writing. In the Bitcoin blockchain network, there are more than 7,000 nodes at the time of writing. Why is this important? Every node that is online has a current copy of the working blockchain. If you lose a few nodes, it's no big deal since there are thousands of other nodes that maintain a copy. In the Ethereum network, when a transaction is written to the ledger, it also is written to more than 1,600 other nodes. Does a centralized database maintain 1,600 copies of its database? Of course not.

Figure 1.4 shows the vast Ethereum network with the Etherstats.io service. You can view many different data points of the Ethereum blockchain, as Etherstats provides transparency into the Ethereum blockchain.

**FIGURE 1.4**
Ethereum network
Etherstats.io

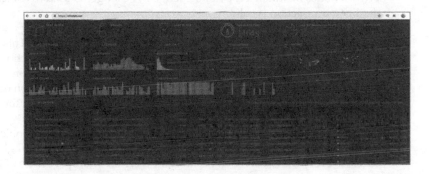

An enterprise would likely be interested in using the Ethereum virtual machine (EVM) for running its off-chain smart contracts or for a token platform that is being built for a distributed application known as a *dapp*. It would then look at the Ethereum Explorer referenced in Figure 1.4 and review the hash rate or the gas numbers.

The Ethereum ledger is also great for keeping track of transactions and providing transparency to your customer base. In Chapter 2, I will cover Ethereum in much more detail and explain why enterprises are interested in Ethereum.

What is the biggest difference between a database and distributed ledger or a blockchain? Well, the decentralized and distributed nature of the blockchain is what makes blockchain ledgers unique compared to traditional databases such as SQL. Databases and ledgers are generally centralized, meaning that there is a centralized administrator or centralized node structure that can create, delete, modify, or update the database. Some common databases include Microsoft SQL, Oracle PL/SQL, and IBM DB2.

In the traditional database world, objects are used as a data structure, and these objects are *mutable*, meaning that they are able to be modified or deleted. In a blockchain, an object is not modifiable after it has been created, and therefore it is considered *immutable*.

### Distribution of Trust

The primary solution that blockchain technologies really provide as compared to a traditional database is around the distribution of trust. In a traditional database, the trust is centralized; in a blockchain, the trust is distributed among nodes of the blockchain.

Distribution of trust means that not only does one blockchain node have a copy but every blockchain node maintains a copy. For example, if there are 1,000 nodes in an enterprise blockchain, then at its truest form the blockchain acts as a "truth agent." The likelihood that 1,000 nodes could be hacked or controlled is statistically impossible with blockchains that are true blockchains since the ledger is a distributed ledger.

### Consensus and Trust

Blockchain ledgers are decentralized, distributed, and immutable. This is critical to trust, which is built on the fact that they can't be modified or deleted.

*Consensus* is an approach that is utilized on a distributed ledger network where all the network nodes maintain a copy of the ledger. The ledger is used to come to an agreement on whether a transaction is valid.

For example, in Ethereum, the ledger, which is distributed among nodes in more than 100 countries at the time of writing, is used for blockchain transactions. This ledger is distributed globally and can be accessed from anywhere with an Internet connection. To access the ledger, you would need the public keys that Ethereum uses for authentication.

Figure 1.5 provides more insight into how an Ethereum transaction occurs at a high level. Jamie is being sent $100. This amount will be deducted in ether from the sender's wallet and deposited into the receiver's wallet.

Remember, the nodes in the blockchain network in most permissionless (enterprise) blockchains have a copy of the whole blockchain. This means that every single node on the network processes every transaction that occurs, and there are multiple copies of that ledger. There is now consensus (an agreement) that this transaction is valid.

### Summary of Differences Between Ledgers and Traditional Databases

You now know that blockchains have ledgers, and these ledgers are different from traditional databases in the following ways:

◆ Legacy architectures in databases are basically centralized repositories of managed data. This data, though, is usually structured and controlled centrally. Blockchains are decentralized and distributed between nodes on the blockchain network. Data is managed by consensus and not centrally controlled.

◆ SQL or NoSQL are common legacy database applications. SQL is the most widely used database. Blockchains do not use SQL or relational database structures.

◆ Whether centralized or distributed, traditional databases use client-server network architecture. Blockchains are decentralized and distributed data structures.

◆ Database processing speed is referenced as transactions per second (TPS), and legacy databases are much quicker in most cases compared to blockchains when it comes to TPS.

◆ Control of the database remains with a designated authority in a legacy database, whereas in a blockchain there is no centralized authority.

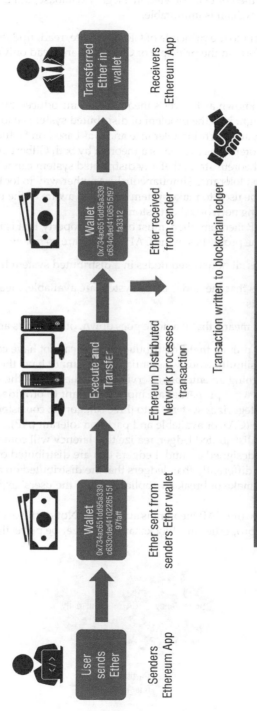

**FIGURE 1.5**
Ethereum transaction

◆ Data can be modified or even deleted in a legacy database, but in a blockchain this cannot occur since a blockchain is immutable.

◆ Databases conform to the principle of CRUD (create, read, update, and delete), and blockchains conform to the principle of CR (create and read only).

## Cap Theorem

The CAP theorem, also known as Brewer's theorem, was introduced by Eric Brewer in 1998, and provides significant insight into the problem of distributed systems had around maintaining consistency, availability, and partition tolerance and was based on factual evidence at the time.

In 2002, the CAP theorem was proven as a theorem by Seth Gilbert and Nancy Lynch, respectively. The CAP theorem states that any distributed system cannot have consistency, availability, and partition tolerance simultaneously. Another way to look at the CAP theorem is that it is a tool that can be used to make system designers aware of the possible property trade-offs while designing networked data stores.

According to the CAP theorem, there must be some property that is reduced to provide for the other two properties. The properties in the CAP theorem are as follows:

◆ *Consistency* means all networked nodes in a distributed system have the same view.

◆ *Availability* means that the nodes in the system are available, meaning they are online and accepting requests.

◆ *Partition tolerance* means that if a node goes down, other nodes are fine.

Note that it has been proven that a distributed system cannot have consistency, availability, and partition tolerance simultaneously. Essentially, you cannot have them all in a distributed system, and when designing an enterprise service—whether or not the service is a blockchain—you will need to choose what properties are more important to provide to your customer.

The CAP theorem categorizes systems into three categories: consistent partitioned (CP), consistent and available (CA), or available and partition tolerant (AP).

When considering a distributed ledger, realize that latency will come into the picture to some degree and needs to be designed around. Ledgers that are distributed over a local data center will, of course, perform differently than ledgers that are distributed on a cloud provider's regions and zones. Latency can make or break an application and the users' experience with the application.

Figure 1.6 shows how the CAP theorem is structured. Notice the overlap between the three properties. These three properties in a blockchain will never be perfectly aligned.

**FIGURE 1.6**
Cap theorem

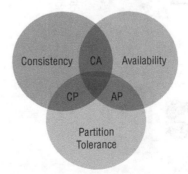

For example, it is important to appreciate the three CAP theorem as applied to your block-chain network.

◆ Consistency is achieved only if all nodes have the same shared state, meaning that they have the same up-to-date copy of the data.

◆ Availability is achieved only if all nodes are up and running and are responding to transaction requests for the latest copy of data on the ledger.

◆ Partition tolerance is achieved between two nodes or more only if they are able to communicate with each other. Communication on any network is subject to latency, jitter, and TCP protocol challenges.

Consistency is achieved in blockchain networks using consensus algorithms that ensure all nodes have the same copy of the data. This form of consistency is similar to replication, but in the IT world we would call this *state machine replication*. The blockchain is a means for achieving state machine replication, and this can be accomplished in several ways based of course on the blockchain.

There are two types of faults that a blockchain node can experience on a distributed network.

◆ The first type of fault is called a *fail-stop fault*. This type of fault occurs when a node has merely crashed. Fail-stop faults are the easier ones to deal with of the two fault types. The Paxos protocol can be used to resolve this concern. (Paxos is a protocol suite that solves consensus challenges in a network of inconsistent nodes.) Basically, networks have challenges such as latency that can greatly worsen the more a network is distributed.

◆ The second type of fault is one where the faulty node exhibits malicious or inconsistent behavior arbitrarily. This fault is difficult to handle since it can create arbitrary results.

Consistency on the blockchain is not achieved simultaneously with partition tolerance and availability, but it is achieved over time. Since the consistency is achieved over time and is not immediate, it is called *eventual consistency*. Distributed networks are slow, and maintaining this consistency needs to be addressed.

The concept of mining was introduced in Bitcoin for this purpose to maintain the consistency of the blockchain network. *Mining* is a compute-intensive process that facilitates the achievement of consensus by using the proof-of-work (PoW) consensus algorithm.

Mining can also be defined as a process that is used to add more blocks to the blockchain as a result of the consensus method. PoW and other common consensus methods are covered in detail in Chapter 4, "Understanding Enterprise Blockchain Consensus."

## Common Properties of Permissionless Blockchains

Permissionless blockchains are blockchains that open to the public and have no permissioning meaning the users do not need authorization to use the platform. The right customer may very well be a business-to-consumer model where the customer may want visibility into a special order such as a custom necklace that is being sourced overseas and is moving thru the logistical processes which would provide the customer "visibility" or in blockchain what we would call "transparency".

Table 1.1 shows the more commonly referenced features of what a blockchain provides. As you can see, there are a handful of common features that blockchain provides.

**TABLE 1.1:**    Common Blockchain Features

| FEATURE | NOTES |
| --- | --- |
| Global computer network | Distributed nodes, with no centralized control of nodes. |
| Ubiquitous access | Can access the resources with only an Internet connection from anywhere. |
| Censorship and tamper-proof ledger | No entity can modify or delete data, which makes the blockchain immutable. Immutability provides data compliance since it cannot be deleted or modified. |
| Open source | Uses programming languages that are portable, which allows ease of development. |
| Compliance | Comes with smart contracts that are validated. The blockchain ledger also is verified by audits. |
| Multiple users | No limitations to who can join the blockchain, and the accounts scale. |
| Trust | Trust in the code (smart contracts), which means that users place trust in the blockchain technology. |
| Guarantees | Atomicity, synchrony, and provenance. |

Blockchain and traditional databases have properties that are similar to each other but also have properties that are not similar to each other. For example, both a blockchain and a traditional database replicate data. However, the way replication is initiated, achieved, and handled is actually very different from a comparative standpoint.

Perhaps the most important difference is how blockchains and databases handle operations on the ledger. Blockchains will only insert operations to the ledger, meaning that the transaction is one-way. In a database, the transactions can be any transaction from an insert or delete operation, meaning create, update, or delete.

Figure 1.7 compares properties of a blockchain to a traditional database: operations, replication, consensus, and invariants. When comparing a database to a blockchain, the property difference is significant.

**FIGURE 1.7**
Blockchain vs.
traditional database
comparison

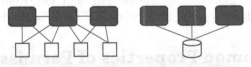

| Properties | Blockchain | Database |
| --- | --- | --- |
| Consensus | Agreement reached by nodes | Based on database rules for commits |
| Operations | Create and read operations(CR) | All transactions (CRUD) |
| Replication | Ledger is replicated to every other blockchain node | Depends on administrative configuration |
| Transparency | Open to public for reads | Security controls, closed system |

It is important to note that the blockchain allows for two specific functions only in its truest implementation.

◆ The validation of a transaction

◆ The writing of a new transaction

Notice that modifying data and deleting data are not functions blockchains support. Blockchains append to the blockchain, and that is the only function that should be supported. Blockchains are stateful programs and thus have some mechanism to keep track of and update state. They maintain the past and thus remember previous transactions that may affect the current transaction. The term used in blockchain transactions is *append*. (I will be covering this in detail throughout the book.)

## Why the Blockchain Is Considered Revolutionary

During the course of the last 100 years or so, the advancement of life-changing technologies has been dramatic. It is also reasonable to say that the potential of newer technologies such as artificial intelligence, machine learning, and blockchains will all impact our lives significantly. Technology often can be revolutionary, and the blockchain technology looks like it will be one of those.

The blockchain technology is revolutionary in several ways, as listed here:

◆ The blockchain technology is a syncing of technologies that now make sense to implement strategically.

◆ Trust is at the center of blockchain technology and through the use of consensus removes intermediaries from the network and thus creates new efficiencies that companies can really benefit from, such as providing transparency, a root of trust, a reduction in labor costs, and numerous other benefits.

◆ The blockchain technology in its true sense, as specified by Nakamoto, is a "tamperproof public ledger of value." The Bitcoin platform enabled citizens of the world to make transactions without the need of intermediaries.

The blockchain technology is disruptive to the status quo since legacy applications and business processes are being phased out with blockchain applications.

Blockchain is a platform with numerous use cases for enterprises. The number and quality of organizations investing in blockchain testing, implementation, and production specifications is impressive.

## Blockchain Principles

Clearly, the principles implicit in blockchain technology have lent themselves to the redesign of software, businesses, organizations, and even governments. The principles of blockchain have renewed trust in users in an era of digital economics and intrinsically fair social systems.

◆ Trust is provided through the implementation of technology. The technology used in a blockchain for establishing trust is provided through encryption and code which validates the transaction requirements and will determine if a transaction is securely accepted or rejected.

◆ Integrity is provided through the blockchain network where there is no centralized authority or failure point, and every transaction is recorded.

◆ Incentives are distributed to all stakeholders to the participants that produce blocks, and these participants are called *miners*.

◆ A blockchain is decentralized, meaning that the data is distributed among thousands of nodes and there is no centralized point of control.

◆ Privacy means that users are in control of how the data is handled. There is no requirement for compliance such as know your customer (KYC), for example.

◆ Equal access/inclusion is in effect in the manner that everyone in the world should have the ability to participate in the blockchain network.

## Trust or Trustless

Blockchains do not actually eliminate trust; rather, they minimize the amount of trust required from any single actor/participant on the network. They do this by distributing trust among different actors in the system via an economic game that incentivizes actors to cooperate within the rules defined by the protocol. The economic incentives are presented for participating in the permissionless blockchains such as Ethereum or Bitcoin; miners produce blocks and obtain rewards for mining.

Blockchains define a secure communication protocol that allows two individuals to transact with one another in a "peer-to-peer" manner over the Internet. This means there are no intermediaries facilitating transactions.

When you digitally transfer value from one account (wallet) to another account (wallet) on the blockchain, you're trusting the underlying blockchain network to enable that transfer and to ensure the sender's authenticity along with the cryptocurrency's validity. *Authenticity* means that the sender is who they present themselves to be electronically via public key encryption usually implemented through certificates and keys. *Validity* means that the sender has the correct wallet and has funds in that wallet to actually send the correct amount of funds.

For example, in the centralized approach, you may need to use Western Union to send funds from the United States to Peru. The cost to do this as well as the time to perform this transfer could be substantial in some cases; it could be a few hours, a few days, or longer. In addition, the transfer fees can be 10 times or more than using cryptocurrencies on a blockchain network.

Basically, you are "trusting" the intermediary to validate the transaction, send the transaction, and confirm the transaction has completed. You might use this service because you expect the transfer to be valid and authentic since the intermediary is performing a fiduciary responsibility. People clearly trust banks, nonbanks such as PayPal, and other entities such as Western Union to send funds to people who request them. However, that trust can come at a cost, whether financial or otherwise.

*Trustless* is generally used to describe "distribution of trust" where the trust is not placed in a centralized concentration but is actually distributed in a decentralized manner to all the participants in the blockchain.

With blockchain consensus methods, this approach allows participants to share digitally distributed "truth" that is stored on a distributed ledger that is not centralized. The truth could be a list of transactions, voucher IDs, customer addresses, or any assets or information that can be written to a blockchain.

## TRUST BLOCKCHAINS

Trust is at the center of all blockchains whether permissioned or permissionless, albeit they approach trust differently.

A blockchain is a truth machine because of the implementation of the technology used, and this implementation of the ledger maintains the truth since the ledger is an immutable record of trust.

In its most basic form, a blockchain is an immutable record of transactions. These transactions can be any type such as movement of money, products, or even services. Blockchains are designed to store information in a way that makes it virtually impossible to add, remove, or change data without being detected by other users.

When considering blockchain technology, it is imperative to understand how trust is established with blockchains. The following list highlights some important considerations:

◆ The blockchain technology is about storing some kind of data—for example, transactions such as in the case of the Bitcoin blockchain or tokens in Ethereum. The platform is trusted to perform these transactions because of the code and encryption utilized. Trust is distributed between the blockchain nodes on the Ethereum platform.

◆ The blockchain technology is essentially transferring trust from an intermediary to technology (software code).

◆ Storing data in the blockchain happens through cryptographic functions such as certificates and keys.

◆ Private keys/public keys are used to secure transactional data written to the ledger through Public Key Infrastructure (PKI).

When considering the reasons why users can trust a blockchain, there are two main considerations.

◆ All transaction data on a blockchain is assumed to be trustworthy because the blockchain protocols are enforced and encryption is used.

◆ The blockchain users base this trust in a blockchain on the following:

　◆ The blockchain data has not been tampered with and is being managed by nodes producing blocks on the blockchain.

　◆ The blockchain ledger that contains the data is immutable and therefore cannot be deleted, modified, or moved.

Trust is at the epicenter of how blockchains function and the value it creates for enterprises and users.

## TRUSTLESS BLOCKCHAINS

When considering blockchains, the model that is used is considered a trustless model where trust is transferred from an intermediary to technology.

A trustless model does not require "trust" in order to safely interact and transact as trust is considered inherent in the technology platform. A trustless blockchain, in reality, is a transfer of trust to the blockchain technology from humans in centralized organizations (banks, governments, corporations).

Blockchains are built on the premise that transparent code (smart contracts) essentially removes the need for intermediaries. Smart contracts can essentially reduce the need for accountants, lawyers, bankers, and so on. Essentially, trust is transformed. "Trustless" in blockchain essentially creates the trust by default, which means when users utilize a blockchain, they are "trusting" the technology to perform as it should.

## Transparency and Blockchain

The blockchain technology is decentralizing information dissemination and providing transparency that has never been seen before. Blockchain's main focus on ledger management and immutable records makes it a perfect technology candidate for the decentralized tracking of resources, which could provide transparency to an enterprise customer purchasing something of value, for example.

Consumers increasingly require more transparency into the services and products they purchase. The following list are some areas of focus where the blockchain industry is seeing significant demand for use cases, proof of concepts, and implementations:

◆ Food supply traceability

◆ Labor credential validation

◆ Logistics and supply chains

◆ Customs compliance

◆ Corporate governance

The transparency of a blockchain comes from the openness of the blockchain transactions viewable to anyone. This transparency, in Ethereum, for example, is accomplished using a blockchain explorer such as Etherstats. A blockchain explorer provides insight into the transactions on a blockchain. For example, in Ethereum your wallet address is what links the transaction to the blockchain user. There is no identifying information, such as name or address of the wallet holder.

The transparency provides insight into how many Ether was sent and received, to what wallet address, and other critical information such as the block height or transaction ID. However, it is important to note that transparency does not provide an identify of who actually sent the ether.

For example, this blockchain explorer translates the ledger and provides some privacy in the sense that a wallet address is displayed (transparency) but the owner of the wallet is not provided publicly (privacy).

*Pseudonymous* is used to reference a blockchain transaction, where the sender and receiver are not directly identified.

Here are some examples of blockchain applications that provide this transparency:

◆ Ledgers stored in the blockchain make it easier to track ownership and liability during transit, limiting liability protecting practitioners and pharmacists who administer drugs to patients

◆ Blockchain technology can be applied to several different aspects of the healthcare space such as managing electronic health records (EHRs), which will be used for validating patient data, and even tracking research methods used to make safer drugs across clinical trials.

- The blockchain technology in the logistics industry, for example, has numerous in-production use cases. One of the more widely publicized is focused in the jewelry industry, which has traditionally been known for high levels of fraud, child labor issues, false metal mining, and a clear lack of transparency.

- A precious metals consortium with IBM has established a blockchain initiative to bring transparency to the consumer. For example, consumers can validate that their purchases are ethically sourced from sustainable resources without the involvement of child labor.

Some common consumer advantages of transparency in blockchain technology include the following:

- Blockchains are open for viewing and validating transactions, meaning that they are transparent for customers, consortium members, and the enterprises.

- Blockchains provide a pseudonymous feature for participants that allows the transactions to be transparent but the users to be unidentified by direct means such as name or address. A wallet address is used, but the name of the wallet owner is not clarified.

- Participants share the same ledger and establish a shared consensus service that can be referenced by the stakeholders.

- Blockchains provide integrity opportunities for businesses that provide services in a logistic blockchain. Integrity means that customers can validate if the business is actually performing the tasks that they say. For example, is your favorite children's cereal company actually buying corn without GMO seeds?

Using a blockchain can result in financial transparency and reduce the need for intermediaries. Other considerable benefits of blockchain solutions in the logistics sector include the following:

- Transparency to the consumers about the supply chain concerns such as farm to table

- Incentives or responsibility from the suppliers to act responsibly and ethically

- Mileage verification for truckers and their drivers to meet the government agency reporting requirements

- Labor verification where no children are used in the mining or processing of jewelry

- Validation of ethical sourcing from suppliers such as fish processors

- An immutable shared view of the ledger that can be viewed by customers of a baby formula manufacturer

**NOTE**  "Dubai's adoption of blockchain technology at a city-wide scale is a testament to its commitment to positively transform government, from service provider to service enabler . . . . We believe blockchain technology, with its built-in efficiency, accountability and security, holds a key to achieving our vision." —Dr. Aisha Bin Bishr, director general at Smart Dubai Office (`https://www.unlock-bc.com/news/2017-12-19/the-transformed-role-of-government-in-the-blockchain-era`)

## Blockchain Transaction Basics

Blockchain transactions are processed in somewhat different ways depending on the platform. For example, Bitcoin processes transactions differently from Hyperledger Fabric, which should be expected since the use cases are very different.

The focus of this section is to cover consensus and how transactions work at a generic level. Chapter 4, "Understanding Enterprise Blockchain Consensus," covers specific details around transactions for Ethereum, Hyperledger Fabric, R3 Corda, and Quorum.

### Consensus

Consensus is effectively the foundational principle of a blockchain and is how the network nodes come to agreement. All nodes in the blockchain network maintain a copy of the ledger, and each node can source historical transactional data from the network to validate requests.

Consensus, simply put, is a way an "agreement" is reached for the distributed ledger nodes on the network. This agreement effectively states how this will be done and what needs to be verified to be a valid transaction.

This approach to an agreement, especially when considering a permissionless blockchain network, is critical since all nodes on the network need to agree on the validity of a transaction. In a permissioned blockchain, this consensus algorithm can be modified or even manipulated through policies.

For example, in Hyperledger Fabric, which is a permissioned blockchain, we can effectively specify how many nodes (peers) need to approve a request. The number of peers can be a single peer, ten peers, or all the peers.

Consensus (agreement) is reached through the implementation of a consensus mechanism, protocol, method, or algorithm. In reality, a mechanism, method, or algorithm are all referring to the same thing, which is how a distributed ledger platform reaches an agreement.

For the purpose of this book, I will mainly reference the *consensus algorithm* since most blockchain technology vendors seem to have standardized on that approach.

Every blockchain has a different blockchain algorithm that provides specific instructions on how the distributed ledger network comes to an agreement and approves transactions.

Proof of work (PoW), proof of stake (PoS), and many other consensus algorithms will be covered in Chapter 4, "Understanding Enterprise Blockchain Consensus," which discusses consensus algorithms in more detail.

### Blocks

Blockchain transactions are recorded on the blockchain network and rely on user verification to be fully authenticated. The transactions executed during a given period of time are recorded into files called *blocks*. Blocks form the foundation of many blockchain networks, as each new block is linked to the previous block of transactions that form the blockchain network.

A transaction is a transfer of cryptocurrency value that is broadcast to the entire network and collected in blocks, as previously mentioned. The recipient of the transaction is represented by the address, which is a string of 26 to 35 letters and numbers. Once verified using the private (secret) key, these transactions are then recorded on the network ledger where this transaction is publicly available. The blocks of transaction information make up the blockchain, with each block's height representing the number of blocks preceding it.

Figure 1.8 shows how a Bitcoin transaction occurs in block sequence. You can trace how block 1 is written first, then block 2 is written, and so on. Note that the hash is referenced in the blockchain, and therefore block 1 would have its hash referenced by block 2, then block 3 would reference block 2's hash, and so on.

**FIGURE 1.8**
Bitcoin blockchain

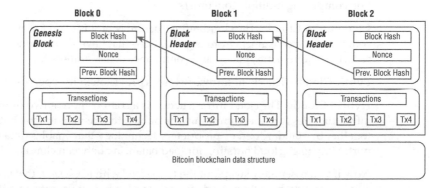

## Types of Blockchains

Blockchains come in various architectures and can provide for different use cases. Blockchains when appropriately designed will meet the requirements of the enterprise customer and meet the use case required. Enterprises generally prefer blockchains such as Hyperledger Fabric or R3 Corda, which are enterprise focused.

In this section, I will cover blockchain types and deployment concerns and also compare blockchains to cloud computing services.

### Public, Private, and Hybrid Blockchains

Blockchains are generally considered infrastructure in most enterprises. *Infrastructure* means that the organization maintains production applications and maintains the application whether directly or indirectly through a service provider.

I generally compare the deployment of blockchains to cloud computing. In cloud computing, there are *deployment models* and *service models*.

A deployment model is essentially a business model. Let's review what NIST states about cloud computing and then let's apply this definition to blockchains.

> *Cloud computing is a relatively new business model in the computing world. According to the official NIST definition, "Cloud computing is a model for enabling ubiquitous, convenient, on-demand network access to a shared pool of configurable computing resources (e.g., networks, servers, storage, applications and services) that can be rapidly provisioned and released with minimal management effort or service provider interaction."*

```
https://www.bartleby.com/essay/
Cloud-Computing-A-Profitable-New-Business-Model-P3S6F9L29BQQ
```

The National Institute of Science and Technology (NIST) defines deployment models as follows (`https://nvlpubs.nist.gov/nistpubs/Legacy/SP/nistspecialpublica-tion800-145.pdf`):

**Private Cloud**   The cloud infrastructure is provisioned for exclusive use by a single organization comprising multiple consumers.

**Community Cloud**   The cloud infrastructure is provisioned for exclusive use by a specific community of consumers from organizations that have shared concerns (e.g., mission, security requirements, policy, and compliance considerations).

**Public Cloud**   The cloud infrastructure is provisioned for open use by the general public.

**Hybrid Cloud**   The cloud infrastructure is a composition of two or more distinct cloud infrastructures (private, community, or public) that remain unique entities but are bound together by standardized or proprietary technology that enables data and application portability (e.g., cloud bursting for load balancing between clouds).

Now if you essentially swap out the term *cloud* with *blockchain*, this is exactly what a blockchain can perform, how it can be deployed, or even how it fits into an enterprise use case.

The notable exception is that in blockchain speak there are no "community" blockchains; however, there are "consortium" blockchains, which are serving the same deployment use case.

These consortium blockchains, which really are "communities," are implemented by likeminded organizations sharing a blockchain. A good example of a consortium blockchain is Ripple, which is used exclusively by the financial industry for interbank payments, for example.

Figure 1.9 illustrates the common cloud computing deployment model. The different service models correlate to the level of effort that is provided by either the provider or the consumer. This model could be used as well for blockchain deployments. For example, blockchains could be deployed in the cloud as a platform or software as a service.

**FIGURE 1.9**
Cloud computing
deployment model

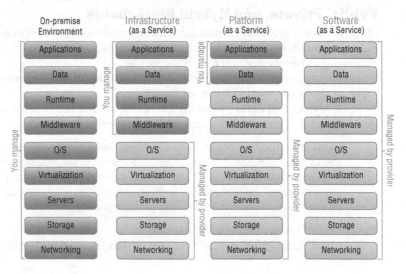

Blockchains are commonly deployed in the cloud and could be deployed as infrastructure/ platform/software as a service in a cloud service. Providers such as AWS, Azure, and IBM, for example, provide services that are deployed in all three service models. AWS blockchain templates are considered an IaaS deployment, while IBM Blockchain Platform has two versions: one that is a SaaS and another that is more of a PaaS.

In terms of comparing cloud computing to blockchain, it is important to note that cloud computing at its truest form is a "centralized" approach to computing. Blockchains in their truest form are a "decentralized" form of computing. Anyone who has been in technology understands that when a technology is developed for one use, it generally can be adapted to other use cases. Blockchains are no exception, and as you will read throughout the book, blockchains have many different use cases, exceptions, and variations; some are centralized, and some are decentralized.

For example, Ethereum is essentially a decentralized global computer that processes smart contracts. Ethereum's CTO Gavin Wood describes blockchains as a "global computer." A computer is simply a computational machine; it takes inputs, processes these inputs using certain instructions, and creates outputs.

Blockchains run on computers that are "decentralized" in a permissionless blockchain. In Ethereum, this global computer consists of thousands of nodes that are distributed in more than 100 countries.

**NOTE**   Cloud computing is essentially a business model, and you can choose to deploy that model in several ways. Consider looking at blockchains as a business since they really are just that, a business model. They can be deployed exactly as a cloud computing infrastructure, if that's what the company determines. Private, public, or hybrid deployments are all in use in blockchains today.

Blockchains that are open to anyone are generally considered public, permissionless blockchains. Blockchains that are closed are generally considered private or permissioned blockchains.

## PUBLIC BLOCKCHAINS

Public blockchains are also referred to as permissionless or open blockchains that are open to anyone. Bitcoin was the original permissionless blockchain, as specified and developed by Satoshi Nakamoto. Transactions are processed by all nodes in the blockchain, and those transactions are publicly viewable (transparent) in the blockchain. These transactions are also widely distributed. For example, Ethereum at one time had more than 6,000 nodes worldwide, and each node maintains a copy of every transaction. In Chapter 2, I cover the Ethereum blockchain and its infrastructure in more detail.

Public blockchains are open to anyone, meaning that you can participate in the blockchain. If you want to run an Ethereum node, you simply go to GitHub and download the blockchain. This assumes, of course, that you have the resources to run the blockchain and the technical knowledge to install and configure the blockchain.

Figure 1.10 presents the high-level structure of a permissionless public blockchain and how a trustless peering is imposed on the network—that is, there is no centralized control of membership or participation on the blockchain network.

**FIGURE 1.10**
Public blockchain
example

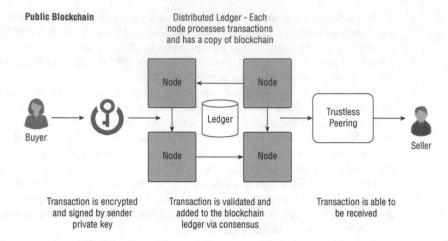

**Public Blockchain**

Distributed Ledger - Each
node processes transactions
and has a copy of blockchain

Buyer

Ledger

Trustless
Peering

Seller

Node   Node

Node   Node

Transaction is encrypted
and signed by sender
private key

Transaction is validated and
added to the blockchain
ledger via consensus

Transaction is able to
be received

Public blockchains have some benefits as compared to private blockchains, as listed here:

◆ Open read and write

◆ Widely distributed ledger

◆ Censorship resistant

◆ Secure due to mining (51 percent rule)

**NOTE** Some common public blockchain examples are Bitcoin, Ethereum, and Monero.

### PRIVATE BLOCKCHAINS

Private blockchains are also referred to as *permissioned blockchains* or *enterprise blockchains*. These private blockchains are a hybrid of a true blockchain since they are not decentralized but are more centralized. Centralization is at the core of an enterprise blockchain since one entity or a consortium maintain access to the blockchain. Accessing the blockchain network requires permissioning, meaning that one or all transactions are permissioned or authorized to proceed.

These blockchains can be open source, consortium, or privately developed blockchains.

Transactions are also handled differently in a permissionless blockchain. Transactions are processed by select nodes in the blockchain. For example, some blockchains, such as Hyperledger Fabric, can utilize channeling. Channeling can also be used to filter nodes, even in a permissioned blockchain, to keep them from participating in specific transactions that they have no direct interest in.

Transactions are not publicly viewable (transparent) in the blockchain. The transparency of transactions can be permissioned as well. (I will discuss use cases in Chapter 8, "Blockchain Use Cases.")

The transactions are also generally locally distributed, meaning that the blockchain is in a centrally controlled data center. This approach is essentially the opposite of a permissionless blockchain, where the nodes are processed worldwide on Ethereum blockchain nodes that are in uncontrolled servers.

Figure 1.11 presents the high-level structure of a private blockchain and how a trusted peering is imposed on the network. A private blockchain uses a trusted peering approach, which is different from a public blockchain. The consortium members, for example, will control membership and/or participation on the blockchain network.

**FIGURE 1.11**
Private blockchain
example

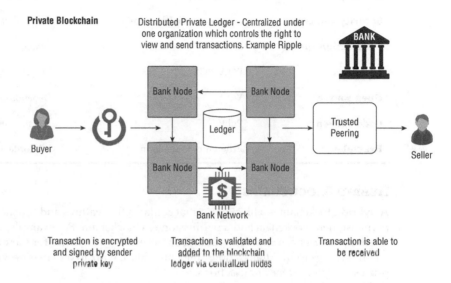

Private blockchains have some benefits compared to public blockchains, as listed here:

◆ They are enterprise permissioned and are controlled for privacy and security.

◆ They have faster transactions because of fewer nodes and a simple distribution of the nodes such as a limited geography. Node locality and scalability can directly affect performance.

◆ They have greater scalability because of the configuration flexibility and membership control.

◆ They have compliance support because of the permissioning and controlled distribution of data storage in appropriate regions.

**NOTE**  Some common enterprise blockchains are Hyperledger, R3 Corda, and Quorum.

Table 1.2 compares the main comparison points of public and private blockchains, including significant differences in security, ledger access, identity, and other features that would be important to consider when designing a blockchain. Private blockchains create value to enterprises through various factors, such as membership, privacy, and even performance.

**TABLE 1.2:**   Public vs. private blockchains

|  | PUBLIC (PERMISSIONLESS) | PRIVATE (PERMISSIONED |
|---|---|---|
| **Access to ledger** | Open read/write | Permissioned read/write |
| **Identity** | Anonymous | Known identities |
| **Security and trust** | Open network (trust free) | Controlled network (trusted) |
| **Transaction speed** | Slower | Faster |
| **Consensus** | POW/POS | Proprietary or modular |
| **Open source** | Yes | Depends on blockchain |
| **Code upkeep** | Public | Consortium or managed |
| **Examples** | Ethereum, Multichain | R3 Corda, Quorum |

## HYBRID BLOCKCHAINS

A hybrid blockchain is a blockchain that contains the features and functions of both a private, permissioned blockchain and a permissionless blockchain. For example, a company may require intense performance requirements and strict security adherence for their internal employees, but when it comes to B2C transactions, they may place it on an off-chain service (channeling) to process cryptocurrency transactions.

In a nutshell, you may want to consider a hybrid blockchain as similar to a hybrid cloud environment where you take features of both and provide a solution that meets your enterprise's requirements.

Control, performance, transparency, compliance, and other features can be carefully orchestrated in a hybrid blockchain solution. I compare hybrid blockchains to hybrid cloud solutions. A hybrid cloud essentially comprises the best of both worlds in cloud computing.

In a hybrid cloud solution, you can extend our on-premises data center to a cloud computing platform such as AWS. When extended to AWS, your data center can provide many benefits such as cost efficiency by reducing capital expenditures, short time use such bursting services during peak hours, or taking advantage of availability options.

Blockchains when deployed as a hybrid solution can be similar. A company can extend, for example, a Hyperledger Fabric blockchain that is on-premises to AWS or IBM BaaS. The main benefits could be to extend off-chain, to meet compliance requirements, or to extend a blockchain network.

**REFERENCE**   Chapter 7 covers blockchain as a service (BaaS) extensively with step-by-step instructions with AWS Templates and IBM Blockchain.

**NOTE**   "Until now we've seen a proliferation of both public blockchains like Bitcoin and private blockchains like Hyperledger Fabric. Going forward, I think we'll start to see the rise of hybrid blockchains, which combine the best of both worlds." —Stefan Thomas, CTO at Ripple and cocreator of the Interledger payment protocol (https://bravenewcoin.com/insights/hybrid-blockchains-the-best-of-both-public-and-private)

Figure 1.12 presents a decision tree for deciding whether to implement a public, private, or hybrid blockchain solution. A hybrid blockchain is an offshoot of a private and permissioned blockchain. A hybrid blockchain can also extend to a permissionless blockchain.

**FIGURE 1.12**
Blockchain deployment decision tree

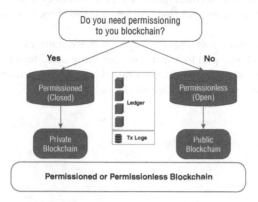

When choosing a blockchain type, another factor to consider is cost. I cover the cost of blockchain deployments extensively in Chapter 6, "Enterprise Blockchain Economics."

Large enterprises will generally require the benefits that blockchain technology can deliver without the associated elevated risks of a public blockchain. If this is the case, then a hybrid solution may provide the enterprise with the right solution for the right use case.

In Chapter 3, "Architecting your Enterprise Blockchain," I will discuss how private-public blockchain-focused projects such as Hyperledger, R3 Corda, and Ethereum Enterprise Alliance can enable organizations to be properly scoped around a blockchain solution.

## PERMISSIONED OR PERMISSIONLESS BLOCKCHAINS

In this book, you will notice that *public* and *private* are sometimes used interchangeably with permissioned and permissionless blockchains. To be fair, these terms can in some cases have somewhat different use cases or meanings to different blockchain companies and organizations.

During my years of solutions selling, architecting, and implementing, it's more than fair to say that specific vendors, service providers, and the media make things more difficult than they need to be. Even with the maturity of cloud computing, most vendors add their own twist on top of the industry-wide acceptance of the NIST cloud computing definitions.

Earlier in the chapter I covered public, private, and permissionless blockchain types. Now I'll cover what a permissioned blockchain is. Permissioned blockchains are a form of blockchain that allow only authorized members to join the blockchain. Permissioned blockchains are ideal for enterprises that want some of the benefits of a blockchain such as an immutable ledger but do not want transparency, open membership, or smart contracts. Permissioned blockchains invariably change the initial purpose of what a blockchain originally should be. That is, blockchains originally were open and permissionless, which essentially means they are open to the public.

# Summary

Satoshi Nakamoto essentially combined computers and economics to create a blockchain platform called Bitcoin that changed how people needed it to interact with legacy institutions such as banks. Bitcoin came about as a direct result of the financial crisis of 2008.

The blockchain technology is revolutionary, especially for the financial sectors and the logistical sectors. As you learned in this chapter, a blockchain is a type of distributed ledger for maintaining a permanent and tamper-proof record of transactional data.

Enterprises are just starting to understand the potential of blockchains for use in their organizations, for their users, and for their customers, and some have already begun adopting blockchain technology.

There are several definitions and several types of blockchain, depending on who you are talking. Blockchains that are open to anyone are generally considered public or open blockchains. Blockchains that are closed are generally considered private blockchains. Finally, enterprise blockchains are generally private, permissioned blockchains.

# Chapter 2

# Enterprise Blockchains: Hyperledger, R3 Corda, Quorum, and Ethereum

In this chapter, I will cover the technical merits of the following enterprise blockchains, how they are structured, and where they fit into the enterprise:

- Hyperledger
- R3 Corda
- Quorum
- Ethereum

The technical merits covered in this chapter include security, consensus, virtual machines, features, and functions that are critical to understanding the blockchain platform. This chapter will cover the architecture at a fundamental level so you can understand the blockchain network and services. In Chapter 3, "Architecting Your Enterprise Blockchain," I will focus on the steps of designing a blockchain network as well as architecture best practices for the specific blockchains.

## Comparing Enterprise Blockchains

Blockchains are used in two main categories of IT solutions.

- Public, permissionless blockchains
- Private, enterprise, permissioned blockchains

A third approach, considered a hybrid solution, combines a myriad of private and public blockchain services. Hybrid blockchains will be discussed as a use case in Chapter 8, "Blockchain Use Cases."

Enterprise blockchains have different requirements than public blockchains such as Ethereum. I will be discussing the merits of enterprise blockchains throughout the book.

As discussed in Chapter 1, "Introduction to Blockchain Technologies," public permissionless blockchains use a networking protocol called the Internet Protocol (IP) to communicate with nodes on the blockchain network as well as to manage the distribution of transactions. Nodes are other virtual machines that are running the blockchain protocol.

A blockchain will run a variation of protocols, and they can be somewhat different from each other on each platform. Ethereum uses a peer-to-peer network protocol, for example, whereas R3 Corda uses a point-to-point network protocol.

Consensus is also vastly different between blockchains, and I will discuss this at a high level in this chapter. It will also be covered in more technical detail in Chapter 4, "Understanding Enterprise Blockchain Solutions."

Table 1.2 shows how different public and private blockchains can be when it comes to the features and functions of the platform. Choosing the right blockchain platform may come down to just one feature.

**REFERENCE**   During the use case sections in Chapter 3, I will discuss how to choose a platform, as well as considerations for architecting your blockchain services, in more detail.

## HYBRID BLOCKCHAINS

In a permissionless blockchain, the ledger is open read/write, meaning that anyone can access the transaction records. This would be done through a blockchain explorer, for example. Other features such as identity, security, and trust are, of course, handled differently.

Enterprise blockchains such as Hyperledger Fabric, R3 Corda, and Quorum are distributed ledgers in which all participants are known and permissioned to be on the blockchain network. Transactions are role-based and determined by consensus in the network. Enterprise blockchains generally introduce a form of centralization to blockchains but may also be decentralized over a membership consortium. Modular components such as consensus or key management systems enable enterprises to determine what fits their use cases. Tokens or cryptocurrencies are generally not needed in a controlled blockchain ecosystem where membership is controlled. Some consortium blockchains such as Hyperledger may provide this capability later.

Enterprise blockchains can utilize "off-chain" data storage services, such as the Interplanetary File System (IPFS), to reduce costs. Created by Protocol Labs, IPFS is a peer-to-peer protocol where each node stores a collection of hashed files. IPFS is actually a fascinating approach to blockchain storage that can provide costing efficiencies and programmatic efficiencies. IPFS clearly refers to files by using hashes, therefore allowing for much richer programmatic interactions.

**REFERENCE**   I cover IPFS in more technical detail in Chapter 7, "Blockchain as a Service (BaaS)."

Enterprise integration may not require middleware or API changes to establish enterprise services. For example, with Enterprise Ethereum and Quorum, there is already some capability to extend the blockchain as a hybrid solution. A hybrid solution means that the blockchain can be extended from a permissioned to a permissionless chain such as Ethereum.

Enterprise blockchains are generally accepted to fall into one of several categories, the most common of which are as follows:

◆ *Private enterprise blockchains* are managed by a single organization. The participants are normally internal users.

◆ *Consortium enterprise blockchains* are managed by multiple trusted organizations. Access requires consensus by multiple participants in the consortium.

◆ *Hybrid enterprise blockchains* are generally used for extended off-chain capabilities. Hybrid blockchains can be a myriad of private and public extensions.

> **NETWORK CONSENSUS**
>
> Consensus varies significantly among the enterprise blockchains. It is important to appreciate that even though these consensus methods may be different, they still attempt to provide a method for reaching an agreement. Consensus also will provide for reliability and may protect the blockchain network from vulnerabilities.

When considering blockchains from a presale's perspective, it is imperative that you understand the use cases for the different enterprise blockchains. Not every enterprise blockchain has the ability to meet every use case. I will now cover the major enterprises blockchains to give you an idea of how they actually compare and contrast. I cover each in more technical detail throughout the book and also compare and contrast these enterprise blockchain features and use cases.

The really convenient part of getting into the enterprise blockchain space today is that there aren't many enterprise blockchains to learn—no more than five, even if you include Ripple, which is a payment network for banks. I do not cover Ripple in depth in this chapter, mainly because it is a banking and payment network service and Ripple does not support smart contracts. Smart contracts provide essentially the main benefits for enterprise organizations around blockchain use cases.

Instead, this book will focus on Hyperledger, R3 Corda, Quorum, and Ethereum. Table 2.1 shows the five major enterprise-grade blockchains and how they compare based on industry, ledger, consensus methods, smart contracts, and cryptocurrency support.

You can view the full chart online at https://www.horsesforsources.com/top-5-blockchain-platforms_031618. It provides insight into how many solution providers out of 50 surveyed actually have engagements in the enterprise blockchains.

**TABLE 2.1:**     Comparing enterprise blockchains

|  | **ETHEREUM** | **R3 CORDA** | **QUORUM** | **HYPERLEDGER** | **RIPPLE** |
|---|---|---|---|---|---|
| **Industry** | Cross-industry | Financials | Cross-industry | Cross-industry | Financial |
| **Ledger** | Permissionless | Permissioned | Permissioned | Permissioned | Permissioned |
| **Consensus** | Proof of work | Pluggable | Majority voting | Pluggable | Probabilistic voting |
| **Smart contract support** | Yes | Yes | Yes | Yes | No |
| **Cryptocurrency** | Ether (Eth) | N/A | N/A | N/A | Ripple (XRP) |

# Introducing the Hyperledger Project

The Linux Foundation hosts Hyperledger and provides a governance structure and oversight to the Hyperledger community. It is a global open source project and the result of collaboration from technology leaders. Linux Foundation also embraces a modular umbrella approach to enterprise blockchains. Hyperledger is an open source software licensing model, which allows the user to model code and distribute it in an appropriate manner.

As shown in Figure 2.1, Hyperledger uses an umbrella approach to manage its open source projects. As an organization, Hyperledger manages more than 100 open source collaborations (projects). The Hyperledger structure has three modules: Infrastructure, Frameworks, and Tools.

You can see that Hyperledger has six frameworks and six tools and utilities. I will focus mainly on Hyperledger Fabric for this book because of its wide development base and the significant enterprise use cases in play now. The umbrella strategy, also referred to as the *greenhouse strategy*, is a proven model that the Linux Foundation has used repeatedly in the other projects it maintains. Historically, the Linux Foundation provides excellent management and insight into how to manage an open source project for consortium members.

## Hyperledger Frameworks

As mentioned, Hyperledger has six frameworks at the time of writing. Each framework is a blockchain. The Hyperledger consortium of members realized that one blockchain framework would not meet the requirements of all its members. The five frameworks ensure its consortium members have the features, functions, and other requirements to deploy an appropriate block-chain for its members' use cases.

Table 2.2 presents the five blockchains that make up the Hyperledger frameworks. I will focus on the Fabric framework, which is a permissioned blockchain that supports channels. Channels allow for controlled transactions that are private.

As mentioned, Fabric will be the focus of the book but the other frameworks in the Hyperledger blockchain family such as Burrow or Sawtooth will be referenced throughout the book mainly as a comparison for use cases.

Hyperledger as an organization empowers its members through the project's blockchain frameworks, tools, and organizational infrastructure. Hyperledger Fabric is by far the most widely used of the frameworks. For example, if you go to the Hyperledger GitHub project, you will see that Fabric has the most forks. GitHub is a collaborative web-based platform for software development projects that use the Git revision control system. Git is the standard for software development and is the most widely used platform.

Figure 2.2 shows that Fabric has more than 4,700 forks. A fork is when developers make a copy of the repository, which is a good sign since it shows that developers are making changes to code, testing the code, or using the code.

It's clear that Fabric has the most activity as compared to the other frameworks. This is mainly because it's the framework that meets the most use cases. Fabric provides some significant features, such as modularity of consensus and encryption key management, but it also supports private channels. This book focuses on the power and flexibility of Hyperledger Fabric specifically.

### Hyperledger Indy

Hyperledger Indy was created and contributed by the Sovrin Foundation. The Sovrin Foundation is a private-sector, international nonprofit that was established intentionally to govern the world's first self-sovereign identity (SSI) network.

Indy is a Hyperledger project made to support independent identities on distributed ledger platforms. Indy provides a wide breadth of tools, libraries, and reusable components for providing digital identities rooted on blockchains or other distributed ledgers. The benefits are that the digital identities provide an interoperable capacity to enterprises across administrative domains, applications, and any other silos.

# The Hyperledger Greenhouse

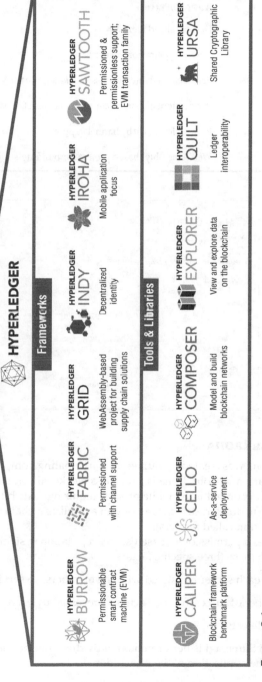

**FIGURE 2.1**
Hyperledger approach (Linux Foundation)
Graphic courtesy of Linux Foundation

**TABLE 2.2:**      Blockchains in the Hyperledger framework

| FRAMEWORK | APPLICATION |
|---|---|
| Indy | Decentralized identity |
| Iroha | Mobile application focused |
| Sawtooth | Permissioned and permissionless support; EVM transaction family |
| Burrow | Permissionable smart contract machine (EVM) |
| Fabric | Permissioned with channel support |
| Grid | Web Assembly–based project for building supply chain-based solutions |

**FIGURE 2.2**
Hyperledger Fabric
GitHub forks

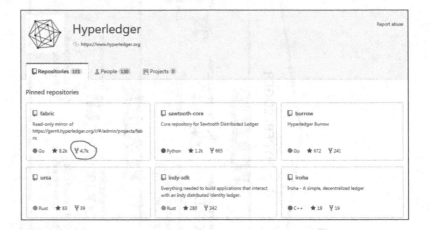

## HYPERLEDGER IROHA

Hyperledger Iroha was created by numerous participating companies, such as Soramitsu, Hitachi, NTT Data, and Colu. Iroha is a business blockchain framework specifically designed to be efficiently incorporated into mobile projects requiring distributed ledger technology. Iroha features a modern, domain-driven C++ design as well as a chain-based Byzantine fault-tolerant consensus algorithm called Sumeragi.

Sumeragi uses a permissioned-based server reputation system that calculates the reliability of servers based on these three specific factors:

- The time each server registered with the membership service

- The number of successful transactions processed by each server

- Failures detection

Consensus in Sumeragi is performed on individual transactions and on the global state resulting from the application of the transaction.

## HYPERLEDGER FABRIC

Hyperledger Fabric was mainly developed by IBM. Fabric is clearly intended as a foundation for developing applications or solutions with the modular architecture that enterprises require. Hyperledger Fabric allows for essentially a modular approach to components, such as consensus and membership services, and leverages containers to host smart contracts called *chaincode* that comprise the application logic of the system.

The permissioned nature of Hyperledger Fabric provides for privacy of operations for the participants. The need for privacy does not exclude the need for identification and audit ability from regulators. Basically, the encryption of identity (membership) is done in a manner that remains "private" from other blockchain participants. Auditing is effectively built in and also provides for compliance requirements, which is a major concern for enterprises.

Hyperledger Fabric does not perform mining, although cryptocurrency support is possible via chaincode by referencing an off-chain exchange.

## HYPERLEDGER SAWTOOTH

Hyperledger Sawtooth was built by Intel and is closer to a proprietary blockchain than an open source blockchain. Sawtooth is a modular platform for building, deploying, and running distributed ledgers, and it is considered Hyperledger's second most widely accepted blockchain framework.

Hyperledger Sawtooth includes a varied consensus algorithm called *proof of elapsed time* (PoET), which targets large distributed validator populations with minimal resource consumption. This essentially means that it can target distributed consensus efficiently.

**REFERENCE**    Chapter 4 covers PoET in greater detail.

## HYPERLEDGER BURROW

Hyperledger Burrow is a permissionable smart contract machine that was the first of its kind when it was released in 2014. Burrow's main value point is that it provides a modular blockchain client with a permissioned smart contract interpreter that was built to the specification of the Ethereum Virtual Machine (EVM). Burrow was specifically built to be a lightweight, efficient, and fast permissioned smart contract machine. Burrow accomplishes this goal by leveraging the hardened and speedy Tendermint protocol for consensus working with the Burrow's Apache-licensed EVM.

Smart contracts should perform the same across different blockchains that support smart contracts. This is really useful for portability since users can easily start with Hyperledger Burrow and over time migrate their smart contracts to another platform.

From this chart, it's clear that Hyperledger as a portfolio of blockchain frameworks has some similar capabilities, but the frameworks have some substantial use case differences between them as well.

# Introducing Hyperledger Fabric

Hyperledger Fabric has wide acceptance as an enterprise blockchain and is Hyperledger's most active project. The number of developers using the GitHub repository is clearly well above other blockchain frameworks in Hyperledger.

However, I will compare Hyperledger Fabric to Burrow, Sawtooth, Iroha, and Indy since those frameworks all have very specific use cases but also have some functionality that overlaps in the framework portfolio as well that are worth noting.

Hyperledger Fabric as a project was started by Digital Asset and IBM and has now emerged as a collaborative cross-industry venture that is currently hosted by the Linux Foundation. Hyperledger Fabric was actually the first blockchain to exit the "Incubation" stage and achieve the "Active" stage in March 2017 within the Hyperledger Project.

Hyperledger Fabric is a blockchain implementation that is designed for deploying a modular and extensible architecture. It has a modular subsystem design so that different implementations can be added over time. The modular architecture of Hyperledger Fabric separates the transaction processing workflow into three different stages, as listed here:

1. Chaincode invocation and initiation where the client application requests access to the blockchain network.

2. Transaction processing and ordering, where the transactions are processed in order first and then validated.

3. Transaction validation and commitment, where the transactions are validated and then committed to the blockchain ledger. The world state is updated as part of this step.

These distinct steps provide multiple benefits to the enterprise such as a reduced number of trust levels and verification, which improve network scalability and performance. In other blockchains such as Ethereum, transactions are processed differently in the sense that they are deterministic, meaning they always yield the same result given the same input and the same logic.

Figure 2.3 shows a typical Fabric network structure. As part of the structure you would have a client application, organizations, various types of peers, ordering peers, and membership services provider.

**FIGURE 2.3**
Hyperledger
Fabric overview

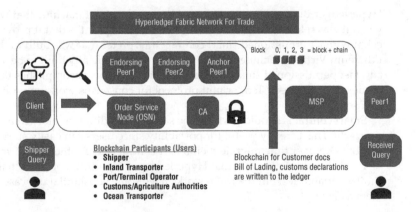

This figure shows a simple Fabric network setup with different peers, two organizations, and a client application. Hyperledger Fabric can scale to hundreds of peers, for example. I will be discussing scalability and performance around the enterprise blockchains in much more detail in Chapter 3.

**HYPERLEDGER FABRIC DEFINITIONS**

The following definitions will be useful to know as you read this book:

*Block*—This is an ordered set of transactions that is cryptographically linked to the preceding block(s) on a channel.

*Chain*—The ledger's chain is a transaction log structured as a hash-linked block of transactions.

*Chaincode*—Also known as a smart contract, this is code that is invoked by a client application external to the blockchain network.

*Channel*—This is a private blockchain overlay that allows for data isolation and confidentiality.

*Consensus*—This is a broader term, overarching the entire transactional flow, that serves to generate an agreement on the order and to confirm the correctness of the set of transactions constituting a block.

*Endorsement*—This is the process where specific peer nodes execute a chaincode transaction and return a proposal response to the client application.

*Genesis block*—This is the configuration block that initializes the ordering service or serves as the first block on a chain.

*Gossip protocol*—A gossip data-dissemination protocol performs three functions: manages peer discovery and channel membership, disseminates ledger data across all peers on the channel, and syncs ledger state across all peers on the channel.

*State database*—Data is stored in a state database for efficient reads and queries from chain code. Hyperledger-supported databases include LevelDB and CouchDB, depending on your use case.

*World state*—Also known as the *current state*, the world state is a component of the Hyperledger Fabric ledger. The world state represents the latest values for all keys included in the chain transaction log.

Source of these definitions: `https://hyperledger-fabric.readthedocs.io/en/release-1.4/glossary.html`.

## Hyperledger Fabric Ledger

The Hyperledger Fabric ledger is an immutable record of blockchain transactions. State transitions are initiated by chaincode invocations that are *transactions*. A transaction may also be considered a *request* to update the ledger.

The result of each transaction is a set of asset key-value pairs that are committed to the ledger as a create/read/update/delete (CRUD) operation. This is also a transaction log.

A key-value pair is an effective way to represent and identify an asset in the Fabric ledger. For example, you would specify a key-value pair that is an asset such as a car whose data is stored in the Fabric ledger. The data is stored in a key-value pair.

Here's an example of a key pair:

```
'color' : 'purple'
```

In this example, "color" is the key, and "purple" is the value of the color. This key-value pair is then stored on the ledger, which maintains a record.

Assets are tracked, identified, or updated via a ledger request (transaction) such as a query or update. Simply put, the ledger is the actual blockchain. The ledger is a file-based ledger that stores serialized blocks. Hyperledger Fabric has some interesting capabilities that are outside the standard behavior for a blockchain. For example, the state database can always be rebuilt from reprocessing the ledger, and a transaction can be rolled back, for example, if a transaction is deemed not valid.

There are currently two options for the state database in Fabric as well. First is an embedded database called LevelDB. You can also choose an external CouchDB as another option.

Hyperledger Fabric Ledger has two distinct parts.

◆ State data is a representation of the current state of the assets on the blockchain. Asset state data can be changed upon changes to the state of the data.

◆ Transaction logs record all the transactions in the order they are received that modified the state data. Once the data is written to the transaction logs, they are immutable and cannot be modified or deleted.

**REFERENCE**    Chapter 10, "Hands-on Blockchain Development," covers the database options for Fabric in more detail around modular choices, complex queries of the database, and compliance requirements to address in the development cycle.

## Hyperledger Fabric Consensus

Hyperledger Fabric's consensus is extensively broad and covers the whole transaction flow from start to finish.

In Hyperledger Fabric, nodes and peers can be somewhat confusing since they both have several roles. This is in stark contrast to Ethereum, for example, since the roles and tasks of nodes participating in reaching consensus are identical to each other. In a nutshell, every node in Ethereum does the same thing, but in Hyperledger nodes are very different in their missions on the blockchain network.

I discuss Hyperledger nodes in the "Nodes" section later in this chapter.

Consensus algorithms under Hyperledger are pluggable, meaning that users may select the algorithm of their choice during deployment.

Hyperledger Fabric 1.4 supports the following consensus methods at the time of writing:

◆ Kafka/Zab

◆ Raft

◆ SOLO

Chapter 4 covers the options for consensus methods for Hyperledger, Ethereum, Corda, and Quorum.

## Hyperledger Fabric Transactions

Transactions in Hyperledger are requests to the blockchain to execute a function on the ledger. The function is implemented by chaincode, which is a decentralized transactional program running on the validating nodes. Chaincode transactions are time-bounded and configured during chaincode deployment, which is similar to a database call or a web service invocation.

If a transaction times out, for example, it is considered as an error and will not cause state changes on the blockchain ledger. One chaincode function can call another chaincode function if the called function has the same restrictive confidentiality scope. Basically, a confidential chaincode can call another confidential chaincode if they share the same group of validator nodes.

As transactions are run in a new block, a delta from the world state in the last block on the blockchain is maintained. A delta is a change in the world state of the blockchain. For example, if the last block is block 27000 and there is an update to the ledger, then the world state changes. Simply put, a new block equals a new state.

Hyperledger supports two types of transactions.

◆   A *code-deploying transaction* is basically the initialization (`Init`) function of the blockchain application. `Init` is called when you first deploy your chaincode to the blockchain.

◆   A *code-invoking transaction* is called when you want to call (Invoke) chaincode functions to perform transactions on the blockchain. These transactions will be captured as blocks on the blockchain effectively.

Hyperledger Fabric is generally considered by the blockchain community as one of the simpler platforms for developing applications. This is because of the flexibility of the blockchain development support.

**REFERENCE**   In Chapter 10, I cover the basics of how to deploy a blockchain smart contract in Corda, Hyperledger, and Ethereum, so please review that text to find out more about smart contracts with those blockchains.

Transactions in Hyperledger Fabric have the following workflow. This can be significantly different from other blockchains.

1.  A transaction proposal that will trigger chaincode is initiated by the client application.

2.  The transaction proposal will then transmit to the appropriate peers for endorsement as specified in policies.

3.  The endorsing peer will execute the chaincode and will write the actual transaction to the ledger.

4.  The endorsing peer will sign the transaction and return it to the proposer.

When comparing Hyperledger Fabric to Ethereum around the transaction workflow, you know that, for example, Ethereum uses the sequential execution style, whereas Hyperledger Fabric uses a nonsequential execution style for transactions.

Figure 2.4 shows the contrast between common blockchain transaction execution styles. You can see that the two different execution styles vary. For example, one difference between the two is that the execute phase is started first non-sequentially. This could provide efficiencies in a permissioned blockchain that controls its membership but also could provide a response to the requester sooner.

To sum up the Hyperledger Fabric transaction process, the process starts with a transaction proposal, which is initiated by a client. A client is a blockchain user with a chaincode application requesting access to the blockchain network. Then this transaction proposal is transmitted to the

**FIGURE 2.4**
Comparing blockchain
execution styles

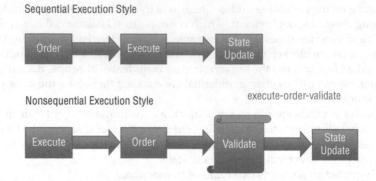

appropriate peers for endorsement as specified by an endorsement policy. An endorsing peer executes the chaincode, which results in an actual transaction for the ledger to maintain. The client receives the confirmation from the peers/nodes.

In summary, the Fabric network has a clear transaction order that needs to be maintained.

For more information on transactions, refer to the white paper "Hyperledger Fabric: A Distributed Operating System for Permissioned Blockchains" (https://www.hyperledger.org/wp-content/uploads/2017/08/Hyperledger_Arch_WG_Paper_1_Consensus.pdf).

## Hyperledger Fabric Nodes

The concept of a node is common in all blockchain technologies. The node becomes the communication endpoint in the blockchain technology.

Nodes connect to other nodes, creating a decentralized network. Nodes use a form of a peer-to-peer protocol to keep the distributed ledger in sync across the network. In Hyperledger Fabric, nodes need a valid certificate to be able to communicate to the network, and the participants use applications that connect to the network by way of the nodes.

Remember, Hyperledger Fabric is a permissioned blockchain and membership, identity, and certificates are validated before transacting on the blockchain. A participant's identity is not the same as a node's identity and could be an organization. For example, when a participant executes or invokes a transaction, their certificate is used for signing that transaction and therefore validated as well.

It is important to note that not all nodes in Hyperledger are equal, unlike other blockchains where every node maintains a copy of the same ledger. In Hyperledger Fabric, there are three distinct types of nodes:

◆ *Client nodes* initiate transactions for the client applications.

◆ *Peer nodes* commit transactions and keep the data in sync across the blockchain ledger.

◆ *Ordered nodes* are the communication backbones and responsible for the distribution of the transactions.

## Hyperledger Fabric Business Networks

A business network models participants, assets, registries, and transactions. Transaction processors implement business logic on these elements. Access control lists (ACLs) define privacy and sharing settings.

The most efficient way to deploy a Hyperledger Fabric business network model is by using Composer Playground, an interactive web tool for testing and deploying business networks. Blockchain developers can opt to install it on Docker as well as locally if they choose.

The business network archive (BNA) is created by using Hyperledger Composer. Composer is a tool that allows blockchain developers to package a few different files and generate an archive file, which can then be deployed onto a Fabric network. Composer is free for your developers to use and has a version that is available on IBM Cloud called Composer Playground.

**REFERENCE**    I discuss the Hyperledger Fabric business models in greater detail in Chapter 10.

## Hyperledger Fabric Chaincode (Smart Contracts)

*Chaincode* is the term to describe a smart contract in Hyperledger Fabric. Smart contracts are fully supported on Hyperledger Fabric, and Golang and JavaScript are supported at the time of writing.

Chaincode is application-level code stored on the ledger as part of a Hyperledger transaction. These transactions also modify the ledger state, which is known as the *world state*.

Chaincode is instantiated specifically on a channel or can be installed on several channels. A channel is a specific communication path used between peers looking for privacy. For example, if you have two channels, you can effectively deploy two versions of the code, and that code will not be accessible to the other code from another channel.

Client applications interact with the blockchain ledger through the chaincode methods Init and Invoke. The chaincode needs to be installed on every peer that will endorse a transaction and be instantiated on the channel. Specifying your membership policies would also be part of this chaincode strategy.

When creating chaincode, there are two methods that you will need to implement.

◆   Init is initially called when a chaincode receives an instantiate or upgrade transaction.

◆   Invoke is called when the invoke transaction is received to process any transaction proposals.

If you are developing a blockchain application, you will need to understand that creating both an Init method and an Invoke method within your chaincode is important.

**REFERENCE**    I cover more about Hyperledger Fabric chaincode development in Chapter 10.

## Hyperledger Fabric Development Tools

Hyperledger Composer is a development framework that is used for writing a blockchain network's chaincode and also is used for deploying the business network in Hyperledger Fabric.

There are two versions of Hyperledger Composer.

◆   A downloadable local version, called Composer, that you would install on premises in a cloud platform.

◆   An online version hosted by IBM Cloud called Hyperledger Playground.

You can download Hyperledger Fabric Composer from GitHub at `https://hyperledger.github.io/composer/latest/`.

You can access Hyperledger Fabric Composer Playground at `https://composer-playground.mybluemix.net/`.

**REFERENCE** Chapter 10 covers Hyperledger Fabric Composer in much more detail, including examples.

Figure 2.5 shows the initial login screen to Hyperledger Composer Playground.

**FIGURE 2.5**
Hyperledger Fabric
Composer Playground
web version
initial screen

Composer Playground is a web-based user interface that you can use to model and test your business network. Playground is good for modeling simple proof of concepts, as it uses the browser's local storage to simulate the blockchain network.

However, if you are running a local Fabric runtime and have deployed a network to it, you can also access that using Playground. In this case, Playground isn't simulating the network; it's communicating with the local Fabric runtime directly.

There are REST-based application programming interfaces (APIs) that can be used by client applications and that allow you to integrate non blockchain applications in the network. Representational State Transfer (REST) technology is an architectural style and services approach used in web services development.

There are also two software development kits (SDK) available for Hyperledger Fabric v1.4: Java and Node are the supported languages at the time of writing. Other development languages such as Python and Go will likely be supported according to the Hyperledger wiki.

SDKs are used to build applications for the blockchain and enable developers to have an onramp to the blockchain network to facilitate rapid development.

**REFERENCE** Chapter 10 covers SDKs and APIs in more detail.

## Hyperledger Fabric Governance

Because Hyperledger Fabric is a private validator network protocol, all entities are required to register with membership services to obtain an identity. This identity provides access and a transaction authority on the network. Certificates are issued to members. Two certificates are required: enrollment certificates and transaction certificates.

Hyperledger Fabric has permissioning governance built into every layer of the architecture. Operations such as starting a new consortium, adding or evicting members, defining a new channel, adding and evicting participants from channels all require collecting approval signatures from the appropriate organizations. The overarching policy model is enforced throughout the blockchain network.

Hyperledger Fabric has two levels of permissioning, and governance support based on either the consortium or the channel. A consortium is a membership-based network services made up of the membership of the organization.

Channels are supported as well, providing enhanced privacy or transactions through a point-to-point connection. Channels also provide a separate blockchain transaction ledger and network services. Chapter 9, "Blockchain Governance, Risk, Compliance (GRC), Privacy, and Legal Concerns," covers governance around Fabric in detail.

# Introducing R3 Corda

R3 is an enterprise blockchain software firm being developed by a broad ecosystem of more than 200 members and partners across multiple industries from both the private and public sectors. Corda is an open source blockchain platform, and Corda Enterprise is a commercial version of Corda blockchain platform for enterprise usage with Corda support.

The Corda platform was developed in close collaboration with a vast network of financial institutions, trade regulators, trade associations, professional services firms, and technology companies to leverage the power of blockchain to address specific business challenges. Corda was designed to meet the highest standards of one of the most complex and highly regulated industries in the world, which is the financial sector.

However, its blockchain services can be applied to other areas of business. Corda allows you to build interoperable blockchain networks that transact in strict privacy from other members.

Corda's smart contract technology (CorDapps) allows businesses to transact directly with industry-leading security features. I believe that Corda improves on the traditional custodial model that legacy financial services organizations have of acting as intermediary.

For example, it defines a standard approach and format for expressing financial assets and liabilities. The following are the main benefits of the enterprise market utilizing R3 Corda.

- ◆ Corda smart contracts can be written in Java and other JVM languages and can accelerate the development process for enterprises with in-house expertise.

- ◆ Corda has a flow framework to manage communication and negotiation between network participants. This network of participants is communicating via a direct peer-to-peer protocol where each node runs the Corda software as well as Corda applications known as CorDapps.

◆ Corda has a unique "notary" infrastructure to validate uniqueness and sequencing of transactions without global broadcast to all network participants.

◆ Corda enables the rapid development and deployment of distributed apps called CorDapps. CorDapps take the structure of a set of JAR files containing class definitions written in Java and/or Kotlin.

◆ Corda was specifically designed to maintain a balance of trade-offs for business problems and domain concerns around the financial sector such as scalability and security.

◆ Corda has a pluggable consensus, which allows blockchain developers to address trade-offs such as performance, scalability, security, and privacy.

The financial sector is one of the most regulated industries not only in the United States but also around the world. Handling customer data while dealing with privacy and compliance concerns is a burdensome task for these organizations.

R3 Corda handles these challenges with trade-offs that regulated financial institutions may find favorable. These trade-offs include the following:

◆ Scalability

◆ Security

◆ Privacy

◆ Confidentiality

◆ Complexity

◆ Performance

◆ Compliance

Handling these trade-offs is exactly what R3 Corda was developed to address and does well through its structure of CorDapps.

Corda is a strictly engineered shared ledger fabric network for financial services use cases that can be deployed within existing legal frameworks and that relies on proven technologies that the financial sector depends on. R3 Corda has a strict and well-defined philosophy that can be broken down into three categories according to the Corda white paper (`https://docs.corda.net/_static/corda-introductory-whitepaper.pdf`).

The three categories are:

◆ Engineering for the requirements of institutions

◆ A focus on nonfunctional requirements

◆ Extensibility

There are essentially two direct approaches to deploying a blockchain network with R3 Corda.

◆ **Corda** is the open source blockchain platform, enabling businesses to transact directly and in strict privacy, reducing transaction and record-keeping costs and streamlining business operations.

♦ **Corda Enterprise** is an enterprise-ready commercial distribution of Corda specifically optimized to meet the demands of enterprises.

As shown in Figure 2.6, the stack of Corda is actually quite simple. Corda has two versions: an enterprise or open source version with blockchain network services and on top of the stack is the CorDapp.

**FIGURE 2.6**
Corda stack structure

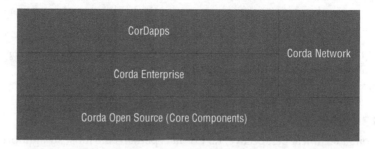

R3 Corda certainly has a niche in the financial and insurance sectors but is expanding its use cases, for example, to other sectors. Currently, Corda would not be a good fit for a logistics company or a government services organization because of the overhead it would have compared to other blockchains such as Hyperledger. I will discuss more about R3 Corda and its use cases in Chapter 8, "Enterprise Blockchain Use Cases."

## CORDA DEFINITIONS

The following definitions, quoted here from the Corda glossary at https://docs.corda.net/glossary.html, will be useful to know as you read this book:

*AMQP*—The serialization mechanism used within Corda for everything except flow checkpoints and RPC.

*Artemis*—The message queuing middleware used within Corda.

*CorDapp*—Corda distributed application (dapp).

*Cordformation*—A Gradle plugin that can be configured via your Gradle build scripts to locally deploy a set of Corda nodes.

*Counterparty*—The other party in a financial or contract transaction.

*Gradle*—Industry-standard build and deployment tool, used extensively within Corda.

*Kotlin*—The language used to code Corda and is fully compatible with any JVM language.

*Kryo*—The serialization mechanism used within Corda for flow checkpoints and RPC.

*Input*—In Corda terms, a state that is used and consumed within a transaction. Once consumed, it cannot be reused.

*JVM*—The Java virtual machine, which is the "computing machine" that Corda is executed within.

*Node*—A communication point on the Corda network and also the provider of the virtual machine in which Corda runs.

*Notary Service*—A network service that guarantees that it will only add its signature to transactions if all input states have not been consumed.

*Output*—In the Corda model, a state generated from a transaction (note that multiple outputs can be generated from one transaction). They are then used as inputs for subsequent transactions.

I've listed only the definitions required to understand this book. For additional development-specific terms, see the Corda glossary.

## R3 Corda Blockchain Fundamentals

From a technical perspective, R3 Corda is perhaps the most straightforward enterprise blockchain to understand. In my experience, there are several reasons for its clear success. The R3 Corda consortium has clearly defined the features, functions, and use cases with their consortium members. Corda is a platform for blockchain applications for financial enterprises where many applications share similarities with an IOU (payment/debt) use case. Corda maintains a vendor approach to development, training, and marketing that is well maintained, professional, and directed.

Corda documentation is clearly defined and professionally developed but also maintained by experts assigned by Corda. Finally, R3 Corda is the only enterprise blockchain to have a demo tool, Corda DemoBench.

The Corda DemoBench tool lets you drive transactions in a blockchain. It is useful for performing demos and is free to use.

**REFERENCE**   Chapter 5, "Enterprise Blockchain Sales Engineering," covers Corda DemoBench in greater detail.

## R3 Corda Network

The Corda network is a fully connected "graph" network and does not use a gossip protocol. Corda communications actually occur point to point and, therefore there is somewhat less network overhead as compared to a gossip protocol, where broadcasts are sent to all network peers. Peers use a specific peer-to-peer Advanced Message Queuing Protocol (AMQP). AMQP is an open-standard Application layer protocol that is message-oriented and uses TLS for secure communications.

For privacy concerns, the peers do not broadcast to all other network peers, but instead they direct to the network peer required in the transaction.

**NOTE**   I discuss specific security and encryption topics in Chapter 11, "Hands-On Blockchain Security."

Corda is a permissioned network that is specifically designed to address regulated financial institutions' concerns and is a natural fit for the banking sector, trading sector, and even the insurance sector.

Figure 2.7 shows an example of how a Corda blockchain network would be set up with the affiliated Corda components. These Corda components are generally easy to plan and deploy. The main difference is that Corda has a somewhat different approach to naming components such as with a notary or a CorDapp.

**FIGURE 2.7**
Corda network

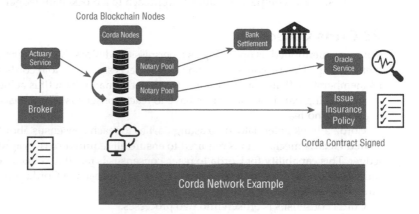

Chapter 3, "Architecting Your Enterprise Blockchain," covers the deployment and architecture in more detail.

**NOTE**   "Our platform considers non-financial applications to be out of scope." —R3 Corda white paper.

## R3 Corda Ledger

R3 Corda is a targeted distributed ledger technology (DLT) platform that uses an effective global broadcast and gossip network protocol to propagate data to other members in the block-chain network.

Corda uses a point-to-point messaging protocol (called AMPQ) where the broadcast is targeted and is not broadcast to all members on the network. Being that the protocol is point to point, only the nodes participating in the transaction will be privileged to the transaction ledger activity. This provides the main benefits of privacy to the members.

The Corda ledger has some significant differences from other blockchains that are noteworthy.

◆   The Corda ledger allows for the management and synchronization of business agreements between multiple parties that can be designed as a legal contract. The Corda ledger was specifically designed to address interparty contracts that are regulated financial institutions, which other blockchains just cannot address efficiently.

◆   There is no centralized ledger operating on behalf of all the nodes on the network, which can very different from other blockchains. Instead, each node on the network maintains a vault containing all of its known facts. A vault is storage space that maintains a secure area for protecting the known facts.

◆ The Corda Ledger is subjective from each peer's perspective, meaning that the ledger will be accessed differently by each peer depending on membership participation. What is somewhat unique is that not all on-ledger facts have to be shared by each member for all the other blockchain network members to view. Think about this as a "need-to-know" basis or a "compartmentalized" approach to a blockchain ledger.

## R3 Corda Consensus

Corda, as mentioned, is operating as a permissioned blockchain ledger for its financial-sector membership. This provides more fine-grained access control to records and enhances privacy for its membership. It also fair to assume that a performance benefit is achieved, as only parties (nodes) taking part in a transaction have to reach consensus. The transactions are not distributed to all other nodes.

Corda allows potentially distrusting parties to reach consensus about the state of a set of shared facts. A mechanism is required to ensure all required parties agree on the state of the ledger. This capability for Corda to reach consensus is facilitated via a verification consensus or uniqueness consensus in Corda. This consensus approach in Corda is remarkably different from other blockchains.

Corda consensus is broken into two processes.

◆ Transaction validity means that the parties involved can reach certainty that a proposed update transaction defining output states is valid by checking that the associated contract code runs successfully. It also has all the required signatures and that any transactions to which this transaction refers to are also valid.

◆ Transaction uniqueness is when the parties can reach certainty that the transaction in question is the unique and correct consumer of all its input states. That is, there are no other transactions around validity and uniqueness that will consume any of the same states.

Parties can agree on transaction validity by independently running the same contract code and validation logic.

### Corda Notary

A *notary* is a network service that is unique to Corda. The notary service provides what is effectively a uniqueness consensus. One more way to view a notary is that it acts as a trusted party that guarantees a particular state is consumed only once. You can think of a state similarly to a funding in a wallet in Ethereum or the world state in Hyperledger Fabric.

The notary provides the point of finality in the system and is similar to an intermediary. The process a notary goes through to validate uniqueness is called *notarization*. Parties cannot be sure that an equally valid but conflicting transaction is regarded as a valid attempt to spend the given input state until the notary signature is obtained.

For example, each state will have an appointed notary and this notary will notarize the transaction only if it is the appointed notary of all the transaction's input states. Simply put, notaries are intermediaries who can both block transactions and resolve conflicts.

Corda has pluggable uniqueness services that can improve privacy, scalability, legal-system compatibility, and algorithmic agility. For example, a single service may be composed of many mutually non-trusting nodes coordinating via a Byzantine fault tolerant algorithm or it could be a very simple virtual machine.

These uniqueness services are required only to attest to whether the states consumed by a given transaction have previously been consumed; they are not required to attest to the validity of the transaction itself, which is a matter for the parties to the transaction.

**NOTE**   Corda supports two types of consensus: uniqueness consensus and verification consensus.

What this really means is that the uniqueness services are not required to see the full contents of any transactions. This will significantly improve privacy and scalability of the system compared with alternative distributed ledger and blockchain designs. This Corda design decision represents an impressive choice as to the acceptable trade-offs in shared ledger architectures.

In short, the point of finality is reached once the notary service signs the transaction. However, there can be exceptions. If a transaction has no input states or timestamps, then the "uniqueness" of those properties clearly cannot be confirmed nor denied. A notary must be assigned to the transaction, but a notary signature is only needed when there are input states and/or timestamps.

**NOTE**   Remember, there is no central ledger in Corda. The ledger is "subjective" from other nodes' perspectives. Essentially, the ledger is distributed but not shared.

## R3 Corda Nodes

The Java Virtual Machine (JVM) is used for contract execution and validation in Corda. This JVM provides several benefits because of the widespread use of Java and ease of development. The main point to realize before developing with the virtual machine is that it has been augmented with a customized sandbox that is more restrictive than the ordinary JVM sandbox. This restrictive virtual machine enforces security requirements.

In a nutshell, a Corda node is a JVM runtime environment with a unique identity on the blockchain network that hosts Corda services and CorDapps.

Corda nodes can have four broad categories of functionality, which can be any of the following:

◆  Network map provides a way to resolve identities to physical node addresses and associated public keys.

◆  Notary acts as a "witness" to the transactions and has the final say in whether a transaction is a double-spend.

◆  Oracle is an access point that links the ledger to the outside world by providing facts that affect the validity of transactions.

◆  Regular mode starts protocols communicating with other nodes, notaries, and oracles, and evolves their private ledgers on the network.

## R3 Corda States

One of the differentiators between other distributed ledger technologies and Corda is how the state of blockchain ledger is actually handled. Corda uses the term *state* to mean a representation of immutable objects with shared facts such as an agreement or contract at a specific point in time.

The terms *shared facts* and *states* can essentially mean the same thing and are generally used interchangeably. Let's clarify what a *state* can be in Corda from a ledger perspective. A state may represent anything that the member agrees upon, such as a bank note, invoices, and so on at a specific time. This is similar to a world state in other blockchains. A static state means that there is no change to the representation of the object being defined.

For example, if you are familiar with the financial sector, then you can have states representing the following:

◆ Collateralized debt obligations (CDOs)

◆ Collateralized loan obligations (CLOs)

◆ Invoices or statements

◆ Bank credits

◆ Credit default swaps

◆ Rate swaps such as interest rates

◆ Bonds

Basically, in Corda the state model can be used to represent literally anything that is part of an agreement. A state can be used to represent financial instruments or multilateral agreements, assets, or liabilities.

Different types of states can contain different attributes. For instance, a trade bond could have a coupon date, a redemption date, and so on. States are immutable and therefore cannot be changed to another state after created. States contain data about shared facts at a specific point in time.

## R3 Corda Transactions

Transactions in R3 Corda are very specific in the sense that it's clearly defined which command is to be issued. For example, in Corda, we would declare intent as "Issue" or "Agree" in a CorDapp, and the CorDapp would determine whether the transactions are valid.

Assume your organization wants to declare which type of transaction is being agreed upon. When you design a CordApp, you need to identify the type of transactions appropriately.

Transactions in R3 Corda are propagated around the network but are not broadcast to every node. The broadcast is verified more on a need-to-know approach. This allows members to ensure that they maintain privacy around transactions.

This transaction approach is comparable to channeling in Hyperledger where you have nodes in the network that can be placed on a channel to communicate for privacy concerns.

## R3 Corda Client Applications

When considering client applications to integrate with R3 Corda in your enterprise, you must realize that Java or Kotlin is used for the Corda APIs. This is not exactly a showstopper but something to be aware of. Corda, however, does provide a full client library that allows your developers to write clients in a JVM-compatible language to interact with the running nodes.

Corda has provided a sample CorDApp for those that would appreciate a tutorial in Corda. You can find it at `https://docs.corda.net/tutorial-cordapp.html`. For community-driven applications, visit `https://www.corda.net/develop/samples.html`.

**NOTE**   Chapter 6 covers how to develop blockchain applications in greater detail.

## R3 Corda Smart Contracts

In R3 Corda, smart contracts are also referred to as *contracts* and may be legally enforceable when the legal prose has been agreed upon by the participants in the CordApps. Comparatively, in Ethereum, a smart contract is a singular program and not an enforceable contract.

In Corda, these contracts are deployed via a CorDapp, which is simply a collection of contracts working together as an application. In Ethereum this is called a *distributed application* (dapp).Realize that these contracts are somewhat different from the smart contracts of other blockchain platforms such as Ethereum. In Corda, these contracts are not stateful objects representing the current state of the world but more like real-world contracts that may have legal prose attached as well.

States can contain arbitrary data, allowing them to represent facts such as a stock trades, bank notes, or loans, for example.

R3 Corda smart contracts (CordApps) consist of computer code but also can contain legal prose that is attached. This is a big differentiator between other blockchains since this feature was clearly planned for its members.

Above the smart legal contracts is specific legal prose that are formulated in a way that they can be expressed and implemented in smart contract code. The rationale behind this is to give the code legitimacy that is affiliated in the associated legal prose.

This specific construct historically has been called a Ricardian contract in the financial sector. The Ricardian contract was devised by Ian Grigg in 1996, as a method of recording a document as a contract of law and linking it securely to other systems, such as accounting, as an issuance of value.

In the blockchain world, Ricardian contracts are nothing more than digital documents that define the detailed terms and conditions of a contract. These contracts are usually signed and agreed to by both parties. This Ricardian contract approach is used to mitigate current contract issues but also provides clarity to any contract challenges in the future.

To summarize, a CorDapp is a Ricardian contract that is written with the standard legal prose that is required in court and then is cryptographically hashed to be available for usage by the application. Corda also has an interesting approach that allows a regulatory body to actually be given oversight access. This regulatory body can also be brought into the network to act as an observer to verify the contract as well (see Figure 2.8).

**FIGURE 2.8**
Corda smart contract
with legal prose

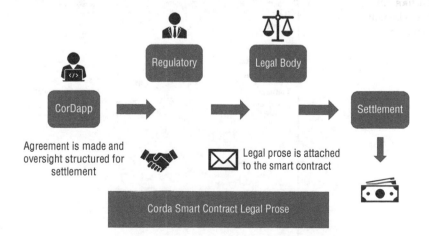

**NOTE**   R3 Corda was intentionally designed to account for the highly regulated environment of the financial services industry.

The following are the benefits of smart contracts (CorDapps) in Corda specifically for financial institutions that use Corda:

◆   Smart contracts regulate and streamline the workflow between the participating decentralized firms.

◆   These CorDapps also include supervisory and regulatory nodes that provide an observer responsibility.

◆   The consensus algorithms are limited & to the firms involved.

◆   Access to the data within an agreement is limited to the permissioned parties involved.

◆   The CordApps also validate the transaction solely between the two parties that are participating.

## R3 Corda Development Tools

R3 Corda, being a private consortium that was built from the ground up to develop enterprise blockchains for its consortium members, has a wealth of documentation, tools, and services. Corda has a large following of developers, and Corda as an organization provides, in my opinion, superior community events that really help drive development.

**Corda DemoBench**   DemoBench is a stand-alone desktop application that makes it easy to configure and launch local Corda nodes. It is useful for training sessions, demos, and experimentation. To learn more, visit

`https://www.corda.net/discover/demobench.html.`

Figure 2.9 shows the starting window after you launch Corda DemoBench. We can configure our node and also determine the type of notary in Corda Demobench. After you download and install DemoBench, you can start adding nodes and notaries.

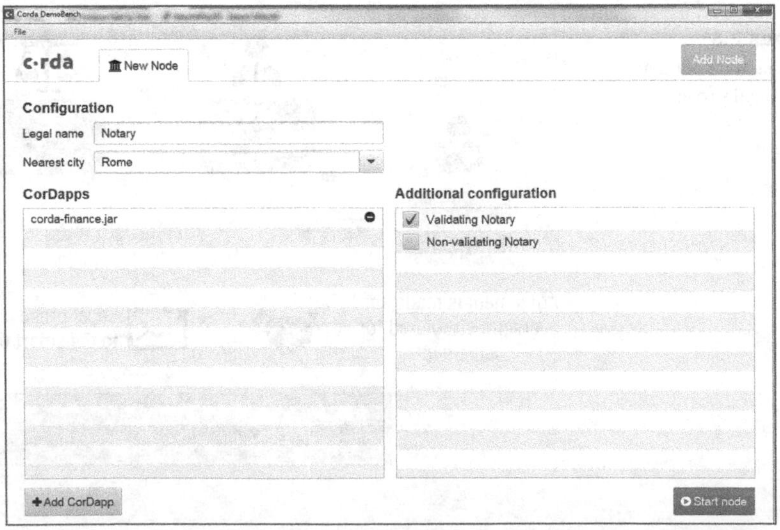

**FIGURE 2.9**
Corda DemoBench
initial screen

I cover the installation, configuration and walk thru a demo in Chapter 5.

**Node Explorer**   "The Node Explorer provides views to the node's vault and transaction data using Corda's RPC framework."

```
https://ci-artifactory.corda.r3cev.com/artifactory/corda-releases/net/corda/
corda-tools-explorer/3.2-corda/.
```

**Blob Inspector**   With Corda 3, R3 Corda has guaranteed a wire stable AMQP serialization format. As a binary format, it has various advantages over text-based protocols but also has the same downside: lack of human readability. The Blob Inspector fills this gap. Given a file path or URL, it will display the contents of Corda blobs in YAML or JSON.

You can find documentation for the Blob Inspector here:

```
https://docs.corda.net/head/blob-inspector.html.
```

You can download the Blob Inspector from here:

```
https://ci-artifactory.corda.r3cev.com/artifactory/corda-releases/net/corda/
corda-blob-inspector/3.2-corda/corda-blob-inspector-3.2-corda.jar.
```

**Network Bootstrapper**   "This is a tool that scans all the node configurations from a common directory to generate the network parameters file, which is then copied to all the nodes' directories. It also copies each node's node-info file to every other node so that they can all be visible to each other. You can find the documentation for the Network Bootstrapper here:"

```
https://docs.corda.net/head/network-bootstrapper.html.
```

"You can download the latest version from here:"

```
https://ci-artifactory.corda.r3cev.com/artifactory/corda-releases/
net/corda/corda-network-bootstrapper/3.2-corda/corda-network-
bootstrapper-3.2-corda-executable.jar.
```

## R3 Corda Governance

Governance in Corda is clearly an important priority because of the nature of its financial sector clients where compliance and liability are a great concern to its consortium members.

Corda uses a unique approach to transaction oversight through the use of a notary oversight procedure. A notary is considered a trusted party that guarantees that a particular state is consumed only once in Corda. This guarantee of state in Corda from the notary eliminates challenges such as any double spending issues, over drafting your account, and even can deal with currency exchange–based issues.

Notaries are the main blockchain network's governance structure in a sense because they validate the transaction uniqueness and the participation in the network.

In Corda, there is no unified blockchain that contains a record of all the transactions. Corda has a different approach where the Corda nodes will see only those transactions in which they are directly involved or which they depend on historically for validation purposes.

Lastly, the Corda nodes are responsible for checking transaction correctness and authorizing the transactions. The Corda nodes fully rely on notaries to verify the uniqueness of transactions and provide governance of the blockchain, which is a critical part of the governance structure.

# Introducing Quorum

Quorum is an open source blockchain solution built by enhancing the existing Ethereum blockchain. Quorum is based on the official Go implementation of the Ethereum protocol, which provides almost a mirror of Ethereum features and benefits.

Quorum provides an additional layer on top of Ethereum that enables it to perform private transactions but also makes it more flexible by using different consensus algorithms. Quorum overall was designed as a permissioned implementation of Ethereum that supports the enterprise requirements of transaction privacy and contract privacy.

The main use case for Quorum is that it can achieve data privacy through the introduction of a new "private" transaction identifier with modifications to the Ethereum codebase. These modifications are provided in the Go-Ethereum codebase, which includes modifications to the block proposal and validation processes. Data privacy in Quorum is achieved through cryptography and also through an intentional segmentation of the nodes similar to sandboxing.

**NOTE**   Quorum is a fork of the Ethereum blockchain.

The main reason an enterprise would choose Quorum over Ethereum is privacy; a secondary reason is that Quorum is based on Ethereum, which has a robust and active development base making it easy to find expertise.

Quorum supports private transactions and private contracts through public and private state segmentation. Quorum supports privacy by using a newer messaging exchange called Constellation. Constellation is a peer-to-peer encrypted message exchange used for the targeted transfer of private data to network participants. This messaging exchange is similar to what we have in Hyperledger with the implementation of Kafka.

Quorum offers options for consensus mechanisms that are considered desirable for a consortium use case. For example, Istanbul Byzantine fault tolerance and a Raft-based consensus are two consensus methods that support enterprise features such as fault tolerance and availability.

Quorum Chain is a new consensus that is based on a majority voting and time-based mechanism that supports Ethereum-based transactions that can be propagated through the network.

**NOTE**   I cover these consensus mechanisms in greater detail in Chapter 4.

Figure 2.10 shows the high-level components of the Quorum blockchain. You can see that there is a Quorum node with Go-Ethereum, which extends the capabilities to the Ethereum network.

**FIGURE 2.10**
Quorum blockchain components

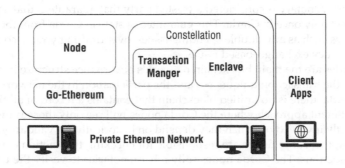

Constellation is a mechanism for submitting information and allows encrypted communication between peers. Constellation consists of two parts: a transaction manager and Enclave.

Permissions at the node level are governed by smart contract code. The main benefit is that it provides a higher level of performance compared to the public Ethereum blockchain.

The primary features of Quorum over public Ethereum are as follows:

◆ Transaction and contract privacy

◆ Multiple voting-based consensus mechanisms

◆ Network/peer permissions management

◆ Better performance and scalability because of its simple consensus

In Quorum, a transaction has to be either public or private. If the transaction is private, all the data within that transaction is private for that set of entities in the blockchain.

In a nutshell, Quorum is open source and more approachable for some organizations than implementing a custom private blockchain on other platforms.

Quorum aims to be a platform that allows integration and experimentation with not only the financial industry, but also other companies interested in the blockchain technology using a proven platform on Ethereum.

---

### QUORUM DEFINITIONS

Like other blockchains and distributed ledgers, Quorum has its own set of terminologies and definitions to learn.

*Constellation* is a newer general purpose messaging system for submitting information in a secure way. It is comparable to a network of message transfer agents (MTAs) where messages are encrypted with PGP.

A *Quorum node* is intentionally designed to be a lightweight fork of Go-Ethereum to take advantage of the R&D happening in the ever-growing Ethereum community.

A *private contract* in Quorum is a contract that was created by a private transaction.

A *private transaction* is a Quorum transaction that takes a list of public keys that identify the parties of the transaction and therefore make the transaction private to those parties.

*Sharding* basically segments the validation of transactions so that not every node in the network is validating every transaction that occurs.

---

## Quorum Blockchain Fundamentals

Quorum is a private/permissioned blockchain platform based on the official Go implementation of the Ethereum protocol with an enterprise focus. Quorum was built on top of an existing Ethereum blockchain and inherits the maturity of the production-hardened "go-Ethereum" code base. Quorum has brought together the public and enterprise development communities on a common protocol to work for the financial sectors.

Quorum uses a voting-based consensus algorithm extremely effectively and then achieves data privacy through the introduction of a new "private" transaction identifier.

One of the clearly stated design goals of Quorum was to reuse as much existing technology as possible from Ethereum to minimize the changes required for Go-Ethereum to work efficiently.

Strategically, for example, this plan actually reduced the effort required to keep in sync with future versions of the public Ethereum codebase. Much of the logic responsible for the additional privacy functionality resides in a layer that sits on top of the standard Ethereum protocol layer.

Based on its official description, Quorum is essentially an extension of Ethereum through a strategic fork of its code base. The Quorum blockchain has many similarities to Ethereum. Quorum has a clear mission to provide the best features of a permissionless blockchain with the added privacy, security, and performance of a permissioned blockchain for a targeted audience.

Quorum was developed by J.P. Morgan Chase and its consortium members. Quorum is one of the first major steps toward the common adoption of blockchain among financial industries.

Essentially, Quorum functions similarly to Ethereum but has four very significant differences or areas to appreciate when compared to native Ethereum.

- Network and peer permissions management to sandbox transactions on a private Ethereum platform

- Increased transaction and contract privacy through private transactions

- Voting-based consensus mechanisms not available in Ethereum

- Higher performance due to limited nodes

## Quorum Ledger

This system has two distinct types of possible transactions in Quorum, which are public and private transactions. *Public transactions* are transactions where the payload is fully visible to all participants. These publicly viewable transactions are the standard Ethereum transactions you're expecting on the Ethereum blockchain.

*Private transactions* are different where the payload is visible only to participants whose public keys are specified in the `privateFor` parameter of the transaction.

## Quorum Consensus

Consensus in Quorum is somewhat more flexible than other blockchains. For example, Quorum offers options for consensus mechanisms that are considered desirable for consortium use cases.

These consensus choices are as follows:

- Istanbul Byzantine fault tolerance and raft-based consensus are consensus methods that support enterprise features such as fault tolerance and availability.

- Quorum Chain is a newer consensus based on a majority voting and time-based mechanisms that support Ethereum-based transactions that can be propagated through the network, for example.

There exists two blockchain states in Quorum. The first state is the public state shared by all nodes of public transactions, and the second state is the private state local to each node for the private transactions the nodes are authorized for.

## Quorum Smart Contracts

As previously mentioned, Quorum is based on Ethereum and is a fork of the Ethereum blockchain. With that being said, implementing and using Ethereum smart contracts will be quite familiar to Ethereum developers.

Quorum uses the standard Solidity language for writing smart contracts. This provides immense value since you can design as you have been in Ethereum.

One of the differentiators is that smart contracts can be either public or private to one or more network participants on the Quorum blockchain network.

**NOTE**    Quorum does not introduce new smart contract types; rather, it introduces a smart contract based on the transaction's type, which is public or private.

The main difference is that with Quorum you can send a private transaction using the Ethereum network protocols. In Quorum, you can send a private transaction by coding your smart contract to address this requirement for a private transaction.

On a Quorum network you would send a standard Ethereum transaction but set the `private-For` parameter on the message to be the public key of the participant that should be able to view and execute the transaction or contract code.

Figure 2.11 shows a private transaction in a know your customer (KYC) use case.

**FIGURE 2.11**
KYC private transaction
in Quorum

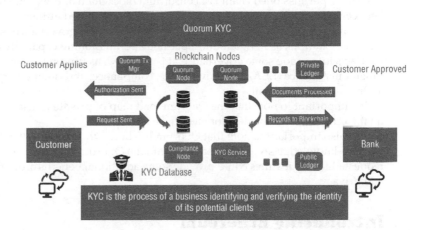

For more on this, go to `https://github.com/jpmorganchase/quorum/wiki/Using-Quorum`. Private contracts cannot update public contracts. This is intentional, as not all participants will be able to execute a private contract. It is important to note that once a contract has been made public, the contract cannot be made private later. For a public contract to become private, it would need to be deleted from the blockchain and a new private contract would have to be created.

**REFERENCE**    Smart contract development is discussed in more detail in Chapter 10, "Hands-On Blockchain Development."

## Quorum Tools and Utilities

Quorum is based on Ethereum, as we already know, so this allows smart contracts to be built with Solidity. Quorum also shares some core development tools with Ethereum. One of those tools is Truffle, which is exactly what the majority of Ethereum developers are likely using already.

Essentially, an Ethereum developer will have very little development ramp-up time and learning curve for integrating the Quorum blockchain solution due to the use of Ethereum tools and utilities.

One tool that was built specifically for Quorum is called Cakeshop. Cakeshop provides an easy-to-use graphic interface (GUI) for working with Quorum networks, smart contracts, and Quorum APIs. Cakeshop can start up a Geth node, which you can then interact with using the Cakeshop front end or can be connected to an Ethereum-like node, such as Quorum, that you already have running. The given Cakeshop instance will connect with only one node on the blockchain network you specify.

You can download the Cakeshop GUI from `https://github.com/jpmorganchase/cakeshop/wiki/Cakeshop-Overview`. For more about Quorum development and tools, please refer to Chapter 10.

### Quorum Governance

Quorum's permissioned chain is a consortium blockchain and was devised to be implemented between participants who are pre-approved by a designated authority.

Because Quorum is a fork of the Ethereum blockchain, governance is not exactly supported well. For example, as in Ethereum, a per-node permissioning capability can be set up via smart contracts to provide some governance. It is expected, as funding comes from the Enterprise Ethereum Alliance (EEA), that governance, compliance, and other enterprise concerns will be addressed more in detail.

It's important to note that the Quorum road map of private transactions and smart contracts is on the project list for the development team to work on.

It is also important to note that Quorum has been working with the Zcash team to integrate the zero-knowledge security layer (ZSL) into the Quorum protocol. These important and highly requested future features could provide some additional benefits around compliance, security, and privacy.

## Introducing Ethereum

Ethereum is an open source platform based on blockchain technology that enables developers to build and deploy decentralized applications (smart contracts).

Ethereum is essentially a world computer that is distributed between thousands of nodes. This computer of many distributed nodes is accessible to anyone, anywhere, with Internet access. There are no membership requirements to address, and it is truly a public blockchain.

The first public beta prerelease network was known as Olympic. The Olympic network provided users with a bug bounty of 25,000 Ethers for stress testing the limits of the Ethereum blockchain. Ether is the token utilized for using the Ethereum network.

Ethereum is software running on a network of world computers that ensures that data and small computer programs called *smart contracts* are replicated and processed on all the computers on the network, without a central coordinator. The founders' vision was to create an unstoppable censorship-resistant self-sustaining decentralized world computer. For example, if you download Ethereum to your computer, it will become an Ethereum "node" on the network, running an EVM, and will behave equivalently to all the other nodes.

Note that Ethereum is a peer-to-peer network, and there is no centralization; therefore, all computers have equivalent status to other nodes. Figure 2.12 shows the peer-to-peer decentralized network of Ethereum. The network nodes for Ethereum run the Ethereum virtual machine. Note that the network structure is not flat or hierarchical, like in common networking.

**FIGURE 2.12**
Ethereum peer-to-peer
decentralized network

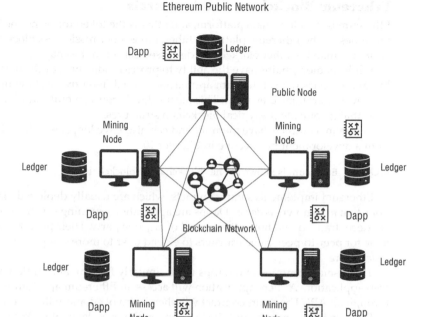

**NOTE** "When I came up with Ethereum, my first thought was, 'OK, this thing is too good to be true.' As it turned out, the core Ethereum idea was good, fundamentally, completely sound." — Ethereum Inventor, Vitalik Buterin (https://www.genesis-mining.com/what-is-the-ethereum-blockchain).

---

## ETHEREUM DEFINITIONS

Like other blockchains and distributed ledgers, Ethereum has its own set of terminologies and definitions.

*Dapps* (decentralized applications) are essentially one or more smart contracts that are working together to run an Ethereum application. These applications run on a P2P network of computers, instead of one computer.

"*Ether* is the native token of the Ethereum blockchain and is used to pay for transaction fees, miner rewards, and other services on the network."

"*Gas* is a measurement roughly equivalent to computational steps for Ethereum. Every transaction is required to include a gas limit and a fee that it is willing to pay per gas; miners have the choice of including the transaction and collecting the fee or not. Every operation has a gas expenditure on an EVM. I will discuss gas in more detail in Chapter 3."

Source: https://bigmarketnews.com/crypto-dictionary/.

*Node* is a device, program, or virtual machine that communicates with the Ethereum network. Nodes are also known as *clients*. A node runs the blockchain services and maintains the ledger.

## Ethereum Blockchain Fundamentals

Ethereum is the blockchain platform, and ether is the token for using the Ethereum virtual machines on the Ethereum platform. Ethereum is a permissionless blockchain and has a different approach than the other blockchains discussed earlier in the chapter.

While all blockchains have the ability to process code, most of the blockchains are severely limited by restrictions. Ethereum approaches code differently by allowing developers to create whatever operations they want. This means developers can build thousands of different applications that go outside the typical blockchain structures.

Ethereum contracts have memory and can also have loops, which I will address in more detail from a development perspective in Chapter 10.

**NOTE**    Ethereum is known as the "blockchain of blockchains."

Ethereum implements smart contracts, which are usually deployed via distributed applications that are known as *dapps*. Dapps are applications running directly on the blockchain. They are decentralized and not in the control of any one party. Their purpose is clearly to use simple logic for peer-to-peer value transfers to extend over to more complicated token structures and much more.

These smart contracts and dapps work similarly from an application perspective to any other web application. A client application will access an Ethereum application via the HTTP protocol through an API. The smart contract will then be invoked and will run on the EVM.

Because the economics and the logic are on the same layer, it makes value transfer extremely easy. You can save hardware and configuration by deploying the logic directly on the blockchain.

**NOTE**    Bitcoin is a blockchain 1.0, and Ethereum is a blockchain 2.0.

Ether tokens are created by a schedule that was set by its 2014 presale structure. Ether tokens are mined and thus require a miner. For example, 5 ether tokens are created for every block mined, which is approximately every 15 seconds. These 5 ether tokens are sent to the miners that mine the block. Ether can also be sent to another miner that participates in the transaction since it is possible that several miners to compete for the mining of the blocks. Ether is considered the "fuel" that runs the Ethereum network.

**NOTE**    Ethereum is the platform. Ether is the cryptocurrency built into the platform.

### PROOF-OF-WORK MINING

In proof-of-work (PoW) mining, the miners compete to create valid blocks by spending electricity to find solutions to a mathematical puzzle. Ethereum's PoW math challenge called Ethash works slightly differently than Bitcoin's PoW mining. This allows common hardware to be used for mining and lowers the barrier to mining at least from a cost perspective. The downside to this is that it reduces the efficiency edge of task-specific hardware known as ASICs, which are common in Bitcoin mining.

There is a plan to move from energy-intensive PoW mining to a more energy-efficient proof-of-stake protocol called Casper. This was scheduled to start to occur in 2018 and early 2019, but was postponed because of several factors. The updated version of the Ethereum software will be called Serenity.

## TOKEN STANDARDS

In Ethereum, tokens must adhere to token standards, which define a common list of protocols that an Ethereum token has to implement. The most common token standard is the ERC20 standard.

The ERC20 standard is basically a set of six functions that can be recognized and identified by other smart contracts for interactions with the smart contracts. Some of the functions are to get the total token supply, get the account balance of the wallet, and so on.

This token standard gives developers the ability to program behavior of new tokens within the Ethereum ecosystem. Second, this approach is common with crowdfunding companies via initial coin offerings (ICOs). An ICO is a similar concept to an initial public offering (IPO) in stock markets.

You can find out more about ether tokens at `https://etherscan.io/tokens`.

## Ethereum Ledger

In Ethereum, consensus is when the distributed ledger has been updated and all nodes maintain their own identical copy of the ledger. This architecture allows for a new capacity as a system of record-keeping that goes beyond being a simple database. Blocks form a chain by referring to the hash or fingerprint of the previous block and are written to the ledger.

Remember that every node in the network holds a copy of the transaction and smart contract history of the network. The nodes also keep track of the current "state" on the ledger. Every time a user performs some action, all the nodes on the network need to come to agreement that this change took place and have it written to the ledger.

For example, every time a program (smart contract application) is used, a network of thousands of computers processes it. Contracts written in a smart contract–specific programming language that are compiled into what is called *bytecode* will be read by the EVM. Then all the nodes execute this contract using their EVMs, which in turn update the ledger.

## Ethereum Node EVM

The Ethereum Virtual Machine (EVM) is computer software that runs on an abstraction layer right above the underlying hardware that is deployed such as a physical server or a container.

Ethereum uses a virtual machine to deploy the blockchain services. This virtual machine type is considered a Turing complete virtual machine that will run and compile the code directly. Turing complete means the software is agile enough to run any code defined by the developer. In the development world, this Turing complete machine is also considered a flexible virtual machine.

Ethereum itself is a protocol defining how the communication should work. It is neither proprietary software nor patented. Instead, it is open, and there are several different implementations of the Ethereum protocol.

Two of the most popular implementations are Go-Ethereum ( Geth), which is written in Go, and Parity, which is written in Rust.

Ethereum nodes communicate with each other using the Ethereum protocol. There are several different ways to connect to an Ethereum node.

You can connect via HTTP and IPC protocols; WebSocket connections as well may be supported.

The Ethereum node accepts requests in a JSON-RPC format via HTTP. This is a standardized way of communicating with Ethereum nodes from clients. Using this approach, any software that implements the JSON-RPC calls should be able to connect to the blockchain via an Ethereum node.

Here are some important notes about the EVM:

♦ The only real limitation the EVM has that a typical Turing complete machine does not is that the EVM is intrinsically bound by gas.

♦ The power of the EVM is limited only by the amount of gas that is provided by the developer request.

♦ The EVM is a stack-based VM, meaning that it uses an ordering structure that processes last-in, first-out ordering.

♦ Flexibility around the development of smart contracts can be in Python, Java, or C++ at the time of writing.

♦ Isolation is achieved when fully deployed since smart contracts are fully isolated from the blockchain network.

Figure 2.13 shows how the EVM fits into the stack.

**FIGURE 2.13**
EVM in the
Ethereum stack

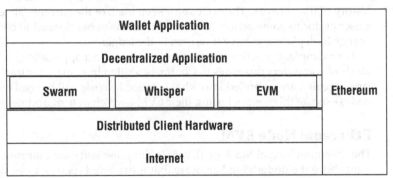

When joining the Ethereum network, you have some options from a blockchain node perspective.

♦ **Light nodes** are nodes that do not verify every block or transaction and do not have a copy of the current blockchain state. These nodes are generally used for development.

♦ **Full nodes** verify every block that is broadcast onto the blockchain network. When you set up a full node, the full blockchain is also downloaded to that node. This could be significant storage space since at the time of writing is more than 180 GB.

♦ **Archive nodes** are full nodes that preserve the entire history of transactions and could be used for compliance requirements in some cases.

Ethernode.org displays the current state of network nodes connected to the blockchain. At the time of writing, there are more than 13,600 nodes. The site also displays the mainnet and testnet. To find out the current Ethereum nodes on the blockchain, visit https://www.ethernodes.org/network/1.

## Ethereum Client Apps

Developing applications to interface with the Ethereum APIs is straightforward. Generally, the following front-end development languages are used with Ethereum:

◆ HTML

◆ CSS

◆ JavaScript

The following backend tools are commonly used:

◆ Solidity

◆ Truffle

You can download Solidity or compile with your browser.

**REFERENCE**   See Chapter 10 for more information about these tools.

### SOLIDITY

Solidity is the development language behind Ethereum and is specifically designed to utilize the EVM. Developers who are working on the Ethereum-based applications will be developing their smart contracts in Solidity.

Solidity uses a large number of programming features, concepts, and methods that exist in other development languages. For example, Solidity has, as you would expect in a programming language, specific variables, functions, classes, and so on.

One common API used with Ethereum is the JSON API, which is a lightweight data-interchange format that can represent numbers, strings, ordered sequences of values, and collections of name-value pairs.

**NOTE**   "Although the Ethereum blockchain is a public blockchain, it is great to see private and consortium blockchains using the Ethereum codebase actively under development." —Vitalik Buterin, Ethereum inventor (`http://www.icofestival.de/post_220118.html`).

The following are some additional tools and applications used with Ethereum:

◆ **Languages**—Solidity, Serpent, Mutant

◆ **IDEs**—Solidity Browser, Ethereum Studio

◆ **Clients**—Geth, eth, parity, Ethereum Wallet

◆ **Storage**—IPFS, Swarm, and Storj

◆ **Dapp Browsers**—Metamask or Mist

◆ **Testing**—Testnet, TestRPC

Chapter 10 includes more details about these toolsets as well as Solidity.

## Ethereum Transactions

Transactions in Ethereum are the way the external world interacts with the Ethereum network. A transaction is used when you want to modify or update the state stored in the Ethereum network. It is important to note that Ethereum is an account-based blockchain implementation, which is different from other blockchains such as Hyperledger.

There are two types of accounts used in Ethereum to be aware of from a development perspective: an externally owned account (EOA) and a contract account.

An externally owned account is effectively an individual user in the external world like a buyer and a seller. This user in the Ethereum network is represented by a 20-byte (160-bit) address.

The contract account has some similarities and differences to the EOA. A contract account is created by referring to a deployed contract. This contract account is identified by a contract address, and an EOA account is still represented by a 20-byte address (160 bit). This is the address that interacts with this deployed account.

The contract account can also keep ethers when appropriate to the business logic at hand. The contract is the "smart contract" capability in the Ethereum network, which is where the business logic is actually implemented.

Figure 2.14 represents the high-level steps an Ethereum transaction takes for a blockchain user to authorize and access an Ethereum application. You can see in the diagram that a user is initiating a web application hosted on Ethereum, so this is not particularly complex. From a technical perspective, this is what would be expected when invoking an Ethereum application and would require "ether" to be able to run an application on the Ethereum blockchain. Ether, of course, is required to power the EVM through the use of "gas."

**FIGURE 2.14**
Ethereum authorization
transaction overview

Chapter 4 provides a deeper dive into Ethereum consensus and how transactions are handled from a smart contract invocation.

## Ethereum Smart Contracts

Smart contracts are contracts that can be converted to code, stored, and reproduced on the network nodes. With smart contracts, you can exchange money, shares, property, and anything that is valued in a transparent manner without the services of an intermediary. For example, through the use of an Ethereum smart contract, you could provide payment for products and have an immutable record of the transactions. Smart contracts define the penalties and rules surrounding an agreement just like traditional contracts would when properly designed.

When you deploy several smart contracts together as an application, it is known as a *distributed application* (a *dapp* in Ethereum).

Smart contracts in Ethereum provide some significant benefits to the users of the platform, including the following:

◆ Autonomy

◆ Trust

◆ Backup

◆ Safety

◆ Speed

◆ Savings

◆ Accuracy

The basics of Ethereum state are that all modifications to a contract's data must be performed by its code. Modifying a contract's data requires a blockchain user to send requests to its code. This process kickoff determines whether and how to fulfill those requests. Smart contracts on the Ethereum network run on the Ethereum Virtual Machine.

Dapps running on the Ethereum network are basically complex smart contracts. Ethereum smart contracts have some properties to be aware of, especially when your development team is designing a smart contract for an application. First, Ethereum smart contracts are deployed in an automated fashion and can act as a complement to an agreement between two parties.

Second, the terms of the smart contract are to be clearly written in a computer language as a set of instructions recorded to an immutable distributed ledger.

Smart contracts when deployed on Ethereum will act as triggered events. For example, when a user sends funds of $100 to another Ethereum user to pay for, let's say, tickets to a concert, these tickets will be sent to the buyer only after the $100 is received from the buyer and deposited in the seller's Ethereum wallet. If the $100 is not received from the buyer, then the smart contract will not be triggered, and the contract process is stopped.

Figure 2.15 shows the workflow of an Ethereum transaction. There are four main steps to a transaction in Ethereum, and each step must be executed properly for the next step to continue. Settlement of the transaction can occur only if the execution of the smart contract occurs as programmed.

**FIGURE 2.15**
Smart contract workflow

When writing smart contracts in Ethereum, developers use a programming language called Solidity. Chapter 10 covers smart contracts and the basics of Solidity in more detail.

**NOTE** Ethereum is the most efficient and developed platform for decentralized applications.

Essentially, a smart contract in the implementation of Solidity is a collection of code and data residing at a specific address on the Ethereum blockchain. Solidity is a programming language native to Ethereum that was specifically designed for Ethereum and was released to the development community in 2015.

**REFERENCE** For more on Solidity and Ethereum smart contracts, see Chapter 10.

## Ethereum Wallets

One significant difference between Ethereum and the other enterprise blockchains is the fact that Ethereum is a permissionless platform, and it also has a cryptocurrency (token) called *ether*. As mentioned, ether is the token that is used for running your smart contracts on the Ethereum platform. To send and receive ether, you need to have a wallet.

A *wallet* is a program that allows you to gain access to, send, and receive cryptocurrency on the blockchain networks. There are several types of Ethereum wallets, including hardware, software, and web wallets.

Common Ethereum wallets include MyEtherwallet, Jaxx, and Metamask. You can also go to an online exchange, such as Coinbase (which is focused on the US market at the time of writing) to get an online wallet (`www.coinbase.com`).

**NOTE** "There is nothing that Bitcoin can do that Ethereum can't. While Ethereum is less battle-tested, it is moving faster, has better leadership, and has more developer mindshare." —Fred Erhsam, Founder of Coinbase.

**NOTE** This book does not discuss how to buy, sell, or trade cryptocurrencies or tokens. There are plenty of other books that focus on the consumer part of the blockchain market.

## Ethereum Tools and Utilities

Ethereum has a robust ecosystem of tools and utilities because of its large developer base and because it's the most successful permissionless smart contract blockchain. Finding what you need in the Ethereum ecosystem as a developer won't be an issue.

Let's review some of the top tools and utilities that are almost required to get going on Ethereum.

**Mist Browser Wallet (Deprecated)** Mist Browser Wallet was used to store ether, send transactions, and deploy contracts but has recently been deprecated. Because of the wide usage of Mist, it clearly deserves a mention. Historically significant as well is that Mist was the first GUI wallet and was clearly the standard token base at the time.

You can download Mist Browser Wallet from `https://github.com/ethereum/mist/releases`.

**Geth and Eth**   These are command-line tools for the Ethereum Network. Essentially these command-line tools will allow you to connect your Ethereum server to or run your application on the Ethereum blockchain. Geth and Eth are two separate command-line tools that can run a full Ethereum, public or private, node. Both of these software tools provide multiple user interfaces.

You can download the Geth CLI tools from `https://www.ethereum.org/cli`.

**Parity**   Party is an advanced Ethereum client written in the new low-level language Rust. Parity was created by Dr. Gavin Wood, who is the former CTO of Ethereum.

You can download the Parity client from `https://www.parity.io/`.

**Metamask**   Metamask is a Google Chrome browser extension that allows you to experience Ethereum in your browser today.

What is really useful is that it allows you to run Ethereum dapps right in your browser without running a full Ethereum node.

Figure 2.16 shows the Metamask interface. You can see that there is an ether balance and that there have been some contract interactions. Contract interactions are essentially using the EVM on the Ethereum mainnet.

**FIGURE 2.16**
Metamask interface

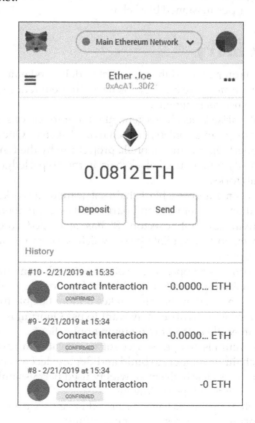

You can download the Metamask extension from `https://metamask.io/`.

**Truffle**    Truffle is a well-tested and utilized development environment, testing framework, and asset pipeline for blockchains using the EVM.

You can download the Truffle framework from `https://truffleframework.com/`.

Note that this is not an inclusive list of tools. However, I will be discussing in more detail Ethereum tools and development-focused frameworks in Chapter 10.

### Ethereum Governance

Enterprise Ethereum clients must superimpose a permissioning layer since it's based on a decentralized platform, which is permissionless. At the time of writing, the Enterprise Ethereum Alliance (EEA) is working on version 3.0 of the standard specification where chain-wide permissioning configuration and enforcement will be enabled.

However, a per-node permissioning capability can be set up via implementation through smart contracts to provide some governance. Because funding comes from the EEA, it's expected that governance, compliance, and other enterprise concerns will be addressed in more detail at the organization's pace. In a nutshell, if you need strict governance, then you may need to consider permissioned blockchains.

## Summary

This chapter covered the four most widely used enterprise blockchain platforms and distributed ledgers. Enterprise blockchains have different requirements than public permissionless blockchains such as Ethereum.

Enterprise blockchains generally fall into one of several categories: private permissioned, public or permissionless, or even hybrid such as Quorum.

Hyperledger is the umbrella project run by the Linux Foundation, and Hyperledger Fabric is the mostly widely used blockchain in the Hyperledger portfolio according to the number of GitHub forks.

R3 is an enterprise blockchain software firm working with a broadly targeted ecosystem of more than 200 members and partners. These members are across multiple industries from both the private and public sectors. R3 has developed Corda, which is an open source blockchain platform, and Corda Enterprise, which is a commercial-grade version for enterprise usage with support.

Quorum is an open source blockchain solution built by enhancing the existing Ethereum blockchain. It provides an additional layer on top of Ethereum, which enables it to perform private transactions but also makes it more flexible by using different consensus algorithms. The main reason enterprises may want to use Quorum is for the privacy and performance capabilities that can easily extend to Ethereum applications.

Ethereum is an open source software platform based on blockchain technology that enables blockchain developers to build and deploy decentralized applications (smart contracts). Ethereum is clearly the most widely used permissionless smart contract blockchain platform and has a wide developer following.

Each of the blockchains discussed have very different technical merits and use cases for the enterprise, so consider each one carefully.

# Chapter 3

# Architecting Your Enterprise Blockchain

This chapter discusses architecting enterprise applications as well as architecting blockchain services with enterprise best practices. I also cover enterprise blockchain integration, scalability, and security. When architecting a blockchain service, note that your design will be mainly focused on an enterprise blockchain. As you know, blockchains are distributed ledgers and flat non-SQL databases that scale differently. When compared to traditional relational databases such as SQL, blockchains are slower from a performance perspective, which we must consider in our use cases.

**THIS CHAPTER HAS BEEN BROKEN DOWN TO COVER EACH BLOCK-CHAIN INDIVIDUALLY AND THUS KEEP CONTINUITY FOR THE READ-ERS. THE FOLLOWING BLOCKCHAINS ARE COVERED:**

- Hyperledger Fabric
- Corda
- Ethereum
- Quorum

For information about additional blockchains, including Multichain, NEO, and others, please refer to the book's website (www.wiley.com/go/blockchainsolutions) for updated content.

## Blockchain Technology Focus Areas

Blockchain technology has the core characteristics of decentralization, accountability, and security. These characteristics are important to understand when designing a blockchain service.

Blockchains are used in two main categories of IT solutions, either public permissionless or private enterprise permissioned blockchains. Another approach is to combine both private and public blockchain services into a hybrid solution. Whether you are working at a private enterprise, a federal government agency, or a nonprofit entity considering blockchain ledger technology, there may be several viable use cases to consider for a blockchain in your organization. One blockchain use case may be a good fit for a nonprofit entity, but that same use case may not be a viable use case for a private enterprise.

## Blockchain Success Areas

One of the main areas I believe blockchains will succeed in are specific industries that work closely together in a collaborative format, such as in a consortium. For example, the insurance industry is a big proponent of the blockchain mainly because blockchains allow not only the sharing of data but also the sharing of costs, actuary data, and responsibilities such as compliance, and the enablement of their stakeholders. The insurance industry sees blockchains as a new business opportunity and even a new business model especially with actuary-related services.

Another industry that clearly will be big winners in the blockchain arena are the "financials," such as interbank transfers, currency exchanges, derivatives, or even risk mitigation practices. Why? Because there are numerous layers of intermediaries that essentially are considered overhead to these financial institutions. I have never been reluctant to state that the financial sector will go mainstream with blockchain technology. This is actually starting to happen with numerous announcements from JP Morgan, HSBC, Goldman Sachs, and more than 30 large international banks announcing blockchain projects. Blockchains will be used as a method for cost cutting as well as risk mitigation.

Employees are considered overhead by executives and company shareholders; thus, that "burdened" salary is clearly costing the company shareholders. Traditional roles such as corporate attorneys, accountants, or other intermediaries with routine tasks essentially will be targets in the coming years.

One of the main benefits that blockchains can certainly provide through the proper implementation of smart contracts is cost efficiencies. Smart contracts can reduce mistakes in manual processes, reduce fraud, and reduce costs per transaction, while actually providing improved customer experiences and meeting compliance requirements.

Figure 3.1 shows an example consortium-based blockchain trading application where the seller (exporter) is being paid in Bitcoin and the buyer (importer) is converting USD for trade.

**FIGURE 3.1**
Blockchain trade
application

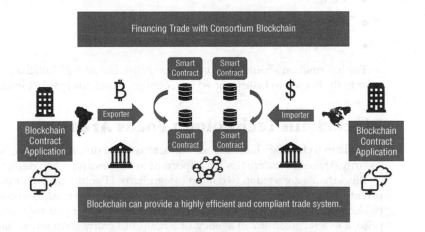

In the scenario shown, the exporter is converting Bitcoin into USD. This cryptocurrency to fiat currency conversion could be done efficiently with a smart contract. Note that there would be a payment gateway interface as part of a smart contract to exchange Bitcoin for fiat currency such as USD. This scenario would also provide increased efficiency for trade due to the automation of the blockchain, removing the need for costly manual processes. The ledgers would be immutable and would also provide immediate compliance adherence due to the blockchain data structure. The blockchain architecture allows for the trade information to be sent as digital information, which is distributed, rather than copied. This distributed ledger data structure provides transparency, trust, and data security for the members of the consortium.

Blockchain technology is being used successfully in the financial services industry. Financial services companies are using this technology for record-keeping, digital notary services, payment services, interbank transfers through the use of solid distributed applications, and smart contracts.

## Blockchain Compliance

Blockchains are excellent for maintaining an immutable history for several reasons whether for ensuring compliance such as for Global Data Protection Regulation (GDPR) or for managing a chain of trust. The GDPR is a compliance requirement that mandates businesses to protect the personal data as well as privacy of European Union (EU) citizens for transactions that occur within the EU member states. This law also extends to other countries that have EU citizens as customers. Blockchains could be used, for example, for GDPR requirements that can be held on the blockchain. Then for facets such as the "right to be forgotten," a blockchain would not be suitable but could be integrated with an off-chain database to adhere to the GDPR requirements. Certain data may or may not be appropriate to store even within a permissioned blockchain network.

For more information on GDPR and other common compliance requirements, refer to Chapter 9, "Blockchain Governance, Risk, and Compliance (GRC), Privacy, and Legal Concerns."

**NOTE**  "Just as the Internet made "frictionless commerce" possible by connecting buyers and sellers in online marketplaces, blockchains could provide the frictionless fabric for value exchange within discrete digital business networks." —IBM Blockchain Services

Lastly, every organization will likely have different business drivers for going to a blockchain ledger platform. Whether this business driver is focused on compliance, collaboration, cost efficiency, providing digital assets, or providing transparency, as blockchain architects we must be able to put these drivers together and match them to a proper blockchain ledger technology solution use case and ultimately a working design.

# Architecting a Blockchain Solution

One of the first exercises we need to perform is to consider whether we have a strong use case for a blockchain. This would seem to be a one-question step. However, there will likely be customers who have potential requirements that would be a good use case for a blockchain and then perhaps one change in a stakeholder requirement could actually remove that requirement.

My main point is that this exercise of determining whether a use case is valid is not always a direct yes or no answer. However, it would likely be easy to determine whether or not you do have a solid use case after a few initial scoping questions.

Generally, we want to understand what the pillars are for determining a valid use case that would be sustainable. Then we want to understand the enterprise architecture it would be integrated into. Another step may be to walk through a checklist or a questionnaire to address detailed information and assign a score to establish validity.

The following section walks you through processes of designing a solution that meets your customer requirements.

## Blockchain Design Workflow

Having a workflow can certainly provide significant instructions to help facilitate the design of a blockchain solution. Blockchain design can be complex, especially when you have compliance requirements or detailed use case objectives to meet in your design.

Following is the eight-step blockchain design workflow. Note that it may not be necessary to address the blockchain decision score spreadsheet (step 5). If the stakeholders have already decided on a specific blockchain platform, then proceeding to design would make sense.

1. Address the stakeholders.

2. Address the use case.

3. Address the blockchain decision tree.

4. Address the enterprise architecture tenets.

5. Address the blockchain decision score spreadsheet.

6. Address the blockchain design.

7. Address the blockchain implementation.

8. Address the blockchain tasking.

Lastly, we want to determine a proper platform that would provide a solid use case that could be implemented into the enterprise architecture.

## Use Case Potential

When considering whether a blockchain is a strong use case or not, we should review the pillars of that potential use case. The more pillars we have checked off, the stronger the use case. For example, if a customer does not have a requirement for a distributed and decentralized ledger, then our potential use case has been removed.

Several of the more compelling areas of accepting blockchain technology are the financial, logistics, and government sectors. These sectors show no signs of slowing down in their acceptance of blockchains as well as their investments in the technology.

Blockchain is on the radar for many other organizations and industry verticals no matter what may be discussed in the media. The challenge that the enterprise blockchain community has is that the enterprise technology is sometimes wrapped up in the same discussion as cryptocurrencies and the failed initial coin offerings (ICOs).

### STAKEHOLDERS

Stakeholders are, of course, a critical area of focus not only from a pre-sale and post-sale perspective. In a sales-driven environment, it is all about providing stakeholder assurance of trust in the technology and the resulting value of the blockchain solution. Discussions around pain points but also discussions around prospective solutions should be addressed. Note also that stakeholders are generally going to be in one of three categories.

When speaking to technical, business, and legal audiences, we would want to clearly understand and address their concerns and ensure our responses are appropriate. For a technical audience, we should focus on implementation, development, and security. For a business audience, the focus should be on the value proposition, TTM, TCO, and ROI. For a legal audience, focus on compliance, privacy, and corporate governance.

## PILLARS OF A STRONG BLOCKCHAIN USE CASE

A *pillar* is a foundational principle or a baseline that supports the use case for even considering a blockchain. For example, if the data requirements specified are used by only one organization, then the data requirements would not be a strong use case for blockchain technology since a single organization would be a great use case.

However, a strong use case would be when you had a consortium requirement, for example, that required an immutable shared ledger utilizing smart contracts for international trade.

Figure 3.2 shows the commonly accepted four pillars of blockchain. You can see that the need for a ledger is clear and that the ledger really needs to be permanent and distributed. Smart contracts need to provide business value, and the blockchain network needs to provide a distributed network with no single point of failure.

**FIGURE 3.2**
Four pillars of strong blockchain use cases

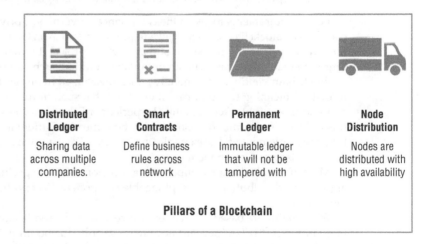

From the four pillars we can derive that if our use case requires an immutable record store, then proceed with considering a blockchain platform. On the other hand, if our use case does not require an immutable record store, then we should likely drop the consideration for a blockchain.

## USE CASE PERSPECTIVES

When considering use cases for an enterprise blockchain, it is imperative to understand that there is no single blockchain platform for every use case available. Even though some blockchain vendors sometimes will tout they are "cross industry," you must realize that there are significant technical considerations that merit distinction. The reality is that some use cases are viable on one or more blockchains. On the other hand, if your use case points toward Ripple, then it's really only a good use case for that distributed ledger because Ripple is a financial-sector platform that does not support smart contracts.

When thinking of the blockchain, there are business requirements, technical requirements, and even legal or governance requirements. It's more than possible that a stakeholder's perspective could change or a new government policy such as GDPR could derail a block-chain project.

The following are two common ways a blockchain project and use case could be derailed:

♦ Business requirements could be more focused on TCO or ROI and even time to market. Not being able to properly show a favorable TCO or ROI could derail the block-chain project.

♦ Technical considerations are generally more detailed, and the wrong understanding of the technical merits could derail the enterprise blockchain project. Integration into current enterprise infrastructure could also place challenges on your potential use case.

Legal requirements focus on the compliance, governance, privacy, and legal enforcement concerns of blockchains. Compliance requirements such as GDPR have been documented to remove the possibility of a successful blockchain project. Privacy concerns such as the right to be forgotten may not be met with an immutable solution such as a blockchain.

Blockchain vendors are generally either specialized in one sector such as financials or "cross industry," meaning that they can fit use cases that span industries. For example, Ripple is clearly a financial-sector blockchain, while Hyperledger Fabric is a cross-industry blockchain. Because of this industry focus, the components may be somewhat different in nomenclature as well as how they are implemented. For example, in Corda we have a notary, but in Hyperledger we do not have a notary as a component.

Most of the blockchain components are customized for specific use cases, such as consensus algorithms, distributed ledgers, pluggable components, encryption methods, and licensing models.

Blockchains are based on an open source approach, and it shows in the blockchain development industry. "Tribal" support is more noticeably due because developers are working on specific features and feature sets that are "requested" or "sponsored." In some blockchain platforms, features can also be pluggable or modular. This is true especially in some enterprise blockchain frameworks such as Hyperledger.

Features that are pluggable or modular allow for some choices to be tested such as consensus algorithms. Blockchains that are more flexible in some areas may present themselves as a better solution. Use cases need to be established, and the use case can be challenged once there is a significant change whether its business, legal, or technically driven.

## BLOCKCHAIN DECISION TREE

There are significant numbers of blockchain decision trees that have been floated out by the academic, corporate, and even governmental agencies. The main focus is to really understand your use case and try to determine if the appropriate blockchain decision tree will work in your sales organization and your customer base. If your customer base consists of dedicated financial companies, you may want a separate decision tree and even checklist for nonfinancial customers.

I like to address decisions that have multiple choices or a decision tree approach to making a platform decision. Anything that can give a clear decision around choosing a blockchain platform is excellent.

Figure 3.3 shows a decision tree that represents my personal approach, which should enable you to decide between a private, hybrid, or public blockchain. There are two end decisions, and we will come to one depending on our requirements. Do we need privacy or not for our transactions? If so, then go with a permissioned blockchain if our transaction will not be public.

**FIGURE 3.3**

Blockchain decision tree

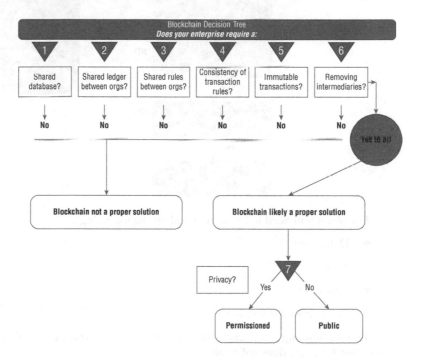

When it comes to making decisions for a specific blockchain, I generally like to look at charts that show features and functions to get me on the path of determining whether the customer should use Hyperledger Fabric or R3 Corda. The decision between two blockchains could be based solely on having channels versus not having channels.

Figure 3.4 shows an alternate example of a blockchain decision tree.

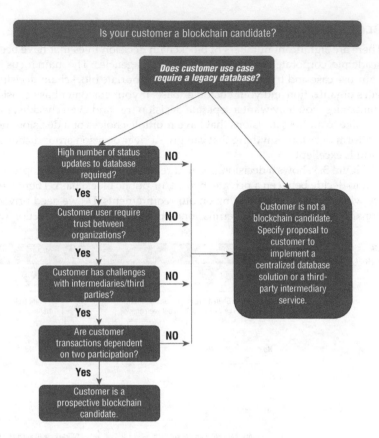

**FIGURE 3.4**
Alternate blockchain
decision tree

Decisions will need to be made based on the following:

◆ Databases

◆ Trust

◆ Third parties

◆ Transaction interaction

When following any decision tree, you will want to consider whether it makes sense in your use case. One size does not fit all.

## BLOCKCHAIN DECISION CHECKLISTS

When it comes to making decisions, sometimes a good old Excel spreadsheet can help. When considering a spreadsheet, it is advisable to establish a few different versions to address your customer base. In reality, there is no one size fits all for blockchain questions, and you would want to be creative and address your audience in an appropriate manner.

# Blockchain Structure and Components

Blockchains are structured differently from the traditional architecture of the World Wide Web, which uses a more centralized client-server network. The structure and the components of the blockchain network will be different and will vary between blockchain solutions.

In the case of the permissionless distributed network of blockchain architecture, each participant (node or a user) within the network maintains, approves, and updates new entries. The system is controlled not only by separate individuals but by everyone within the blockchain network. Each member ensures that all records and procedures are in order, which results in data validity and security.

Figure 3.5 compares a client-server topology to a P2P topology. This P2P network consists of several nodes (computers), and they are running a virtual machine that would have blockchain protocols.

**FIGURE 3.5**
Comparing client-server topology to P2P topology

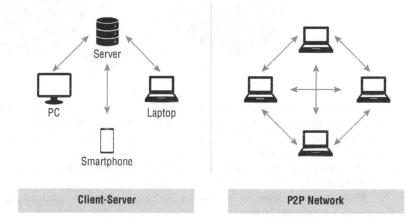

For more information on blockchains compared to traditional databases, please refer to Chapter 1, "Introduction to Blockchain Technologies".

## Blockchain Structure

The structure of blockchain technology is represented by a list of blocks that are ordered, with these blocks represented as transactions in a particular order. These ordered lists can be stored as a flat file or in the form of a document database using NoSQL such as Cloud Datastore in Google Cloud Platform or DocumentDB in AWS.

There are two important data structures that are used in blockchain, and they are referred to as the *pointers* and the *linked lists*. The main purpose of this section is to address how a permissionless blockchain might handle a block of data and write to a blockchain. In the individual blockchain sections for Hyperledger Fabric, Corda, Ethereum, and Quorum, I will highlight specifics as to how these blockchain ledgers address the data structure in more detail. So, take these examples as more of a generic structure than a one-size-fits-all kind of structure.

Figure 3.6 shows the relationship between data structures in blockchain ledgers. We can see the direct relationship between the pointers and the linked lists in the data structure. When considering a blockchain solution, we would want to understand how these data structures are handled from a latency perspective, for example. Your blockchain developer would, of course, want to be aware of this when developing the blockchain application and connecting to the blockchain network.

**FIGURE 3.6**
Blockchain data structures

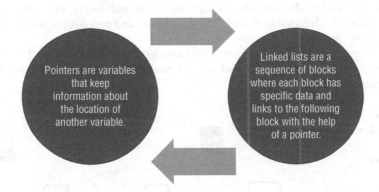

The blockchain data structure is a back-linked record of blocks of transactions that are ordered links. Each block may be recognized by a hash, created utilizing the SHA256 cryptographic hash algorithm on the header of the block. Each block will refer to the previous block, which is identified as the parent block, in the "previous block hash" field.

The following represents common terminology in distributed ledger technology around the blockchain ledger data structure.

The *index* represents the location of the block on the blockchain ledger and essentially an address for locating blocks.

◆ The *hash* is the function that facilitates the rapid classification of data in the dataset that is provided in the blockchain ledger.

◆ A *nonce* is a random number that is assigned as part of a hash on the blockchain. Nonces provide for increased security in the sense that it can be used only once in a blockchain and make it hard to replay the transaction.

◆ Pointers are known as *hash pointers* and are used to build a linked list for the blockchain.

◆ A *record* is the block transaction written to the blockchain and then committed to the ledger. These records are considered immutable in most enterprise blockchain ledgers.

◆ A *timestamp* will save the time aspects of when the block was built as well as when it was transacted in some enterprise blockchains.

◆ A *Merkle tree* is a summary of the hashing list of the blockchain and provides for the efficient verification of the blockchain.

◆ A hashing list is descriptive list of hashes of the data blocks in the blockchain.

Figure 3.7 shows the linking of the blocks that create the data structure. We can see that there are records. These records are written to the blockchain. The pointers are building the linked list.

Hashing is involved; you should note that each hash points to the previous hash as part of this linking. The first block does not contain the pointer since this one is the first in a chain and known as the *genesis block*.

**FIGURE 3.7**
Example of a blockchain data structure

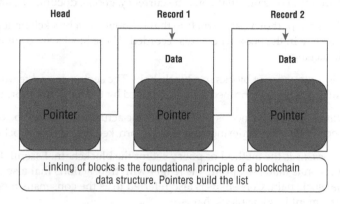

Linking of blocks is the foundational principle of a blockchain data structure. Pointers build the list

Figure 3.8 shows a detailed blockchain sequence diagram, which is a connected list of records. We can see hashing is involved where each hash points to the previous hash as part of this linking. The Merkle root is the top part of the Merkle tree. The leaves are data blocks, and the nodes further up in the tree are the hashes of their respective children.

**FIGURE 3.8**
Blockchain sequence

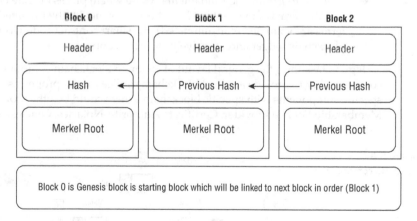

Block 0 is Genesis block is starting block which will be linked to next block in order (Block 1)

There are certainly more concepts around blockchain transactions to understand, but for the purpose of this book, the main goal is to provide insight into how these blockchains manage transactions. The upcoming sections will provide insight into how Hyperledger Fabric differs, for example. From a design perspective, this could affect transactions per second (TPS) if one blockchain orders transactions before validating.

## Blockchain Core Components

This section covers the main core blockchain components. This list is not specific to any blockchain platform but more of a vendor-neutral component list. For example, Hyperledger and Ethereum have vastly different components in some respects.

*Nodes* are generally virtualized users' components, applications, or servers within the blockchain architecture.

◆ *Transactions* are the smallest building block of a blockchain network, and they keep track of anything of value that could be currency, goods, documents, and so on.

◆ *Blocks* are part of a data structure that is known as a blockchain ledger. Blocks are similar to a page in the book where it is recorded. These blocks are ordered and are what form a blockchain.

*Chain* is a sequence of blocks in a blockchain. The sequence and features of the chain of blocks that are supported is determined and maintained by the blockchain protocol.

◆ *Miners* are specific nodes that perform the actual work on a blockchain. They provide block validation, ordering, and even record-keeping for the blockchain.

◆ *Consensus* is the method or policy set for the blockchain. Essentially, consensus is how the decision is made to update the ledger with transactions that also determines the state of the blockchain. Consensus is also referred to as the consensus mechanism or consensus agreement in some blockchains.

◆ *Validity rules* (validation) state how the user and the transactions will be validated. This validation process sometimes may occur before a transaction is ordered and written to the blockchain depending on the blockchain.

◆ *Smart contracts* are the fundamental value where pieces of code can automatically check that the terms of the contract have been fully met by the involved third parties. Once the terms are validated (consummated), the smart contract code would record it against the blockchain ledger and effectively close the contract.

Figure 3.9 shows the general layout of common blockchain components. All these components come together to provide a robust blockchain service for the proper use case. When it comes to specific components with specific blockchains, there could be other components such as a Membership Service Provider, Certificate Authority, Notaries, Oracles, and so on.

**FIGURE 3.9**
Blockchain components

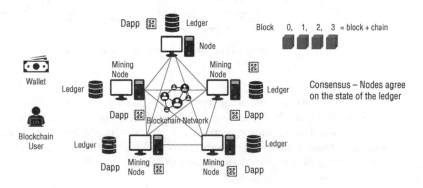

# Enterprise Blockchain Architectures

Enterprises have strict requirements and therefore tend to choose applications and services that support those requirements. Blockchains were not initially developed for enterprise applications and were more focused on cryptocurrency transactions. Of course, this has changed with the release and the evolution of consortium blockchains such as Hyperledger and R3 Corda that have an active corporate user base.

Blockchains also were originally developed as permissionless platforms such as Bitcoin. Ethereum came along and expanded upon blockchains as not only a cryptocurrency platform but also as a use-case platform or a development platform. Ethereum was designed to be a permissionless blockchain, but now with the advent of channeling and off-chains. Off-chains mean that your application is extending out of the enterprise blockchain for a specific purpose such as a payment gateway. For example, Ethereum can now be extended to the enterprise for specific use cases quite simply and effectively.

When it comes to architecting solutions for blockchains for an enterprise, it is important to understand how enterprise architectures have been approached. Consider your current enterprise architecture best practices and reference any of the enterprise architecture frameworks.

In some widely accepted enterprise architecture frameworks, there are four pillars or domains focused on architecture. The purpose of the enterprise architecture framework domains is to guide your organization's business, information, process, and technology decisions in order to enable the organization to execute its business strategy and meet your customer's requirements.

TOGAF is the most widely used out of the common enterprise frameworks. These frameworks include ISO, DoDAF, and UPDM. I will focus on TOGAF enterprise domains for this book since it's the most widely accepted and actually can correlate to blockchains as well.

## TOGAF Domains

Before diving into blockchain architectures, it makes sense to establish a baseline of what enterprise architecture is. The best starting point is to review the TOGAF standard. A baseline in enterprise architecture (EA) is a critical point for organizations. Without a baseline, essentially business outcomes would not meet the objectives or even work out for that matter.

TOGAF is a well-known acronym for the Open Group Architecture Framework, which was developed by the Open Group. The Open Group is a not-for-profit technology industry consortium that continues to update and reiterate the TOGAF enterprise architecture domains. The TOGAF standard is the de facto standard for enterprise architecture frameworks. TOGAF provides the specific methods, processes, and standards for enabling the acceptance, production, use, and maintenance of an enterprise architecture.

The first version of TOGAF, released in 1995, was based on the Technical Architecture Framework for Information Management (TAFIM) specification developed by the US Department of Defense (DoD).

DoD gave the Open Group explicit permission to create TOGAF by building on TAFIM, and TOGAF has been continuously evolving since then.

Essentially, without a framework, connecting corporate enterprise strategy to projects online would be challenging. Blockchain projects are more complex because of the lack of knowledge and expertise in the area.

The four domains of the TOGAF enterprise architecture are as follows:

**The business architecture domain** states how the enterprise is organizationally structured. This domain also provides insight into what functional capabilities are necessary to deliver on the business vision.

**The application architecture domain** provides insight into the enterprise applications and relationship to the core business processes of the enterprise.

**The data architecture domain** provides insight into the structure of an organization's data assets as well as insight into the data management resources available.

**The technology architecture domain** states the requirements needed to actually implement the enterprise applications.

## What, Who, and How of Enterprise Architecture

When it comes to architecting solutions, it is important to establish the "what, who, and how" of enterprise architectures.

◆ What is the organization's business vision, strategy, and objectives that guide this creation of a blockchain service?

◆ Who is responsible for executing the defined blockchain services?

◆ How are any previously defined business services or capabilities implemented with blockchain services?

Simply put, knowing your customers' history and interests can matter in your blockchain design.

## Tenets

Tenets are organizationally defined rules and guidelines that the organization uses for accomplishing its mission.

Figure 3.10 highlights common enterprise architecture tenants that can be used around blockchains. When it comes to discussing the enterprise architecture (EA) tenants with your customer, you may want to address them by whiteboarding them with the customer. These tenants could be valuable in your discussions with stakeholders and may be used in application design. The defined tenets should guide application governance and provide concise architectural review. Perhaps they can even enhance your enterprise blockchain adoption performance.

In a nutshell, you should consider approaching a blockchain application as an enterprise application. This means determining which enterprise architecture framework makes sense in your organization and applying the basic tenets that correlate to the enterprise architecture. The blockchain application may or may not be deployed enterprise-wide or even integrated enterprise-wide for the initial deployment. Addressing enterprise concerns ahead of time could certainly enhance stakeholder acceptance, adoption, and delivery of a blockchain solution.

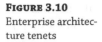

**FIGURE 3.10**
Enterprise architecture tenets

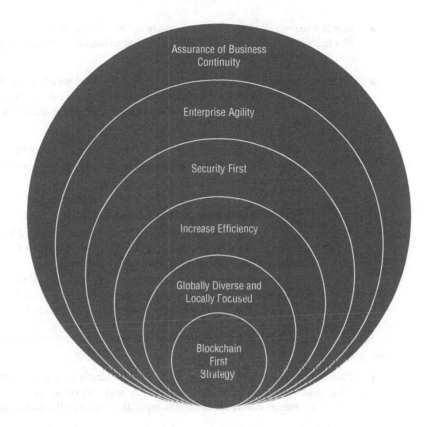

## Blockchain Design

When designing any enterprise blockchain application, it is critical to establish the requirements, baselines, features, functions, and scalability of the blockchain that is being evaluated or proposed.

From an architecture perspective, you want to consider some of the common permissionless blockchain features and determine which features are important to your enterprise when evaluating blockchain services.

◆ Blockchains are generally decentralized, and thus there are no centralized points of failure, at least theoretically. All information transiting through the blockchain is visible to every node, and information cannot be removed from the blockchain because of immutability.

◆ Blockchains holistically are defined by peer-to-peer networks with peer-to-peer resources that are distributed as well as decentralized. Blockchains in their true form are not centralized databases.

◆ Blockchains are inherently secure due to the security built in with encryption and also can enhance privacy and security. They can even enhance compliance requirements for an organization.

◆ Blockchain networks scale horizontally quite well by adding nodes to the network, but blockchains do not scale well vertically due to latency that can be imposed, for example, by the virtual machines.

◆ Transaction processing is dependent on consensus algorithms such as proof of work, proof of stake, or any of the other options you may choose. The choice of consensus and the blockchain platform used can have a significant effect on the outcome of the blockchain services.

Traditionally, enterprises have been focused on the centralized control of resources, and in specific regard to blockchain using a permissioned blockchain makes sense where the enterprise could benefit from a blockchain.

## Enterprise Blockchain Adoption Challenges

As previously mentioned, there are three ways to approach defining a blockchain. Blockchains should be defined according to the audience you're speaking to, and this simple approach can help facilitate acceptance and adoption of the blockchain proposal.

During stakeholder meetings, calls, or emails, remember the audience and how to specifically address the audience at hand. If you're speaking to the technical engineering group, then speak technically such as "speeds and feeds" of the blockchain. If you are speaking with corporate counsel, then use legal jargon when discussing application.

Some challenges for the enterprises around blockchain adoption are focused on the audience you're speaking with.

◆ *Business challenges* can include business costs, funding requirements, corporate governance, executive vision, stakeholder buy-in, and corporate culture. It's also reasonable to expect a company to react to how competition utilizes the blockchain.

◆ *Legal challenges* can abound, especially in sectors such as finance, insurance, and logistics that may not adjust well to the "disintermediation" of financial services. This means that trust or acceptance may not be fully realized because of compliance requirements, such as PCI, SOX, or GDPR. In the case of GDPR, using a true blockchain solution can be a challenge since blockchain nodes may be distributed out of the regulatory body jurisdiction or not centrally managed.

◆ *Technology challenges* can be around performance such as transactions per second (TPS), integration with legacy applications, middleware, application stakeholder buy-in, and addressing technical issues around privacy and security.

Note that this is not an inclusive list of challenges around enterprise blockchains.

## Risk Management

If you work for a government integrator, you may be familiar with the Risk Management Framework guidelines specified in NIST 800-37. The Risk Management Framework provides an essential connector that integrates both the critical security and risk management activities into the system development lifecycle.

This documentation can also be used by nongovernmental organizations to help them establish a risk-based approach to security control selection and specification considerations.

There are some activities related to managing organizational risk that are critical to an effective information security program. What is really useful is that they may be applied to both new and legacy systems within the detailed context of the system development lifecycle and the Federal Enterprise Architecture. This applies to blockchains as well even though there are no current best practices for blockchain in the federal government documented by NIST.

The following are the risk management activities a federal integrator may become familiar with:

1. Categorize the system.

2. Select controls.

3. Implement controls.

4. Assess controls.

5. Authorize the system.

6. Monitor controls.

For more information on the NIST Framework, refer to Chapter 9.

### Blockchain as a Hammer

Anyone reading posts on LinkedIn, Medium, or Quora may assume that blockchains can solve every problem known to man. Some vendors, bloggers, and consultants constantly are shouting out that their blockchain solutions are solving epic world problems all the time.

Honestly, blockchain technology is no panacea, and in reality, it seems that blockchain technology is a "hammer in search of nails in a sandbox." Blockchains must be considered as a targeted solution and must be effectively focused as a laser.

Lasers are finite tools that directly apply pulses of light that target an expertly focused area. One of the challenges that I continually run into is discussing with customers and students why their use case may or may not be a good blockchain use case. As a blockchain specialist, you must be able to address scenarios where a proposal for a blockchain is not appropriate, whether it is because the customer really needs the features of a centralized database, or because there is no consortium interest in a blockchain platform.

The lesson learned should be that blockchains are no panacea and we must use blockchain solutions effectively in a directly focused manner such as a laser and not as a handyman with a hammer in search of a nail.

## Enterprise Blockchain Design Principles

When it comes to designing your enterprise blockchain services, there are some key design principles, approaches, and even feature requirements to address.

You can certainly use software design approaches that work in your organizations such as ISO or Agile to help facilitate known enterprise practices. The reality is that blockchain design, development, and deployment are in their infancy.

From that perspective of infancy, I approach blockchains as if I were deploying a cloud application. You can expect to accommodate the same level of resources, requirements, and specialized expertise in most cases. Deploying a cloud service such as a database on AWS is similar and different all at the same time than if we were deploying a SQL database on GCP. SQL code may import and take the same structure, for example; however, both AWS and GCP support different versions of SQL differently.

In a nutshell, design is about bringing the requirements together for a blockchain application and placing them on a platform that meets those requirements. This platform can be on your enterprise's local premises or in a cloud provider's remote data center.

When considering a blockchain architecture for your enterprise, you would want to understand some of the features, benefits, and even trade-offs, listed here:

◆ Trust

◆ Consistency

◆ Availability

◆ Security and privacy

◆ Performance

◆ Compliance

**REFERENCE** Chapter 5, "Enterprise Blockchain Sales and Solutions Engineering," discusses blockchain architecture and these features, benefits, and trade-offs to be made around blockchain engineering.

## Enterprise Blockchain Design Requirements

In Chapter 1 we briefly reviewed aspects of blockchain design. This section builds on the first chapter and provides additional insight into making the proper design requirements. Design requirements, although fairly baseline in some industries, could be very different in other industries. For example, some companies may rate integrity higher on the requirements list than consistency. Understanding your customer design as well as enterprise architecture tenets, use cases, and pain points should help come to a solid blockchain architecture.

### DESIGN FOR INTEGRITY (IMMUTABILITY)

Integrity can mean several things to different organizations, so let's clarify that integrity can also infer "trust" due to the immutability properties of the blockchain ledger. Immutability in the world of the blockchain really means that once something has been written to the blockchain, it cannot be modified, deleted, or tampered with by anyone or anything. On the other hand, we know that databases are centralized, whereas the blockchain is a truth agent that is decentralized.

When considering blockchain technologies, it is important to realize that the main reason blockchains were developed was centered around the lack of trust in legacy institutions such as banks and government institutions.

When designing a blockchain, it's critical to consider the user and enterprise requirements. Maintaining user trust is critical to the design and your customer's business. Organizations in industries from the financial sector to the defense industry rely on trust.

## DESIGN FOR CONSISTENCY

When considering the enterprise user experience, it is important to appreciate how the end user is accessing the blockchain application. You can likely approach this by understanding how the rest of the enterprise approaches enterprise application development for their legacy application. Providing a solid workflow for the users of the blockchain application would certainly help the adoption of these blockchain services.

Consistency should be focused not only on the application development but also on the user experience (UE). Blockchain application users should understand how the solutions work at least at a high level, which is more of a process level than a transactional level. Provide an experience that the users will want to participate in. In Chapter 10, "Blockchain Development and Programming," we discuss areas of usability, consistency, and trust, all of which are critical part of the application experience for the users.

## DESIGN FOR AVAILABILITY

Enterprises require a level of resilience where the blockchain networks should assume that failures are bound to happen. The enterprise must be prepared to keep the blockchain networks running during these situations.

High availability (resilience) requirements may vary by an enterprise vertical or line of business, blockchain application requirements, project funding, and many other factors based on the enterprise needs.

Enterprises should approach blockchain availability the same way that traditional enterprise applications handle redundancy. They often utilize service replication and redundancy to make sure that they stay available.

Enterprise blockchains need to deploy redundant peer nodes and clustered ordering services and also replicate other working blockchain network components to work seamlessly without any hindrances to blockchain application availability.

## DESIGN FOR SECURITY AND PRIVACY

Privacy and security concerns in the enterprise are no real surprise to enterprise architects. When designing your blockchain applications, it is recommended you approach privacy and security concerns with caution when anything is connected to a public network or even a private network that you may not control.

The need for enterprise-level blockchains is even greater than perhaps early on since enterprises generally deployed their blockchains in a private instance away from public networks. However, there are now more options that have been presented such as channels, off-chains, oracles, and the expanding new possibilities presented by blockchain, so it is imperative that companies get security and privacy correct.

Why? Blockchains are connected to a network whether or not it's a private or public network. Chances are that the network is generally connected to the Internet like just about every network I am familiar with. The one exception where a network is not connected to the Internet is in the case of a government classified Secret or Top-Secret network.

Connecting your network to the Internet will expose your network to possible exploits whether or not you have the most updated network security posture.

Most companies should not want an exposure such as the far-reaching Equifax breach occurring on their enterprise network or blockchain.

**NOTE** "The Equifax breach occurred due to hackers who had used an Apache Struts vulnerability, a months-old issue that Equifax knew about but failed to fix and gained access to login credentials for three servers. They found that those credentials allowed them to access another 48 servers containing personal information." —Alfred Ng, CNET (`https://www.cnet.com/news/equifaxs-hack-one-year-later-a-look-back-at-how-it-happened-and-whats-changed/`)

The Equifax hack exposed vulnerabilities but also the lack of responsibility companies routinely have around company data, which in turn is actually personal data. This is important especially because the confidence, trust, and reputation a company has essentially can be devastated by a lack of responsibility.

It is fair to say that data exposure with blockchain services should be considered just as risky as any Internet-based applications. That is, blockchains run on servers—specifically, Linux servers that contain open source software and those are the same servers that power the Internet. Anyone remotely familiar with Linux or Docker containers has the base knowledge to look for vulnerabilities.

Digital identity is a concept in blockchain that could aid in the critical area of data privacy. Using specific digital identities could aid in the evolution of enterprise-grade protection on the blockchain.

The blockchain can also provide privacy without secrecy in another important way: through smart contracts. Put simply, a smart contract is logic that is programmed to ensure that if certain conditions are met by the requests that something particular will happen, such as a blockchain transaction, a message event being triggered, or funds being sent as a result of a contract signed.

Since these are permissioned blockchains used by most enterprises using blockchains, all members must be known entities that are carefully vetted before they enter the enterprises membership ecosystem.

Permissioned blockchains will have specific restrictions regarding who can actually participate in the blockchain. Access for new participants is handled in specific scenarios by specific conditions being met such as being provisioned by a membership certificate or transaction certification or being enabled by a policy.

The following are common schemes used in enterprise blockchains to grant membership to a blockchain network:

◆ Company employees or partners enrolled through the use of directory services such as LDAP or AD (directory services).

◆ A consortium of companies that agree to participate in a membership schema that is funded by the member companies directly (membership fees). For example, an insurance consortium that shares actuary data between insurance consortium members.

◆ Consumers granted access for reasons such as enrollment, employment, or being a consumer of the enterprise.

◆ Regulators that are part of a government entity, trade association, or other regulatory body that needs to provide oversight in compliance areas such as SOX, GDPR, AML, or KYC.

**NOTE** "Blockchain ensures that everyone's private information will be owned by the user themselves. The data is protected by the technology, thus ensuring that no sensitive personal data will ever be leaked." —Eric Gu, CEO and founder of Metaverse (`https://www.coinspeaker.com/blockchain-technology-the-ultimate-data-privacy-solution/`)

During the course of this book, I will be diving deep into the area of privacy and security concerns specifically related to enterprise blockchains. Security focused examples as well as designs are presented in the Chapter 11, "Blockchain Security and Threat Landscape."

## DESIGN FOR PERFORMANCE

Blockchain performance is clearly a highly focused area where there is much debate on whether blockchains can scale to the levels we can attain with a traditional centralized database. The reality is that blockchains were never built or even considered for high performance. Blockchains were built for security, privacy, and immutability on a network that is decentralized as well as distributed.

Blockchains are inherently slow and should not be compared to platforms such as Visa, SWIFT, or PayPal. Blockchains are being developed that will scale somewhat closer to Visa, but in reality, they would not be a blockchain but more of a Hashgraph.

However, the use case for competing with Visa for a higher number of transactions is really not there at this time when properly scoped use cases are considered.

Permissioned blockchains can certainly scale greater than permissionless blockchains because the number of nodes is controlled (permissioned) and the network node distribution is controlled as well.

Comparing a centralized application to a decentralized application is not exactly comparing "apples to apples." It would not be fair to expect blockchains to compete in TPS with a legacy application due to its significantly different architecture.

## DESIGN FOR TRUST

Just because you have a blockchain solution won't likely mean that people will immediately trust the systems, data, or processes. When designing a blockchain, you should consider your user base and appreciate that trust is more than a word; it's a feeling and an experience.

As an architect and developer, I generally want to verify that the processes are actually working as planned as well as that the data is sanitary. Sanitary means that the data has not been compromised, data is secure, and transactions are kept private as specified if required.

**NOTE** "Just because blockchain technology is built to eliminate the reliance on trust doesn't mean users will trust the machine or network." —Jonny Howle, UX/UI Designer

## DESIGN FOR COMPLIANCE

From a privacy compliance perspective, it matters greatly whether the blockchain is generally accessible or accessible only to users who are members of a closed group.

For instance, privacy concerns may influence the assessment of whether data is transferred to countries that do not ensure adequate protection. For example, in the European Union there is a fairly new standard to meet called the General Data Protection Regulation (GDPR).

This marvel of a compliance structure is a legal framework that clearly defines guidelines for the collection and processing of personal information from individuals who live in the European Union (EU).

These EU regulations apply to every business regardless of where websites are based. The regulation must be applied by all sites that attract European visitors, with no exception, even if they don't specifically market goods or services to EU residents.

For more information about the GDPR, see `https://www.bloomberg.com/news/articles/2018-03-22/is-your-blockchain-business-doomed`.

**NOTE** "Some blockchains, as currently designed, are incompatible with the GDPR." —Michèle Finck, Lecturer in EU, Oxford University

In addition, it is possible that each party to the blockchain network has specific access only to part of the information stored via the blockchain and not off-chain. Each party has its own copy of the entire blockchain that is effectively restricted by encryption. Depending on how a blockchain is deployed, it may or may not meet compliance requirements that the enterprise needs to consider. Design for node locations, networking infrastructure, and enterprise integration all need to be considered. In Chapter 9, I cover GDPR extensively around blockchain-related concerns.

### Other Concerns—Deployment Model

Blockchains can be hosted on-site in the enterprise architecture, in a shared model such as cloud computing Blockchain-as-a-service (BaaS) models, or in a managed service hosted, for example, with a VAR.

BaaS is a newer solution that has started to provide enterprises with options for deploying their blockchains for developing and testing and can be used for a proof of concept.

If you are deploying a blockchain in your own data center, then you already have a good idea of the costs of that data center space, upkeep, and procedures to consider. Most blockchains are deployed on various versions of Linux-based servers and virtual machines. Linux is the best-known and most-used open source operating system.

When it comes to deploying Linux in your enterprise, there is no shortage of expertise available. The challenge will be on deploying your blockchain and the client applications that connect your blockchain networks. One area of expertise shortages is commonly around middleware, which acts as a translator from a legacy application to a blockchain application. During the course of this book, I will be discussing this in detail around both planning and deploying blockchain applications both on-premises and in the cloud.

## Hyperledger Fabric

This section covers Hyperledger Fabric, a permissioned cross-industry blockchain that has a pluggable framework. The following topics are covered:

- Hyperledger Fabric selling points
- Hyperledger Fabric design considerations
- Hyperledger Fabric design example architecture

Other than Ethereum, Hperledger Fabric is by far the most widely covered, discussed, and accepted blockchain platform. Finding information on Hyperledger Fabric will likely be fairly easy for whatever your project is because of its wide acceptance.

The global collaboration, hosted by The Linux Foundation, includes global leaders in aeronautics, finance and banking, health care, Internet of Things (IoT), supply chain, manufacturing, and technology. It currently boasts more than 222 members, and many of these members are actually competitors of each other.

So, what does Hyperledger Fabric actually do so well, and why does it have such great acceptance? Hyperledger has been enterprise focused from its inception as a consortium. Consortium members play a critical role in the development, planning, and implementation of its blockchain frameworks.

## Hyperledger Fabric's Main Selling Points

Hyperledger Fabric has several selling points, and these usually follow your design, meaning that you can choose to implement it as required.

◆ Modularity, which is perhaps Hyperledger Fabric's main selling point.

◆ Wide acceptance of Hyperledger Fabric from a cross-industry perspective

◆ Privacy through implementation of channels that partition the blockchain network and create a separate ledger

◆ Scalability and performance due to the ability to scale on demand

## Hyperledger Fabric's Blockchain Design Considerations

Hyperledger Fabric was intended for developing solutions with a modular architecture. Hyperledger allows the components to be essentially plug-and-play.

Hyperledger Fabric is a private and permissioned blockchain system and therefore needs to be designed differently. We would need to account for additional nodes, policies, a certificate authority (CA), and a membership services provider (MSP).

Hyperledger Fabric also offers a distinct approach to enable privacy through the use of channels. Channels allow for a group of participants to create a separate ledger of transactions and also maintain privacy. Hyperledger Fabric currently supports two database options for different use cases. The two current database options are CouchDB and LevelDB for storing the world state of the blockchain.

## Hyperledger Fabric's Advantages

Since Hyperledger Fabric is a permissioned blockchain, it has some major advantages over other blockchain systems.

**Permissioned Membership**   Permissioning a blockchain clearly provides advantages of security, privacy, and even performance of the blockchain. Permissioned blockchains such as Fabric can also provide benefits around compliance requirements when properly designed.

**Performance and Trust**   Fabric is a modular platform and can enable greater flexibility for an enterprise around transaction processing Data on Demand.

Ledger data is clearly maintained and can easily be queried for compliance reasons, data analytics, and even security analysis.

**Historical Queries** The ledger has been designed for transaction queries, and the choice of databases can enable deeper insight. With CouchDB you can run a complex query and gain deeper insights into your data.

**Modularity** Hyperledger provides the options for your enterprise blockchain to be as close to a plug-and-play model as a blockchain can be. You have the ability to choose the CA, HSM, consensus method, and APIs.

**Hardware Security Module (HSM)** Identity and Access Management flexibility is achieved with Hyperledger Fabric through the implementation of different key management options. Choosing your HSM can provide significant enhancements in your enterprise's security stance.

The following are the key features of Hyperledger Fabric that fulfill its promise as a customizable enterprise blockchain. It is important to understand these terms since the design example architecture will reference them.

◆ **Assets** are whatever is actually traded on the blockchain that is valuable.

◆ **Chaincode** is another name coined by IBM for a smart contract.

◆ **Ledger features** provide flexibility around ledger queries and distinct ledger privacy measures through channels.

◆ **Channels** enable private transactions between two parties and through channels enable a separate channel specific ledger.

◆ **Security and membership services** provide for access to the blockchain and full auditing capacity.

◆ **Consensus** choices are available for implementation, which allows for different performance, security, and privacy measures as part of reaching an agreement.

## REFERENCE ARCHITECTURE

Hyperledger Fabric has a well-referenced architecture. It clearly defines the four specific areas of design: Identity, Ledger and Transactions, Smart Contracts and APIs, and Events and SDKs.

The architecture is modular and allows the blockchain designer to determine specific modules in the design such as consensus, certificate management, and even the database option for the ledger.

Figure 3.11 references the Hyperledger Reference Architecture.

In the Hyperledger Reference Architecture you can see there are distinct modules. The current architecture separates the trust assumptions for chaincodes. What this means is that your policy creation capacity is really based on how you decide the ordering service handles blockchain transactions. Ordering nodes are commonly referred to as an *ordering service node* (OSN). Hyperledger Fabric provides for different network roles based on the type of peer node deployed. Consensus modularity is also apparent and allows pluggable consensus implementations for your enterprise. It is important to note that you cannot change the consensus after you deploy your ordering service.

FIGURE 3.11
Hyperledger Reference
Architecture

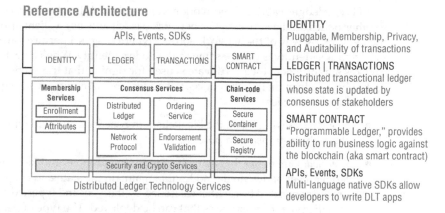

**Reference Architecture**

IDENTITY
Pluggable, Membership, Privacy,
and Auditability of transactions

LEDGER | TRANSACTIONS
Distributed transactional ledger
whose state is updated by
consensus of stakeholders

SMART CONTRACT
"Programmable Ledger," provides
ability to run business logic against
the blockchain (aka smart contract)

APIs, Events, SDKs
Multi-language native SDKs allow
developers to write DLT apps

**NOTE** For more information on the Hyperledger Fabric Reference Architecture, refer to `https://hyperledger-fabric.readthedocs.io/en/release-1.4/architecture.html`.

## ORGANIZATIONS

Hyperledger Fabric from a design perspective requires planning for organizations. An *organization* is a membership-driven security domain and is considered a unit of identity and credentials.

An organization governs one or more network peers and depends on a membership service provider to issue identities and certificates for the peers as well as clients for smart contract access privileges. There is also a node that is referenced as an ordering service, which is the cornerstone of a Fabric network, and is typically assigned its own organization.

Figure 3.12 shows a high-level organization overview. Org1 is the exporter, and Org2 is the importer. Both organizations agreed on the terms, and Org1 has sent the clothing to the United States. As part of the importing process, a customs declaration must be recorded. After the transaction has been declared and authorized, the transaction is recorded on the blockchain.

FIGURE 3.12
Organizations in a
Hyperledger Fabric
blockchain

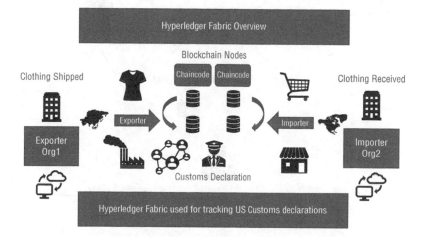

In Hyperledger Fabric, the network nodes need a valid certificate to be able to communicate to other nodes on the network. The network participants use a client application that connects to the network by way of the network nodes. Hyperledger is a permissioned blockchain, and the participant's identity is not the same as the node's identity. When a participant executes or invokes a transaction, their certificate is used for signing that transaction.

In Hyperledger, there is the concept of nodes, and all nodes are *not* equal. There are three distinct types of nodes.

◆ *Client nodes* will initiate the blockchain transactions and will represent the end user through the transaction process.

◆ *Peer nodes* are nodes that actually commit transactions and keep the data in sync across the ledger. Peer nodes are the nodes that maintain the state and copy of a shared ledger. Peers are authenticated by certificates issued by the MSP. In Hyperledger Fabric, there are three specific types of peer nodes that can be deployed. The type of peer node deployed depends upon the assigned roles such as a peer, an endorsing peer, or an ordering peer.

◆ *Ordered nodes* are the communications backbone and are responsible for the distribution of the transactions.

## PRIVACY

For privacy, a "channel" could be used between two members of the blockchain network. A channel is a private blockchain overlay that allows for data isolation and confidentiality. Note that a channel-specific ledger is shared only across the peers in the specific channel.

Figure 3.13 references a simple example of what a channel would accomplish. Three participants are in the blockchain network. Participants A and C create a channel to ensure privacy from the rest of the blockchain, leaving out participant B. This direct method removes the propagation of a transaction from the rest of the blockchain network, and this is how privacy is handled in Hyperledger Fabric.

**FIGURE 3.13**
A channel in
Hyperledger Fabric

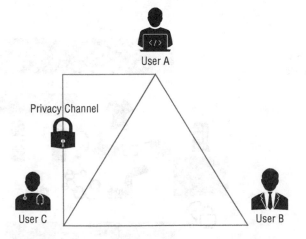

The Hyperledger Fabric framework is implemented in Go. The Hyperledger Framework was made specifically for enabling Hyperledger Consortium blockchains with different degrees of permissions, use cases, and integration capacity. Fabric uses smart contracts called *chaincode*. This chaincode is installed on any nodes that will be operating the chaincode. These peers of the blockchain networks run in a locked-down Docker containerized environment.

Figure 3.14 illustrates a typical Hyperledger Fabric peer network structure with clients, peers, MSPs, and logical organization groupings. The end user will be invoking a blockchain application, which in turn "invokes" an API call, which will invoke chaincode, which is a smart contract.

**FIGURE 3.14**
Hyperledger architecture structure

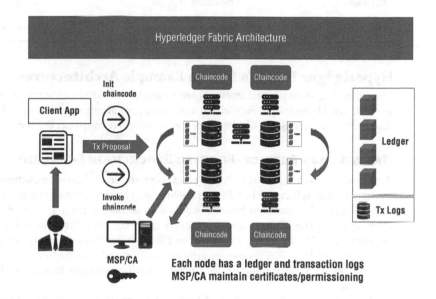

## LEDGER DATABASE OPTIONS

Fabric Ledger has two parts to its structure, which is very different from other blockchains.

◆ State data is a representation of the current state of the assets. Asset state data can be changed upon changes to the state of the data.

◆ Transaction logs record all of the transactions (in the order they are received), which modifies the state data, and once the data is written, it is immutable and cannot be modified.

You have two choices in Hyperledger Fabric when it comes to the database for your ledger: LevelDB or CouchDB.

The main reason to choose one database over another is if your requirements need complex queries for binary data. The ledger system in Hyperledger Fabric uses LevelDB. By definition, LevelDB allows concurrent writers to safely insert data into the database by providing internal synchronization. State database options include LevelDB and CouchDB.

Table 3.1 displays the options for the Hyperledger Fabric ledger. There are two choices for the state database. However, LevelDB is available only for the transaction logs. Transaction logs are also immutable and allow only create and read operations.

**TABLE 3.1:**      Hyperledger Fabric Ledger Options

|          | TRANSACTION LOGS   | STATE DATA (WORLD)          |
|----------|--------------------|-----------------------------|
| **Type**     | Immutable          | Mutable                     |
| **Operations** | Create, Read       | Create, read update, delete |
| **DC**       | LevelDB            | LevelDB/CouchDB             |
| **Attitude** | Embedded in peers  | Key-value paired (JSON, binary) |
| **Query**    | Simple             | Complex                     |

## Hyperledger Fabric's Design Example Architectures

The following example architectures are meant to provide insight into a customer request scenario for Hyperledger Fabric that a presales consultant may run into. There are likely many different solutions that could be scoped and designed based on the requirements.

### HEALTH CARE PRIVACY–FOCUSED BLOCKCHAIN SCENARIO

A customer has asked your IT integration company to design a blockchain network for their customer base, which are health care customers. Health care privacy is, of course, a significant requirement. The customer has also stated the customers are mainly in the United States and must abide by Health Insurance Portability and Accountability Act of 1996 (HIPPA) compliance requirements. HIPPA was enacted by the 104th United States Congress and signed by President Bill Clinton in 1996. HIPPA has security provisions and requirements for data privacy to keep patients' medical information safe. The act contains five titles that cover different facets of the legislation.

Since the customer has specified compliance requirements that are focused on HIPPA and health data security, blockchain technology can have a great impact here since we could use certificates and encryption keys to protect the data. From a session perspective, we could use channels, which Hyperledger Fabric supports remarkably.

The architecture shown in Figure 3.15 allows mobile users to access a blockchain service that is hosted on a cloud provider. The application that is being used is meant to provide mobile users with updates for their health care needs.

You can see that we are using cloud computing, and this blockchain cloud is serving the application for the mobile users. There are channels provided, and users are using their own channel. Fabric uses a public key infrastructure (PKI) to generate cryptographic certificates that are tied to an organization. Channel access is allowed only to the permissioned users, which is exactly required for privacy.

**FIGURE 3.15**
Health care blockchain
with Hyperledger Fabric

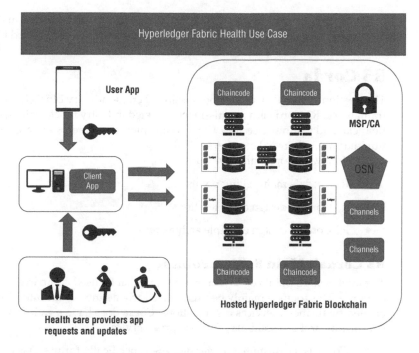

## CONSORTIUM BLOCKCHAIN FOR INTERNATIONAL TRADE SCENARIO

A customer has asked your IT integration company to design a blockchain network for their logistics application. The customer has stated this blockchain would be a consortium blockchain and would also entail some compliance requirements. There are no cryptocurrency requirements, and the customer stated that it was an international blockchain.

Figure 3.16 proposes a Hyperledger Fabric network that handles international trade. Various parties are involved in the blockchain network. The blockchain ledger has any nonfinancial activity written to the blockchain. There are several peers in the network as well as a dedicated MSP, OSN, and CA. This solution would be fine in most scenarios where the transactions per second would be low, such as 2,000 TPS or less.

**FIGURE 3.16**
Hyperledger Fabric
network for trade

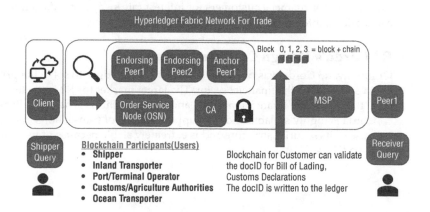

Hyperledger Fabric is a flexible, secure, and well-utilized cross-industry blockchain. The developer community is robust when compared to other permissioned blockchains.

# R3 Corda

This section covers R3 Corda, a permissioned cross-industry blockchain that has a pluggable framework. R3 Corda is a permissioned targeted industry blockchain. Its real merits shine in the financial and insurance sectors. Corda is an enterprise-grade software company, and the consortium has more than 200 members.

The following topics are covered:

◆ R3 Corda's main selling points

◆ R3 Corda's design considerations

◆ R3 Corda's design example architectures

## R3 Corda's Main Selling Points

The main selling points of R3 Corda are somewhat focused compared to Hyperledger Fabric, for example. This focus is mainly because of a clearly defined distributed ledger focused around and created by financial services organizations. Corda does have a well-funded backing from the R3 consortium and is a solid play for enterprise services.

◆ Corda is a distributed ledger designed specifically for use cases in the financial sector.

◆ Corda has expanding use case for insurance and other industries.

◆ Corda has a unique feature where there is direct support for legal prose in smart contracts.

◆ There is easy enterprise integration due to JVM flexibility.

◆ Enterprise support is unmatched by other blockchains because of its corporate structure and funding mechanisms.

R3 Corda is an ever-evolving ledger platform that provides clear value to its user base. R3 Corda leverages industry-standard protocols that provide what is considered seamless integration for operating the JVM that also maintains a robust toolset. Corda also has customized experiences for financial customers for interest rate swaps, standard initial margin model calculations, interbank settlements, and even reinsurance.

## R3 Corda's Design Considerations

Originally, R3 Corda was designed as a distributed ledger to solve the privacy issue of a blockchain solution for the financial sector. The target market for R3 is the financial industry, specifically the wholesale financial markets, and therefore this is what we will be discussing.

Corda is highly scalable and can support billions of transactions in a deployment. It is secure because of its security structure and is extremely stable because of its professionally developed codebase.

## CORDA ADVANTAGES

Corda's main advantages are focused on the increased efficiency for reducing manual tasks, as well as its capacity for introducing legal prose. As one would expect, smart contracts in Corda are detailed agreements whose specific execution is automated through computer code. The code works based on the inputs received. One distinct feature that other enterprise blockchains do not have is the manner that the contract law is encoded (attached) into the smart contracts, which may be legally enforceable.

One main advantage of using smart contracts with Corda is that they link the business logic and business data to the associated legal prose. A second advantage is that these Corda contracts define a specific part of the business logic on the blockchain ledger and are considered mobile contracts.

## PRIVACY

Corda was designed for privacy, as we stated in the previous chapter. It does this by sharing only the transaction within that customer network (no broadcast data propagation). Essentially it was designed to be a distributed ledger that addresses privacy and interoperability, which are still fundamental design principles of Corda. Notaries were designed in Corda to be clusters of distrusting nodes operating a BFT algorithm.

R3 Corda provides an impressive return on investment (ROI) for recording, managing, and automating financial agreements that are manual processes with low efficiency.

## SMART CONTRACTS

The Corda platform supports smart contracts with an interesting twist. That twist is through the implementation of legal prose designed into the platform.

The smart contracts on Corda are called CorDapps. A CorDapp is usually developed in Java or Kotlin, and the legal prose is an optional attachment.

R3 Corda has done some detailed work of addressing the "contract" part of "smart contracts." What do I mean by this? One of the challenges of any agreement in computer code is to be able to address legal prose. Corda essentially supports the inclusion of legal prose when the contract code may not be sufficient to address legal concerns.

In CorDapps, each contract will refer to a legal prose document that states the rules governing the evolution of the state over time in a way that is compatible with traditional legal systems. The benefit to the business is clear with a transparent chain of provenance for a legal document's full life cycle from partial settlement to full maturity. This transparent chain of provenance is a game-changer. I am not aware of any other blockchain capability with this maturity in a legal prose sense that is integrated. If you can connect your smart contract text to business logic through a template, then your enterprise can commoditize your legal documents.

**NOTE**   Legal prose, as it is known in the legal industry, is an approach to legal writing as a step-by-step process.

R3 Corda has an excellent video on legal prose that can be viewed on Vimeo at `https://vimeo.com/213879293`.

## LEDGER OPTIONS

The ledger in R3 Corda Ledger was built for financial markets and was designed to focus on the following:

◆ Data privacy

◆ Consensus

◆ Regulatory

◆ Smart contract

◆ Integration with bank systems

The Corda ledger differs from other blockchains from each peer's viewpoint. Essentially, the Corda ledger has no single central store of data. What it does have is that each node maintains a separate database of known facts. Known facts are really a view of the world state that the node can view. Each peer sees only a subset of facts on the ledger, and no peer is aware of the ledger in its entirety.

In Corda the ledger is *not* a central ledger and is a shared fact store. Network peers maintain a vault of facts, and these facts are not shared with all.

Figure 3.17 shows the relationships of a state in Corda and the views of the participants. We can see three participants, Joe, Greg, and George. The shared facts' view of the ledger in this example are A and B. Joe and Greg share fact B, and Greg and George share fact A. Facts D and C are not shared between participants.

**FIGURE 3.17**
Corda ledger facts

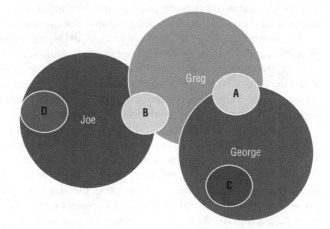

## KEY CONCEPTS

Corda is a permissioned peer-to-peer network targeted toward the financial sector. Corda uses a pluggable notary model for managing consensus rather than using traditional Practical Byzantine Fault Tolerance (PBFT) mechanisms such as proof of work (PoW). Corda uses notary pools, which enable greater performance and scalability via parallelism. Multiple notary pools can implement alternate consensus algorithms on the same network as well.

Corda has an extensive and unique terminology base that must be understood before considering designing a Corda network. Refer to the master documentation as needed.

♦ Consensus is when parties reach an agreement on a shared fact.

♦ Flows are light-weight processes used to coordinate interactions needed for the peers to reach consensus about a shared fact.

♦ The doorman acts as a front to a certificate authority. It accepts POSTs of PKCS#10 certificate requests and returns a string that can be used to poll the server until a zip file of certificates is ready.

♦ Oracles are a means for Corda contracts to reference off-ledger data in the controlled and deterministic manner that's required for the smart contracts sandbox.

♦ State objects are immutable objects that represent facts such as a financial agreement or contract at a specific point in time.

♦ Transactions are input states, and these states create output states. The output state that was created replaces the input that is "historic." This is similar to appending the blockchain.

♦ Notary is a Corda network service that provides a distinct service for the uniqueness consensus. The notary accomplishes this by attesting that the transaction is unique, which in Corda means that the proposed input states have not been consumed. The notary pool provides what is known as the point of finality in the system and is perhaps the most unique part of Corda.

♦ Vaults are databases that track all the current and historic states that the vaults are aware of.

## Consensus

Corda has "pluggable" uniqueness services to improve privacy, scalability, legal-system compatibility, and algorithmic agility.

The pluggable uniqueness service in Corda and the use of shared cryptographic hashes to ensure restrictive viewing of transactions both tackle the scalability and privacy issues.

Consensus, used for determining whether a proposed transaction is a valid ledger update, involves reaching two types of consensus.

♦ Validity consensus, which is checked by each required signer before they sign the transaction

♦ Uniqueness consensus, which is checked by a notary service only for the uniqueness of a transaction

For more information on Corda consensus, please refer to the Corda master documentation at `https://docs.corda.net/key-concepts-consensus.html`.

## Transactions

A transaction is a proposal to update the ledger. A financial transaction is an agreement between buyer and seller parties to exchange one or more assets for the payment of monetary value.

Examples are the purchase of products or services, loans and mortgages, bank deposits and withdrawals, credit and debit card purchases, chargebacks, interest accrual, tax payments, royalty payouts, and so on.

A nonfinancial transaction is an agreement that involves no transfer of monetary value between parties. Examples are a change of postal address or appointing a CEO at a given annual salary.

Corda's view of the world is driven by the intent of the transaction.

◆ Financial transaction: Agreement to exchange assets for payment of monetary value

◆ Nonfinancial transaction: Agreement that involves no transfer of monetary value

In Corda, transactions are defined by the use of commands to indicate their intent in Corda. Figure 3.18 shows a simple example of how to define a transaction.

**FIGURE 3.18**
Corda transaction commands

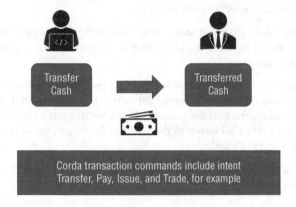

Transactions represent assets that are fungible assets, which are homogenous assets that are divisible, mergeable, and interchangeable, and also nonfungible assets, which are unique assets that represent something that is not divisible, mergeable, or interchangeable.

## R3 Corda's Design Example Architectures

The following example architectures are meant to provide insight into a customer request scenario for Corda that a presales consultant may run into. There are likely many different solutions that could be scoped and designed based on the requirements.

### CROSS-BORDER PAYMENTS SCENARIO

A customer has asked your IT integration company to design a blockchain network for their customer base, which consists of financial organizations. This organization would like to have Corda reduce intermediaries and provide efficiencies around cost and process time. The application will send payments in USD but will use a foreign exchange service to convert to EUR.

Figure 3.19 presents an example architecture for transferring value between two banks. It shows two banks, Bank A and Bank B, which are in a CorDapp to transfer value by using a foreign exchange to convert USD into EURs. The contract has the cash payment, public key, and address.

**FIGURE 3.19**
USD to EUR CordApp
for cross-border
payments

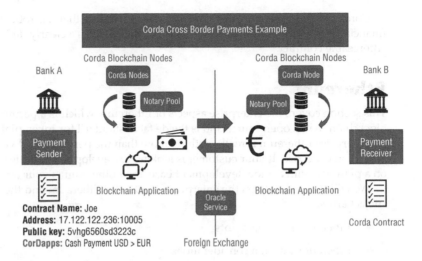

**INSURANCE CONSORTIUM SCENARIO**

A customer has asked your IT integration company to design a blockchain network for their customer base, which is an insurance consortium. The customer's consortium has decided that it would need to ensure that it uses legal prose in the deployment of their smart contracts.

Figure 3.20 shows an insurance solution that uses a CorDapp to issue policies. An insurance broker is using a consortium-based Corda blockchain network. Before the policy is issued, the broker uses an actuary tool that assesses risks against the policy before a decision is made and issued. Once a positive result is issued, the broker can issue a policy via a CorDapp Issue Policy, which would issue the policy and validate payment.

**FIGURE 3.20**
Insurance solution

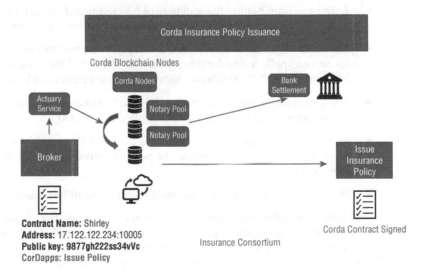

Corda is a professionally developed blockchain ledger that has robust use cases for the financial sector. Corda has built-in legal prose that enables a clearly defined and even legally enforceable contract.

# Ethereum

This section covers the enterprise aspects of Ethereum, which is a permissionless cross-industry blockchain that is open source and is the de facto standard for token platforms.

Enterprise Ethereum is really nothing more than the permissioned version of the public Ethereum codebase. If your customer is looking to develop a distributed application that is based on a platform with a wide development base, then Ethereum is your target.

We will focus mainly on the enterprise benefits for Ethereum and the enterprise around these subject areas:

- Ethereum's selling points

- Ethereum's design considerations

- Ethereum's design example Architectures

## Ethereum's Selling Points

Ethereum has several "selling points," and they are focused on an enterprise use case for Enterprise Ethereum. Note that Enterprise Ethereum is a term that refers to how enterprises use Ethereum and that Enterprise Ethereum is not exactly a specific product and is more focused on hardening the codebase.

The following are the main selling points of Ethereum. They relate to why enterprises could use Ethereum in their enterprises even though it is a permissionless token-based platform.

- Enterprises can deploy the codebase of Ethereum and modify the code to meet an enterprise blockchain use case and can take advantage of the whole Ethereum ecosystem.

- Ethereum is the most widely used token platform, and this makes Ethereum a good choice for an enterprise to use for the digitization of assets. Ethereum is the most widely accepted because of the ERC-20 tokens utilized on public Ethereum blockchain.

- The Ethereum ecosystem is the largest of the blockchain ecosystems and has a community of developers that is estimated to be more than 250,000.

- Enterprise Ethereum is faster due to the privatized, permissioned, and hardened code-base. It is many times faster than the public Ethereum network, which averages no more than 20 TPS.

- Private transactions are implemented with the use of channels.

The Enterprise Ethereum Alliance (EEA) is actually the world's largest business blockchain consortium and somewhat bigger than the competitive Hyperledger Consortium.

The Enterprise Ethereum Alliance has more than 450 members including Microsoft, JP Morgan, Accenture, Intel, and so on. The consumer and enterprise focus areas of Ethereum are developing standards to promote interoperability and guiding regulations to ensure the future success of the Ethereum blockchain. Consensus is an organization that promotes blockchain success and they have a paper on Ethereum that one should read.

**NOTE**   To find out more about the Ethereum blockchain fundamentals of ConsenSys, see `https://media.consensys.net/the-state-of-the-ethereum-network-949332cb6895`.

## Ethereum's Blockchain Design

In this section, we will cover the main aspects of Enterprise Ethereum, which is a hardening of the widely used permissionless blockchain platform that has its main use case focused on the digitization of assets, which is also known as *tokenization*.

Ethereum is a decentralized network of independent blockchain nodes, which means it is not controlled by any single governing entity. Ethereum is also referred to as a *global computer*, where you can write code that controls digital value, that runs exactly as programmed, and that is accessible from anywhere in the world.

From a historical perspective, the majority of business networks have been built on a centralized system of control and oversight. This approach has been used by governments and businesses for hundreds of years and has also been proven time and time again. This approach was needed since having an "intermediary" was required such as when sending funds from one bank to another bank.

A centralized system means that any single entity can control the blockchain network, but it also means there is a single point of failure, which makes apps and online servers utilizing this system extremely vulnerable to hostile takeovers, hacking, and instability.

Ethereum, being the exact opposite of a centralized system, is a decentralized system. This decentralized system is fully autonomous and is not controlled by any one person or organization. Ethereum also has no central point of failure since it is being run from thousands of nodes in more than 100 countries (at the time of writing).

**NOTE**   "I am seriously looking forward to when the cryptocurrency community basically passes away with proof-of-work." —Vitalik Buterin, Ethereum inventor

From a design perspective, Ethereum is the simplest because of its permissionless structure and limited enterprise-ready capabilities. For more sample designs, please reference the book's website.

Enterprise Ethereum increases the privacy level with the implementation of private P2P transactions that increase scalability and performance. It also introduces different consensus protocols other than proof of work. It allows customers to choose, for example, their network size, block size, and gas limits.

### ENTERPRISE ETHEREUM ARCHITECTURE STACK

The Enterprise Ethereum Alliance (EEA) has a stack layer that you should be aware of. The EEA stack and specification are meant to accelerate the deployment of Enterprise Ethereum solutions and motivate businesses to deploy EEA standardized solutions by providing interoperability among multiple vendors of choice.

The following are the main areas of the EEA stack:

◆   The Application Layer is the top layer, under which are three sublayers: Dapps, Contracts and Standards, and Smart Contracts and Tools.

◆   The Tooling Layer is the next layer, under which are three sublayers: Permissions and Credentials, Integration and Deployment Tools, and Client Interfaces/APIs.

◆ The Privacy/Scaling Layer is the third layer, under which are two sublayers: Privacy and Scaling.

◆ The Core Blockchain Layer is the next layer, under which are three sublayers: Storage and Ledger, Execution, and Consensus.

◆ The last layer, the Network Layer, is the foundation layer and contains only one sublayer: Network Protocol.

When designing your enterprise blockchain, it is important from an integration standpoint to understand how the stack could affect your design and integration planning.

**NOTE** For more information on the Ethereum Enterprise stack, refer to `https://entethalli-ance.org/technical-documents/`.

## PRIVATE TRANSACTIONS

One the main points of using Enterprise Ethereum solutions is the implementation of private transactions, whether on the chain or off the chain. When the "chain" is referenced in Ethereum, it is referring to the main public blockchain network. Enterprise will want to have both on-chain and off-chain transactions to get the most benefits of the Ethereum blockchain ecosystem. Range proofs or ring signatures can be used. ZK-SNARKS is also on the road map for possible improvements to privacy for the blockchain.

Private transactions are based on a mix of symmetrical and asymmetrical cryptography applied on event sourcing architectural scheme.

Symmetric encryption is used for information several parties want to share. A private key signature is used to identify the origin of the data, and public key encryption is used for sharing the symmetric encryption key and notifying one party. Each transaction actor must install and run the Ethereum Privacy node.

Figure 3.21 shows how a private transaction could occur with Ethereum. Two or more business partners would have private nodes installed and would connect to the public Ethereum network. For example, the private key signature is used to identify the origin of the data and then the public key is used for sharing the symmetric encryption key. The business partners would be notified of a transaction, and it would be written to the Ethereum blockchain.

**FIGURE 3.21**
An Ethereum private transaction

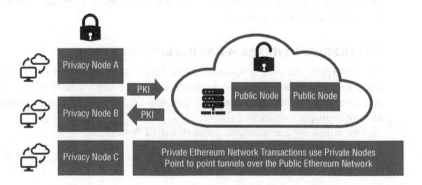

Creating a private transaction means installing a simple stand-alone program that interacts with the public blockchain and encrypts and decrypts all data regarding a business contract between two business parties.

## Scaling Transactions

Unlike the traditional Ethereum platform codebase, the Ethereum Enterprise codebase has two types of transaction-scaling approaches instead of one. These are on-chain and off-chain transactions.

*On-chain* scaling occurs at layer 1 of the Enterprise Ethereum architecture. It changes the Ethereum protocol to suit the transactional needs better. *Off-chain* scaling happens at layer 2 of the architecture stack of the Enterprise Ethereum.

The main purpose of using Enterprise Ethereum is to extend private transactions using the public network. This of course provides some benefits to companies that may not want to invest in a private blockchain infrastructure. The main proposal allows businesses to connect into the public Ethereum blockchain, pay for the use of the public infrastructure, and transact with each other via standard smart contracts, using their standard technology, which is public key infrastructure to identify their business partners.

# Ethereum's Design Example Architectures

The following example architectures are meant to provide insight into a customer request scenario for Enterprise Ethereum that a presales consultant may run into. There are likely many different solutions that could be scoped and designed based on the requirements.

## Corporate Finance Blockchain Scenario

The customer has asked your IT integration company to design a blockchain network for their corporate finance application regarding letters of credit. Customer has stated they would not invest in a member-based blockchain and want a public blockchain that has reasonable privacy technology implemented. There are no cryptocurrency requirements, and the customer has stated that there is trading between numerous parties and they want this trading to be economical.

Figure 3.22 shows how private transaction would occur via the public Ethereum blockchain. We have two business partners that are using privacy nodes. From a deeper technical perspective, the privacy nodes compress and then sign the transaction data with its RSA private key, generate a one-time use symmetric AES 256 key, and lastly encrypt the signed transaction. The symmetric key is then encrypted with the public key for each of the target nodes. The keys are published into the *PrivateTransactions* smart contract on the public Ethereum blockchain.

## Diploma Issuance Blockchain Scenario

Your customer, the School of Blockchain, has asked your IT integration company to design a blockchain application that will publish certification credentials and diplomas to a public blockchain. The customer has stated they will not invest in a member-based blockchain and just want the diplomas published to the public blockchain. They also want to extend this capability to other consortium schools in the future. These certification credentials and diplomas will be public viewable but will require a private contract to publish to the blockchain.

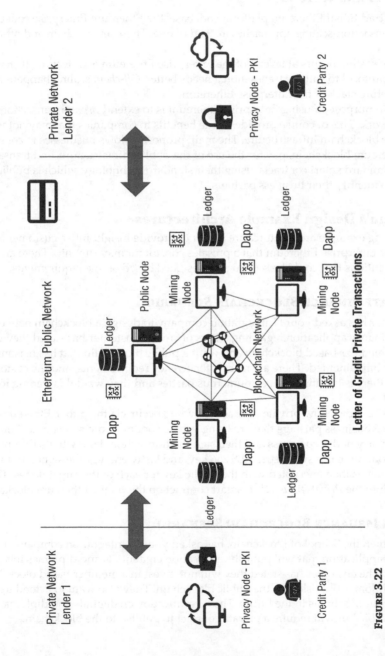

**FIGURE 3.22**
Letter of credit issuance with private transactions

Figure 3.23 shows a credential-issuing blockchain of a school and a student using private transactions with Ethereum. The school is publishing the credentials to the Ethereum public network and has sent the student a private link that is essentially a public/private key pair to authenticate an issuer as well as a recipient. The student also can generate a key pair and share the credentials with an employer, for example, if requested.

Ethereum is a flexible and well-utilized cross-industry public blockchain with private extensions. The developer community is robust compared to other permissioned blockchains, and the use cases abound with potential.

# Quorum

This section covers Quorum, a hybrid cross-industry blockchain that has a pluggable framework. Quorum is an open source private permissioned fork of Ethereum designed for enterprise deployment. The following topics are covered:

◆ Quorum's selling points

◆ Quorum's design principles

◆ Quorum's design example architectures

What is really useful about Quorum is that if you already know Ethereum, you're learning curve for Quorum is no more than an hour. The only challenge with Quorum is not technical since it's a fork of the Ethereum blockchain but is more about its limited user base and acceptance challenge JP Morgan has attracted more than 220 banks to its Quorum-based Interbank Information Network.

Some differences between Ethereum and Quorum is that Quorum was meant to be deployed as a private Ethereum-based network or be extended to a public network. There is no mainnet as with Ethereum, and it was created through a joint effort by JP Morgan and engineers from the Ethereum Foundation, which brings it significant support. Consensus algorithms used in Quorum are based on voting and does not involve mining at all like in Ethereum.

The developer base overall is lower compared to Ethereum and Hyperledger, and the number of applications is just a fraction of what you may find on Ethereum. However, a well-versed Ethereum developer will easily take an Ethereum distributed application and convert it to work with Quorum.

## Quorum's Selling Points

Quorum is an enterprise-focused, private permissioned blockchain infrastructure specifically designed for financial use cases. Quorum is built from a fork of Ethereum called Go Ethereum.

Quorum functions similarly to Ethereum. The similarities include network and peer permissions management, increased transaction and contract privacy, voting-based consensus mechanisms, and higher performance. When considering Enterprise Ethereum or Quorum for a particular use case, it is important to consider Quorum for financial sector customers.

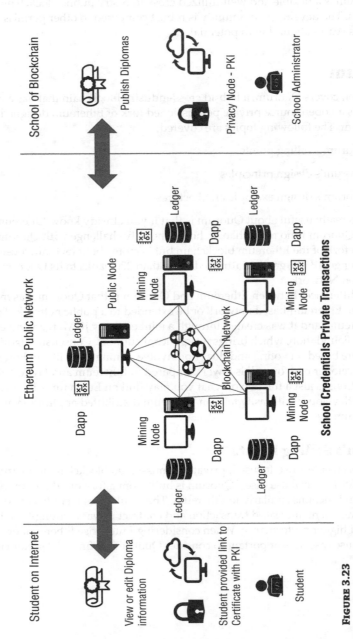

**FIGURE 3.23**
Credential issuance blockchain

The main points to consider with Quorum are the following:

◆ Private transactions are supported, and private contracts through public/private state separation are available over a private network or a public network.

◆ Quorum provides for solid security and a high throughput of transactions in a private blockchain deployment. A transaction speed increase is a result of the simplistic consensus mechanisms.

◆ Alternative consensus mechanisms are available with multiple consensus mechanisms that are more appropriate for consortium chains instead of the proof-of-work consensus with Ethereum.

◆ Quorum takes advantage of the Ethereum ecosystems and maintains similarities in some respects. This provides for a rapid development experience for Ethereum developers.

◆ Quorum is a fully supported blockchain by a consortium network led by JP Morgan.

## Quorum's Blockchain Design Principles

Quorum is a permissioned decentralized platform that allows you to deploy dapps on top of it. It's hybrid in the sense that it can support dapps created using one or more smart contracts. Quorum is a fork of the Ethereum codebase that provides for some similarities to Ethereum but also differences to Ethereum. From a design perspective, the differences are around the consensus protocols Quorum uses, the encrypted storage, and a new Geth client.

In Quorum, the smart contracts can be written in the usual Ethereum developer language solutions such as Solidity, LLL, or Serpent. Solidity is by far the most accepted with the widest reach, so it is preferred. In Quorum, there can be multiple instances of a smart contract. Each instance is identified by a unique locater address, and you can deploy multiple dapps on the same Quorum network. Remember, we are not deploying Quorum over the Ethereum mainnet but rather over a private corporate network or another publicly shared consortium network.

### QUORUM COMPONENTS

Quorum has the following main components in its architecture:

◆ Quorum Node, which is a modified Geth client. It has features that provide for some significant modifications. The main modifications made to the EVM node are a P2P layer that allows connection with permissioned nodes, validation changes to handle private transactions, removal of gas pricing, and newer consensus methods.

For current information on the Quorum Node, refer to the Quorum GitHub repository at `https://github.com/jpmorganchase/quorum`.

◆ Constellation, which is actually two separate components—Transaction Manager and Enclave.

◆ Transaction Manager is responsible for transaction privacy of the chain. This component is what actually stores and then provides access control to encrypted transaction data. Constellation also utilizes Enclave, which is the other component of Constellation for cryptographic functionality.

◆ Constellation Enclave provides a distinct separation of concerns. Enclave also has an impact on performance improvements through the parallelization of specific crypto operations.

Figure 3.24 provides a high-level overview of Quorum.

**FIGURE 3.24**
Quorum block-
chain overview

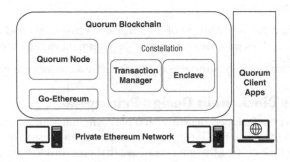

Quorum is fairly simple at a high level. The first thing to note is a fork of the Ethereum blockchain. It uses go-ethereum, and this provides some benefits around integration.

## CONSENSUS

Quorum supports three consensus protocols at the time of writing: QuorumChain, IBFT, and Raft. QuorumChain is a majority voting protocol. From my point of view, Raft and IBFT are the most widely used and useful for most enterprise implementation.

Consensus is handled by a set of nodes that are relegated by voting rights, and all have voting rights and also confer voting rights to others. A smart contract in Quorum is used within the genesis block to assign voting rights. The smart contract tracks the current status of all the voting nodes within the blockchain network as it updates them. The voting process is triggered by a voting smart contract that pings or samples voting nodes. When a proper block height is reached, the transaction is committed.

Raft-based Consensus provides for faster transaction finality and also on-demand block creation.

Istanbul BFT consensus algorithm provides for perhaps the most important duty of a block-chain, which is transaction finality. Istanbul BFT provides for peer permissioning, which is essentially node/peer permissioning using smart contracts and ensuring only known parties can join the network.

Quorum offers significantly higher performance than the public Geth (Ethereum) of the main Ethereum network and provides the look and feel of Ethereum that Solidity developers know.

## QUORUM LEDGER

Quorum maintains two state databases for the world ledger. One is the public state database, and the other one is the private state databases. Note that both have their world state committed over the same single ledger.

## PRIVACY

Privacy is perhaps the main advantage over Ethereum, and that's the main use case for Quorum. Privacy was intentionally built in through the development process of the Quorum blockchain. The Quorum blockchain manages much of its secure message transfers through its implementation of Constellation.

Quorum supports two mechanisms to achieve security as well as privacy.

◆ A zero-knowledge security layer protocol, which provides zero-knowledge proofs (ZKPs). A ZKP is a fancy way of defining transactions as a branch of mathematics. This allows one party in a transaction to prove knowledge of some secret value or information without conveying any detail about that secret.

◆ Private contracts, which enable the transaction to be disclosed between two parties.

Privacy models are changing, and the old way of banking privacy is also changing. With the implementation of Quorum's permissioning layer, the financial institutions are ensured that only authorized parties can join their private Ethereum network.

## TRANSACTIONS

Constellation, Quorum's privacy module, uses parameters to allow participants to exchange private transactions and ensures that confidential transaction data remains confidential between parties.

Transactions include a global transaction hash. This transaction hash consists of all transactions in a block, the public state root hash, and the block maker's signature.

## Quorum's Design Example Architectures

The following example architectures are meant to provide insight into a customer request scenario for Quorum that a pre-sales consultant may run into. There are likely many different solutions that could be scoped and designed based on the requirements.

### INTERBANK TRANSFER PRIVATE BLOCKCHAIN SCENARIO

Your customer who is a banking consortium has asked your IT integration company to design a blockchain application that will provide for interbank transfers over a private permissioned network. The customer stated this is not going to extend to the mainnet, and no oracles are needed, for example, to validate foreign exchange information.

Figure 3.25 shows a simple private blockchain. This private blockchain has a consortium and is used for sending payments. The consortium manages a distributed ledger and has imposed trusted peering.

### KNOW YOUR CUSTOMER BLOCKCHAIN SCENARIO

Your customer, a large international bank, has asked your IT integration company to design a blockchain that will provide for privacy but also meet the requirements for validating customer identities.

**FIGURE 3.25**
Private blockchain
with Quorum

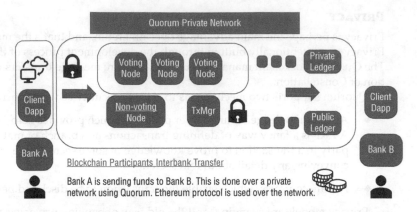

Figure 3.26 shows a Know Your Customer (KYC) blockchain. Quorum nodes process transactions and provide updates to both a private ledger and a public ledger. As part of this deployment, a KYC service is deployed to authenticate against known identities. A compliance node is maintained to ensure compliance around maintaining identities.

**FIGURE 3.26**
Know Your Customer
blockchain

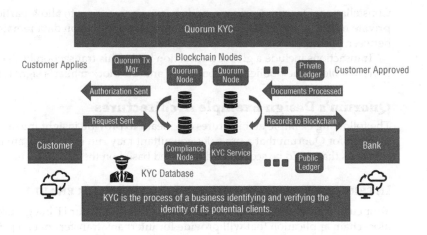

Quorum is a flexible private network-focused blockchain with private extensions based on the Ethereum blockchain. Privacy is perhaps the main advantage over Ethereum and is the main use case for Quorum.

## Summary

This chapter discussed the four most widely used enterprise blockchains and distributed ledgers and several use cases for each.

Enterprise blockchains have very different requirements from each other, both technically and from a business perspective. Corda is very different from Hyperledger and Ethereum.

Enterprise blockchains generally fall into one of several categories: private permissioned, public or permissionless, or hybrid solution, such as Quorum.

Hyperledger is the umbrella project run by the Linux Foundation, and Hyperledger Fabric is the mostly widely used blockchain in the Hyperledger portfolio. Hyperledger Fabric is a flexible cross-industry blockchain that presents many options for enterprises to deploy.

Corda was first built mainly to target the financial industry, where recording, managing, and automating financial agreements are manual processes with high inefficiencies. The platform was designed and built considering requirements such as data privacy/confidentiality and transaction scalability of financial institutions.

Ethereum is an open source software platform based on blockchain technology that enables developers to build and deploy decentralized applications (smart contracts). Ethereum is the most widely used permissionless blockchain and has a wide developer following.

Quorum is an open source blockchain solution built by enhancing the existing Ethereum blockchain. It provides an additional layer on top of Ethereum, which enables it to perform private transactions but also makes it more flexible by using different consensus algorithms. The main reason enterprises may want to use Quorum is for its privacy enhancements and performance capabilities.

Example architecture designs were presented for each of the four blockchains presented. As part of the design module, we covered best practices, considerations, and technical concerns.

# Chapter 4

# Understanding Enterprise Blockchain Consensus

This chapter will cover the most common consensus methods used for blockchains and distributed ledger platforms. The chapter will cover how blockchain consensus came to be and will provide insight into the historical challenge of the Byzantine Generals Problem and how it compares to the computer science challenges with distributed systems. The main focus of the chapter will be on the consensus methods used in the enterprise blockchains Hyperledger Fabric, R3 Corda, Quorum, and Enterprise Ethereum.

You will learn about the enterprise blockchain consensus algorithms used in the major enterprise blockchains. I will cover the most common blockchain consensus algorithms; however, I won't be able to cover every blockchain consensus method. There are at least 40 consensus methods, and most are not viable for enterprise requirements, mainly because of the blockchain they were developed for or the lack of enterprise features.

The goal of the chapter is to give you a technical presales perspective on why the blockchain consensus methods vary and how this could play into an enterprise's decision to implement a specific blockchain ledger platform. The chapter was not designed to provide you with a doctorate in blockchain consensus where you can trace transactions like an actual blockchain developer would.

Note that blockchains such as Bitcoin and Ethereum can be moving targets since the changes made to them are routine and expected. For an experienced blockchain and cryptocurrency expert, it should come as no surprise that a fork to these blockchain occurs almost annually. Another way to view a blockchain fork is that it is essentially a collectively agreed upon software update to the blockchain nodes. The main goal of a fork is to create two parallel blockchains, where one of the two is the winning blockchain.

Keeping in line with the mission of this book, I will focus on the enterprise-ready features, speeds, and feeds of the consensus methods that are used in enterprise blockchains.

**NOTE**  "Consensus is the backbone of the blockchain and any other decentralized and distributed technology." —Collin Thompson, cofounder of Intrepid Ventures

As mentioned, during the course of this chapter, you will look at each of the enterprise blockchains and distributed ledger consensus methods that are used in Ethereum, R3 Corda, Hyperledger, and Quorum. I will also cover the enterprise aspects of these enterprise blockchains and ledgers that have pluggable or modular components to enable your customers to have flexibility with the consensus approach.

You will see that both proof of work (PoW) and proof of stake (PoS) are commonly used as comparisons throughout the book. The reality is that it is hard to compare consensus mechanisms without a reference point of comparison to Bitcoin's PoW since it was the original consensus method. PoS is also widely used in blockchain platforms and can make for interesting comparisons as well. The chapter also will review what consensus is, why is it important, and how the Byzantine Generals Problem came about and how it was solved with a form of consensus called Byzantine fault tolerance.

Specifically, the following consensus methods are covered in this chapter:

- Proof of work

- Proof of stake

- Proof of elapsed time

- Delegated proof of stake

- Delegated Byzantine fault tolerance

- Practical Byzantine fault tolerance

- Istanbul Byzantine fault tolerance

- Raft-based directed acyclic graphs

# Blockchain Consensus Methods from a Historical Perspective

This section covers the concept of consensus from a historical perspective. The following topics are discussed:

- The importance of consensus

- The Byzantine Generals Problem

- Bitcoin's solution to the Byzantine Generals Problem

- Byzantine fault tolerance

## The Importance of Consensus

Consensus, as you know, means the method used to come to an agreement. So, consensus in a blockchain is how the blockchain nodes "come to agreement" over the blockchain transactions that will be written to the blockchain ledger. Consensus can be viewed as an agreement on the last state of the blockchain ledger's "world state," which is similar to a snapshot or picture of the current transactions written. Consensus validates transactions and also orders them.

More specifically, a consensus algorithm is a process used to achieve an agreement, for example, for a transaction on a distributed network. The primary concern to the blockchain network's operation is the maintenance of the consensus of the information being recorded on the blockchain within the blockchain network. Consensus algorithms inherently have a trade-off. The trade-off is between transaction security and performance in most scenarios. Performance in blockchains is measured in transaction throughput, which is also known as *transactions per second* (TPS). For example, the nature of Ethereum is trustless and is addressed by using the well-known proof-of-work algorithm. The Ethash consensus algorithm used in Ethereum makes attacks both prohibitively expensive and unlikely to occur. However, Ethereum is slow compared to other database technologies.

Consensus can also impact the parameters and security of the blockchain ledger operations. Understanding the strengths and weaknesses of the blockchain consensus being deployed is advisable since exposure to known vulnerabilities can be avoided with some basic knowledge. Also, the blockchain network could have rogue actors that could facilitate greater exposure to vulnerabilities.

Enterprises require availability and consistency at a minimum. By the end of this chapter, it should be clear that specific consensus algorithms were designed to achieve reliability in a network involving multiple unreliable nodes. Solving the consensus problem as it is known in the industry is quite important in distributed computing and for that matter enterprise services.

Consensus in a blockchain follows the same requirements as distributed computing and must satisfy the following two properties to guarantee an agreement among network nodes:

- Safety is referenced in most blockchain platforms as being able to provide a finality to a blockchain transaction. In a blockchain, this can mean that each node will have the same output for each input.

- Liveness is referenced to availability. In a blockchain, this means that each nonfaulty node will eventually receive every submitted transaction.

Two types of blockchain consensus are generally accepted in the industry: voting-based and lottery-based. Voting-based consensus should be chosen based on the following:

- **Finality**—Voting-based algorithms are considered beneficial since they provide what is considered low-latency finality. This is accomplished by a majority of nodes validating a transaction or block.

- **Strict rules**—Rules are strictly enforced, especially in a PoW consensus method as used in Ethereum.

Lottery-based consensus should be chosen based on the following:

- **Fairness**—The function should distribute leader election across the broadest possible population of participants.

- **Investment**—The cost of controlling the leader election process should be proportional to the value gained from it.

- **Verification**—It should be relatively simple for all participants to verify that the leader was legitimately selected.

## Byzantine Generals Problem

The Byzantine Generals Problem comes from the world of traditional computer science. In this scenario, the involved parties must come to an agreement for a strategy in order to avoid a complete failure of operations. It could also be that some nodes in the network could be corrupt and effectively spreading unreliable requests or information.

**NOTE** The Byzantine Generals Problem was originally referenced in a paper by Leslie Lamport, Robert Shostak, and Marshall Pease of SRI International. See `https://www.microsoft.com/en-us/research/publication/byzantine-generals-problem/?from=http%3A%2F%2Fr esearch.microsoft.com%2Fen-us%2Fum%2Fpeople%2Flamport%2Fpubs%2Fbyz.pdf`.

Before telecommunications, encryption, and general information technology (IT), the only way to really communicate with other people was through other people who were messengers. This form of communication was clearly dangerous for both the army and the messenger. Messengers could be captured, for example, and the message stolen, which could place the army in a vulnerable scenario. Sure, other forms of communications were available such as smoke signals or mirroring. However, smoke signals were not accepted as a way to be secretive.

Perhaps the city is strong enough to defend itself against one or two of the enemy army brigades, but it may not strong enough to defend against three and definitely not against seven. So, the general's seven brigades need to have "consensus" and must agree on how, when, why, and where to attack with precision.

How do the generals attack at the same time? How do they know a message sent from another brigade was not tampered with? How do they communicate so it's not intercepted?

Now let's get back to computer science and specifically discuss how consensus affects blockchain technology. In the world of blockchains, nodes are essentially virtual machines running the blockchain networking protocols, code, and messaging services on a distributed network. These blockchain nodes need a way to reach an agreement when it comes to writing to the blockchain ledger. This is where consensus comes in to handle how these blockchain nodes come to an agreement in this distributed network.

Figure 4.1 shows a blockchain network with Ethereum Virtual Machines. This distributed network has six nodes connected in a mesh network style. Blockchain ledgers are not updated on one node at a time but are actually propagated to all the nodes at the same time in most distributed ledger platforms.

**FIGURE 4.1**
Ethereum node network

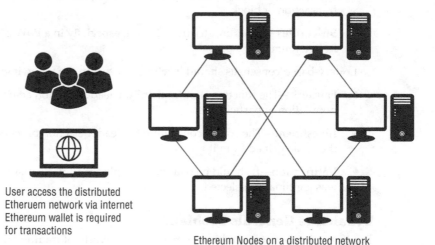

User access the distributed
Etheruem network via internet
Ethereum wallet is required
for transactions

Ethereum Nodes on a distributed network

It is critical that the agreement between all of these blockchain nodes on how to write to the blockchain ledger is strictly defined. This strictly defined agreement in blockchain is called reaching a consensus.

The true solution to the Byzantine Generals Problem is not a straightforward solution where "one size fits all" in the world of consensus. These blockchain ledger solutions need to involve specific types of hashing, intense computing work, and a latency-tolerant peer-to-peer communications protocol between all the nodes to verify the transactions. You can think of nodes as generals when applying the Byzantine Generals Problem to blockchains.

### Byzantine Fault Tolerance

Byzantine fault tolerance (BFT) came about since it represents a valid solution to the Byzantine Generals Problem. BFT is a crucial part of an effective blockchain platform, and there are multiple ways in which tolerance can be implemented. In your role as a presale's specialist or IT architect, you need to understand the various consensus methods available based on the enterprise blockchain platforms you're considering.

Figure 4.2 goes through the step by step of how the Byzantine Generals Problem works. First, General A gets a message to attack, while General B does not get this message. Because General B does get this message, this creates a problem where the city that was being attacked could foil the whole attack.

**FIGURE 4.2**

Byzantine fault
tolerance workflow

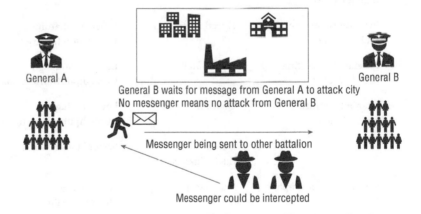

General A

General B

General B waits for message from General A to attack city
No messenger means no attack from General B

Messenger being sent to other battalion

Messenger could be intercepted

I will be discussing various forms of Byzantine fault tolerance, such as PBFT and other forms of BFT, in the remaining parts of this chapter.

## Comparing Enterprise Blockchain Consensus Methods

One of the main challenges that you can run into when understanding blockchain consensus is how vastly different the consensus algorithms can be for different blockchain ledger platforms. For example, Bitcoin and Ethereum both use a form of PoW, which is an amazingly costly and resource-intensive consensus method. Other enterprise blockchains use a form of voting for their consensus approach.

Table 4.1 references the most common blockchains and the consensus methods they employ. Each consensus method has a specific use case and its own pros and cons. Most of the blockchain consensus methods were developed to work on a private permission blockchain such as the various versions of BFT and more specialized proprietary consensus approaches such as Raft-based directed acyclic graphs and proof of elapsed time.

**TABLE 4.1:**    Common blockchain consensus methods

| CONSENSUS METHOD | USED IN | PRIMARY PROS | PRIMARY CONS |
| --- | --- | --- | --- |
| Proof of work | BTH, ETH, LTC | Widely tested | Slow and resource intensive |
| Proof of stake | Peercoin, ETH Casper | Energy efficient | Nothing at stake |
| Proof of elapsed time | Hyperledger Sawtooth | Participation cost | Specialized hardware |
| Delegated proof of stake | Steemit, EOS, LISK | Fast and efficient | Witnesses/not centralized |
| Delegated Byzantine fault tolerance | NEO | Fast and scalable | Root chain control |
| Practical Byzantine fault tolerance | Hyperledger Fabric | Efficient, sharding transaction finality | Centralized |
| Federated Byzantine fault tolerance | Ripple, Stellar | Low cost and high throughput transactions | Centralized |
| Istanbul Byzantine fault tolerance | Quorum | Low cost, high throughput transactions | Centralized |
| Raft | Quorum, IPFS, Clusters | Faster block times | Permissioned only |
| Directed acrylic graph | Iota, Hashgraph | Fast, energy efficient finality | Oracle requirements |

## Proof-of-Work Consensus

Bitcoin was the first practical and successful cryptocurrency platform, and it introduced the proof-of-work (PoW) consensus method as part of the platform. The proof-of-work protocol involves block miners solving complex cryptographic puzzles. As part of participating in the challenge of solving complex problems, miners are compensated by receiving rewards in the form of Bitcoin in the case of the Bitcoin blockchain platform, or Ether in the case of the Ethereum blockchain platform. Proof of work is like a running a marathon for the blockchain miners in the sense that the first node to produce the longest chain will win the block rewards, which are cryptocurrency or tokens depending on the platform.

Proof of work is the most widely used consensus method. This is mainly because it was the original protocol and has proven its resilience against internal and external attacks. Basically, PoW demonstrates that a participant has done some work and gets a reward for solving a problem.

A high-level overview of the PoW consensus in Bitcoin is that a block including relevant parts of the transaction is hashed, and a random nonce is added to it so that the resulting hash is below a certain value, which is called the *difficulty level*. Another way to consider the mining process is to look at it as an operation of inverse hashing, which is a cryptographic approach. This inverse hashing determines a random number (nonce) so the cryptographic hash algorithm of block data results in less than a given threshold, in other words, the difficulty level. This difficulty level is what the miners use to gauge the level of compute power and resources needed to mine Bitcoin, for example, and if it would be profitable.

Figure 4.3 shows the high-level process of a PoW transaction where it references the previous block's hash.

**FIGURE 4.3**

Transaction process in proof of work

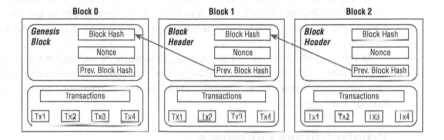

The second block is referencing the first block's hash, and then the third block references the second block's hash. For a block to be written to a blockchain, significant work has to be done by the miners.

Proof of work's main characteristics are the following:

♦ It provides hard-to-predict blocks, which can add to the competitiveness of the blockchain for miners but also security for the blockchain network. Essentially, the math problem gets more difficult as required by the difficultly rate.

♦ It provides an easy way to validate the correctness of blocks by validating who manages to solve the problem through predefined values.

One main challenge with PoW is that a lot of energy is considered "wasted" or "consumed." When you have thousands of nodes on a network such as Bitcoin, you will have thousands of nodes working to solve a problem. Consumption of resources is the main concern. Along with that, the cost to mine a Bitcoin has skyrocketed as well to over $1,000 or more. Mining cryptocurrencies requires intense electrical power requirements. To successfully mine Bitcoin, for example, you would need to purchase a "mining rig" that would likely have an application-specific integrated circuit (ASIC), which is a microchip designed for a special application such as Bitcoin mining. Mining is a competitive business, and an ASIC can provide a competitive edge and provide efficiency, performance, and even security in the blockchain mining arenas.

For example, in Bitcoin, a miner needs to be competitive, and this is done by continuing the testing of different unique values. These unique values are known as *nonces*. Once a miner manages to solve this complex problem, the miner will receive the prevalent bitcoin rewards. The miner then may add the block into the Bitcoin blockchain by broadcasting to the blockchain network that the block has been mined by this node.

Mining serves two main purposes for a blockchain. First, mining is used to verify the legitimacy of a transaction and because of this, helps to avoid the so-called double spending issue. Second, mining facilitates the creation of rewards and disbursement to the miners on the Bitcoin network.

**NOTE** "You called bitcoin a fraud. I'm a bitcoin miner. We create bitcoins. It costs over $1,000 per coin to create a bitcoin. What does it cost to create a U.S. dollar? Which one is the fraud? Because it costs whatever the paper costs, but it costs me and other miners over $1,000 per coin. It's called proof of work." —John MacAfee on CNBC replying to a James Dimon comment about Bitcoin

If you're an enterprise or your customers are enterprises, then you're likely not going to be using a PoW-based blockchain such as Bitcoin. You may want to use Ethereum, for example, as a token platform or perhaps to extend a payment gateway for a cryptocurrency platform as well.

In the case of Quorum and Enterprise Ethereum, however, you may have a good use case to consider those blockchains as well because of their hybrid enterprise solutions. Chapter 8, "Enterprise Blockchain Use Cases," covers the more common use cases for Quorum and Enterprise Ethereum.

## Proof-of-Stake Consensus

Proof of stake (PoS) is a consensus algorithm that is commonly used by cryptocurrencies to validate blocks and is very different from proof of work from a consensus standpoint. Proof of stake was created in 2011, and the first cryptocurrency to implement it was Peercoin in 2012. Essentially it was created as a way of avoiding the well-known economic and environmental issues with PoW, such as intense energy consumption and cost of mining.

Proof of stake implements an approach where the creator of the next block is determined by a randomized system that is logically dictated by how much of an investment a user is holding or how long they have been holding that particular currency. This is a different approach from the "computational power" in PoW, for example, where the probability of creating a block and receiving the associated rewards is proportional to a user holding the underlining token or cryptocurrency on the network.

Proof of stake is an interest-based approach to handling a blockchain where a node's interest is directly proportional to its investment. Another way to look at proof of stake is that it is a deterministic way that is essentially based on wealth, defined as *stake*. A greater investment in a cryptocurrency stake equates to greater influence.

Proof of stake's main characteristics are as follows:

◆ A stake may change due to economics.

◆ Votes are based on economics.

◆ Nodes need to be online to vote.

+ Votes are final.

+ Multiple votes are not allowed.

Ethereum has a planned Casper release, which is a fork of the Ethereum blockchain. This fork would be to change from a PoW consensus to a PoS consensus. Note that if Ethereum moved to a PoS consensus, it would be a major disruptive move, since Ethereum would go from a mining consensus to a validator consensus.

The PoS system is well enabled for platforms with a static coin supply. For example, most crowd-funded platforms leverage this approach to distributing tokens based on investment. This is exactly where Ethereum is going. However, what makes Ethereum different is its PoS-based finality system capable of overlaying an existing PoW blockchain. This overlay on top of PoW is essentially a hybrid PoW/PoS approach called *Casper Friendly Finality Gadget (FFG)*. However, this update has been delayed because of technical challenges and security concerns.

One of the main advantages of using proof of stake is that it has a significantly lower energy requirement; therefore, you can get a better return on investment (ROI).

It has been documented that each Bitcoin transaction, which uses a PoW system, can require as much electricity as an average Dutch household does in two weeks. This is both ineffective and unsustainable.

Proof of stake is considered a more efficient consensus protocol as it requires far less electricity to operate and can run on less strict hardware requirements such as ASICs instead of GPUs.

Also, PoS has less of a need to release many new coins, which has been a means of incentivizing miners to maintain the network. This helps keep the price of a particular coin more stable and therefore provides incentive for more blockchain participation.

## Comparing Proof of Work and Proof of Stake

Now that you have a general understanding of both PoW and PoS, let's review PoW versus PoS to understand how disruptive it would be for Ethereum to move from PoW to PoS.

+ **Proof of work**—PoW relies on miners running nodes on the network to solve computationally difficult math problems to validate new blocks of a transaction. Miners are compensated for their work.

+ **Proof of stake**—PoW relies on validator nodes on the network to take turns proposing and validating the next block in the chain. The value of the validator's node—and the size of its reward—depends on the amount of coins staked in the verification process. Essentially, the more you deposit, the bigger the potential return.

PoW is work intensive and requires miners (nodes) to write to the blockchain transactions. Miners are costly, and the mining process is hideously intensive economically and from an energy standpoint.

According to a recent Cointelegraph article (https://cointelegraph.com/news/bitcoin-mining-uses-more-power-than-most-african-countries), it was estimated that just the Bitcoin network uses 0.14 percent of the global energy consumption. Bitcoin mining now potentially consumes more electricity than the bottom 750 million electricity users, which is more than 10 percent of the population of the world.

PoS requires a different type of investment than PoW and is less energy intensive. PoW offers the following pros:

♦ It is a historically proven consensus method that is widely used for cryptocurrency and is a stable platform.

♦ It's secure because of the high cost and low probability of a 51 percent attack. (A 51 percent attack is where the pool of mining nodes is taken over by a group of miners controlling more than 50 percent of the network's mining hash rate.) This type of attack is unlikely because of the immense hash power and the requirement for the number of nodes to control.

PoW has the following cons:

♦ Transaction processing is slow compared to other consensus approaches. For example, in Bitcoin it can take several hours to get a transaction confirmation.

♦ The 51 percent attack concern is still real, meaning that 51 percent or more than 51 percent of nodes in the network can be exploited.

♦ Mining is a time-consuming process because of the work that has to be done to produce blocks.

♦ Mining is an expensive process from both an economic and environmental perspective. For example, Bitcoin mining uses so much power it is frequently banned by municipal power companies.

PoS offers the following pros:

♦ It is energy efficient compared to proof of work since there is no need to mine coins, making it an environmentally friendly option to cryptocurrencies such as Bitcoin.

♦ A PoS system has a lower barrier to entry because no mining rigs are required, and it allows more users to take part in the staking and forging processes.

PoS offers the following cons:

♦ Someone can monopolize the network. With PoS you know that an increased stake in the network means increased leverage. This can be a concern if someone forges most of the future blocks and centralizes the rewards.

♦ Hackers can steal your wealth but also your stake in the network. When someone loses their "wallet" with the coins, then they also lose their ability to vote in the blockchain network.

As with any blockchain requirement you're trying to establish, reviewing the benefits and drawbacks should enable you to determine the right solution.

## Proof of Elapsed Time

Proof of elapsed time (PoET) attempts to address the problem of proof of stake where the random election of participants proposing blocks can occur and also ensures that every participant has a fair chance to propose a new block and then participate in the voting process.

PoET was developed by well-known computer chipmaker Intel to be a production-grade protocol capable of supporting large network use cases. PoET requires a special CPU instruction set called *Intel Software Guard Extensions (SGX)*, which provides for a trusted environment called TEE. Trusted code runs in an environment that is private from the rest of the application. This means the rest of the application will not interfere with the memory space of the trusted code, for example. Think of this as a container in cloud computing or a sandbox.

PoET essentially mitigates concerns about the PoW consensus by electing what is considered a leader and implementing a two-tier process. PoET attempts to correct the issue of PoS, which will arbitrarily determine that the members proposing blocks are expected to guarantee that each member has a reasonable opportunity to offer a block.

Every participant in the network is assigned a random amount of time to wait, and the first participant to finish its wait time will have the opportunity to commit the next block to the blockchain.

PoET imposes a hold-up time from its local reliable enclave of node members. The node member with the shortest hold-up time is next to "offer" a block only after the expiration of the hold time. Each privately trusted enclave signs the potential requests. The results are then validated by other members so they can confirm that no other nodes have skipped the waiting time.

There are valid concerns that because PoET relies heavily on SGX for the foundation of the protocol, the SGX enclave could be hijacked. This has been proven with the recent Foreshadow vulnerability. Still, Hyperledger Sawtooth utilizes the PoET consensus algorithm, which leverages Intel's SGX to implement this leader-based lottery system.

**NOTE** To find out more about PoET, visit the Sawtooth document repository at `https://sawtooth.hyperledger.org/docs/core/nightly/0-8/introduction.html`.

PoET is a specialized use case. Its main benefit is that it is a trusted proprietary platform from Intel.

PoET offers the following pros:

♦ Trusted environment that is essentially a plug-and-play consensus on Hyperledger Sawtooth

♦ Lower energy usage than a PoW consensus that has mining costs such as hardware and energy

♦ Solves the random leader selection problem without being resource intensive or requiring incentives

PoET has the following cons:

♦ Lack of portability due to reliance on Intel's proprietary hardware and software requirements

♦ Higher costs than other blockchain platforms due to the proprietary hardware requirements

As you can see, the pros and cons could certainly be acceptable for enterprises that are seeking a targeted solution and not expecting to go outside of that solution.

## Delegated Proof of Stake

Delegated proof of stake (DPoS) was invented by Daniel Larimer, cofounder of Steem and CTO of EOS, both of which use DPos. DPos is an offshoot of its relative PoS.

DPoS uses a real-time voting system and a reputational system to achieve consensus. The DPoS blockchain consensus protocol allows the blockchain token holders to leverage their coin balances to elect delegates that are called *witnesses*. These witnesses have the opportunity to stake blocks of new transactions and then will be authorized to add them to the blockchain network.

Interestingly, the voting power is determined by how large the token holdings are of the specified blockchain stakeholders. The stakeholders who have more coins or tokens, for example, will have a greater impact on the network than those with fewer. Generally, this impact of the stake is directly proportional to the stake that has been placed into the system's network.

DPoS is considered to be the least centralized consensus protocol compared to all others as it is the most inclusive.

There are significant variations of DPoS where a delegate needs to show commitment by depositing funds into what is similar to a time-locked security account. Each of these blockchains also has a different protocol for how the consensus method is implemented and maintained.

There are typically 21 to 101 delegates elected in the various blockchain networks using the DPoS consensus algorithm. For example, at the time of writing, in EOS and also Steemit there are 21 block producers. In Bitshares, there are 101 block producers. In a DPoS network, it is up to the consensus rules of that chain to determine the variables of choosing a block producer.

Essentially, there are several benefits such as availability and performance, which are just two differentiators as compared to other blockchain algorithms. These are clear benefits to using a DPoS consensus.

DPoS offers the following pros:

◆ DPoS consumes significantly less energy than PoW and is considered to be very energy efficient.

◆ DPos provides incentives to participate in the network and provides delegates with a way to be voted out if they misbehave on the network.

◆ DPos scales greater than PoW and PoS and has faster transaction processing due to less overhead.

◆ There is a fair reward distribution where it is considered a "democratized" reward schema.

DPoS has the following cons:

◆ A 51 percent attack is clearly possible because fewer people are in charge of ensuring the network stays secure.

◆ Centralization of control could occur if the delegates with the most tokens gain strength, which in turn could allow a "cartel" approach to network control.

Some of the blockchain projects that use a DPoS consensus include Steemit, EOS, Bitshares, and Lisk.

## Delegated Byzantine Fault Tolerance

Delegated Byzantine fault tolerance (dBFT) was developed by the NEO team to overcome the Byzantine Generals Problem. NEO is similar in many respects to Ethereum, but I chose not to cover NEO as one of the blockchains due to its low usage and unproven platform at the time of writing.

It is, however, important to note that NEO does have some features that would be useful for enterprises, so covering it here will be useful.

The system comprises nodes, delegates, and a speaker. dBFT essentially works in a similar fashion to a country's government structure, with its citizens, delegates (representatives), and speakers (politicians) to ensure that the country (network) is functionally correct.

dBFT has some unique terms compared to other blockchain consensus, so it's important to clarify some terminology before moving on.

- *Citizens* are essentially NEO token holders and are considered ordinary nodes. A token holder is anyone who holds a cryptocurrency token and maintains an interest in the blockchain by voting.

- *Delegates* are bookkeeping nodes and elected to the role to file requests.

- *Speakers* are randomly chosen delegates to follow the citizens' requests by proposing the requests.

dBFT is a unique consensus algorithm developed for NEO with what can be considered a perfect finality. Perfect finality means that all transactions are 100 percent confirmed to be final after the first confirmation.

Interestingly, the blockchain cannot fork with dBFT, and this can remove some friction for stakeholders. dBFT is totally focused on the enterprise since it was clearly built with both regulatory and business use cases in mind.

dBFT offers the following benefits:

- NEO offers immediate finality after confirmation as well as being an almost impossible protocol to launch a 51 percent attack.

- NEO has fast and efficient protocols since a new block on the chain takes between 15 and 20 seconds.

- The NEO dBFT network cannot be forked and, therefore provides stability for participants.

dBFT has the following disadvantages:

- There is high centralization due to the low node count of the NEO network.

- Centralization is clear since the bookkeepers are controlled by the NEO council.

- The NEO network cannot actually be forked, which may be a concern if a disagreement occurs between members.

- The NEO user and developer bases are still small compared to Ethereum, which makes expertise harder to find.

NEO is a nonprofit community-driven blockchain project. It utilizes blockchain technology and digital identity to digitize assets and automate the management of digital assets using smart contracts. To find out more about NEO and dBFT, go to https://neo.org/.

## Practical Byzantine Fault Tolerance

Practical Byzantine fault tolerance (PBFT) has been the most widely used permissioned blockchain platform protocol at the time of writing. PBFT was introduced by Miguel Castro and Barbara Liskov at the MIT Laboratory for Computer Science in 1999. PBFT is also one of the several potential solutions to the Byzantine Generals Problem, which was discussed earlier in the chapter.

PBFT consensus decisions are determined based on the total decisions submitted by all the generals (nodes). PBFT addresses the challenges without the extensive expenditure of energy required by proof of work. It is important to note that PBFT works only on a permissioned blockchain and thus does not allow anonymity like in Ethereum.

PBFT has the main purpose of deciding whether to accept a piece of information submitted to the blockchain. Essentially, is the information being proposed from an honest and reliable source?

PBFT offers the following two benefits:

◆ Rapid transaction finality that does not wait for confirmations to log transactions

◆ Lower power consumption compared to PoW

PBFT has the following disadvantages:

◆ Initially designed for a limited use case because of the high load of network traffic between nodes

◆ Can be susceptible to sybil attacks where a single party can create or manipulate a large number of network nodes, compromising the network

Blockchain projects such as Zilliqa, Hyperledger Fabric, and Ripple currently are using PBFT as their primary algorithm or have it as a choice in their portfolio.

## Istanbul Byzantine Fault Tolerance

Istanbul Byzantine fault tolerance (IBFT) is a hybrid form of BFT and is an efficient alternative to PoW, which is currently used in the Ethereum network. IBFT is an implementation of the PBFT algorithm with some significant modifications to the blockchain code. These modifications provide for benefits that include efficient settlement finality and reduced infrastructure.

For example, in its use case with Quorum, IBFT uses a pool of validating nodes operating on a private Ethereum network, which will determine whether a proposed block is valid to be proposed for addition to the blockchain network.

The next step in the process that occurs is that one validating node is arbitrarily selected as the proposer and will be responsible for constructing a block at the block interval. It then will share this block with the group.

Effectively, if a "super-majority" of the node validators accept the block to be valid, the accepted block is then written to the blockchain.

Lastly, at the completion of the consensus process, these validator nodes may select a new proposer. This proposer then will be responsible for providing the next candidate block at the next block interval in the process.

IBFT is a Byzantine fault-tolerant solution offering immediate transaction finality that reduces the required blockchain infrastructure that other platforms may require. IBFT offers substantial benefits when used on a private blockchain where the validator pool is trusted and held accountable.

Lastly, IBFT really provides for what is a predictable transaction processing rate that enterprise blockchain must have.

The most significant implementation of IBFT is in the Quorum blockchain.

## Raft Consensus

Raft is a consensus algorithm that is designed to be easy to understand by most IT professionals in the sense that it has a simple ledger structure with little overhead. The main difference is that Raft has been simplified into relatively independent processes, which are known as *"subproblems."*

The Raft processes are as follows:

◆ Raft provides for a leader election process, where a new leader is elected in case of the failure of an existing one.

◆ Raft provides for a log replication service for the leaders, which provides high availability.

◆ Safety is the process that is implemented if one of the servers has committed a log entry at a particular index and, comparatively speaking, no other server can apply a different log entry for that specific index.

Raft has provided several useful resources to help you learn Raft efficiently. For an interesting and interactive Raft visualization that you can view in your browser, visit `https://raft .github.io/`.

For more information about distributed consensus, the leader election process, and Raft processing, visit `http://thesecretlivesofdata.com/raft/`.

Figure 4.4 provides a visual of the Raft processing resource. As you can see, there are five servers in a Raft cluster that is running in a browser. What is interesting is that you can interact with the utility.

**FIGURE 4.4**
Raft consensus
visualization overview

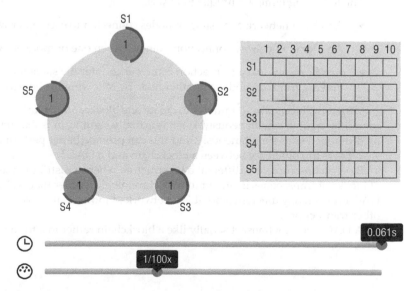

Raft offers the following benefits:

◆ Raft has a very simple ledger and network structure that you can comprehend quickly.

◆ Raft has been well known since it is a "sister" version of Paxos. Raft is used as a backend data structure for containers.

◆ Raft uses a randomized election timeout process that ensures that "split votes" are minimized.

◆ Raft consensus does not mint blocks unless there are pending transactions, which can provide for some efficiency.

◆ Raft transactions have a faster block time as compared to IBFT consensus used in other blockchains.

Raft has the following disadvantages:

◆ Raft has a somewhat limited use case in the sense that it is not used directly with cryptocurrencies.

◆ Raft also has a limited enterprise blockchain ledger that is available to work with significant enterprise use cases.

The Raft consensus is an option used in the Quorum blockchain

## Directed Acyclic Graph

Directed acyclic graphs (DAGs) may become more prevalent in ledger technology's future based on several factors. Some of these factors are greater performance and significant scalability, which in reality blockchains do not do well.

A DAG is a very different data structure than what a blockchain is. A DAG has traditionally been used in computer science to solve challenges around data modeling and data analysis.

Before moving on, it is important to understand some definitions when discussing the DAG platform. DAG's have some unique terms compared to other blockchain consensus methods.

The following terms are unique to DAGs:

◆ A *web* is a network consisting of nodes connected to each other with edges.

◆ An *edge* is a one-way connection point between one or more network nodes.

◆ *Acyclic* means that a transaction cannot encounter the same node for the second time when moving from one node to another node by following the edges of the network.

Generally, it can take 10 minutes to create one block, and it's important to note that blocks cannot be created simultaneously. What is actually significant is that transactions can be running on different chains simultaneously, and this can provide better performance.

What is the difference between a blockchain and a DAG?

Blockchains are a very different data structure where a distributed ledger forms a linear chain of blocks of transactions in an immutable chronological order that is clearly timestamped. A DAG is effectively different since it is a network of individual transactions linked to any multiple other transactions.

A DAG does not transact serially like a blockchain rather in a form of a parallel ledger data structure.

A blockchain is a linked list of blocks, but a DAG is a tree where transactions branch out from one transaction to another. This is considered a graph that travels in one direction without cycles connecting the other edges. A simpler way to look at a DAG is a "web of network nodes" where each network node is interconnected but is running one-way communications to the other network nodes.

Figure 4.5 compares visually a typical blockchain structure to a DAG structure in Hedora Hashgraph. The structure of a blockchain is more linear and hierarchal as well. One of the main benefits of DAGs are that these networks are faster because of how the transactions are validated and then processed in a parallel approach. In a blockchain, transactions are processed in a serial approach.

**FIGURE 4.5**

Blockchain vs. Hedora Hashgraph data structures

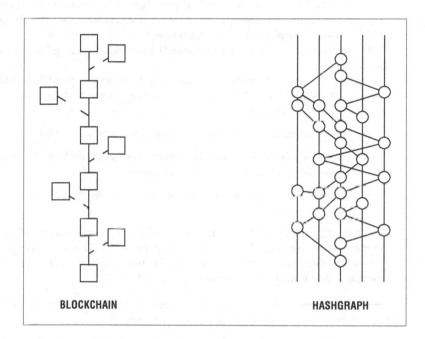

BLOCKCHAIN

HASHGRAPH

DAGs offer the following advantages over a blockchain:

◆ DAGs are fast and can scale with more transactions.

◆ Transactions can be validated in a parallel or simultaneous manner, compared to a blockchain that validates in a linear fashion.

◆ Lower transaction fees may be realized because of efficiencies in protocols.

DAGs have the following disadvantages over a blockchain:

◆ Considered complex to learn from a historical perspective

◆ Limited uses cases where blockchains may not be appropriate such as with Internet of Things (IoT) data

Ledger platforms that use DAGs are IOTA, Hashgraph, and Nano.

## Blockchain Consensus Evaluation

There are many more forms of consensus that are used in various platforms such as proof of authority (PoA), proof of burn (PoB), and many other variations of BFT consensus. For the purposes of this book, I have limited the discussion to the most common enterprise-ready consensus methods and blockchain platforms implemented in Ethereum, Quorum, Corda, and Hyperledger.

When making a design decision around enterprise blockchains and the appropriate consensus methods that can be used with a particular blockchain, it is critical to understand the three main comparison points between permissioned-based consensus and proof-of-work consensus.

Even with Quorum, Corda, and Hyperledger, there is some "modularity" that is supported around consensus. For example, in Quorum you choose between Raft, Quorum consensus, or IBFT consensus implementations. Choosing one consensus form over another may provide for better performance of transactions (speed), but when choosing IBFT, you may experience greater scalability.

The main features that require some consideration are speed, scalability, and finality. Generally, voting-based algorithms are advantageous in that they provide low-latency finality as compared to the following:

◆ Speed is the amount of time a transaction takes to complete.

◆ Scalability is a reflection of how many nodes the blockchain network can accommodate. Generally, scalability and speed are inverse.

◆ Finality is how long the voting-based algorithms are advantageous in that they provide low-latency finality.

Table 4.2 compares different types of consensus algorithms according to three main features that an enterprise needs to evaluate. Both permissioned consensus types (lottery and voting) provide better speed over proof of work. Finally, scalability is good in both proof of work and permissioned lottery-based consensus methods.

**TABLE 4.2:** Comparing consensus algorithms

|  | **PERMISSIONED LOTTERY-BASED** | **PERMISSIONED VOTING-BASED** | **STANDARD PROOF OF WORK (BITCOIN)** |
| --- | --- | --- | --- |
| **Speed** | Good | Good | Poor |
| **Scalability** | Good | Moderate | Good |
| **Finality** | Moderate | Good | Poor |

Choosing the proper consensus when designing your enterprise blockchain can be confusing at first, but the consensus choices are limited to two or three choices at best. Essentially, you'll want to determine the proper blockchain platform and then consider the proper consensus method to address speed, scalability, and finality.

# Summary

This chapter covered the most widely used enterprise blockchain and distributed ledger consensus methods. Enterprise blockchains depend on a method of consensus for many reasons such as reaching an agreement on validating transactions or establishing trust. The consensus methods vary widely on how consensus is reached, how a stake is arrived at, the terminology that is used, and the blockchain for which it was developed.

Enterprise blockchains generally use a form of Byzantine fault tolerance or an approach to consensus such as distributed proof of stake. Proof-of-work consensus is used mainly in cryptocurrencies and from an enterprise perspective is expensive because of the cost of electricity to support mining. This PoW overhead is not required in enterprise applications because the nodes are trusted by the organization.

Proof of stake uses a different approach than the computational power in PoW. For example, the probability of creating a block and receiving the associated rewards is proportional to a user's holding of the underlining token or cryptocurrency on the network. Proof of stake is an interest-based approach to handling a blockchain where a node's interest is directly proportional to its investment.

Proof of elapsed time attempts to directly solve the issue of proof of stake, which will arbitrarily determine the members proposing blocks by guaranteeing that each member has a reasonable opportunity to offer a block. Hyperledger Sawtooth utilizes the proof-of-elapsed-time consensus algorithm that leverages Intel's Software Guard Extensions to implement a leader-based lottery system.

Delegated proof of stake uses a real-time voting system and a reputational system to achieve consensus. The DPoS blockchain consensus protocol allows token holders to use their coin balances to elect delegates, called *witnesses*.

Delegated Byzantine fault tolerance is a consensus algorithm developed by NEO with perfect finality, meaning that all transactions are 100 percent final after the first confirmation, which adds to its high transaction capacity.

Practical Byzantine Fault Tolerance is the most popular permissioned blockchain platform protocol. PBFT was introduced by the MIT Laboratory for Computer Science in 1999. PBFT is one of the potential solutions to the challenging concerns of the Byzantine Generals Problem.

Lastly, Raft is a consensus algorithm that is designed to be easy to understand as well as utilize. DAGs are considered transformational since transactions are "linked" from one to another, meaning one transaction confirms the next, and it continues.

In the upcoming chapters, I will be covering some of the consensus methods in more detail, mainly regarding security, membership, and development concerns.

# Chapter 5

# Enterprise Blockchain Sales and Solutions Engineering

This chapter covers the solutions sales cycles of typical enterprise blockchain engagements and how you as a VAR, IT vendor, or even solutions integrator can participate in the blockchain sales cycles. Blockchain solutions selling has a heavy focus on application development, compliance, and enterprise integration, so a focus on those areas is advisable. However, your organization is already likely helping clients in these areas of application development, compliance, and enterprise integration successfully, and therefore translating your existing skill base should not be difficult with the proper focused training of how blockchains provide value and can integrate with the organization.

Throughout the chapter, I will discuss specific details of selling blockchain solutions and the professional services that can come with the solution selling. Then I will dive into gathering requirements and identifying potential use cases.

The goal of the chapter is to give you a technical presales perspective on how to sell blockchain services, software, and hardware. Part of my "mission" is to help enable you to sell blockchain solutions. I want to ensure that you are aware of all the following: historical references, business and technical resources, conceptual and nonconceptual patterns, and lastly routine presales tasks such as RFPs, demos, whiteboards, readiness assessments, and proof of concepts.

**NOTE**  Blockchains differ when it comes to sales cycles, margins, and vendor engagement.

## Enterprise Blockchain Sales Cycle

Blockchain sales cycles can certainly mimic, in some cases, the sales cycles for enterprise IT hardware, software, and professional services. In some scenarios, the process of selling blockchain solutions is more straightforward than for traditional IT solutions. This is because of the significant lack of valid production blockchain options, especially in the financial sectors.

However, in other cases, there may be some new aspects in solutions selling, especially when it comes to blockchain development. Regardless, whether you understand blockchain technology or not, your main goal should be to provide value to your customer. If this means this means you need to step out of the process and bring in a "blockchain developer," then that should be acceptable to both your organization and your customer.

In most complex sales cycles, you'll need to go through a "discovery" phase where you discuss, understand, and then translate the customer requirements; then ideally you go on to the exploratory and engagement phases and perhaps the commitment phase as well.

Figure 5.1 shows the high-level sales cycle that is commonly accepted by IT-focused VARs, vendors, and integrators. Note that there is also a seven-step sales cycle that is used; however, in an attempt to focus more on the technical aspects, we will [concentrate] on the four steps that happen after the funnel work has been done.

**FIGURE 5.1**
High-level solutions
sales cycles

This four-step process is consistently used for IT-focused solution selling as well as blockchain technology selling. When considering a solution to place in a prospective enterprise customer environment, these are the steps:

1. Identify a problem the client would like solved; in the blockchain industry, you will identify areas that blockchain technology could provide a solution for such as security, privacy, and compliance.

2. Investigate the causes of the problem and then build proposals for the customer on how to solve the problem.

3. Engage with the customer around possible solutions. In this step, I provide several options for the proposed solutions with benefits, costs, and risks. Providing the customer with these three facets will establish you as a trusted advisor.

4. Work with the customer and facilitate ways of validating the proposed solutions. These methods of validation could be technical, business, and legal validations. For the technical merits, use a demo, proof of concept, or even trusted customer references. For the business side, it's important to work with return on investment (ROI), total cost of ownership (TCO), and any other customer metrics that will facilitate a sound decision. From a legal perspective, the corporate counsel will evaluate what is a myriad of regulations and data protection laws that apply to the blockchain applications. Corporate counsel has met with IT to avoid noncompliance, penalties, and other impacts.

Experienced sales executives understand that enterprise buying is a complex, consensus-building process that is rarely transparent and is usually lengthy. Selling blockchain and distributed ledger technology could take a few weeks or up to a year in my experience. It can be a lengthy process for several factors.

◆ Customers are still learning what exactly blockchains are and where blockchains may fit into the enterprise. Customers who are technically adept will be better prospects for blockchains.

◆ There are a limited number of uses for blockchains that have flexible enough use cases. If the organization cannot identify a specific problem that a blockchain can solve such as compliance, data integrity, cost efficiencies, and so on, then the sales cycle will likely stall.

◆ Legacy applications may not integrate well and therefore present additional challenges. Can they be ported over easily or require middleware or reworking? Applications that are cloud native make good candidates for blockchain integration.

◆ Political challenges can arise from stakeholders, especially in the case where the stakeholder's roles may be in jeopardy.

◆ No two organizations are the same, even if they are both Fortune 100 financial institutions. Everything from political climates, training, corporate governance, business models, and so on, can present challenges to the sales cycle.

Blockchain sales cycles take patience, especially when the enterprise does not have an immediate use case, the budget, or technical capabilities on hand. Note that blockchain presales engagements are not at all similar to selling a cluster of network edge switches to a network engineer who already has established the enterprise use case to expand their network. Generally, in cases where the technical knowledge exists, it's a "speeds and feeds" discussion, whiteboard, and pricing exercise for the sales teams working with the network teams.

Selling blockchain technology requires a significant interaction with the development group. Developers are different in the way they think than your typical network engineer, for example. They are detailed, clearly identify with coding languages, use specific jargon, and like to solve problems. Developers are also going to be the one group of stakeholders who know how an application works from start to finish. They understand the runtime environments, the database structures, integration with the endpoint services, and the logging for compliance, for example. When presenting to the development stakeholders, you'll need to present a technical discussion, so you are well advised to bring talent who can discuss areas of focus. These areas include application programming interfaces (APIs) such as REST or Open APIs; development languages such as Go, Java, and Node; and integration options for distributed business applications that may run on smart contracts such as Enterprise Resource Planning (ERP), Know Your Customer (KYC), Anti Money Laundering (AML) and Customer Relationship Management (CRM) cross-border payments, and so on.

The stakeholders who are developers in some organizations are in departments called dev, development, DevOps, or in one engagement I encountered emerging technologies. Therefore, you should know that the stakeholders who may be in a blockchain project are not exactly "one size fits all."

It is also important to mention that stakeholders, decision-makers, or approvers will likely consist of the legal counsel and financial groups that blockchain projects can impact. You will likely want to brush up on compliance requirements before discussions with corporate counsel, which I cover extensively in Chapter 9, "Blockchain Governance, Risk, Compliance (GRC), Privacy, and Legal Concerns."

In a nutshell, selling blockchain is a "development exercise" for the most part, and you must be knowledgeable as a sales organization to effectively position blockchains. In that blockchains and distributed ledgers are newer technologies with a limited knowledge base, your role as a presales engineer will be more "evangelist" or even a "trainer" to ensure that your prospects understand the value of the solution and how the solution will integrate into their organizations.

## Blockchain Roles (Stakeholders)

It's important to cover the roles that will likely have a "sales play" in blockchain and ledger-focused solutions. In this section, I'll identify the stakeholders who will be part of the substantial discussions about blockchains.

This is important because in most cases blockchains are not a general hardware or software sale. It is also important to appreciate that solutions selling around blockchains could expand past the usual CIO, IT director, and network or database administrator you commonly work with. IT roles in this new world of blockchains, consensus, frameworks, smart contracts, and distributed applications are an evolving area of focus for enterprises. Some roles may require dedicated blockchain expertise, and some may only require that blockchain technology is a "nice-to-know" area of focus.

The following roles are commonly found in the enterprise blockchain arena. The definitions are provided more as a guide for general understanding, as one would likely expect that in some cases, titles and actual job responsibilities vary widely from company to company.

**Blockchain Developer**   A blockchain developer is focused on developing smart contracts or chaincode, designing distributed applications (dapps), or integrating front-end user web interfaces that will interface with the blockchain network applications. Traditional developers who have advanced skillsets around Java, JavaScript, Python, Solidity, Go, or even C++ development experience do well in blockchain development. The demand for a solid experienced blockchain developer has never been higher.

**Blockchain Architect**   A blockchain architect is a client-facing role that essentially will collect the customer requirements, translate the requirements into a working platform, and turn the platform over to the blockchain developers to work on their smart contracts, dapps, and client applications. In many organizations, a blockchain architect can also be called a solutions architect or a consulting engineer.

**Blockchain Administrator**   A technical lead handles the post-sales management of a blockchain platform. Generally, a blockchain administrator has managed other platforms such as cloud computing or telecommunications.

**Blockchain Operator**   A blockchain operator is a role that handles the management of certificates and accounts and the permissioning of a blockchain. In smaller organizations, the blockchain operator and blockchain administrator roles might be merged.

**Blockchain Legal Counsel**   In organizations that take blockchain compliance seriously, this role is required. The attorney (counsel) usually establishes "legal prose" for smart contracts and consortium partnerships, maintains compliance/governance requirements, and performs due diligence on various blockchain-related concerns. From what I have seen, in organizations that are focused on initial coin offerings (ICO), this role is focused on structuring deals.

**Solutions Architect**   This is a technical role that is client-facing and is considered to be one of the most critical technical roles for most VARs, vendors, or resellers. The goal of the solutions architect is to take a blockchain solution and solve a business problem. The solutions architect and presales engineer roles often overlap.

**Presales Engineer (Architect)**   This is a client-facing role that is critical to the organization and works in a "before the sale" capacity. They essentially pave the way for the more technical leads when applicable. The presales engineer is really focused on how blockchain products can translate into a solution and explain this to the customer. It is important to note as well that most large training companies and professional services organizations may also have a presales-focused role that is specialized on blockchain or professional services or development. It is also extremely common to see a presales engineer or architect role be the same or overlap in responsibilities as a solutions architect. Presales engineers and architects are considered to be "revenue-generating" roles and thus critical to the organization. If you like people, want to actively generate revenue for the company, and get rewarded for this "front-line" participation, then this role could be for you.

**Blockchain Marketer**   The blockchain marketer role is nontechnical and more focused on "relaying" the business benefits of the blockchain solutions and services to the prospective customers. This role usually is well represented at trade shows, conventions, and networking events. events, and is really focused on actively looking for leads and prospects for the company. In some smaller companies, for example, I have seen inside sales and account executives have the responsibility of a blockchain marketer.

**Blockchain Project Manager**   This role is nontechnical and more focused on keeping the blockchain implementation on schedule as well as on budget. Generally, any project manager who manages IT projects will likely be successful in this area. The one area that I have found to be new for some project managers is understanding the complex processes of interfacing with cryptocurrency exchanges.

**Blockchain Trainer**   This role is focused on enabling customers to work with blockchain technology. A blockchain trainer should be both technical and customer centric. Generally, technical requirements will be focused on networking, application development, business processes, and training, but also could be responsible for setting up proofs of concept.

## IT-Based Sales Cycles

Although blockchain technology may be complex, in reality the blockchain sales cycle follows the typical sales cycle you follow to sell telecommunications gear, data storage arrays, cloud computing platforms, or CRM solutions.

The seven steps shown in Figure 5.2 make up a typical sales cycle process (although some vendors use an eight-step system). For this book, I focus mainly on the blockchain sales cycle, for which there is no official sales cycle. However, I provide insight into how I handle different parts of the sales cycle to adapt it to the blockchain technology. After the sales cycle, I then move on to the design and implementation phase.

Every IT vendor, systems integrator, and consulting firm has its own view of what the sales cycle world is. After working successfully for more than a decade for several large organizations (Brocade Communications, Hitachi Data Systems [HDS Federal ViON], 3Par Data, and Dimension Data), I realize that every industry vertical looks at solutions selling in a vastly different manner, which drives revenue differently. That is, some organizations are front-heavy with a dedicated team approach (1:1 ratio of sales executive and sales engineer/architect), whereas other organizations are less heavy (two or more sales executives to one sales engineer/ architect). The ratio may be as high as 5:1, which can be directly related to the industry vertical or geographic region.

Presales engineers often sell solutions that are considered expensive and also as capital expenditures such as IT networking equipment or data storage hardware or software. It is common as well to spend a considerable amount of time in most of the stages of the sales cycle as a sales executive would. This can be different from sales cycles of less expensive products or services where the sales cycle may be traversed more quickly. Presales engineers really should not be fully engaged in every phase but clearly communicated with by the account executives.

**FIGURE 5.2**
The seven sales cycle phases

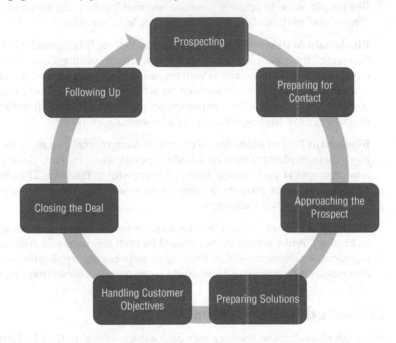

Generally, as a presales engineer, it's important to get involved in the discovery aspects of what the pain points are for the customer and what is creating these pain points. An experienced presales engineer should know when to get in and when to get out—for example, when to turn over the technical aspects to a blockchain-focused solution engineer. Basically, know your boundaries as a presales engineer and engage the post-sales teams as needed.

The following phases, to identify both sales and technical aspects, should be handled efficiently, effectively, and professionally to ensure that the customer receives what they need exactly when they need it.

The areas of a seven-phase IT sales cycle are defined with my own input for each:

1. **Prospecting (relationships):** This step involves obtaining client leads through various means such as conventions, trade shows, and even referrals from other customers. Traditionally vendors have group that can provide leads as well a qualified inside sales. This phase is more about establishing the relationship and building trust with the customer. Lastly, requests for proposals are another way some companies (especially in the government and education sectors) may prospect for customers.

2. **Preparation (intelligence gathering):** This step involves preparing to meet with the customer either in person or online, gathering information about the customer and the enterprise. Collect some use cases that you can leverage for their industry (financial, energy, insurance, government, and so on). Also, a great account executive should be identifying pain points, identifying any additional stakeholders and business decision-makers, and perhaps identifying project funding.

3. **Approach (initial meeting):** In the approach stage, your account executive will handle the initial face-to-face meeting, webinar, or conference call. The reality is that these initial meetings routinely do not include a presales engineer. In some cases, you as the sales engineer should be "qualifying" the customer and your organization's solutions set. As part of this phase, the technical decision-makers should be identified.

4. **Presentation (second meeting):** During this phase, you as a presales engineer will likely be demonstrating how the blockchain solution works through at least a presentation, a whiteboard, and more than likely a demo or proof of concept (POC).

5. **Customer objections (addressing):** Perhaps the most challenging part of the seven steps of a sales cycle for a sales team is handling objections. Handling objections is actively listening to your prospect's concerns and addressing them in a manner that will provide value so they can make a decision. As a sales engineer you should be working on the "technical close," which is the point where you have provided enough technically valid information around the requirements that the customer feels they can make a favorable decision.

6. **Closing the deal (purchase order):** This is the stage when the the purchase order (PO) is signed by the stakeholders and the sales team management. During this stage the implementation details are worked out, and any required implementation teams are called in.

7. **Follow-up (supporting the relationship):** After your purchase order is signed and weeks after the implementation team is on the ground working with the customer, you should consider it imperative for a sales team to be aware of how the project is going. The sales team should demonstrate to the customer that they are there for them after the PO is signed and the blockchain is implemented.

## Presales Tasks

As part of a sales cycle, it is clearly evident that sales are being driven by a sales team, and you need to appreciate the level of effort that can come into play for the sales team to close a deal. Before any purchase order is received, it is expected that one if not all of the following tasks will be performed to consummate the closing of the blockchain deal:

- Requests for proposals
- Identifying, analyzing, and managing stakeholders
- Blockchain readiness assessment workshops
- Performing demos
- Using vendor demo tools
- Performing blockchain readiness assessment workshops
- Whiteboarding solutions
- Performing proof of concepts
- Enabling the sales process with blockchain as a service

## REQUEST FOR PROPOSALS

A request for proposals (RFP) is commonly used in specific industry segments as the main vehicle for organizations to address procurement for their enterprises, which from a cost perspective is for a mandated cost.

Procurement is also referred to as an *acquisition* in the U.S. federal sector and is regulated by statutes dealing with U.S. federal contracts and the U.S. federal contracting process. Titles 10, 31, 40, and 41 of the U.S. Code are the common references for U.S. federal contracting.

An RFP, whether placed on the market by military, intelligence, or civilian agencies, is known at the federal, state, and local levels as a *solicitation* from the government.

Even large commercial companies will solicit bidders for an RFP. You as a solutions provider or potential vendor may be participating in a blockchain RFP, so let's clarify some terms before getting started with RFPs.

◆   The solutions provider giving a response to the RFP is called the *bidder*.

◆   The customer placing the RFP out for bid is called the *solicitor*.

A portion of my work experience for more than a decade was focused on government contracting (military and civilian agencies) in the metro Washington, DC area. As part of this experience, can assure you that your only way into most federal, state, and local entities is through the RFP process.

I refer to the RFP as a doorman or gatekeeper since you have no choice but to participate in the process. Requests for information (RFIs), requests for quotation (RFQs), and RFPs can be a time-consuming and essentially complex process for both the solicitor and the bidder.

Figure 5.3 illustrates the standard high-level RFP workflow process steps. The workflow starts with an RFI, which is an information-gathering request. Then it proceeds on to the RFP, which is the work for the sales team. Lastly, some companies may bypass the RFI and RFP processes and just publish an RFQ, which is a pricing exercise.

**FIGURE 5.3**
Procurement workflow
process steps

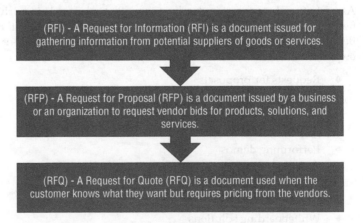

(RFI) - A Request for Information (RFI) is a document issued for gathering information from potential suppliers of goods or services.

(RFP) - A Request for Proposal (RFP) is a document issued by a business or an organization to request vendor bids for products, solutions, and services.

(RFQ) - A Request for Quote (RFQ) is a document used when the customer knows what they want but requires pricing from the vendors.

The procurement process also entails a lengthy workflow for what is referred to as *procurement activities*, which are one of the following: requirements development, pre-award activities, and post-award activities. These processes are usually complex for both the solicitor and the bidder because of extensive government procurement processes, regulations, and bidding processes that are managed by the General Services Agency (GSA). There is also a consistently challenged scoring system that the GSA uses to rate proposals' bids. These challenges are known as *protests* and are usually a result of the GSA's evaluation of the company, which can result in a company score that is less favorable to winning the bid.

When an organization decides to proceed with a bid for a government contract, for example, there are some industry best practices for assessing and responding to an RFP. RFPs are well structured, and from a bidder perspective, they require a team effort to complete thoroughly. Note that there are red teams, blue teams, green teams, gold teams, and pink teams, and each team has specific responsibilities around the proposal development. These teams are essentially a logically represented layered approach to the maturity level of the state of the proposal.

Before even thinking of taking on a blockchain-related RFP, your organization should ensure that they have the right expertise on board and also be willing to fail. From the few blockchain RFPs that are out there, it is important to realize that some of these organizations seem to be using the RFP process as more of an educational process than a procurement process. This is not intentional probably; rather, the solicitor might not be educated in blockchain and therefore not understand the real problems to be solved.

In a nutshell, responding to RFPs can be a spectacular way to waste your companies' resources if you're not carefully reviewing the proposal details. For example, having one response that might not be clear to the solicitor can rule out your organization as qualifying or even winning the procurement whether you're a sub or the prime. In the world of both commercial and government contracting, a *prime* is the primary contractor who holds the contract directly with the customer. A *sub* is a subcontractor who works directly for the contractor, not the customer. The prime contractor and subcontractors will likely work together in proposing the RFP.

You need to clearly appreciate as well that most RFPs are not worth even considering competing or bidding for if the customer has not established a proposed use case. Your organization likely needs to consider the limited resources available and the resources spent on competing, especially if the government really does not know the problem it is trying to solve.

RFPs require detailed technical responses, and these technical responses must address the customers' requirements appropriately. The RFP will certainly provide a list of questions that each bidding company must respond to. These could include business-focused responses, for example, prior experience or company processes, to more technical responses including what type of solution is proposed and even detailed equipment lists.

An RFP may be distributed to all the companies identified during the RFI process or might be made public to solicit additional bidders. During the RFP process, the most important task is the proposal development. This is where the responding company (bidder) will respond to the RFP with its proposed solution.

RFP questions are often detailed technically, and the bidders need to place great care in how they respond to every question. The responses will provide a thorough look at the bidders and their prospective solutions to the solicitor. On the other hand, the RFI will ask a standardized set of questions concerning your company's history, technical capabilities, partnerships, business plans, ownership, and other key details that are less technically detailed.

When it comes to procurement processes, RFPs may or may not be part of your organization's business plan. If they are, then learning how to respond should be a priority and so should finding resources that provide insight into your specific organization's markets such as education, government, or commercial.

Responding to procurements can be time-consuming, even if you're experienced. When considering whether to respond to a U.S. federal solicitation, there are strict requirements, and it is advisable that your organization retain the business and technical talent to create the appropriate responses.

## IDENTIFYING, ANALYZING, AND MANAGING STAKEHOLDERS

Every organization has more than one stakeholder in a project or procurement. Generally, as a project management best practice, if the project is undertaken due to a contractual agreement, it's advisable that the sales team review the contract agreement to find the stakeholders who will be part of the sales process.

A *stakeholder* is a person who may be affected in some manner (directly or indirectly) by a given project. These stakeholders could be employees working on a project, organization, or even partner companies. Stakeholders have different levels of influence, such as being a technical influencer or a business influencer.

Stakeholder identification is, of course, critical to ensure both the sales team and the customer are not wasting their time. Identify both the decision-makers and the end users. The decision-makers need to be involved and should ensure that there is reasonable commitment to engage with you as necessary.

Figure 5.4 presents the stakeholder process workflow. When identifying stakeholders, one of the best places is to identify roles in the organization. The second step is analyzing; you want to understand the role of the stakeholder and understand how they can influence the decision of a blockchain solution. Lastly, you must manage your stakeholders in a manner that facilitates your role as a trusted advisor, and this means responsive, effective, proficient, and honest communication.

**FIGURE 5.4**
Stakeholder process workflow

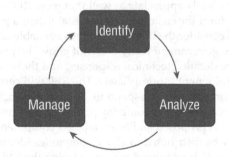

The stakeholder workflow is straightforward. You must first identify who the stakeholders are and then analyze them to determine what level of authority they have. For example, are they technically driven or more business focused? Then you can move on to the last part of the workflow: manage. You engage the stakeholder in the appropriate fashion, such as with meetings, whiteboards, proposals, and then meet the appropriate level of expectations.

As a trusted advisor to your customer base, you must ensure that you represent your organization as professionally as possible. One of the best ways to do this is to clearly understand the stakeholders and what role they play in the organization. This will help you to not only set expectations appropriately but also meet or exceed them. One of the last things you would want to do, of course, is "over promise and under deliver," which is a common quote that is used in sales training.

## BLOCKCHAIN READINESS ASSESSMENT WORKSHOPS

A blockchain readiness assessment workshop is focused on understanding where the customer is in the adoption of blockchain technologies. Generally, a readiness assessment is also known as a *blockchain workshop* by some vendors and partners.

A workshop is exactly what you would expect to offer as a vendor, VAR, integrator, or services firm to help facilitate the knowledge transfer in a highly interactive environment. Whiteboarding is a likely requirement when it comes to assessments and establishing requirements. Whiteboarding is critical to identifying problems and presenting solutions in an interactive manner that is visual for both the vendor and the customer.

Generally, in your role as an engineer you will want to work with the customer to establish the potential blockchain use case for the organization. As part of the process, you will also identify requirements, educate the customer, and provide a summary report with an actual use case that may be applied later.

During a blockchain workshop, you want to review at least the following steps:

♦ Identify the potential opportunities for blockchain technologies by engaging with the stakeholders to facilitate discussions around potential solutions to problems.

♦ Identify and document the potential scale of the blockchain use case for the organization. Some organizations may not be ready for a blockchain as an individual unit or department. Potential customers will be more likely to benefit from working as a "consortium" where sharing the benefits and costs could provide direct value.

♦ Document the stakeholder's functional requirements, which will specify what a blockchain should accomplish from a business perspective such as compliance, reporting, auditing, authorizations, or business focus.

♦ Document the stakeholder's nonfunctional requirements. The nonfunctional requirements specify what the system should do from a performance, reliability, security, or technical standpoint.

♦ Determine customers' perceived risks for blockchain implementations.

♦ Document any compliance requirements such as GDPR, PCI, SOX, and HIPPA, for example, since these requirements are a significant part of a blockchain use case.

♦ Identify any performance requirements such as transactions per second (TPS). Blockchain is not a high-performance platform as compared to client-server technologies.

♦ Provide your customer with any expected next steps in the evaluation process such as follow-up calls or quotes.

## PERFORMING DEMOS

Demos are a required part of most roles for presales-focused engineers. Demos are different in many aspects from proofs of concept, which are performed at a later stage in the sales cycle. Demos need to be direct, timely, efficient, and kept under 30 minutes.

When it comes to performing demos, these are some best practices to appreciate:

♦ Perform the demo on a stable platform that you maintain if possible, whether on your own platform or in a cloud blockchain as a service.

◆ Blockchain demos are "software" focused and in most cases should maintain a "story-board" around this unless required otherwise. A storyboard is an approach used to relay the features and functions in a logical manner.

◆ Identify specific concerns, features, or functions that are of interest to the customer, and avoid a "standard" demo process if possible.

◆ Keep demos to less than 30 minutes to avoid losing the attention of the customer.

◆ Identify your customer's stakeholder base ahead of time and provide a demo that will focus on the audience. For example, a CIO will have different interests than a cloud developer or network engineer.

◆ Provide an interactive demo if the customer wants to "drive" the blockchain transactions.

◆ During the demo, display how the solution resolves "pain points" that the customer identified in previous discussions.

When it comes to performing demos, I like to set up a blockchain as a service (BaaS) with a basic configuration to address the customer interests and provide value around reducing "pain points." For example, if the demo is about Hyperledger Fabric and you're running this in IBM Bluemix, you're basically ready to go. If the customer base is made up of developers, I walk them through how to deploy chaincode (smart contracts). On the other hand, if the customer base involved is more executive level, then I want to focus on creating efficiency, showing the ease of use, and discussing any ROI/TCO savings that could be accomplished with the solution.

Figure 5.5 shows the interface to start the blockchain service in the IBM Blockchain Platform.

**FIGURE 5.5**
IBM Blockchain
Platform

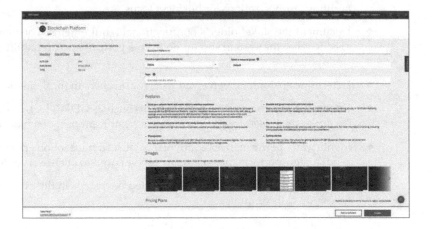

The IBM Blockchain Platform interface enables a sales engineer, developer, or customer to start a Hyperledger Fabric blockchain network in only a few clicks. You can see that the service requires a service name, region, and organization to start a blockchain network in the IBM Blockchain Platform. When performing a demo or proof of concept, you can get started in minutes, and this could provide significant results for organizations.

**REFERENCE**    For more information on performing IBM BaaS, refer to Chapter 7, "Blockchain as a Service."

## USING VENDOR DEMO TOOLS

Some vendors also have additional tools that can show your customer how the interface works, how transactions occur, or how to deploy a node. Having a demo tool available that you can run on your laptop can be invaluable in some cases.

R3 Corda provides a solid demo tool called Demobench. Demobench is a stand-alone desktop application. The goal of Demobench is to make it easy to configure and launch local Corda nodes on your desktop. It is very useful for training sessions, demos, or just experimentation of Corda.

Figure 5.6 shows the network map in Corda Demobench. This specific page is called the Node Explorer, which can be used locally on your laptop. It deploys a JVM and runs an instance locally specifically for demos.

**FIGURE 5.6**
Corda Demobench

## WHITEBOARDING SOLUTIONS

Whiteboarding is one of the most critical skills a customer-facing engineer can have. Whiteboarding is a powerful sales tool that can provide insight to the customer about your understanding of their environment and also provide insight to the customer about the proposed solution. Whiteboarding should clearly build up the decision-making process for the customer in easy-to-understand workflows, diagrams, and figures.

Whiteboarding is best approached by a technical engineer who can relay the proper visualization of component integration, network connections, and application gateways.

As part of a whiteboard session, a discussion about customer pain points is recommended, and then you can visually map them to a specific application. Understanding the challenges and customer requirements deeply will certainly facilitate solid discussions about how blockchain solutions can solve their problems. Remember, whiteboards are social interactions that are visual outlets for recognizing customer pain paints. Proposing solutions should be secondary once the customer knows you clearly understand their pain points.

## PERFORMING PROOF OF CONCEPTS

A proof of concept is a technical exercise most sales engineers will be involved with at one time or another to help identify the specific performance, security, and other factors such as usability that the customer is trying to establish that will work for their use cases.

A POC is essentially a realization of a certain method or idea to demonstrate a solutions feasibility. It's a demonstration process in principle that is usually a "visual" process for the customer to establish that the solution could work. This section contains my best practices with POCs.

First, when I am performing a proof of concept, the critical thing I do is to discuss with the sales team that the customer has been vetted and has a procurement viability. (Has the customer been vetted financially?) As a best practice, your organization's account executives (AEs) should be vetting the proper leads and then following up with appropriate stakeholders to ensure that a POC is a valid and proper exercise for both the customer and the sales organization. From my experience, it's a wise decision to question the AE about customer validation to ensure that a POC is in the company's best interest from technical and business perspectives. It's one thing to perform a packaged 30-minute demo remotely, but it's totally different situation to spend a weekend setting up for a specific use case and two days on-site. You as an engineer are fully responsible for your time and should want to ensure you're not "fishing in a dead lake."

Second, I request that the customer and the sales team work directly with me to establish clear "success criteria" for the POC. This can be done via a conference call, for example, before going on-site. The POC must be clearly defined for you as an engineer; you must be able to state the goals and the desired results that are the success criteria. You can get in your car and drive aimlessly, or you can get in your car and have a destination. It's your choice to control the POC you're running, and I suggest you're clearly identified as the driver.

Lastly, I like to confirm with the sales executive that they have commitment from the customer that if we deliver on the success criteria, we will win the procurement. If the expectation is not set correctly with the customer, then it shows the sales team is weak, and you as an engineer may very well be involved in another exercise in futility.

Generally, you are being asked to perform a POC for a reason. Some of the common reasons to perform a POC are the following:

- To show the customer the functionality of the solution as well as how the solution solves their pain points

- To remove some of the risk of the solutions procurement for your customer

- To leverage the procurement process and establish trust with the potential stakeholders

Enterprise blockchains have different use cases, limitations, and features that as an engineer you need to be aware of. When considering a blockchain POC, it's important to identify the blockchain architecture as well as the application stack. The application stack is where the complexity can come in. The complexity could involve integration of the end-user applications, commercial APIs, decentralized and open source applications, or even compliance implementations. For example, Hyperledger Fabric is based on a three-tiered architecture. The tiers of Hyperledger Fabric are the blockchain network, chaincode, and client application. When performing a POC, your role as a sales engineer may very well be to install chaincode. Chaincode can be written in one of three development languages: Go (Golang), Java, and Node.js.

Developing applications and porting it to the blockchain platform, though, of course, are the responsibilities of the customer development team. In Chapter 10, "Blockchain Development and Programming," I cover this area of development in more detail later in the chapter.

Figure 5.7 provides insight into the three layers of the Hyperledger Fabric development stack. Hyperledger Fabric at the networking infrastructure layer is focused on connecting the blockchain network to the APIs and integrating the nodes with their smart contracts. Chaincode, SDK, and APIs are the "middleware" for putting together blockchain network with the end-user application.

**FIGURE 5.7**
Hyperledger Fabric development stack

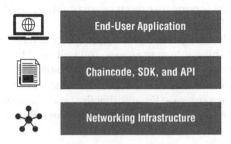

The lesson learned here should be that POCs can be a rewarding opportunity to work with the sales team as well as the customer to provide value around enterprise blockchains. Before executing on a POC, you want to ensure customer stakeholder buy-in and also ensure that valid "success criteria" have been identified.

## ENABLING THE SALES PROCESS WITH BLOCKCHAIN AS A SERVICE

As a well-traveled cloud architect, I can assure you that one of the greatest enabling "gifts" given to any IT sales organization is blockchain as a service (BaaS). This is also known as a blockchain platform as a service (PaaS), for example, in the world of IBM Bluemix.

Sales organizations can consume a cloud service for little or no CAPEX funds and utilize the cloud for their POCs, demos, and training around blockchains such as Corda, Hyperledger, and Ethereum. Sometimes there really is no need to run to the C-level suites to request funding for a CAPEX expenditure for a blockchain infrastructure. Account executives know that requesting CAPEX funds in just about any type of company of even modest size is a time-consuming and frustrating process. In reality, it is likely a *series* of time-consuming processes from my experiences.

In 2009, I remember selling 3PAR data storage arrays to the commercial sector in the Washington, DC metro area. These 3PAR arrays were inexpensive compared to an EMC or HDS array, with the same number of gigabytes or terabytes. We were talking a $50,000 deal versus an $800,000 deal, and we were performing somersaults to obtain a purchase order. In my opinion, you need to understand margin and the cost of a customer acquisition, which I cover in Chapter 6, "Enterprise Blockchain Economics." A root canal could be considered less stressful.

Some companies can even spin up a BaaS for less than $100 USD. It can even be free if you can use "promotional credits" or an "always-free" tier that some providers allow.

In summary, you can also use the resources in the cloud for demos, proof of concepts, and even during training. I like to perform demos as well during a readiness assessment just to get the techies thinking and comparing cloud services to blockchain services. To be honest, utilizing a blockchain as a service is not for every sales organization, and having a dedicated platform can provide efficiencies as well as benefits in many respects when you have both the use case and the transaction volume to justify a substantial investment. A solid use case to having a dedicated blockchain services team, for example, would be when the larger consulting firms, VARS, and vendors do invest in their own dedicated in-house private clouds and can expand services to include a blockchain.

## Selling Enterprise Blockchain Solutions

One of the challenges of selling a blockchain solution is to not oversell the benefits of said blockchain solution. Blockchain technology is still in the "adopter" phase in some markets, and therefore it can be "oversold" as a solution that solves every enterprise challenge. I have seen many blog posts and listened to many convention presentations about how specific blockchain solutions are solving just about every problem, and I would give most of them an A on marketing but an F for viability.

The reality is that blockchain technology is limited in solving problems, providing efficiencies, and establishing robust use cases. You will need to engage both your company's business and technical experts when selling blockchain solutions. For example, if the customer has a use case for supply chain management or compliance, these prospective use cases may be great for establishing a use case for immutability and transparency, but the use case may not effectively provide the customers with performance and security requirements.

### REQUIREMENTS GATHERING

It is critical to capture enough requirements to effectively identify the software solution being built. When gathering these requirements, ensure that they are testable. For example, a requirement that states "The solution must process more than 200 transactions per second (TPS) at peak workload" is clearly viably testable. On the other hand, a requirement that states "The solution should be really high performing to the stakeholders" does not clearly show how it can be tested nor lend itself as a viable requirement.

Your blockchain solution will likely entail some significant software design and development but also entail some hardware requirements and perhaps a blockchain as a service solution. From a historical perspective, you need to understand what the typical best practices have been focused on for requirements gathering. These requirements are identified as functional requirements and nonfunctional requirements. Software system functional requirements state how the solution should accomplish the proposed end results, whereas nonfunctional requirements will determine the constraints on how the solution will accomplish these end results.

Let's define these requirements more specifically and provide an example of each.

◆ Functional requirements will specify functions that a solution, a system, or a specific system component must be able to accomplish for the customer or provide a viable use case for. These functional requirements provide technical details on how the system will accomplish the criteria stated.

*For example*: The stakeholders in the company identify that the e-commerce web application must provide an easy-to-use shopping cart experience that will be intuitive for the consumer to use, highly secure, but also high performing with the goal of increasing revenue for the company.

◆ Nonfunctional requirements are the requirements that specify the criteria that will be established to gauge the operation of a system or its components rather than specific routines. These nonfunctional requirements define external constraints, system restrictions, and other technically specified outcomes. These nonfunctional requirements help to determine the success or failure of the project.

*For example*: The company user base identifies that the e-commerce application will utilize open source solutions from Company A, which provides a hosted e-commerce solution. This solution with an industry-leading SaaS platform integrates "Shopify" shopping carts and provides for more than 2000 TPS with enterprise SSL certificates as part of an integrated solution.

It is also important to note that there are two main categories of nonfunctional requirements.

◆ Execution qualities, for example, are focused on performance and usability, which are considered observable since we document this.

◆ Evolution qualities are testability, maintainability, extensibility, and scalability and are embedded in the static structure of the software stack.

The IEEE-Std 830 – 1993 clearly states "13 nonfunctional requirements" to be absorbed into software requirements documentation. Figure 5.8 shows the 13 requirements as specified by the Institute of Electrical and Electronics Engineers (IEEE).

**FIGURE 5.8**
IEEE 13 nonfunctional requirements

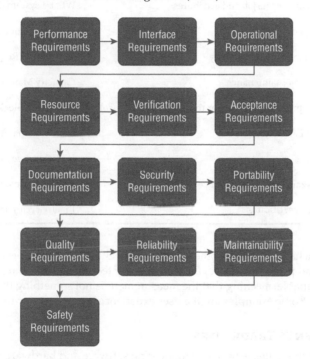

IEEE is a world-renowned nonprofit professional organization founded by engineers in 1884. The main purpose of the organization is to consolidate ideas dealing with electrotechnology. The IEEE plays a significant role in publishing technical works, sponsoring conferences and seminars, providing accreditation, and developing standards.

You can see that there are 13 blocks in the nonfunctional requirements list recognized by IEEE. For the purpose of this book's scope, I won't detail each of the 13 nonfunctional requirements. If you are not familiar with these IEEE nonfunctional requirements, I recommend finding out more from IEEE by visiting https://ieeexplore.ieee.org/document/392555.

A blockchain solution is a software solution with aspects of computer networking, computer security, and business such as compliance. Historically, a software system's functional requirement states how the solution should accomplish something, whereas a nonfunctional requirement will state the constraints on how the solution will accomplish something.

Table 5.1 shows some of the common blockchain-related functional and nonfunctional requirements that a blockchain solution commonly addresses. If your customers are asking about technical specifications, such as which type of consensus is being used, they are concerned about the nonfunctional requirements.

**TABLE 5.1:**      Examples of blockchain functional and nonfunctional requirements

| NON-FUNCTIONAL | FUNCTIONAL |
| --- | --- |
| How a system does its job and attributes. | What a system does or accomplishes. |
| Technical Specifications | Business Requirements |
| Transaction log data redundancy | Compliance Requirements |
| Transaction log maintenance | Capacity Management |
| Transaction processing with peer to peer gossip protocols | Enterprise Blockchain Performance |
| Distributed Ledger version | Data Transparency |
| User Interface | Intuitive ease of use |
| Practical Byzantine Fault Tolerance (PGFT) | Protect against malicious peers |
| Utilize x.509 certificates | Ensure secure membership |

With blockchains there are some clear requirements that can be specified, such as consensus, certificates, and protocols. However, as with every technology, there are also requirements that are not quantifiable, meaning that the measurement is not something that can have a number assigned to it. Some examples are the user experience, ease of use, or trust in a company brand.

## REQUIREMENTS TRADE-OFFS

As with anything in life, especially engineering software and hardware systems, solutions, and components, you can expect trade-offs in your design. Generally, you need to expect trade-offs between performance, security, and resiliency.

Triangles are desirable for understanding trade-offs in three dimensions. Figure 5.9 shows the three design trade-offs to understand in the design of a blockchain.

**FIGURE 5.9**
Design trade-off triad

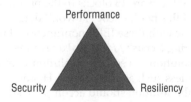

Performance
Security    Resiliency

Performance in blockchains is focused on transactions per second. Security is focused on the risks that may be realized with a platform, such as vulnerabilities. Lastly, resiliency is focused on how the blockchain platform will be available if a network node goes down and is sometimes compared to availability. For example, if your proposed blockchain solution is using Hyperledger Fabric and your design is using eight nodes/peers in a New Jersey data center, your deployment is very local with no geographic resiliency. What happens if the power grid goes down? What happens if there is a weather event? Localized blockchain networks perform as efficiently as possible but provide no resiliency against regional disasters.

When you need to extend your blockchain and deploy additional nodes/peers, then you must consider your new location and the possibility of inducing some latency into your blockchain network. The performance you may have had would not be the same as expected. You now have a blockchain network that is geographically resilient but is not performing with lower transactions per second because of the additional induced network latency.

Another common trade-off is around consensus methods (algorithms) and the commonly consistent issues with these. For example, some consensus methods are strictly used in permissionless blockchains such as proof of work (POW). In a permissionless blockchain, you're essentially giving up your privacy and security and then dealing with performance issues. In permissioned blockchains, your costs and responsibilities are greater, but you're also gaining security, privacy, and, in most scenarios, performance benefits.

Table 1.2 compares public and private blockchains. It's important to clearly relay these differences in design to the customer.

Whether you decide to implement a permissionless or permissioned blockchain, there will be trade-offs. You must weigh the trade-offs in blockchain design as well and choose accordingly. When it comes to requirements gathering and also the blockchain design, there are significant differences between a public blockchain and a private blockchain. For example, if you are discussing KYC, which would of course require identity management as a requirement for the customer, then you would rule out a public permissionless blockchain, since you would not have a mechanism in place to "know your customer."

## TECHNICALLY QUALIFYING A BLOCKCHAIN OPPORTUNITY

As a presales engineer, you may be the sole technical expert in blockchain technology in your sales organization, or you may not be. Regardless, you likely will want to control your time.

Qualifying blockchain opportunities is a must for ensuring that your time and company resources do not get misplaced. One of the challenges that can occur is when you have a sales team or account executive who fully relies on you to qualify the customer for every possible solution. When initially considering if a potential blockchain opportunity is qualified, I examine the following:

♦ Is the customer's potential use case a "conceptual fit" where a blockchain is a valid use case? For example, does the customer require a compliant immutable record of customs declarations that will need to be retained for audit? Or perhaps the customer does not require a high TPS performance use case for their logistics application. Basically, are the properties of a blockchain solution clearly understood, and can they be applied to the customer use case? Determining the "conceptual fit" should be one of your main goals.

♦ Does this customer have stakeholder buy-in? For example, is the current database application that has been identified as being phased out a technical and business challenge that can be overcome by the enterprise? You need to understand if the customer has an environment favorable to new technologies.

♦ Does this customer have one of the industry use cases that have been historically viable, for example, with competitors, and can this past performance provide some insights into the potential benefits and use case validation? Can you actually take the use case and match it up to another company that has documented blockchain success? Doing this makes the solution selling somewhat more convincing to the customer.

## BLOCKCHAIN DECISION WORKFLOW

When you are working with a potential customer on whether the blockchain is going to be a valid solution, it's really important to understand that as an engineer or an architect you need to follow a workflow as well as go through a checklist of potential areas that can make or break a blockchain being a good use case.

The IEEE decision tree provides an easy-to-understand workflow to making a "considerations" decision on whether your use case would benefit from a blockchain. One of the main things I like about the IEEE decision tree is that it starts by asking whether traditional database technology meets your needs. This question really will filter the requirements remarkably easily. One of the challenges that you may also run into is that the blockchain industry is trying to make it seem that blockchains are the solution to every problem by using, a "hammer in search of a nail where every problem is made into a nail." Reality is that if the customer does prefer or requires, for example, high transactions processing (over 1000 TPS), then you just ruled out a blockchain. On the other hand, if privacy, security, and compliance are the main concerns, then you may very well have a potential blockchain application use case.

The decision tree provides insight into questions that should be asked before deciding on whether blockchain is a good fit and then if a permissioned blockchain or a permissionless blockchain would be the right outcome.

◆ The first decision to make is to come to the realization that if a traditional database would work, then a need for a blockchain would likely not be there. If a traditional database is not going to work, then you can proceed.

◆ The second decision to make is to determine whether there will be multiple parties involved. If so, then proceed to the third decision. Generally, blockchains that are consortium-based blockchains are the best use cases.

◆ The third decision to make is around trust and whether a third party could be used.

◆ The fourth decision to make involves security and how you can trust distributed decisions.

◆ The fifth and final decision would be focused on whether you need privacy for your transactions. If you do, then you proceed to a permissioned blockchain, and if you do not, you would proceed possibly with a permissionless blockchain.

Chapter 3, "Architecting Your Enterprise Blockchain," covers this step-by-step process in more detail. For the full context of the IEEE decision tree for adopting blockchain technology, see Morgen E. Peck's article at `https://spectrum.ieee.org/computing/networks/do-you-need-a-blockchain`.

## INDICATORS OF A SUCCESSFUL BLOCKCHAIN USE CASE

By understanding your blockchain indicators, you can determine how to establish a use case. Customers usually appreciate use cases from industries and verticals similar to their industry, even from competitors. The easiest way to establish and justify a use case is of course to have a comparable use case that would be from an industry partner or a competitor.

When you are qualifying a blockchain customer use case, here are some indicators that you're likely to use in a potential valid use case with blockchain technologies:

◆ The customer has a KYC compliance requirement.

◆ The customer requires a distributed ledger that can maintain immutable records.

- The customer does not require SQL database performance, especially around transactions per second.

- The customer has requirements to implement cross-border payments that do not rely on a central authority.

- The customer has contracting requirements that could result in financial disputes such as chargebacks or term disputes that may result in legal concerns.

- The customer understands what legal prose is and intends to incorporate these requirements into a smart contract.

- The customer needs to establish a "farm-to-table" application that provides visibility to their customer base.

- The customer is considering removing intermediaries to reduce costs from their transaction processing business unit.

There are certainly more use cases that can identify a successful blockchain use case. You may want to review the blockchain vendor websites for additional use cases. I cover several more detailed use cases with potential indicators in Chapter 8, "Enterprise Blockchain Use Cases."

## Highlighting Benefits of Blockchains

The benefits of the value creation of the blockchain technology should end in what outcome? For most organizations seeking blockchain benefits, every potential use case will have a different result.

Essentially, a distributed ledger for a logistics company may keep track of shipments coming in overseas and manage provenance for the company's compliance requirements around U.S. Customs. Performance and cost management may not be the main benefits since the application is more concerned about tracking and recording U.S. Customs compliance.

The following list identifies the common benefits an enterprise can realize using blockchain technology:

- CAPEX and OPEX reductions (cost management)

- Permissioned access (security)

- Increased privacy (channeling)

- Efficiency by reducing intermediaries (fewer accountants, attorneys, custom agents, and lenders)

- Risk reduction (less human error)

- Data integrity (immutability)

- Provenance (historical event logging)

- Transparency (trust for consumers)

Blockchains can provide some great benefits related to security. Also, blockchains are specifically suited to data platforms where there is a need for security and redundancy.

## Smart Contracts and Value Creation

When correctly implemented, smart contracts provide significant value to some organizations. As a reminder, smart contracts are computer program codes capable of managing, executing, and enforcing the performance of an agreement using blockchain technologies. The entire smart contract process should be fully automated and can also act as a complement, or substitute, for legal contracts in some scenarios. Corda for example provides immense value in this area.

Blockchain technology makes use of two distinct proprietary characteristics with the deployment of smart contracts: the use of validation rules and their enforcement of these rules in smart contracts. Validation rules define the conditions in which the records and blocks will be included in the blockchain, and the enforcement of validation rules work with an algorithm or protocol that enforces rules that have been entrusted by all parties with contributing data to the blockchain.

Smart contracts can provide that missing autonomy or trust that the organization did not enable before smart contracts. Smart contracts can also provide legal prose on some platforms such as R3 Corda where an attachment is used to clearly define the terms. The terms of the smart contract are recorded and are immutable once deployed on the blockchain.

Following are some of the more common reasons to use smart contracts for value creation. Not every use case for blockchains and smart contracts will experience value in the same way.

- ◆ Autonomy
- ◆ Trust
- ◆ Backup
- ◆ Safety
- ◆ Speed
- ◆ Savings
- ◆ Accuracy

As a sales engineer, you should ensure that you have a solid understanding of the potential value of smart contracts that an enterprise can benefit from.

Table 5.2 shows a comparison of traditional contracts versus smart contracts. Smart contracts are much more efficient for redundant tasks and can provide significant cost savings.

**TABLE 5.2:**     Traditional contracts vs. smart contracts

| TRADITIONAL CONTRACTS | SMART CONTRACTS |
| --- | --- |
| 1–3 days | Minutes |
| Escrow necessary | Escrow may not be necessary |
| Expensive | Fraction of the cost |
| Physical presence | Virtual presence |
| Attorneys required | Attorneys may not be required |

When discussing smart contracts with a customer, you should understand how the customer handles, procurement, contracting, or transactions within the organization. This will provide insight in how to address the potential benefits and also perhaps begin solid discussions on how they provide value. For example, I want to understand the customer's application. Let's say it's a

U.S.-based company that imports tons of products from overseas. I first want to understand how the customer's current legacy solution works and understand the pain points, identify inefficiencies and potential savings, and then draw a potential high-level workflow that utilizes a smart contract blockchain platform.

**REFERENCE**    Chapter 6, "Enterprise Blockchain Economics," discusses smart contracts from a business perspective in much more detail.

### CHALLENGES TO BLOCKCHAIN ADOPTION

As a sales-focused engineer, it's important to appreciate why blockchain is not the Holy Grail for solving every business and technical problem. Challenges to blockchain adoption can be great and for that matter numerous in some enterprise organizations. Furthermore, some industries and verticals are traditionally conservative in their approach to adopting new technology.

The following are some common challenges that I frequently deal with around blockchains and distributed ledgers:

- Industry technology adoption is slow with limited use cases that do not provide a valid TCO or ROI.

- The organization's technology adoption is slow or may be due to some politically related concerns such as job security.

- Regulatory concerns may not have been clearly identified as the proper use case, or the regulatory body may not identify what blockchain solutions are "compliant."

- The migration of services has not been clearly defined and therefore could limit adoption. For example, the process of migrating a legacy application to a blockchain service does not have a defined migration path.

- The hiring environment may be challenging due to the limited skill sets available in Ethereum or in a specific geographic location.

When it comes to blockchain adoption, you must realize that at a high level it might appear easy to justify a blockchain. However, blockchains are new compared to other technologies, and the maturity of the solutions is still not comparable to a "centralized" solution such as SQL, an established database SQL.

## Sales Engineering Success

As an organization that may be considering expertise in the blockchain solutions architecture, there are some basic recommended job requirements to be considered during the hiring process.

### SALES ENGINEERING JOB REQUIREMENTS/RESPONSIBILITIES FOR BLOCKCHAIN SUCCESS

The following are some of the common job requirements for a successful blockchain sales engineer:

- Marketing responsibilities, such as conferences, trade shows, and booth duty

- Developing and presenting technical presentations that will translate the value of the proposed enterprise blockchain services to your prospects

◆ Translating the enterprise business requirements into technical requirements that will realize the business requirements

◆ Providing cost estimates based on technical procurement requirements for RFPs

◆ Supporting solutions demos and POCs including setting up demos and POCs

◆ Performing competitive analysis around major enterprise blockchain platforms and providing recommendations for client success

◆ Creating content such as solutions whitepapers, technical presentations, technical design diagrams, blog posts, and articles

The following are some of the common job experiences that a solid sales engineer should have:

◆ Experience selling IT infrastructure, software, and hardware and professional services

◆ Significant hands-on IT networking experience with TCP/IP protocols around integration

◆ Maintaining a solid understanding of computer programming development languages, software development kits (SDKs), and application programming interfaces (APIs)

◆ Experience with common blockchain development languages such as Python, Go (Golang), Node.js, JavaScript, C++, Rust, and Solidity

## SALES ENGINEERING BEST PRACTICES FOR BLOCKCHAIN SUCCESS

As a customer-facing sales/solution engineer, you will spend most of your time working with a sales team made up of a sales executive, a sales manager, and perhaps a territory manager.

The following recommended best practices are focused on technical solutions selling:

◆ Become a trusted advisor by establishing credibility with the customer base of your organization. Knowing your customer's business requirements as well as their business challenges can make all the difference in your success as a sales engineer.

◆ Ask the right questions to comprehend your customer's business requirements and then take those requirements and translate them into a technical solution that meets or exceeds the customer's requests.

◆ Clearly identify with confidence the use cases that bring value to your enterprise customer base.

◆ Understand the blockchain technology enough to discuss the appropriate blockchain solution and provide value during demos and proof of concepts.

◆ Identify the stakeholders and appreciate that there are different types of people. They may come to decisions in different ways. Do not attempt to be pushy or overly objective. Decisions are made sometimes not based on merit but on political issues in the organization.

◆ Listen to the customer's point of view and address it appropriately.

◆ Know your customer's procurement process enough to ensure you're providing the most efficient solution with the proper responses the customer requires. If you are responding to an RFP, then read all the data points before making a response.

◆ Engage talented application developers who understand software architecture and can provide insight for the customer around specific blockchain programming languages such as Python, Go, JavaScript, and so on.

◆ Perhaps the most overlooked trait is to just be likeable as well as approachable. Being a person who can establish a relationship on a personal level can sometimes be much more valuable to everyone involved. Being a nerd is great around programmers, but discussing other things of interest to the customer such as golf, military service, or their alma mater can enhance likeability and be a competitive edge for you. Know your customer and show them you care about their organization.

## BLOCKCHAIN COMPETENCY READINESS

When it comes to working with any IT-related platforms or solutions, it's important to understand your competencies. Basically, what are your company's areas of expertise? What does your company do well, and what could be improved upon?

Generally, if you're an IT vendor, reseller, or VAR, you may have deep expertise in IT networking and data storage. However, when it comes to application development, your company might not be able to talk about Python programming in an intelligent manner.

That's where you need to do one of the following:

◆ Obtain talent internally (insourcing)

◆ Obtain talent externally through a partner or through direct hire (outsourcing)

◆ Walk away from the opportunity for the appropriate reason

Your sales leadership needs to evaluate a number of blockchain competencies. The first phase is blockchain training. It is always the starting point to understand the technology before proceeding to design, implement, develop, or even support. In my experience, I see application development as being the weakest phase for most companies. Figure 5.10 provides a workflow of activities that solutions based organization should perform to enhance blockchain readiness.

**FIGURE 5.10**
Blockchain Competency
Readiness

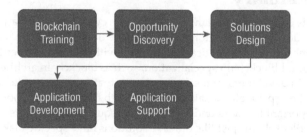

**Blockchain Training**   As a sales-driven organization, the first thing your organization must invest in is training after buy-in from upper management. Identify areas including blockchain basics as well as more advanced areas such as smart contracts, legal prose, performance, and security. Some organizations take the step to educate everyone in the company, while others educate only a few IT professionals to be "enabled."

**Opportunity Discovery**   It's all about driving revenue from your customers and your prospective customers. Generally, most sales-driven organizations handle this phase quite well. You can always count on good account executives to drive at least initial contacts. This phase could also take place at your trade shows and conventions. A confident sales engineer at a booth can make all the difference in engaging technically with attendees. It's all about identifying blockchain opportunities, and your experts must be enabled.

**Solutions Design**   When it comes to designing a blockchain network, it's all about the capabilities and meeting customer requirements. Generally, most organizations I have worked with can design a network quite efficiently. When it came to cloud computing or blockchain, it was clear that these vendors and integrators were lacking in expertise. In this phase, you must be able to create a blockchain network, design highly available systems, specify proper blockchain platforms, determine deployment approaches, and then ensure that these designs meet the customer's expectations.

**Application Development**   This is where the buck stops! Most vendors and VARs perform the preceding phases well. When application development comes into play, this requires more than the sales team. Your sales organization really needs to have application development expertise at the ready to be successful in this area. It's one thing to take a SQL database and upgrade the application hardware, but it's another thing to move from SQL to a blockchain platform. Integration, development, performance, and security requirements all need to be addressed. Smart contracts and distributed applications need to be discussed.

**Application Support**   After the integration and deployment, the blockchain application and the customer relationship need to be supported and maintained. Generally, most of these responsibilities are turned over to the customer. However, your developers and engineers may very well need to be engaged when challenges arise, especially during a POC. For example, with R3 Corda there are two options to deploying Corda. The options are the open source version and the enterprise version. Generally, during a POC you're supporting the customer and not the vendor, which is Corda. When the customer moves to Corda Enterprise, the support, updates, and customer management are handled directly by Corda.

# Summary

This chapter covered the solutions sales cycles of blockchain engagements and how VARs, vendors, and integrators can participate in the blockchain sales cycle. Selling blockchain solutions requires a significant interaction with the development group. There are numerous roles around blockchain specialization, such as blockchain architects, blockchain marketers, blockchain developers, and sales engineers, that focus on blockchains.

Enterprise blockchains will have both functional and nonfunctional requirements. It is important that you understand these requirements when scoping a blockchain engagement.

Blockchains just like other IT solutions have specific tasks during the sales process that you will need to perform or participate in such as requests for proposals (RFPs), demos, and proof of concepts (POCs). Blockchain technology has specific benefits, such as providing transparency, provenance, and immutability, but also specific challenges to its adoption. Discussions with prospective customers and clients will be focused on technical requirements for IT networking, blockchain, and computer programming. Becoming a trusted advisor by establishing credibility with the customer base revolves around knowing your customer's business requirements as well as their business challenges—which can make all the difference in your success. Lastly, I discussed specific blockchain core competencies such as training, solutions design, application development, and best practices.

# Chapter 6

# Enterprise Blockchain Economics

Blockchains and distributed ledgers provide significant opportunities in the areas of cost control, cost reduction, and cost avoidance. In this chapter, I will discuss how blockchains and distributed ledgers can facilitate impressive total cost of ownership (TCO) scenarios and clearly improve return on investment (ROI) for finance-technical (*fintech*) use cases.

If you're an IT vendor, integrator, or VAR, you need to understand the cost models so you can provide value to your customer base. When you are participating in discussions about blockchains, it's imperative to be able to compare legacy systems costing models to blockchain models.

The goal of this chapter is to explain how to justify implementations of blockchain services and hardware from a financial perspective and explain enterprise concerns related to costing.

## Introduction to Enterprise Blockchain Economics

When you consider the economics of a blockchain solution, it is important to realize there are myriad economic decisions that an organization may consider, and those decisions can affect the outcome of a customer meeting significantly. From my experience, companies that are conservative in the risks that they take tend to view blockchain solutions as a gamble. But if you look at how that company would address disaster recovery, for example, where backups and DR testing are on a schedule with little disruptions, you can apply the same decision-making process to blockchain technologies. In other words, that same company will look at the IT-centric numbers around ROI, TCO, and other indicators to determine the likelihood of success of implementing a technology. It's the same process when implementing a blockchain solution.

### Enterprise Ecommerce Business Models

Enterprise business models are important to understand when considering blockchain architectures. The generally accepted models for ecommerce are as follows:

- Business to business (B2B) is ecommerce between two or more businesses.

- Business to consumer (B2C) is ecommerce between a business and the business's consumers.

- Consumer to consumer (C2C) is ecommerce between consumers.

- Government to business (G2B) is ecommerce between government and business.

- Government to consumer (G2C) is ecommerce between government and its citizens.

As a blockchain vendor, integrator, or VAR, it is important that you understand how these models can affect an enterprise's revenue stream. For the purposes of this book, I will be focusing on how an enterprise can utilize blockchain technologies such as payment gateways, for example. I won't be covering how B2B works or other business topics that are out of scope for this book.

**NOTE**   Blockchains and distributed ledgers are providing new business models, trust models, and cost efficiency models. Blockchains are also solving IT "pain points" as well around providing significant ROI and TCO.

## Value Creation

Blockchains can add value in numerous ways such as transforming company operations, transforming the business model, and presenting new opportunities such as using a blockchain for shared cost efficiency. Of course, value from blockchain technologies will be defined differently between different companies, and the results will vary. Blockchain technologies can also open up new markets, for example, with the use of cryptocurrency. It can also reduce some markets or at least reduce opportunities for traditional payment services such as PayPal, Western Union, or global banking systems. Removing these intermediaries creates opportunities for blockchain companies but also removes opportunities from traditional organizations. The world is constantly changing, and history is riddled with important companies that are totally irrelevant today. Companies must constantly innovate and create value or become extinct like Polaroid or Blockbuster, for example.

**NOTE**   "We're changing the world one blockchain at a time, and if we use this technology properly, we're bound to make the world a better place for everyone." —George Levy, CSBCP and CBP

Not only can blockchains provide organizations with new platforms to trade and perform payment services on, but blockchains can also connect to legacy payment gateways. Stablecoins are also an increasing popular solution to consider. Adopting a stablecoin makes sense when the model is business to consumer. (Stablecoins are discussed in more detail in the "Stablecoins" section.)

## Blockchain Payment Gateways

Enterprises that are transacting between businesses or their consumer base may want to consider deploying a blockchain-based platform application for several reasons. First, connecting to a payment processor provides a different means of transacting and making payments, which may very well create new sources of liquidity for the enterprise as well as its business partners. Second, utilizing a blockchain payment gateway could enable the enterprise to lower the cost per transaction (TPC) for ecommerce applications by reducing integration costs and intermediaries, essentially reducing overhead and providing greater efficiency. Third, deploying a blockchain-based payment gateway may reduce the enterprise risks when deploying a blockchain application.

Examples of blockchain-based payment processors include the following:

- Coinbase
- BitPesa
- Aliant

- ◆ MenaPay
- ◆ Go URL

The integration between these payment processors and your enterprise could be accomplished simply with a payment gateway API. These APIs are provided by the payment gateway provider. Some APIs support different features and functions as well. The real benefits are a faster TPS and low cost, typically around 1.5 percent, which is somewhat lower than a credit or debit transaction and is significant for the merchants using a payment gateway.

## Stablecoins

One of the newer ways to provide both economic value and utility value such as price stability is through the implementation of a stablecoin. A *stablecoin* is a cryptocurrency that is collateralized to the value of an underlying asset. An underlying asset could be another cryptocurrency, a fiat currency such as the U.S. dollar, or a metal such as gold or silver.

Stablecoins solve the challenge of the volatility that a cryptocurrency traditionally has. This instability reduces the potential adoption of cryptocurrencies for everyday payment purposes. A stablecoin mitigates the up and down prices of the cryptocurrency that it may be pegged to so that the users can utilize the services.

A more exciting stablecoin project that was announced at the time of writing is the Facebook Libra project. Facebook has more than 2.38 billion monthly active users, and Libra could present some significant opportunities for the "unbanked," meaning people who may not have access to a bank account.

Libra is built on an open source blockchain called the Libra Blockchain featuring its own proof-of-stake protocol. Libra's mission is to reinvent money and transform the global economy so people everywhere can live better lives.

Libra is backed by a reserve of various assets designed to provide intrinsic value to Facebook users. Libra is governed by the independent Libra Association tasked with evolving the ecosystem. The founding members include a varied group of organizations such as Mastercard, PayPal, Stripe, Visa, eBay, Facebook, Lyft, Uber, Spotify, Andreessen Horowitz, Vodafone Group, Kiva, Mercy Corps, and Women's World Banking. The member list is at `https://libra.org/en-US/partners/`.

There are three types of stablecoins at the time of writing, and some of these do have some enterprise adoption for customer-based interaction and ecommerce. The three types of stablecoins are asset-backed off-chain, asset-backed on-chain, and algorithmic. Table 6.1 compares the three types of stablecoins and their funding models.

**TABLE 6.1:**     Stablecoin comparative overview

| TYPE | FUNDING MODEL | EXAMPLES |
| --- | --- | --- |
| Asset-backed off-chain | Fiat or commodity backed | Tether, Gemini, USD coin |
| Asset-backed on-chain | Crypto backed | Steem, Maker, Huabi |
| Algorithmic | Algorithms and smart contracts; known as seigniorage-style stablecoin | Terra, Karbo, Ampleforth |

Table 6.1 references the different types of stablecoins that are common for blockchain-based services and applications. A stablecoin is usually anchored or "tethered" to real-world currencies on a one-to-one basis and backed by reserves. Tether is an active project and is a widely held stablecoin that allows you to store, send, and receive digital tokens. These tokens are pegged or "stabilized" to currencies such as dollars, euros, and yen on a person-to-person level. Stablecoins are commonly used on crypto-based commodity exchanges, for example, to trade commodities.

The most common stablecoins are listed on the Stablecoin index at `https://stable-coinindex.com/`.

Stablecoins provide significant value when a company uses them to interface directly with consumers, other businesses, and even governments to provide stability for the platform.

## Blockchain Funding and Costs

When it comes to funding a blockchain project, you must be aware that the project may be funded by one method initially and then funded by another after the deployment is completed. For example, if a company procures $30,000 in servers and network equipment to deploy Hyperledger Fabric on-premises, the support and maintenance after deployment will probably be funded by another mechanism such as departmental funds.

When an IT project is being proposed, an effective executive sponsor can demonstrate commitment by publicly discussing the reasons why the program is important to the organization. Knowing your stakeholders and then working with the stakeholders will provide immense value to blockchain adoption.

Understanding how your customer's blockchain project will be funded is of course important to understand. This section of the chapter will provide you with a solid understanding of the various project funding concerns.

### CAPEX and OPEX

Companies fund their infrastructure projects and day-to-day operations via different funding methods. These methods will have some impact on the profitability of the company because there are significant tax laws not only in the United States but also in other countries. The costing models most commonly used are the capital expenditure (CAPEX) and operational expense (OPEX) models.

◆ CAPEX is the large financial investment a company makes today to invest in the future. CAPEX funding is a procurement exercise where approvals are required from executives and from the enterprise's procurement departments. This type of funding is planned on an annual basis, and the funding can be time-consuming to get approved and also to receive.

◆ OPEX is the funding used for the smaller, "day-to-day" money a company spends. OPEX is usually disbursed to the business units on a calendar basis with no approvals or procurement exercises required. (Monthly, quarterly, or annually are common calendar schedules.)

A significant difference between these two types of expense schemes is the way they are accounted for in an income statement and the tax benefits that may present to the company. CAPEX spending from an enterprise perspective is used to acquire assets such as a datacenter generator, which would have a useful life beyond the specific tax year it was purchased. From a tax perspective, these expenses normally won't be fully deducted in the year they're incurred (purchased). (They are capitalized, amortized, or depreciated over the asset's lifetime, which in the United States could be 7 to 15 years.)

OPEX spending is used for operating expenses that can normally be fully deducted in the tax year the item was purchased, which can provide significant benefits for shareholders. Most companies prefer OPEX since they can write off these expenses in full and immediately because they are not over an amortized tax schedule.

Table 6.2 provides some examples of OPEX and CAPEX expenditures.

**TABLE 6.2:**     CAPEX and OPEX data center expense examples

| CAPEX | OPEX |
| --- | --- |
| Computers and servers | Cloud Subscriptions |
| Data storage arrays | Blockchain As a Service (BaaS) |
| Networking equipment | Utilities |
| Building requirements | Network bandwidth |
| HVAC requirements | Membership and fees |
| VM/DB/OS licensing | Contract labor and employee wages |
| Internal CRM suites | Rents and leases |
| | Employee training and books |

In a nutshell, any IT service can be deployed in an on-premises data center that is controlled by the enterprise or can be deployed in a colocation data center (*colo*). A colo is a shared data center facility in which an enterprise can rent or lease data center space for its IT equipment. These colocation contracts vary widely, but one differentiator is that you can actually access your equipment; however, in contrast to a cloud computing platform, you have no access to them physically. For example, with ATT, Equinix, and Digital Reality, you can visit and access your equipment, but with AWS, GCP, and Azure this would not be the case.

As a pre-sales engineer, I have been involved in perhaps thousands of hours of discussion around technology choices, and part of those discussions involved funding decisions. Whether to choose CAPEX or OPEX funding is a decision that enterprises take very seriously because of profit-and-loss concerns, tax ramifications, time to market, and perhaps the viability of the project.

From experience, I find that companies almost always choose the OPEX approach for funding. I have run into instances where the company will fund a $120,000 project that would normally be CAPEX via not one funding source but several OPEX sources by breaking purchases into smaller amounts. This is similar to going to the grocery store with $120 to buy groceries and breaking up the purchase into three transactions and then using three debit cards with small limits.

## Cost Considerations

Costs in most IT projects can be both predictable and unpredictable. An example of a predictable monthly services cost is the fee for reserving cloud computing virtual machines. Other examples are leases, support contracts, labor costs, software licensing, taxes, insurance, and so on.

An example of an unpredictable cost is the fee for bandwidth when it is difficult to determine ahead of time the number of queries against a database. Blockchains that are hosted on-site will of course have much more predictable costs, especially if the users as well as the blockchain nodes are local. If you have users who are utilizing a blockchain as a service (BaaS) in AWS, then you can expect certain costs to be unpredictable. Other examples include network bandwidth, transactions fees, utilities, and legal fees.

The following are examples of costs that can be incurred in typical enterprise blockchain deployments:

- Infrastructure (fixed or not)
- Data storage costs
- Data transfer costs
- Legal review
- Implementation costs
- Development costs
- Maintenance and support
- Compliance requirements

The costs will also depend on the type of industries that the blockchain is serving and the amount of risk that the customer is willing to take during implementation and even management. For example, if you have a blockchain deployment that can use a predefined blockchain template in AWS, that would cut several costs significantly. However, by using a blockchain template from any vendor, you are essentially limiting your blockchain's performance, virtual machine configurations, and blockchain versions and regions.

The most important point is to ensure your client understands that blockchains are a newer technology, and they are still evolving. This means an investment made yesterday could very well be wasted if not properly planned from a costing perspective today.

### INFRASTRUCTURE COSTS

Infrastructure costs will be your data center costs whether your company owns it or is leasing. Data centers are quite expensive and require significant CAPEX and OPEX funding to maintain.

Costs for data center space are calculated based on square feet. Also, you may be considering a colocation data center (colo), where the cost is based on a "per rack" approach. You may want to consider density as well.

When it comes to data center costs, the following costs should be considered. Note that these data center requirements can fluctuate based on the enterprise's business model. The costs and utility requirements also will vary significantly based on the tier level that your enterprise requires.

- Leases

- Utilities (power, cooling, UPS)

- Fire suppression

- Insurance

- Maintenance contracts

- Labor costs

- Hardware (servers, storage, network)

- Software licensing (OS, VMs, apps)

- Inspections and audits

- Networking

- Service providers (bandwidth)

- Solutions design

In general, the customers implementing a blockchain such as Hyperledger in their infrastructure are incurring significant costs. To be quite fair, it's not exactly a one-to-one relationship when comparing a blockchain application to a traditional centralized database application. Hyperledger and Oracle Databases have significantly different cost structures and labor requirements, for example.

Customers that want to reduce CAPEX or just avoid CAPEX completely can use a cloud service such as AWS, Azure, or IBM BaaS. There are, of course, several other cloud providers that have some form of blockchain templates or services as well. The pros of using BaaS are that in most scenarios your organization will avoid any CAPEX expenditures and reduce its maintenance and support responsibilities. This will allow your organization to get the blockchain service out to market more quickly.

The cons of using BaaS are that you are limited to the configurations that the cloud provider has available, subjected to network latency, and in reality, you sometimes have no control over your node configurations you deploy.

## DATA STORAGE COSTS

Data storage is a continual cost since the blockchain is a distributed ledger and that distributed ledger is continuously being "appended." Another factor to consider based on the ledger structure being utilized is that the decentralization of blockchain storage can have various additional financial benefits to your enterprise. For example, you may save on bandwidth since files are distributed among nodes and downloaded from multiple nodes instead of from a single node.

Figure 6.1 references the costs of data storage when using a common blockchain cloud provider. The numbers are fictional, and you would need to evaluate each provider as well as the type of storage, region, and other features. For example, data storage can be priced per gigabyte, based on 100GB per month. Also, you should be aware of numerous factors, such as the cloud provider's regions and zones. which could have different costs per gigabyte and numerous other costs such as ingress and egress of accessing the storage.

**FIGURE 6.1**
Data storage costs

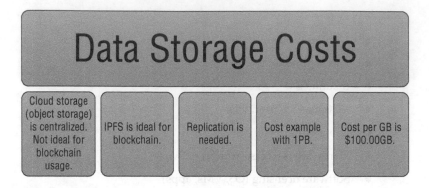

# Data Storage Costs

| Cloud storage (object storage) is centralized. Not ideal for blockchain usage. | IPFS is ideal for blockchain. | Replication is needed. | Cost example with 1PB. | Cost per GB is $100.00GB. |
| --- | --- | --- | --- | --- |

## DATA TRANSFER COSTS

One of the challenges when using any network service is to understand how network costs are handled. For example, when traversing your enterprise's on-premises resources to a cloud provider such as Microsoft Azure, you will need to be aware of bandwidth costs.

Bandwidth costs are broken into two charging traffic mechanisms.

**Ingress**  Ingress is traffic that is directed toward an internal resource from an external resource.

**Egress**  Egress is all traffic that is directed toward an external network from an internal resource.

When you consider a blockchain service that is traversing multiple networks, you need to understand the cost of the potential applications. If you have nodes that are disbursed between two different data centers, whether or not they are cloud services, you're going to need to estimate the costs for these applications.

Figure 6.2 shows the traffic flow for ingress and egress traffic from a company data center.

**FIGURE 6.2**
Ingress and egress traffic
flow from the cloud

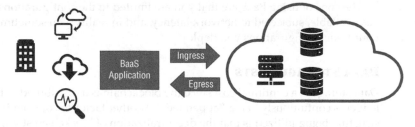

Historically, traffic charges are billed monthly based on a tiered structure, with higher rates for higher data transfers into and out of the cloud.

Blockchains are going to be traffic intensive—that is, the distributed ledger is constantly being appended to, and transaction logs are going to be written to. Some of the factors of blockchain services that could affect traffic charges include the following:

◆ Backups of ledger traffic an/or transaction logs

◆ Disaster recovery

◆ Snapshots of containers and/or virtual machines

◆ Monitoring of blockchain nodes and/or services

Figure 6.3 refers to ingress and egress charges and provides an example of Microsoft Azure and how redundancy as well as the regions could affect costing.

**FIGURE 6.3**

Microsoft Azure data storage costing example

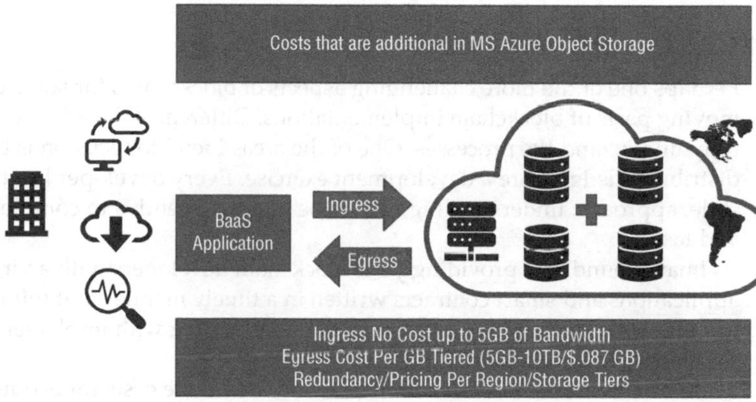

Costs that are additional in MS Azure Object Storage

BaaS Application

Ingress

Egress

Ingress No Cost up to 5GB of Bandwidth
Egress Cost Per GB Tiered (5GB-10TB/$.087 GB)
Redundancy/Pricing Per Region/Storage Tiers

The configuration shown has two regions that are being utilized: North America and South America. The costs for cloud services in both regions vary; you also want to be cautious about replication and bandwidth charges. Plan your blockchain data services appropriately to avoid excessive costs. An area of waste that is typically part of a "cloud spend" problem is that there are virtual machines and storage objects that are not being utilized or are on the wrong tier of service. If your blockchain is running on a cloud provider, then use one of the cloud provider's cloud spending analyzers or calculators to identify waste.

Managed object cloud storage allows you to expand your usage footprint to utilize as much data as your enterprise requires. Your enterprise can store oversized files up to 5 TB on both AWS and Azure, for example. Storage is one area where costs can get out of control, so tread conservatively in your planning and implementation. I have done many cloud and virtual machine assessments and have seen companies waste more than 40 percent of their cloud spend on just redundant data.

## LEGAL COSTS

When considering blockchain transactions that may be "traversing" legal jurisdictions such as states, provinces, and countries, it is important to consider the legal concerns. When you are making transactions across borders between the United States and the European Union, for example, the legal team needs to be involved to review any potential liability risks as well as compliance requirements.

Your legal or corporate team will likely want to validate concerns about how a ledger transaction is handled in a smart contract on R3 Corda from a "legal prose" perspective. *Legal prose* is a term used in R3 Corda to reflect a specific record of an explicit link between human-language legal prose documents and smart contract code. These "documents" may be relied upon in the case of legal disputes.

Some common legal concerns that can create additional costs have to do with legal prose, lack of legal precedence, smart contract compliance, property rights, and chain of custody tracking and compliance. In Chapter 9, "Blockchain Governance, Risk, Compliance (GRC), Privacy, and Legal Concerns," I cover the legal concerns in much more detail. For the purposes of this chapter, be aware that legal costs can be a factor that may need to be considered when discussing blockchain funding.

## IMPLEMENTATION COSTS

Perhaps one of the more challenging aspects of blockchains for some enterprises will be the moving parts of blockchain implementations. Different stakeholders and even the vendors don't fully understand the processes. One of the areas I tend to focus on is that blockchains and distributed ledgers are a development exercise. Every developer has their own programming style, approach, understanding, and to be honest, incentive to completing the requirements and tasks.

I have found that providing your blockchain developers with an incentive to getting the client applications and smart contracts written in a timely manner that follows your application requirements can make or break your project. Costing with implementations will likely never be within 20 percent of the estimates.

Some common costs that can be planned for are the costs for acquiring the skillsets required to develop the blockchain application, resources to be procured, and contractors who will aid in the deployment. Training is also a cost that should be considered for any labor as well for a proof of concept. This is often overlooked and under-budgeted.

## DEVELOPMENT COSTS

Development costs can vary widely when considering TCO and ROI calculations. I prefer to err on the side of conservative estimates. The last thing you want to do is underestimate costs and place your estimates in jeopardy.

The main concern I run into is related to enterprise integrations. For example, how does the organization integrate efficiently its existing client applications into a platform such as Hyperledger Fabric? Another concern is hiring the right blockchain programming talent, which can be challenging. For example, the pool of developers who understand and code JavaScript and Python is somewhat larger than developers who can develop in Golang or Solidity.

Figure 6.4 highlights common development costs.

Blockchain expertise is in high demand worldwide. According to CNBC Blockchain (https://www.cnbc.com/2018/10/21/how-much-do-blockchain-engineers-make.html), engineers are making, on average, between $150,000 and $175,000 in annual salaries. Blockchain development hotbeds such as New York City, London, Singapore, Silicon Valley, Switzerland, and Toronto are seeing blockchain developers command more than $200,000 a year.

When searching for blockchain expertise, it is critical to understand that the job seeker has the upper hand, at least at the time of writing. Therefore, you should be conscious that even though a blockchain developer is a developer, their skills are clearly in demand, and your hiring behavior should reflect this if your enterprise is concerned with filling the vacancy.

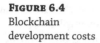

**FIGURE 6.4**
Blockchain
development costs

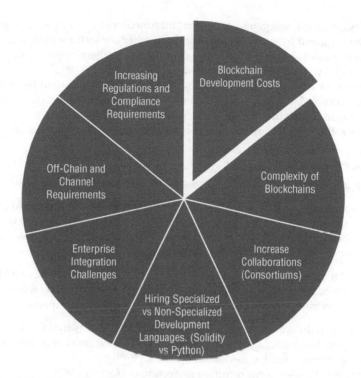

Some of the skills that a blockchain developer needs are related to enterprise skills such as networking, security, Agile, and DevOps. The different blockchains use different programming languages. For example, Ethereum is focused on Solidity, while Hyperledger focuses on Golang. Other common languages are Node.js, Java, Python, C++, and .NET languages. Having experience with open source is also recommended.

Obtaining the right skillsets will be challenging based on the requirements, location, and other factors such as salary and experience requirements.

**REFERENCE**    For more detailed information about blockchain skillsets, demand, and development requirements, please refer to Chapter 12.

# Enterprise Blockchain Cost Models

Blockchains are transforming the way entire industries work, especially in the fintech and logistics industries, with new business models and potentially new revenue opportunities. When it comes to blockchains, it is important to understand that most of the cost savings that will be realized will be through implementing "business logic" into smart contracts.

Business logic delegates your prior "intermediary" tasks to smart contracts or chaincode that will be triggered by events originating from other consortium members. For example, the Ethereum blockchain can resemble a cloud service, where responsibility for processing transactions is shared among distributed nodes.

However, if you must have privacy, security, and specific membership, you can't use a shared permissionless blockchain like Ethereum and must either absorb the full cost of the blockchain or share those costs with other industry members.

The following sections provide insight into a cost's effectiveness on the blockchain solution.

## Return on Investment

ROI analysis is used to compare investment scenarios. Let's look at two high-level scenarios.

◆ An enterprise customer is determining whether to refresh a SAN storage array for three, five, or seven years. An ROI analysis will be requested to help determine which option is better from a "financial perspective." The costs for this hardware are fixed (hardware, software, support, power, and so on).

◆ An enterprise customer is determining whether to implement a Hyperledger Fabric blockchain for three, five, or seven years. An ROI analysis will be requested to help determine which option is better from a "financial perspective."

The main difference here from an exercise standpoint is that the hardware has fixed costs that are easy to determine, and a blockchain has both fixed costs and some not so fixed costs that can be undetermined such as development costs.

Figure 6.5 shows some common reasons to perform an ROI.

**FIGURE 6.5**
Return on investment

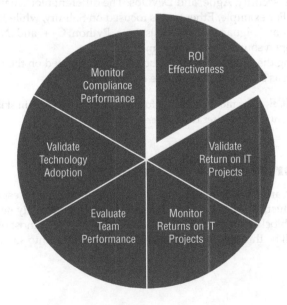

Every organization has different expectations and approaches to how to monitor and manage the effectiveness of an IT project. When evaluating a blockchain opportunity, you want to start establishing what ROI formula to utilize. Essentially, the following is the most direct approach to an ROI number or basic formula for ROI:

ROI = Net Profit / Total Investment * 100

Essentially, net profit is the "return," and total investment is a collection of costs that are incurred from hardware, software, cloud services, consulting, and development.

The basic ROI calculation is also known as the *rate of return* (ROR) or the *rate of profit* (ROP). This ROI return is also known as income gained or income lost on any investment or the profit and loss results. In the accounting world, there are many approaches to calculating the same outcome, especially when it comes to tax assessments. The cost of investment is also known as a capital investment. Specifically, in IT, we would use the CAPEX and OPEX approach to fund IT projects even if they are blockchains.

Figure 6.6 highlights the most common ROI formulas used in IT-focused projects. The number that is arrived at for an ROI will be vastly different based on what inputs you're measuring. For example, if your customer measures net profit or net income differently than another company, then this will skew the results. I have been in large Fortune 100 companies where two different IT-focused departments determined ROI very differently. As a solution engineer, you need to work with the customer to ensure you use the most favorable metrics for the customer's use cases.

**FIGURE 6.6**
ROI costs and formulas

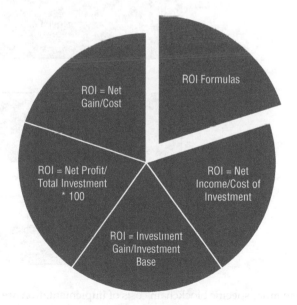

When calculating ROI, I like to use a chart or spreadsheet showing potential benefits present to the customer. These benefits fall into two categories.

**Tangible Benefits**   Tangible benefits are those that can be seen, measured easily, or documented easily. These are known as *hard benefits*. An example is replacing a legacy email system with a cloud service. It's clear that the legacy systems have been decommissioned and the costs recovered.

**Intangible Benefits** Intangible benefits are those that cannot be seen, measured easily, or documented easily. These are known as *soft benefits*. An example of an intangible benefit would be replacing a call center system and experiencing higher customer satisfaction and potential in increased brand awareness.

## Total Cost of Ownership

Total cost of ownership is widely used to estimate costs for a blockchain application. TCO is essentially gathering up all the costs, whether direct or indirect, to estimate a project. Figure 6.7 highlights the high-level cost tiers to consider when you're estimating a blockchain application deployment.

**FIGURE 6.7**
Total cost of ownership

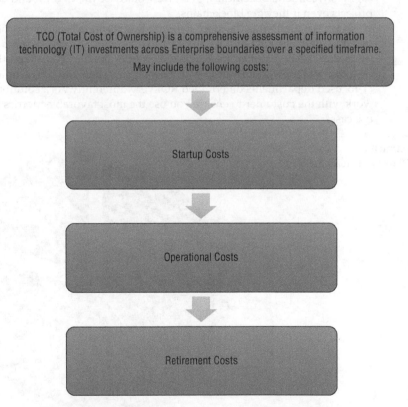

Some more specific blockchain costs of implementation are usually considered "startup costs" such as training for personnel, infrastructure hardware and software, licensing, and consulting services. Operational costs are incurred after startup and when the application is in production. These costs include management and monitoring services, bandwidth costs, and transaction fees. Retirement costs are incurred to "turn off" a service, essentially decommissioning the application.

This could mean archiving data for compliance purposes, removing and disposing of server racks, or incurring tax consequences.

Figure 6.8 covers common TCO costs an enterprise would incur when deploying an application service in a data center.

**FIGURE 6.8**
TCO costs

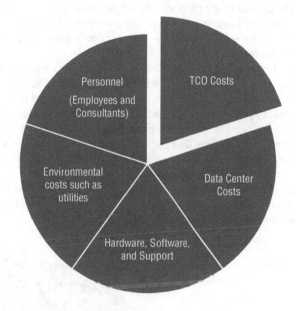

## ROI vs. TCO

The major differences between the two financial analysis models (ROI and TCO) are that the ROI model is a cash flow model and not just a costing model, while TCO is the total cost of acquiring and operating an asset over a period. Also, you should be aware that the costs as well as any savings the investment has produced need to be quantified (itemized).

# Potential Cost Efficiencies

Let's consider some of the typical cost efficiencies that blockchains can introduce into the organization. The cost efficiencies will focus on removing intermediaries that process manual transactions.

## Reducing Burdened Labor Costs

Technology innovations can provide cost savings that are based on transactions, fees, hardware, or software purchases or even governance and compliance. Technologies such as cloud computing, automated intelligence, and machine learning are providing substantial costs in labor, both for employees and for contractor hiring requirements.

For example, cloud computing is known for creating substantial reductions in overhead TCO for hardware, software, utilities, and labor costs. Not only has cloud computing been used to implement aggressive cost cutting in IT around reduction in force (RIF) for traditional legacy IT professionals, it also provides burdened salary cost efficiencies and requires more skilled but also lower-paid IT professionals.

Blockchain technology certainly is no different when you consider the number of potential full-time employees that could be reduced because of their roles as intermediaries. Blockchain technology will likely provide efficiencies from removing manual interactions or transactions that were traditionally required. One example is Know Your Customer (KYC), which is considered to be a time-intensive, manual, and costly procedure that financial institutions are required to participate in.

If your averaged burdened overhead costs per employee (salary, taxes, and benefits) are an average of $150,000 per year and your company has 50 intermediaries validating, auditing, or somehow participating in transactions, then you could consider the legacy solutions a target for blockchain applications. This becomes somewhat more relative when there is a consortium, for example, that could realize the benefits as a collaborative effort.

Some common costs that go into the "burdened" salary are wages, payroll taxes, benefits such as insurance, computers, retirement costs, free snacks, and any human resource or recruiting costs.

Figure 6.9 shows the common costs that go into an employee's salary. From a perspective of a large bank, if they have hundreds of employees, then finding a reason to not keep as many employees is always in the mind of the CEO.

**FIGURE 6.9**
Burdened salary costs

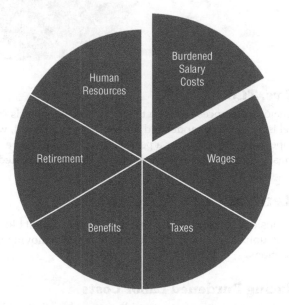

Smart contracts were created to essentially perform "intermediary" (accountant, lawyer, customs reviewer, and so on) duties and provide efficiency based on computer logic. Of course, the potential discussions could revolve around reducing your organization's institutional overhead that typically performs important, manually intensive, costly, but idealistically "redundant and predictable" duties. The best use cases will provide significant cost efficiencies that will document clear savings such as reducing the employee head count.

## Using OPEX over CAPEX

When a company decides to move from CAPEX to an OPEX model for IT funding, it can realize substantial savings. For example, savings can be realized when migrating from the enterprise's on-premises data centers to a cloud computing service such BaaS.

Operating expenditures in the United States can be fully deducted that tax year and thus provide the company with greater revenue realization, better earnings per share (EPS) ratios, and financial benefits for shareholders. Some examples are that all cloud computing–related spending, which is known as *cloud spend*, usually can be fully written off or deducted that year. *Deducted* means subtracted from the revenue when calculating the profit/loss for the enterprise. Please note that I am not a tax advisor or providing financial advice; this is a generalization of corporate behavior of IT costing in the United States.

## Lower Transaction Costs

When a company is processing a transaction specifically for payments, the cost per transaction (CPT) can be drastically reduced via a blockchain application. For example, participants in a marketplace such eBay, Amazon, or Etsy act as intermediaries charging fees and therefore capitalizing on their ability to control transactions taking place within their marketplaces. Lower transaction costs can easily be attained with the right blockchain solution that introduces automated transaction management that is decentralized. Stablecoins, for example, could play a role in a marketplace to help facilitate trade and provide stability for the customer base. This in turn can provide lower costs per unit or transaction for the platform.

**REFERENCE**    I will discuss more use cases that can lower transaction fees in Chapter 8, "Enterprise Blockchain Use Cases."

## Costless Verification

*Costless verification* is a term that is referenced with blockchain technologies to describe the validation of a transaction after the transaction has occurred. The blockchain is a living ledger that is being updated constantly but is also historically an immutable provider of transaction histories. Costless verification can reduce the verification costs of transactions especially when compared to traditional legacy financial systems. Costless verification means that the recorded attributes that need to be verified securely on a blockchain can be referred to at any point on the distributed ledger at no cost to the subscribers.

One more factor to consider is that blockchain transactions are always available and are not centrally controlled. For example, if a company wants to validate the transactions of a shipment of avocados, it simply could "query" the blockchain ledger and confirm instantly any related information to the shipment. In a centralized database system, that was not always the case. Costless verification provides efficiencies, and you should be aware of this as a possible cost efficiency to discuss with your customer.

## Intermediary Roles and Blockchain

The P2P trust economy that blockchains such as Bitcoin have enabled represents an impressive shift of power. Gone are the days you need to go to a bank to send money overseas, for example, thus incurring substantial fees. Now you can send money via any number of cryptocurrency platforms and save money especially as a user.

Figure 6.10 shows a high-level transaction flow through the legacy network of Swift. Note that there is an intermediary such as a bank who collects a fee.

**FIGURE 6.10**
Intermediary example

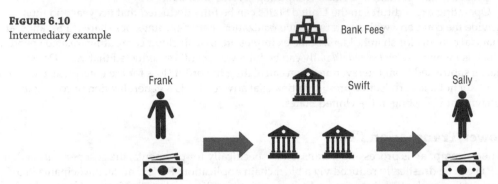

Traditional Model - Frank wants to send funds to Sally but cannot do it directly.
He must use an "intermediary" such as a bank or transfer service.

Perhaps with this new trust economy some enterprises may benefit from a lower cost per transaction by removing the requirements for an intermediary. The one sure thing with blockchains is that every enterprise's "mileage may vary" in the sense of cost savings and benefits that blockchains are able to bring to the table.

When it comes to blockchain cost efficiency, the greatest cost savings could come in the form of "intermediary" reduction or reassignment. Blockchains that are permissionless are open and transparent and allow access to transaction information in the smart contract. Because of this, smart contract automation problems can perhaps be solved more efficiently.

Figure 6.11 shows a blockchain-based solution transferring value. Note that there is no intermediary such as a bank.

**FIGURE 6.11**
Blockchain example

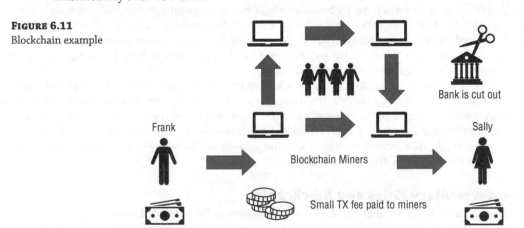

Blockchain Model - Frank wants to send funds to Sally and can use a P2P "cryptocurrency"
to bypass a bank or transfer service's high fees and slow service.

Blockchain technology enables data reconciliation between two independent parties. A database may very well be distributed and highly available. The blockchain ledger is distributed between any number of nodes, and any changes in the database can be managed by parties that are independent or not fully independent. The reality is that depending on the blockchain deployment and whether it's permissioned or permissionless, the benefits may not be fully realized.

In financial institutions, it has been documented that the blockchain is providing efficiencies for intermediary-based role requirements. These requirements revolve around the number of intermediaries required but also the skill levels required. Blockchain is disrupting roles. Following are the common roles that are being affected:

◆ Accountants

◆ Attorneys

◆ Custom inspectors

◆ Fulfillment processors

◆ Settlement agents

Blockchains, like most IT-focused projects, have significant costs, and as a customer-facing engineer, it is important to understand these costs to ensure you set the correct expectations of the project.

## Summary

This chapter covered the various cost models such as B2B and B2C and discussed the main ecommerce models that are common in the business world. When it comes to IT projects, some costs can be predictable, while some costs are not predictable. Companies are relying less on CAPEX funding and more on OPEX funding. OPEX is disbursed to the business units on a calendar approach with generally no approvals or procurement exercises required. There are numerous costs such as infrastructure (fixed or not), data storage costs, data transfer costs, legal review, implementation, development costs, and maintenance and support.

Selling blockchain solutions requires a significant interaction with the development group and various roles of an enterprise. Both TCO and ROI are important financial accounting calculations that need to be utilized in a blockchain assessment. When it comes to blockchain cost efficiency, the greatest cost savings could come in the form of intermediary reduction or reassignment, which could lead to a lower cost per transaction.

# Chapter 7

# Deploying Your Blockchain on BaaS

In this chapter, I discuss why blockchain as a service (BaaS) is a great way to help stand up your enterprise blockchain without all the heavy lifting of having to set up your IT infrastructure to accommodate a blockchain. BaaS provides the added benefit of reducing the capex requirements of standing up resources for your blockchain in your on-premises data center. Then I will walk you step-by-step through how to deploy Hyperledger on IBM and AWS.

BaaS takes full advantage of cloud computing by utilizing both the economic and technical merits of cloud computing to enable enterprises to deploy these services on cloud providers such as AWS, Microsoft Azure, and IBM Cloud.

I will discuss how blockchains and distributed ledgers can facilitate an impressive total cost of ownership (TCO) scenario and improve your return on investment (ROI) models for FinTech-focused use cases.

Deploying a blockchain is a relatively direct, cost-efficient, and manageable task that can be completed in less than a few hours. I will discuss why companies choose to use a cloud service and the main benefits of using a provider such as IBM for your blockchain deployment.

The first part of the chapter provides a concise guide of current BaaS platforms with the main benefits, features, and use cases they provide. I will also discuss how to use BaaS for proofs of concepts and demos especially for presales-focused readers.

In the second part of the chapter, I will walk you step-by-step through deploying a blockchain on the following services:

◆ Amazon Web Services (AWS)

◆ IBM Cloud

The main goal of this chapter is twofold. First, I'll give you a financial perspective for how to justify implementations of blockchain services and hardware as well as present enterprise concerns around costs. Second, I'll explain how to deploy a blockchain on the AWS and IBM Cloud services.

## Blockchain as a Service Overview

The blockchain market is expanding at a brisk pace, and BaaS is no exception. The market leaders in cloud computing have been investing millions in this area as well. From a market perspective, I will focus on AWS, IBM Cloud, and Microsoft Azure, which at the time of writing are the most comprehensive solutions.

**NOTE**  "The global BaaS market will reach USD 30.59 billion by 2024." —Zion Market Research

## Why Use a Blockchain as a Service?

Blockchain as a service is a cloud services offering that allows customers to leverage cloud-based solutions to build, host, and use their own blockchain apps, smart contracts, and functions on the blockchain. In BaaS, the cloud-based service provider manages all the necessary tasks and activities to keep the infrastructure agile and available.

The BaaS market is expected to grow significantly over the next five years. This growth is due to the market's demand for increasing blockchain applications in the commerce sector. International business transactions are getting more secure, fast, and reliable alongside the BaaS model coming into the picture. Because the database is distributed and the trail of every transaction is available, blockchain as a service is eliminating obstacles in international payment processes. Delay in verification and invoice processing increases the cost of business activities, which can be nullified or reduced by using blockchain technology. The technology provides a common chain of information visibility that will be shared across vendors and purchasers. Using BaaS in international business transactions may very well reduce processing time and costs significantly.

In a nutshell, the BaaS model allows companies to access a blockchain provider's services so they can then access, develop, and deploy blockchain-based applications.

The growth of blockchain is clear, and along with that there will likely be the increased utilization of blockchain as a service on platforms such as IBM, AWS, and Azure. Other players such as Oracle, Alibaba, Baidu, Hewlett Packard Enterprise (HPE), Huawei, and Tencent currently have BaaS or will have potential availability shortly.

**NOTE**    "One advantage of partnering with a BaaS provider is how users can leverage the lessons learned by the provider to help make their systems more secure." —Bill Fearnley Jr., IDC research director of worldwide blockchain strategies (`https://www.information-age.com/essential-guide-blockchain-as-a-service-123473581/`)

One of the main benefits of using a BaaS vendor is that they provide all the necessary software deployments for blockchain as well as the infrastructure to the customer in a generally easy-to-consume subscription model. The vendor is then responsible for setting up and maintaining the backend of the blockchain's infrastructure.

To clarify, there are certainly some BaaS platforms that are either a true software as a service (SaaS) or a platform as a service (PaaS) such as IBM Blockchain Platform. For example, IBM supports both SaaS and PaaS solutions quite well.

On the other hand, some blockchains as a service are really infrastructure as a service where you deploy infrastructure templates. For example, AWS Blockchain templates in the AWS Marketplace can help your company create and deploy blockchain networks on AWS using different blockchain frameworks. You would need to create your security groups, deploy CloudFormation templates, and determine networking configurations before deploying the blockchain. There is a level of AWS expertise that would be needed to deploy these templates in a production environment.

## Benefits of Using a Blockchain as a Service

Cloud computing has been around since the early days of Amazon Web Services, which essentially created the market for infrastructure as a service (IaaS) cloud computing. Cloud computing has numerous benefits for an enterprise, a startup, or even a home user. The reality is that IT infrastructure is expensive to procure and to maintain, and finding talented people can be a challenge on a limited budget. Cloud computing has essentially leveled the playing field for both a consultant in Jacksonville, Florida, and a large multinational bank in New York City, thereby allowing them to use the same level of enterprise services on a scaled costing model, for example.

The benefits are realized because BaaS is being deployed on a cloud computing infrastructure that is managed by the cloud vendor. Some of the main benefits of using a blockchain cloud service include the following:

- Lower startup costs over traditional on-premises solutions that support opex funding

- Faster time to market due to no infrastructure lead-time requirements

- Services managed by provider, reducing your management responsibilities

- Support and expertise of service provided by the provider

- Scalability greatly improved by provider services

- Immediate data security benefits realized and managed by the provider

- Compatibility with current cloud services that the enterprise may be utilizing such as monitoring

Cloud services run blockchain applications, and it's clear that the benefits are similar to what you would experience running perhaps your databases or virtual machines in the cloud.

## Negatives of Using a Blockchain as a Service

Cloud computing, as we know, has many benefits, which some enterprises may or may not fully realize. Not all uses cases may realize the benefits due to the application frameworks, cost models, or development models utilized.

For example, while working as a presales architect in the data storage and cloud markets for more than a decade, I can certainly say that customers that do not generally manage resources well in-house will likely not manage resources in the cloud well either. Resource management is a must in using cloud resources effectively and efficiently. I have seen "cloud spend" skyrocket by more than 300 percent in just a few months, and the cloud engineers have no idea why this is happening. The two types of resources that generally take up most of the "cloud spend" are your data storage and your virtual machines.

The following are some of the negative results of using BaaS:

- Cloud spending costs are not managed appropriately, resulting in unexpectedly high cloud spending.

- Resources are centralized, and blockchains by definition should not be centralized for solid use cases.

- There is limited support for blockchain/ledger services on your provider of choice.

- Experienced cloud professionals are in high demand and hard to find.

- Cloud applications may not be portable once placed on a cloud provider.

- Performance issues such as latency may not be acceptable for your applications.

- Compliance violations can arise when the networking nodes are in data centers that are not in appropriate regions.

Cloud services run blockchain applications, and it's clear that the negatives are similar to what you would experience running your databases or virtual machines in the cloud, so you will want to design judiciously.

## Blockchain as a Service for Sales Teams

In Chapter 5, "Enterprise Blockchain Sales and Solutions Engineering," I briefly discussed why using BaaS can enable a sales team by providing a platform for a proof of concept (POC) or for an actual production environment.

When considering a POC or a demo around any major blockchain, such as Hyperledger, Corda, or Ethereum, you can certainly leverage any number of the cloud providers to host your project. Using a POC or demo on a cloud provider can reduce your company's overhead for infrastructure.

From my experience, if you're a VAR, vendor, or systems integrator, you may have an internal platform you can leverage. The main challenge you may have is ensuring that you have the technical expertise to set up and maintain the platform.

In your situation, using BaaS may not be something you will need to be concerned with or need to plan for when hosting a POC or a demo. However, having options is always a great approach to consider for delivery of a POC or a demo.

For example, if you're a partner of AWS at specific levels, you may have available credits to give to your customer to spin up cloud services. This could be very useful because it will allow you as a trusted adviser to essentially give your customer the keys to test it out, and your real role is to provide guidance and answer questions.

For me that was always the best route because anyone in presales can appreciate that even though they are doing endless POCs and demos, in reality, the customer may not be interested in your technology. If your customer is willing to "take the keys" and take initiative to learn, then this is clearly a benefit to everyone.

## Blockchain as a Service Providers

The growth of blockchains has certainly created what seems to be a gold rush for cloud providers, vendors, and even VARs. Vendors and cloud providers are rushing to create their own blockchain services, whether it's an IaaS solution, a PaaS solution, or even a SaaS solution. Note that Google has no current blockchain offering but announced plans for marketplace solutions at its annual conference in 2018.

Table 7.1 shows the mainstream cloud computing providers and the blockchain platforms they support at the time of writing.

**TABLE 7.1:** Comparing BaaS Providers

|                  | AWS                                                          | AZURE                                       | IBM                        |
| ---------------- | ----------------------------------------------------------- | ------------------------------------------- | -------------------------- |
| **Frameworks**   | Ethereum, Hyperledger Fabric, Quorum                        | Ethereum, Hyperledger Fabric, Corda         | Hyperledger Fabric         |
| **Deployment model** | IaaS, PaaS                                              | IaaS, PaaS                                  | PaaS                       |
| **Service**      | Blockchain templates (IaaS) and managed blockchain (PaaS)   | Blockchain workbench, Blockchain templates  | IBM Blockchain platform    |
| **Cost model**   | Pay as you go                                               | Pay as you go                              | Pay as you go              |

As you can see, the cloud providers have different cost models and deployment models. These differences can greatly affect the cost and scalability of the blockchain service.

It is important to note that even if a cloud provider does not have BaaS available, that does not mean you cannot deploy a blockchain on that provider. In that case, you can certainly deploy most blockchains on a container service that supports Docker containers. For example, Google Cloud Platform enables you to deploy Hyperledger Fabric on Kubernetes Engine or the Facebook Libra testnet on Compute Engine.

## Amazon Web Services Options

At the time of writing, Amazon Web Services has two options to deploy blockchains: Amazon Managed Blockchain, which is a fully managed platform (PaaS), and Amazon Blockchain templates, which is essentially using containers that you set up and manage (IaaS). There is also a new distributed ledger technology service called Amazon Quantum Ledger Database (QLDB), which, at the time of writing, is still in prelease mode.

**Amazon Managed Blockchain**   Amazon Managed Blockchain is a fully managed service that makes it efficient to create and manage scalable blockchain networks using the popular open source frameworks Hyperledger Fabric and Ethereum. Amazon Managed Blockchain eliminates the overhead required to create the network and automatically scales to meet the demands of thousands of applications running millions of transactions.

Figure 7.1 shows the Amazon Managed Blockchain service home page that has the introductory service information about the service. The direct link for the Amazon Managed Blockchain service is https://aws.amazon.com/managed-blockchain/. Note that Figure 7.1 looks similar to AWS Blockchain templates. If you choose to go to the search engines instead of the direct links, they may have defaulted to AWS Blockchain templates, not the Managed Blockchain service.

**FIGURE 7.1**
AWS Managed
Blockchain

The Managed Blockchain service makes it easy to manage and maintain your blockchain network. It manages your certificates, lets you easily invite new members to join the network, and tracks operational metrics such as usage of compute, memory, and storage resources.

**Amazon Blockchain templates** This option is for customers who are looking to manage their own blockchain network and just need an easy way to set it up and get started. The AWS Blockchain templates service is the right fit in most instances I have seen.

Figure 7.2 shows the AWS Blockchain templates service and provides a highlight of the services. The following is the current link for Amazon Blockchain templates:

https://aws.amazon.com/blockchain/templates/getting-started/

**FIGURE 7.2**
AWS Blockchain templates

**NOTE** The upcoming instructions will focus mainly on the Blockchain template for Hyperledger Fabric.

The AWS Blockchain templates service deploys the blockchain framework you choose as containers on an Amazon Elastic Container Service (ECS) cluster or directly on an EC2 instance running Docker depending on the deployment model.

The service costs are what you have already been paying for in AWS for basic services, essentially the use of the compute, network, and data resources. Effectively, you pay only for the resources you use, not the blockchain services with the Hyperledger and Ethereum templates.

The AWS blockchain solutions provided are across industries including financial market and commerce, supply chain, insurance, healthcare, and KYC and compliance.

Deploying blockchain services on AWS is relatively straightforward with the Blockchain templates once you get through the AWS required steps for security groups, virtual private clouds, and other networking-related tasks that must be set up before deployment. If the steps are not followed precisely, then the Hyperledger Fabric network will not work.

The instructions are broken down into high-level and low-level (step-by- step) instructions anyone should be able to follow. These instructions are provided as a baseline; cloud providers may change their interfaces, links, instructions, and best practices, so check with AWS before following the instructions here.

The following instructions will reference this template for northern Virginia, as specified:

License: Apache 2.0 (Please do not remove) Apr 19, 2018 (bt-k5nffx4jb)

This template is clearly defined on the AWS template stack page, which I will reference again in the step-by-step instructions.

## AWS Blockchain templates Deployment High-Level Steps

The following are the high-level steps to create a blockchain service on AWS with Blockchain templates:

1. Determine which blockchain (Ethereum, Hyperledger, or Corda) to deploy.

2. Determine which region on AWS to deploy on. Regions in AWS are effectively geographic locations of services.

3. Create a virtual private cloud (VPC), which is a logically isolated set of services in AWS.

4. Create key pairs and a security group, which are needed to access the virtual machines or containers in AWS.

5. Deploy the CloudFormation stack. CloudFormation is the AWS infrastructure deployment tool.

6. Deploy the Blockchain templates as required. Templates at the time of writing are Hyperledger Fabric and Ethereum.

7. Install chaincode for Hyperledger Fabric.

The preceding high-level steps have been simplified to give experienced AWS professionals an idea of what is expected before we progress into the step-by-step instructions.

Assuming that all the steps are followed correctly, that AWS makes no procedural changes, and that no outage occurs on any AWS service, these steps should take approximately two hours to complete. If you are experienced in AWS, you can assume it will take you approximately one hour to configure these services.

For more information about AWS Blockchain templates, refer to https://aws.amazon.com/blockchain/templates/.

At the time of this writing, the templates are available only for Ethereum and Hyperledger Fabric. From a planning perspective, you should understand the regions the templates are deployed in, which are limited at the time of writing.

## Understanding AWS Regions and Availability Zones

Regions are separate geographies, such as US East, US West, or EU Ireland. Availability Zones (AZs) are no more than isolated parts of a region that are logically segmented and maintain separate infrastructure for redundancy. Regions usually have three or four Availability Zones, providing availability for the services deployed in that region.

The limited availability of regions with AWS Blockchain templates could be a showstopper if you're in the European Union or Asia. This would likely be due, for example, to possible latency that could be experienced as well as to meeting compliance requirements.

For more information on AWS regions and availability zones, refer to the following:

https://docs.aws.amazon.com/AmazonRDS/latest/UserGuide/Concepts.RegionsAndAvailabilityZones.html

At the time of writing, templates are available for the following regions:

◆ US East (N. Virginia) region (us-east-1)

◆ US East (Ohio) region (us-east-2)

◆ US West (Oregon) region (us-west-2)

Figure 7.3 shows the AWS Blockchain templates web page. You can choose from Ethereum or Hyperledger Fabric for Blockchain templates. For the purposes of this book, we will choose Hyperledger Fabric.

**FIGURE 7.3**
AWS Blockchain templates https://aws.amazon.com/blockchain/templates/getting-started/

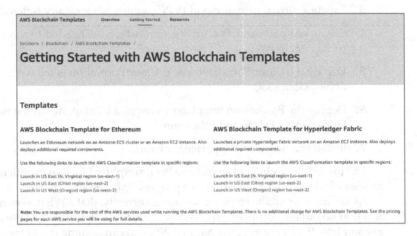

The AWS Blockchain templates use an AWS service called CloudFormation, and we will use this service to create a stack in AWS.

If you are not familiar with AWS CloudFormation, which is AWS's version of infrastructure as code, you can consider CloudFormation as a stack in the development world, which is similar to a deployment workflow.

A workflow is also routinely referenced as a pipeline in many facets of application development. This development workflow will deploy a private Hyperledger Fabric blockchain network on an Amazon EC2 instance and will deploy the required components such as networking, storage, and other required services.

Figure 7.4 shows the first part of the CloudFormation template, including the remaining parameters, such as EC2 key pair, security group, and other parameters. Figure 7.5 shows the second part of the template. A template is a preconfigured stack of resources in AWS. For more information on what a CloudFormation template is, refer to the following:

https://aws.amazon.com/cloudformation/aws-cloudformation-templates/

**FIGURE 7.4**
CloudFormation
template, part 1

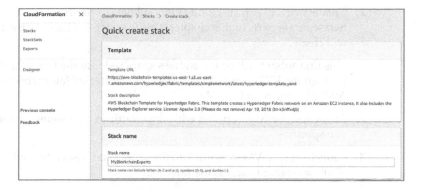

**FIGURE 7.5**
CloudFormation
template, part 2

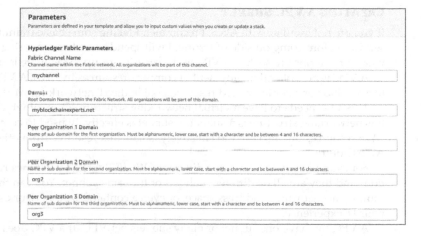

Note that we will not deploy this template yet, as we need to prepare the AWS environment. This discussion was to provide insight into what the template looks for around configuration variables.

## Deploying Hyperledger on AWS

When using the AWS Blockchain templates, you're essentially deploying a Hyperledger CloudFormation template that AWS has made free and publicly available to help facilitate creating a blockchain network hosted on an EC2 instance hosted in AWS.

The word *template*, of course, in most IT realms would seem as if we just have to click and deploy. Well, nothing could be further from the truth in AWS. The template you will use is only going to work after you actually set up the environment for the template, which includes the security groups, subnets, VPCs, and a host of other tasks.

To actually accomplish the proper setup of your AWS Blockchain templates, there are a few things you need to plan beforehand and set up to ensure your template deployment is successful, which we covered in the "AWS Blockchain template Deployment High-Level Steps" section.

1. Create a virtual private cloud (VPC) subnet. To clarify, we will need to create a subnet in two separate parts of this chapter. This first step covers only the first subnet that we will create.

   This first subnet will be the address space used for the blockchain network services through the VPC. The second subnet will be created later when we get to that part of the AWS Management Console.

2. Create a security group that will allow traffic to the instance through only the ports you specify.

3. Launch an EC2 VM instance into the subnet and associate it with an elastic IP. (An elastic IP allows traffic to access the Internet.)

## CREATING A VPC SUBNET

If you are not familiar with AWS, I recommend taking some basic training for using the cloud services before going outside of testing. I will spend some time covering the basics to clarify what some terms are such as a VPC and a security group to facilitate learning these subjects.

A VPC is an isolated deployment of compute resources in AWS. A VPC can also be compared to a sandbox or a containerized resource pool in the IT networking world.

This VPC needs to have a virtual networking structure setup, of which an elementary part of this networking structure is a subnet. A subnet is effectively used to communicate with other AWS resources but also used to effectively isolate that resource from other resources in the AWS Cloud.

For example, say you have ten different AWS EC2 virtual machines running different applications and they are all on different subnets or the same subnet. You can think of a subnet as a routing mechanism, an address space, or even a containerized network schema depending on your IT experience.

A VPC can have one subnet or many subnets per VPC. If a VPC does not make sense still, then I recommend you review the AWS documentation site or take a class in AWS.

**REFERENCE** To get started on the AWS journey with VPC, refer to the following:

`https://docs.aws.amazon.com/vpc/latest/userguide/what-is-amazon-vpc.html`

Now let's get started deploying our cloud resources.

The first thing we would need to do is log in to the AWS Management Console, which is also known as the Cloud Console, Cloud Dashboard, and the AWS Management Console. For this book, I will reference the AWS Management Console to alleviate any confusion.

This book assumes you have an AWS account, which is required to access services on AWS. The instructions on how to set up an AWS account and log into the AWS Management Console are beyond the scope of the book. These instructions are on the AWS website, YouTube, etc., if needed.

The AWS Management Console is currently located at `console.aws.amazon.com`. (However, it is important to note that cloud providers are well known for changing links routinely, so validate any links provided accordingly.)

1. Log in to the AWS Management Console.

   Figure 7.6 shows the AWS Management Console after you initially log in.

**FIGURE 7.6**
AWS Management
Console

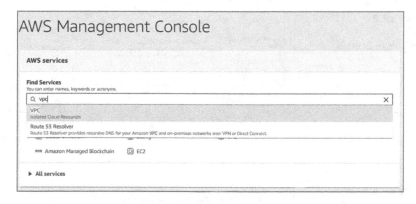

The AWS Management Console is rather simplistic from an aesthetic standpoint. For those of you who may not be familiar with AWS, you can find the VPC dashboard by going to the Find Services box in the middle of console, entering **VPC**, and selecting the VPC Dashboard.

**2.** Select Launch VPC Wizard from the VPC dashboard, as shown in Figure 7.7.

**FIGURE 7.7**
Launching the
VPC Wizard

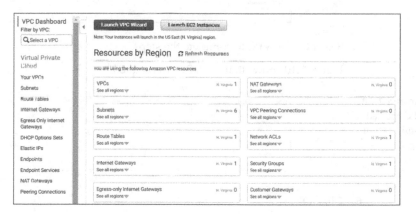

There are several options for creating a nondefault VPC, but this chapter will focus on the following approach.

**3.** Select the VPC with a Single Public Subnet option, as shown in Figure 7.8, and then click Next.

A subnet is needed to ensure traffic is segmented appropriately as an address space on AWS.

**4.** Enter **myblockchain** as the VPC name, as shown in Figure 7.9.

For the purposes of this demo, leave the settings at the defaults. In your deployment, however, you will need to determine more detailed configurations, such as the endpoints, availability zone, hardware tenancy, and the CIDR range l. These configurations settings are beyond the scope required for this demo.

**FIGURE 7.8**
VPC
Configuration dialog

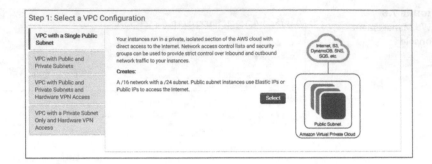

**FIGURE 7.9**
Myblockchain VPC

5. Select Create VPC to complete the steps.

   Figure 7.10 shows that the VPC was created.

**FIGURE 7.10**
VPC-created
confirmation

6. Click OK.

   You will then see the VPC menu, as shown in Figure 7.11.

**FIGURE 7.11**
VPC menu

Your VPC Myblockchain is now created, so you can move on to the next step in the process, creating a security group.

## CREATING A SECURITY GROUP

A security group in AWS is a virtual firewall that helps facilitate proper network traffic to the EC2 instance at hand. You can think of a firewall (security group) as a barrier for your AWS networking resources, enforced by egress and ingress policies. *Egress* refers to traffic leaving the AWS Cloud, and *ingress* refers to traffic entering the AWS cloud. We need to have several ports open in these egress and ingress policies to allow traffic through.

We can configure several layers of firewalls. Effectively, we can configure a security group for our VPC and for our EC2 instance. In this demo, we will configure two layers of firewalls (security groups).

Enough of AWS 101. Let's get to work.

We need to configure rules for outbound and inbound traffic to the instance. To do this, we will configure a security group.

1. Select Security Groups from the left pane, as shown in Figure 7.12.

**FIGURE 7.12**
Security Group menu

2. Select Create Security Group.

   The Security Group dialog box appears, as shown in Figure 7.13.

**FIGURE 7.13**
Security groups

3. Enter the following variables and then click Create:

   ◆ **Security Group Name**: Hyperledgerblockchain

   ◆ **Description**: Hyperledger Fabric Deployment

   ◆ **VPC**: (The name of the myblockchain VPC you created previously.)

   Figure 7.14 shows that the security group was created.

4. Select Close to advance to the Security Group dashboard, as shown in Figure 7.15.

5. View the security group list to validate that the security group you created is in your list.

   Figure 7.16 shows the VPC security group has been created.

**FIGURE 7.14**
VPC selection dialog
completion

**FIGURE 7.15**
Security group
confirmation

**FIGURE 7.16**
Security group listing

Now that the security group is deployed, we need to configure the outbound and inbound firewall rules.

6. Select the Inbound Rules tab from the bottom of menu interface, and then select Edit Rules.

Figure 7.17 shows the VPC Security group has been created and was selected. When it's selected, the Security metadata properties are listed (Description, Inbound Rules, Outbound Rules, and Tags).

**FIGURE 7.17**
Edit Inbound
Rules interface

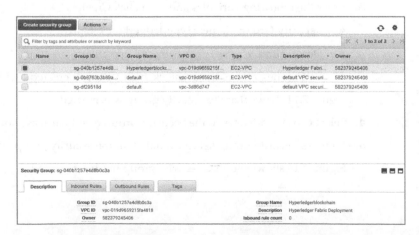

Now that the security group is deployed, we need to configure the outbound and inbound firewall rules.

**7.** Select the Inbound Rules tab from the bottom of menu interface, and then select Edit Rules, as shown in Figure 7.18.

We have no rules, so we need to configure them for the blockchain services.

**FIGURE 7.18**
Edit Inbound
Rules interface

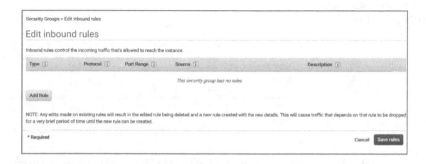

**8.** Select Add Rule from the middle left of the screen.

Figure 7.19 shows the Rule "Custom TCP Rule" on the drop-down menu.

**FIGURE 7.19**
Edit Inbound Custom
Rules initial window

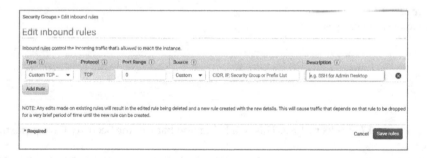

**9.** Create two inbound rules: one for HTTP and one for HTTPS.

Enter the following for the HTTP rule:

◆ **Protocol**: TCP

◆ **Port Range**: 80

◆ **Source**: Custom, leave 0.0.0.0/0

◆ **Description**: http

Enter the following for the HTTPS rule:

◆ **Protocol**: TCP

◆ **Port Range**: 443

◆ **Source**: Custom, leave 0.0.0.0/0

◆ **Description**: https

Note that 0.0.0.0/0 is not a best practice and is effectively allowing access inbound from any address. Before deploying in your enterprise, confirm the proper address source to configure for your AWS deployment.

Figure 7.20 shows the Edit Inbound rules, which is for traffic entering the cloud network.

**FIGURE 7.20**
Edit Inbound Rules with
HTTP and HTTPS

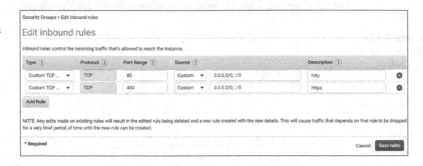

10. Add the firewall rules that allow HTTP and HTTPS traffic from anywhere and then select Save Rules.

Figure 7.21 shows that we have completed the inbound rules.

**FIGURE 7.21**
Inbound rules completed

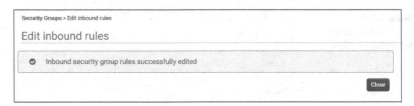

11. Select Close. This will bring you back to the Security Group dashboard (see Figure 7.22).

**FIGURE 7.22**
Rules successfully edited

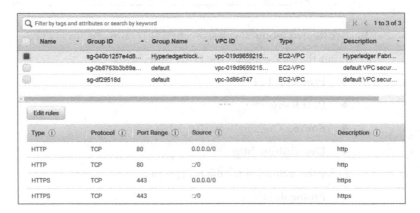

**12.** Select the security group again and view at the bottom of the screen the rules you created for HTTP and HTTPS. You should have only two rules that you created.

Note that in Figure 7.22, I added another rule to show the opposite of allowing all traffic with `0.0.0.0/0` versus disallowing all traffic with `::/0`.

**13.** Select VPC Dashboard to go back to the main VPC dashboard, as shown in Figure 7.23.

**FIGURE 7.23**
VPC Dashboard

## LAUNCHING AN EC2 INSTANCE

In AWS, we call the virtual machines EC2, which stands for Elastic Compute Cloud. EC2 will be used in the following blockchain deployment.

Launching your blockchain service requires you to deploy one or more virtual machines to run the blockchain services. In this book, I will deploy one for demo purposes initially.

To launch EC2 virtual machines, perform the following steps:

**1.** Go back to the main Management Console and select EC2 from Find Services, as shown in Figure 7.24.

**FIGURE 7.24**
Find Services in
Management Console

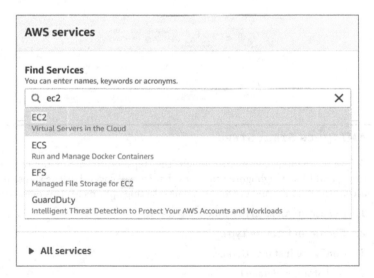

**2.** Select Launch EC2 Instances, as shown in Figure 7.25.

**FIGURE 7.25**
EC2 Dashboard

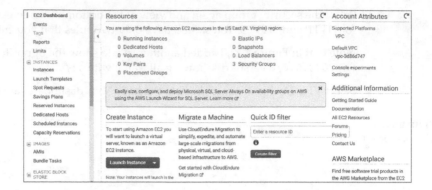

We want to launch an instance that will meet the requirements for scalability and cost. We could use this AMI as the default Amazon Machine Image (AMI) or even a Free Tier Eligible AMI if we choose for demo purposes. In actual development or production, you would want to be cautious about your VM configurations for performance, integration, support, and cost reasons.

Figure 7.26 shows the Choose an Amazon Machine Image (AMI) menu page.

**FIGURE 7.26**
Choose AMI Quick
Start page

### AMI QUICK START STEPS

Before proceeding, I want to highlight the steps located at the top of the screen. There are seven steps, and I have highlighted the ones that we will cover. For the steps that display *default*, we will accept the defaults and proceed without selecting options for this demo only.

1. Choose an Amazon Machine Image (AMI).

2. Choose an Instance Type.

3. Configure Instance Details.

4. Add Storage (default).

5. Add Tags (default).

6. Configure Security Group.

7. Review (default).

**3.** For demo purposes, select the first AMI—the Amazon Linux 2 AMI (default). You could, of course, run the template on other versions of Linux if you choose. At the time of writing, more than 30 versions of machine images are available.

Figure 7.27 shows the configurations available with the Amazon Linux 2 AMI image. We will go with what's available for the free tier.

**FIGURE 7.27**
Selecting the AMI configuration

**4.** Select your image T2 Micro (Free Tier Eligible) if available.

Note that Amazon may not have resources available in all regions at specific times due to the existing workload in the region.

In the next step, we will configure the EC2 instance.

**5.** Select Next: Configure Instance Details.

Figure 7.28 shows the initial Configure Instance Details settings we will configure.

**FIGURE 7.28**
Configuring the instance details

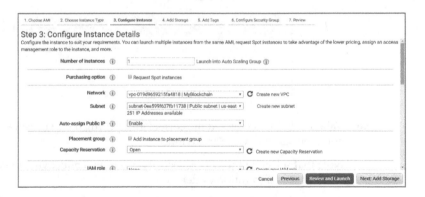

**6.** Select the network that was created—Hyperledger Note.

**7.** Select the subnet that was created—Public Subnet.

Note that your naming would likely be more specific in a development or production deployment.

**8.** Skip steps 4 and 5 and proceed to step 6.

Figure 7.29 shows that the security group that was created is selected. Note that the inbound rules do not show all the rules due to the screen scroll.

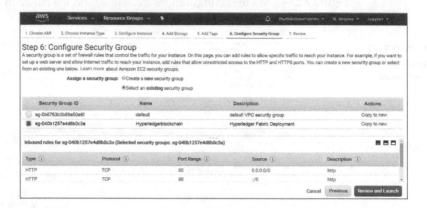

**9.** Select the security group for Hyperledger Fabric named Hyperledgerblockchain, as shown in Figure 7.29.

Figure 7.30 shows the Review Instance Launch page.

**10.** Validate that you selected the correct group, which will be reflected by a blue checkbox, and then select Review and Launch.

Note that selecting the wrong security group will effectively make your instance unusable without reconfiguration or deletion.

After hitting the Launch button, you will be prompted to create or save your key. The key is used for SSH access, so keep it safe on your desktop.

Figure 7.31 shows the key pair of the instance created.

Figure 7.32 shows the launch status of the EC2 instance.

**FIGURE 7.31**
EC2 key pair

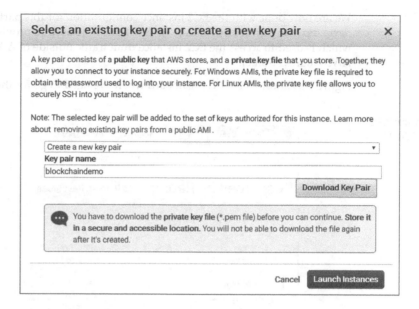

**FIGURE 7.32**
EC2 instance
launch status

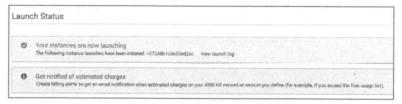

**11.** Select the small blue area with a crypto name that starts with "i."

This will bring you to the EC2 Dashboard.

**12.** Review the instance in the EC2 Dashboard, as shown in Figure 7.33.

**FIGURE 7.33**
EC2 Dashboard

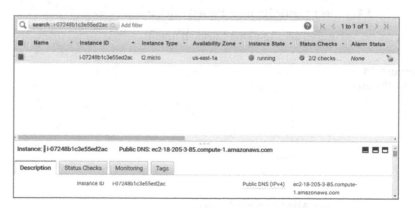

We are now done with the EC2 instance configuration for this part of the process. The next step is to provision an elastic IP. An elastic IP is used to provision a static public IP, which is used to access the EC2 instance from traffic outside of AWS going into AWS (ingress traffic).

Figure 7.34 shows the VPC Dashboard where we need to go for the next step.

**FIGURE 7.34**
VPC Dashboard

13. Select the AWS icon at the top of the console to bring you back to the AWS Management Console. From there, select the EC2 dashboard.

14. Select Elastic IPs from the left sidebar.

   Figure 7.35 shows the Elastic IP menu.

**FIGURE 7.35**
Elastic IP menu

15. Select Allocate New Address.

   Figure 7.36 shows that the allocation for the VPC elastic IP has succeeded.

**FIGURE 7.36**
Allocated new address

16. Select Close to go back to the Elastic IP menu.

    Figure 7.37 shows the IP configuration.

**FIGURE 7.37**
IP configuration

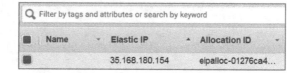

After validating our IP is allocated in the list, we can now proceed to provision a key pair. Key pairs are needed to provide SSH access.

17. Select the AWS icon at the top of the page and proceed to the AWS Management Console to select EC2.

    The AWS Management Console is the home page effectively and also shows the recently visited services such as EC2 and VPC.

18. Select EC2 from the AWS Management Console Recently Visited Services or search for it. Below is the EC2 Dashboard, specifically the resources.

    Figure 7.38 shows the one running instance, which we just launched.

**FIGURE 7.38**
AWS Management
Console

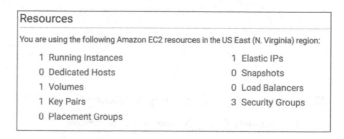

19. Validate your key pair is correct.

    Figure 7.39 shows the key pair created in previous EC2 steps.

20. Go to the Security Group section in the EC2 dashboard, as shown in Figure 7.40.

    We now need to create another security group for the EC2 instance and create rules.

**FIGURE 7.39**
Validate Key Pair
dialog box

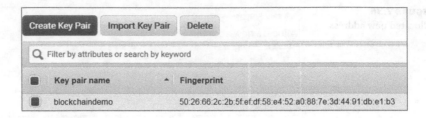

**FIGURE 7.40**
Security
Group dashboard

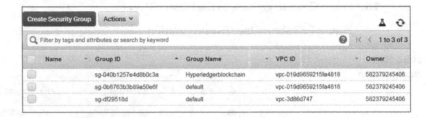

**21.** Select Create Security Group.

The Create Security Group dialog box appears, as shown in Figure 7.41.

**FIGURE 7.41**
Security group
configuration

**22.** Configure the security group as follows:

- **Security Group Name**: Blockchainbook
- **Description**: Blockchain security group
- **VPC**: myblockchain

**23.** Select Create.

The results should be similar to those shown in Figure 7.42 when it completes.

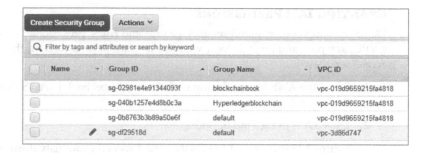

We now need to allow traffic into the security group, so we need to edit the rules of security group.

**24.** Select the blockchainbook security group and then click Edit.

The Edit Inbound Rules screen appears. Add the following to inbound rules, as shown in Figure 7.43:

◆ SSH for access from port 22

◆ Custom TCP for Monitoring port 8080

**25.** Select the SSH and Custom Rule items and also select MyIP, since it will pick up your source IP from logging into AWS automatically.

**26.** Select Save to save the rule and go back to the security group home page.

Figure 7.44 shows the newly created inbound rules.

| Type | Protocol | Port Range | Source | Description |
|---|---|---|---|---|
| Custom TCP Rule | TCP | 8080 | 0.0.0.0/0 | Monitoring |
| Custom TCP Rule | TCP | 8080 | ::/0 | Monitoring |
| SSH | TCP | 22 | 99.69.212.202/32 | ssh |

We can now move on to creating identity and access management rules and policies.

### GRANTING IAM PERMISSIONS

We have created our required security groups and rules, provisioned an elastic IP, and deployed a VPC, key pair, and an EC2. Now we have to grant permissions for the AWS EC2 service to access services.

1. Select the AWS icon at the top of the menu to get back to AWS Cloud Management Dashboard.

2. Enter **IAM** in the Find Services box.

   Figure 7.45 shows the IAM Dashboard. Proceed cautiously during the following steps, as a mistake will not allow the Hyperledger Fabric service to start.

**FIGURE 7.45**
IAM dashboard

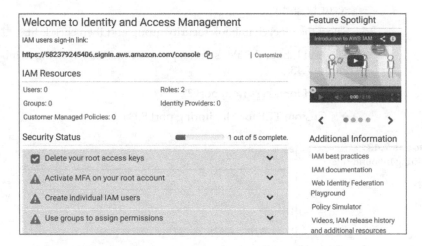

3. Select Policies from the left pane. We want to create a policy for S3 and CloudFormation.

   Figure 7.46 shows the IAM Policy menu. We need to create a policy that allows ECS to access S3.

**FIGURE 7.46**
IAM Policy menu

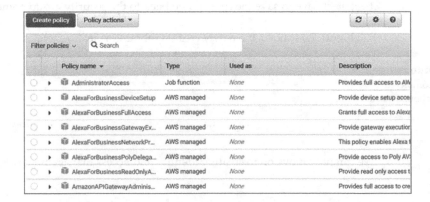

4. Create an S3 policy that allows Full Read Access but limited List by searching for S3 and selecting the AmazonS3FullAccess, as shown in Figure 7.47.

**FIGURE 7.47**
S3 policy search

5. Select the arrow by the AmazonS3FullAccess permissions. We need to ensure S3 has only read-only permissions, so we need to go into the S3 AmazonS3FullAccess policy and reduce the permissions.

   Figure 7.48 shows the limited permissions to select for AmazonS3ReadOnlyAccess. Now we need to do the same thing as earlier for setting up permissions in the policy for AWS ECR.

**FIGURE 7.48**
S3 limited permissions

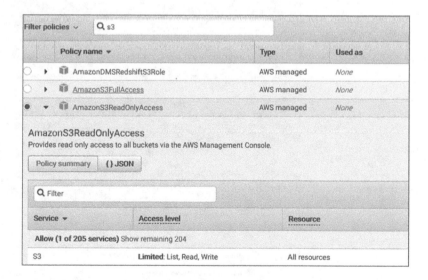

6. Go to Filter Policies and search for *Container*, as shown in Figure 7.49.

7. Select AmazonEC2ContainerRegistryReadOnly.

   Figure 7.50 shows the permission options available with specific services.

**FIGURE 7.49**
Container
Registry search

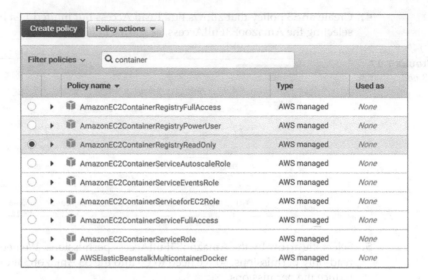

**FIGURE 7.50**
Container Registry
Limited Permissions

**8.** Select Create Policy.

The Create Policy dialog box appears, as shown in Figure 7.51.

**FIGURE 7.51**
Create Policy dialog

We need to add the policy via the policy editor. A policy defines the AWS permissions that you can assign to a user, group, or role. We will add S3 and then ECR.

9. Select the following:

♦ **Service**: S3

♦ **Actions**: Read

♦ **Resources**: All

Figure 7.52 shows the services available in AWS that we can provide policies for in S3.

**FIGURE 7.52**
Add Service Editor

**10.** Select Add Additional Permissions from the bottom of the screen and perform the same routine for ECR as you did for S3.

**11.** Select Review Policy.

The screen shown in Figure 7.53 will appear.

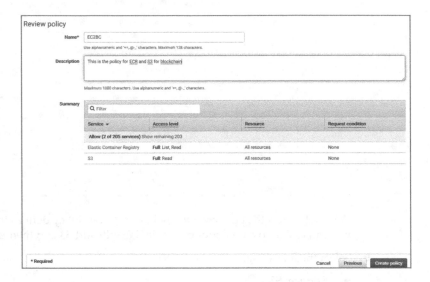

**12.** Enter **EC2BC** as the policy name, and enter **This is the policy for ECR and S3 for blockchain** as the description.

The services in the Summary section should be Elastic Container Registry and S3.

**13.** Select Create Policy.

Figure 7.54 shows the available options. Note the EC2BC policy has completed.

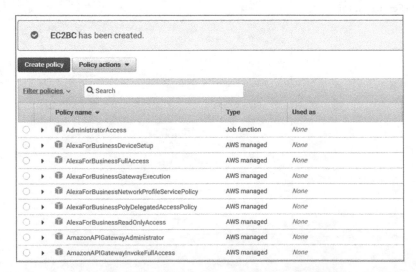

S3 is Amazon's object storage service, and ECR is Amazon's Elastic Container Registry, the container service that the Hyperledger Fabric containers are actually deployed on. I advise you to read the AWS IAM documents before configuring any AWS deployments because of the number of possible security vulnerabilities that could occur with improper setup. Refer to the following:

`https://docs.aws.amazon.com/IAM/latest/UserGuide/access_policies.html`

**14.** Create a role at the IAM Roles dashboard by selecting Roles in the left pane.

Figure 7.55 shows the IAM Roles dashboard, which appears more instructional than anything.

**FIGURE 7.55**
IAM Roles dashboard

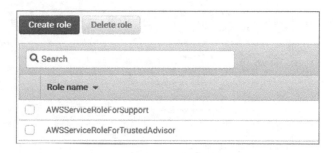

The role we need to create will be for EC2, and we will attach the policy we created earlier called EC2BC.

Figure 7.56 shows the roles creation dialog interface. Roles can be created for both users for what are machine-to-machine operations.

**FIGURE 7.56**
Creating a role

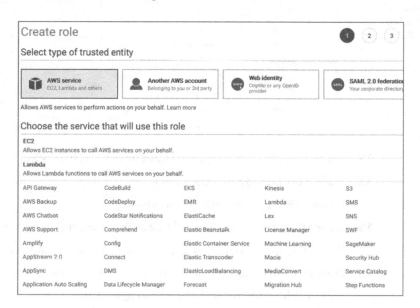

**15.** Select Create Role. The Create Role dashboard appears.

**16.** Highlight the EC2 service, and then select Next: Permissions.

Figure 7.57 shows the Attach Permissions Policies options.

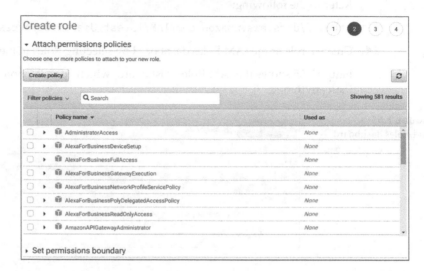

We will now go to the filter policy and add the policy EC2BC we created earlier.

Figure 7.58 shows the Create Role policy option for filtering.

**17.** Search the Filter Policies for the EC2BC policy and then select it.

**18.** Select Next:Tags to add a tag for easy identification.

Figure 7.59 shows the Add Tags window.

**19.** Enter **blockchain** as the key and **EC2** as the value, and then click Next: Review.

Figure 7.60 shows the review panel we will view before proceeding.

**20.** Enter **EC2Blockchain** for the role name and click Create Role.

A list of roles will appear, as shown in Figure 7.61.

**FIGURE 7.59**
Adding tags for
EC2 policy

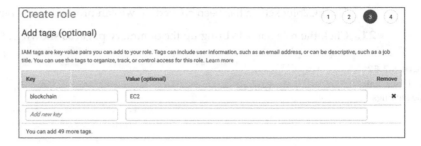

**FIGURE 7.60**
Reviewing tags for the
EC2 policy

**FIGURE 7.61**
EC2blockchain role
among the list of roles

The EC2blockchain has been created, so we can proceed to the next step.

**21.** Click the role name to bring up the Summary page, as shown in Figure 7.62.

**FIGURE 7.62**
EC2blockchain
role settings

Note the ARN, which stands for Amazon Reference Name; it's used to locate specific AWS resources. We can consider this similar to a namespace in the directory services world.

**22.** Validate the new role and note the instance profile ARN, which begins with a format of *arn:awsxxxx*. We will need to reference this ARN address later in the deployment.

We have finally created all the needed permissions, roles, and networking. We can now start to deploy our Blockchain template.

### DEPLOYING THE AWS BLOCKCHAIN TEMPLATE

In this section, we deploy the actual Hyperledger Fabric Template and then log in to our Hyperledger Fabric Deployment.

**1.** Go to the AWS Blockchain template page on AWS (`https://aws.amazon.com/block-chain/templates/getting-started/`).

Figure 7.63 shows the Blockchain template page on AWS. We will be using the Hyperledger Fabric CloudFormation template in this book.

**FIGURE 7.63**
AWS Blockchain
templates

2. Select the Northern Virginia Hyperledger template for Hyperledger Fabric.

   Note that Figure 7.64 and Figure 7.65 are the same template. The image was broken into two images because of the length of the template.

**FIGURE 7.64**
AWS Blockchain templates, part 1

Figure 7.64 shows the stack name and parameters preset in the top part of the template, but we still need to complete the lower half of the template.

3. Enter **blockchainbook** as the name of the stack and optionally enter the channel and the domain (or select Default).

4. Proceed to the lower part of the template by scrolling down.

   Figure 7.65 shows the lower part of the stack page. I preselected the ECC key pair and EC2 security group and entered the ARN number that we noted in step 21 in the previous section. In your case, select the appropriate EC2 instance and available variables that meet your deployment requirements or select the defaults.

**FIGURE 7.65**
AWS Blockchain
templates, part 2

It's important to double-check that we entered everything correctly, as modifying the template later could actually be more work than deploying a new one, depending on the variable misconfigured.

5. Enter the following:

   ◆ **ECC Key Pair**: blockchaindemo

   ◆ **EC2 Security Group**: blockchainbook

   ◆ **EC2 Instance Profile ARN**: Enter the EC2 instance ARN from step 21 in the previous section.

6. Select both the "I acknowledge" checkboxes (if you agree), and then click Create.

   Figure 7.66 shows the status of the Blockchain template deployment. This process could take up to 10 minutes depending on the AWS region workload. However, you can select the blockchainbook2 stack and proceed since the status is updated dynamically.

**FIGURE 7.66**
Stack creation initiated

| blockchainbook | | | | | | | | Delete | Update |
|---|---|---|---|---|---|---|---|---|---|
| Stack info | Events | Resources | Outputs | Parameters | Template | Change sets | | | |

**Events**

Q Search events

| Timestamp | ▼ | Logical ID | Status | Status reason |
|---|---|---|---|---|
| 2019-11-15 10:32:56 UTC-0500 | | blockchainbook | ⓘ CREATE_IN_PROGRESS | User Initiated |

**7.** Select the blockchainbook2 stack to proceed to the stack page shown in Figure 7.67.

The CloudFormation template launched, deployed our blockchain network, and now shows complete. Let's validate via the Event logs.

**FIGURE 7.67**
Stack completed

**8.** Select 4 More Events To Display to expand Events.

Figure 7.68 reflects the CloudFormation event logs and any other current information.

**FIGURE 7.68**
CloudFormation
event logs

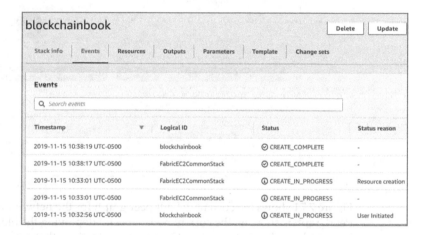

**9.** Select Outputs.

This will provide insight into the components of the blockchain deployment. Figure 7.69 shows outputs of the CloudFormation template.

**FIGURE 7.69**
CloudFormation outputs

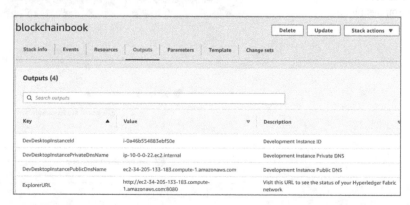

**10.** Select the URL for the ExplorerURL in the Key column. The ExplorerURL is Hyperledger Explorer, the same as a blockchain explorer that is used for traversing the blockchain ledger.

Hyperledger Explorer provides visual insight into the activity on our blockchain network. It also provides detailed status information on the components that are online as well as the peers that are on the network.

Figure 7.70 shows our new network deployment in the Hyperledger Explorer.

**FIGURE 7.70**
Hyperledger Explorer

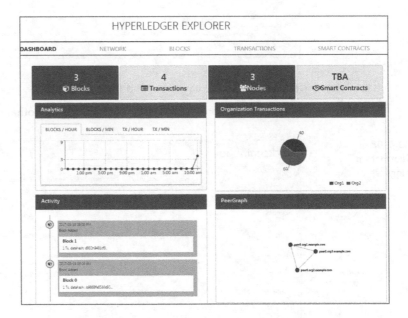

Figure 7.71 shows the current default peer graph for the network that was deployed. PeerGraph is showing the current nodes (peers) deploying the blockchain network. We have nodes online in three orgs. Orgs are organizations that represent a party (user). Because Hyperledger Fabric has just been installed and we have not installed chaincode yet, we won't have any further activity to explore.

**FIGURE 7.71**
PeerGraph explorer

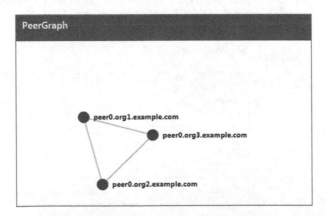

**11.** Select Network to validate that the peers are online.

The Hyperledger Explorer Network tab shows our nodes in Figure 7.72.

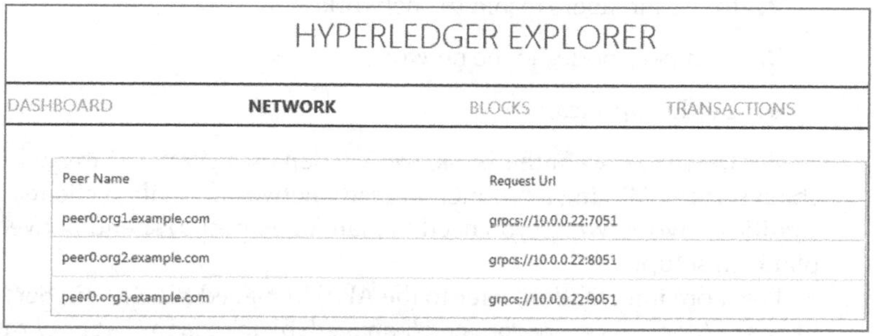

**FIGURE 7.72**
Hyperledger Explorer
Network tab

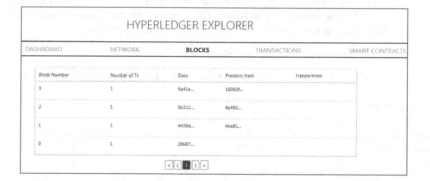

**12.** Select Blocks to validate that the blocks have been written.

Figure 7.73 shows that we have blocks written to the blockchain.

**FIGURE 7.73**
Hyperledger Explorer
Blocks tab

Let's review. We successfully configured a Blockchain template on AWS for Hyperledger Fabric. The process to set up networking, policies, and roles takes some time for the EC2 instance. The CloudFormation template allowed us to deploy a blockchain in only a few clicks after the initial configuration was done.

## Deploying AWS Managed Blockchain

AWS Managed Blockchain is a fully managed blockchain service that makes it easy to create and manage scalable blockchain networks using the open source Hyperledger Fabric and Ethereum frameworks. You can write smart contracts and applications and run them on the blockchain network to transact securely.

The membership in a Hyperledger Fabric network is your identity, which is known as an *organization*. This membership enables you to participate in the blockchain network. The membership rate also includes a Hyperledger Fabric certificate authority (CA) for user management and other shared network costs. You can create multiple network members in a given network.

There are four high-level steps to deploying the AWS Managed Blockchain service.

1. Create a blockchain network.

2. Invite members to join the network.

3. Add peer nodes to the network.

4. Deploy applications.

For the purposes of this book, we will deploy a simple Managed Hyperledger Fabric blockchain service. Having a production-ready network, installed clients, and channels requires significant work, which you need to plan for. Expect to spend between six to seven hours on this platform setup.

For more information, refer to the AWS Managed Blockchain Service documentation at https://docs.aws.amazon.com/managed-blockchain/latest/managementguide/ get-started-create-client.html.

## CREATING AN AWS MANAGED BLOCKCHAIN NETWORK

AWS Managed Blockchain is a relatively simple service that is provided by AWS for deploying a PaaS-based blockchain network. Developers can deploy nodes and then deploy their applications on the platform without worrying about the nodes.

1. Return to the AWS Management Console.

2. Enter **Managed Blockchain** in the Find Services box, as shown in Figure 7.74.

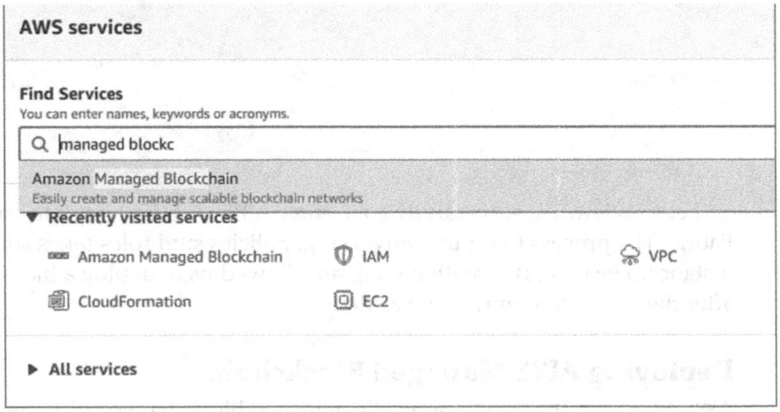

**FIGURE 7.74**
AWS Managed
Blockchain console search

This will bring up the Managed Blockchain service, as shown in Figure 7.75.

3. Click the Create A Network button.

The Create Blockchain Network screen will appear, as shown in Figure 7.76.

**FIGURE 7.75**
AWS Managed
Blockchain

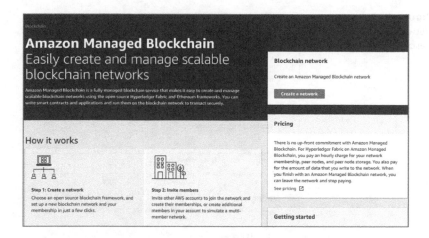

**FIGURE 7.76**
AWS Create Blockchain
Network page

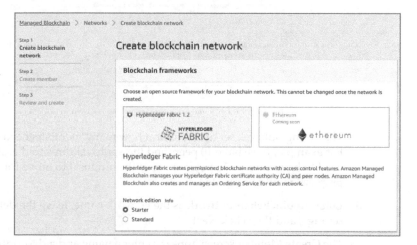

Two templates are available: one for Hyperledger Fabric and one for Ethereum (Coming Soon). There are also two choices for a network edition. A network edition is the subscription model. The network edition will determine attributes of the network, including the number of member, nodes per members, and other resources. The Starter network is limited in the images that can be deployed and the number of members and is considered a testing deployment. For production workloads, select the Standard network. The different editions have different consumption rates associated with the membership. For more information on pricing, refer to https://aws.amazon.com/managed-block-chain/pricing/.

**4.** Select the Hyperledger Fabric template. For demo purposes, we will use the Starter network edition.

The Network Name And Description dialog box appears, as shown in Figure 7.77.

**FIGURE 7.77**
Network Name and
Description dialog box

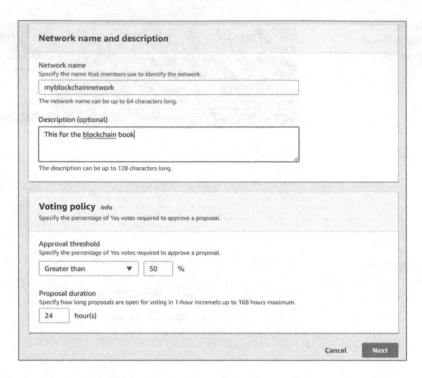

The voting policy is set up to confirm how many members need to approve a proposal. For example, if we have 10 peers and the approval threshold is 50 percent, then we would need to have 6 out of 10 peers approve the proposal to move forward; otherwise, the proposal would be rejected.

5. Enter **myblockchainnetwork** as the network name, leave the defaults for the Voting Policy settings, and then click Next.

   The Create Member screen appears; enter a name and a description (optional).

6. Scroll down to the bottom of the Create Member screen, as shown in Figure 7.78. Enter an admin username and password, and then click Next.

**FIGURE 7.78**
Create Member (CA)
admin settings

**Hyperledger Fabric certificate authority (CA) configuration** Info

Admin username
Specify an alphanumeric string that defines the login ID for the Fabric CA admin user.

    admin

The admin username can be up to 16 characters long. It must start with a letter, and can have alphanumeric characters.

Admin password
Specify an alphanumeric string that defines the password for the Fabric CA admin user

    ...........

☐ Show password

The admin password must be at least 8 characters long, and must contain at least one uppercase letter, one lowercase letter and one digit. It cannot have a single quote('), double quote("), forward slash(/), backward slash(\), @ or a space. The admin password can be up to 32 characters long.

Cancel    Previous    Next

**7.** The Review And Create screen appears, as shown in Figure 7.79. The Review And Create screen has two steps: Blockchain Network and Member.

## Review and create

### Step 1: Blockchain network                    [ Edit ]

**Network options**

| | | |
|---|---|---|
| Framework | Description | Voting policy |
| Hyperledger Fabric | This for the blockchain book | Greater than 50% |
| Network name | Network edition | Proposal duration |
| myblockchainnetwork | Starter | 24 hour(s) |

### Step 2: member                               [ Edit ]

**Member options**

| | | |
|---|---|---|
| Member name | Admin username | Admin password |
| blockchainadmin | admin | **** |
| Description | | |
| member for demo | | |

Cancel    [ Previous ]    **Create network and member**

**8.** Review that the information is correct, and then click Create Network and Member.

This creation process will take approximately 15 minutes to complete. After the wait, we should see a status update from Creating to Available, as shown in Figure 7.80.

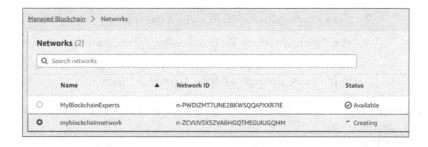

Managed Blockchain  >  Networks

**Networks** (2)

Q Search networks

| Name | ▲ | Network ID | Status |
|---|---|---|---|
| ○ MyBlockchainExperts | | n-PWDIZMT7UNE2BKW5QQAPXXR7IE | ⊘ Available |
| ◉ myblockchainnetwork | | n-ZCVUV5X5ZVA6HGQTMEGUIUGQHM | ⌐ Creating |

Figure 7.81 shows the updated Status now as Available.

**FIGURE 7.81**
Blockchain network
configuration
completion

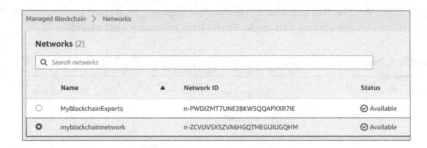

The blockchain network has been deployed and has created a managed blockchain network in AWS. Now we can move on to inviting members to join the network.

## INVITING MEMBERS TO JOIN THE NETWORK

Use the Create Member Proposals pane to remove members from the blockchain network or invite other AWS accounts to join.

1. From the list of networks in Figure 7.81, click your network's name to reveal a set of option tabs. The Create Member Proposals option is on the Members tab, as shown in Figure 7.82.

**FIGURE 7.82**
Network details

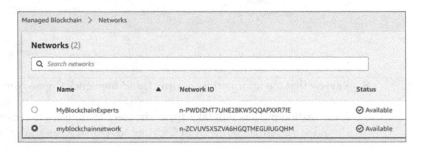

2. Click Propose Invitation to invite a member.

   The Create Invitation Proposal dialog appears, as shown in Figure 7.83.

   To invite a member, you need to have the member's AWS account number, which can be found in the account holder's Account Settings.

**FIGURE 7.83**
Create Invitation
Proposal dialog

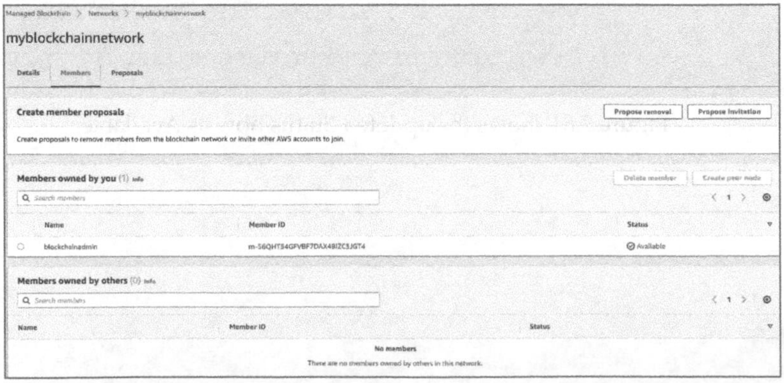

3. In the Submit Proposal As drop-down, choose the member in your account that submits the proposal. (I'm choosing Production because that's the account I am in.)

4. Enter an optional description, which will be displayed to other members.

5. Under "Specify AWS account(s) to invite to the network," enter the account number for the AWS account. Click Add to enter additional accounts. Once all the potential additions are listed, click Create.

6. The member who submits the proposal must also vote on it (the system doesn't assume you vote Yes!), so the next window is the proposal voting dialog shown in Figure 7.84.

   The proposal has various information such as details, status, actions, and more to review before proceeding.

**FIGURE 7.84**
Voting proposal
selection

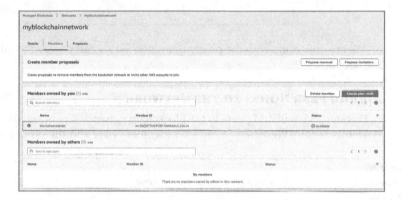

7. Select Propose invitation in the top right corner; you'll be asked to confirm your vote (Figure 7.85).

**FIGURE 7.85**
Vote On Proposal dialog

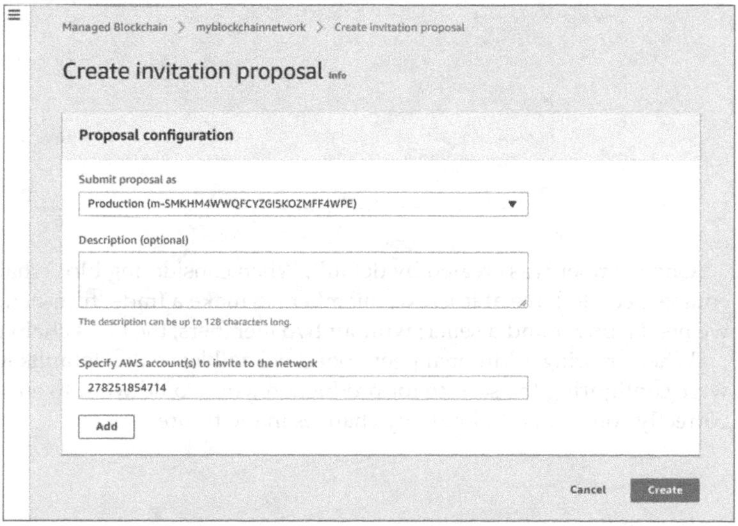

**FIGURE 7.86**
Policy completion

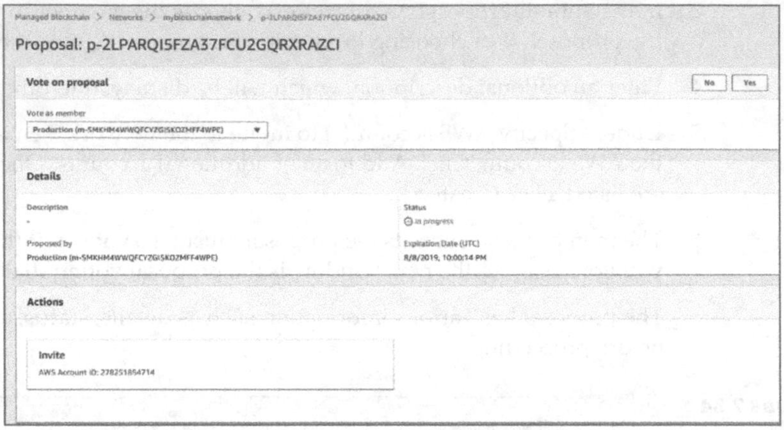

We are now done with the preconfiguration, so we can proceed to adding peers to the network.

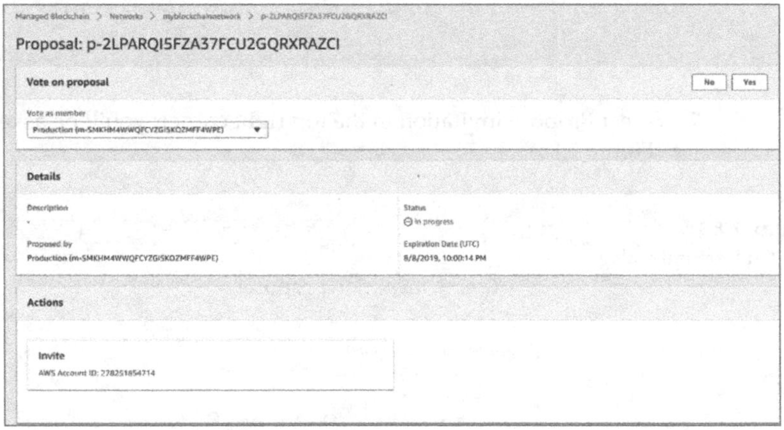

## Adding Peer Nodes to the Network

In this step, we will add peers to the blockchain network. Peers are also referred to as *members* in AWS blockchain. Figure 7.87 shows the members view and the proposal status.

**FIGURE 7.87**
Adding peers to the network

One member was created by default. When considering blockchain transactions, we would, of course, need to have at least two members to make a trade, transaction, purchase, etc. Effectively, we need a buyer and a seller; without two members, the blockchain network provides no value.

When creating additional peer nodes, we will leave the defaults for demo purposes. If you were configuring the service for production, you would want to ensure that the peer nodes are correctly configured to limit any changes in the future.

The steps are as follows:

1. Select Create Peer Node.

   The Create Peer Node screen will appear, as shown in Figure 7.88.

**FIGURE 7.88** Create Peer Node screen

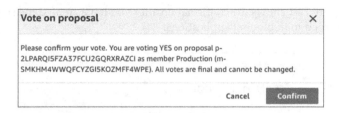

Vote on proposal
Please confirm your vote. You are voting YES on proposal p-2LPARQI5FZA37FCU2GQRXRAZCI as member Production (m-SMKHM4WWQFCYZGI5KOZMFF4WPE). All votes are final and cannot be changed.
Cancel
Confirm

2. Select an instance type and an Availability zone, and then click Create Peer Node. (I am leaving the defaults for the demo.)

   Figure 7.89 shows that the "Creating" process is still in progress. The process could take up to 10 minutes.

**FIGURE 7.89** Node creation process

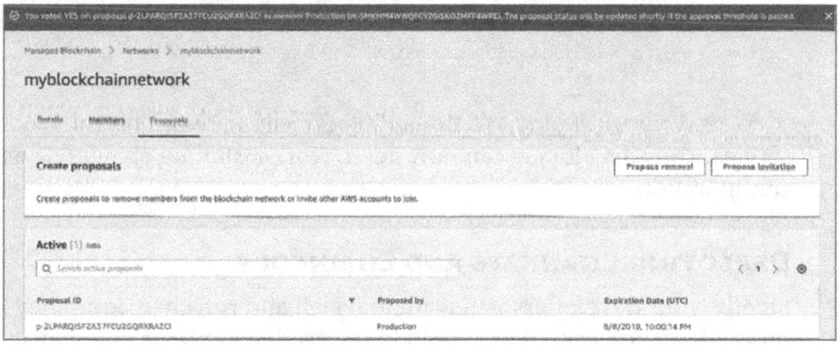

myblockchainnetwork
Create proposals
Propose removal
Propose invitation
Active (1)
Proposal ID
Proposed by
Expiration Date (UTC)
Production

Figure 7.90 shows that the status has changed from creating to completed.

**FIGURE 7.90** Node creation process has completed

myblockchainnetwork
Details
Members
Proposals
Create member proposals
Propose removal
Propose invitation
Create proposals to remove members from the blockchain network or invite other AWS accounts to join.
Members owned by you (1)
Delete member
Create peer node
Name
Member ID
Status
Production

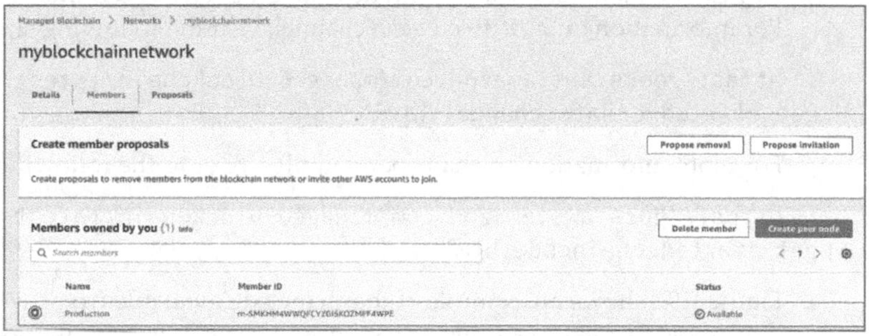

You may want to add additional peers for your development and production networks. You would want to confirm the EC2 instance template and Availability zone ahead of time, as you cannot change the configuration of the peer at the time of writing.

3. Create a second peer node by repeating the preceding steps.

Figure 7.91 shows the confirmation after you have created the second peer. You can now proceed to deploying applications.

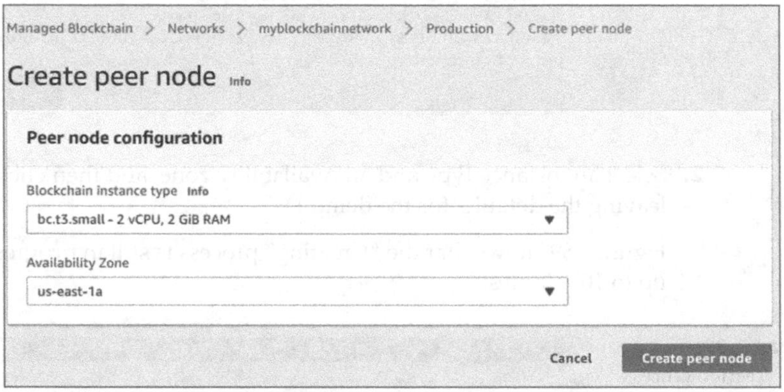

**FIGURE 7.91**
Second node creation
process has completed

We have now deployed a limited blockchain network on the AWS Managed Blockchain service. Your developers can now get to work installing chaincode as needed with further configuration.

## DEPLOYING CHANNELS AND CHAINCODE

Finally, your developers will want to install and run chaincode they have developed. Before proceeding, however, they would likely need to deploy a channel and then add chaincode.

In Hyperledger Fabric, a ledger exists in the scope of a channel. The ledger can be shared across the entire network if every member is operating on a common channel. A channel also can be privatized to include only a specific set of participants. Members can be in your AWS account, or they can be members who you invite from other AWS accounts.

For information on how to create a channel, visit the following site:

```
https://docs.aws.amazon.com/managed-blockchain/latest/managementguide/
get-started-create-channel.html
```

For more information on chaincode samples, refer to the following:

```
https://docs.aws.amazon.com/managed-blockchain/latest/managementguide/
get-started-chaincode.html
```

Figure 7.92 shows an example of the chaincode available from AWS.

The whole process to adding a channel and chaincode can take six to seven hours, depending on how your client setup goes. This is a new service out of preview mode, and, at the time of writing, limited information is available. The service looks promising for companies that want a limited blockchain network structure to get started developing blockchain applications on.

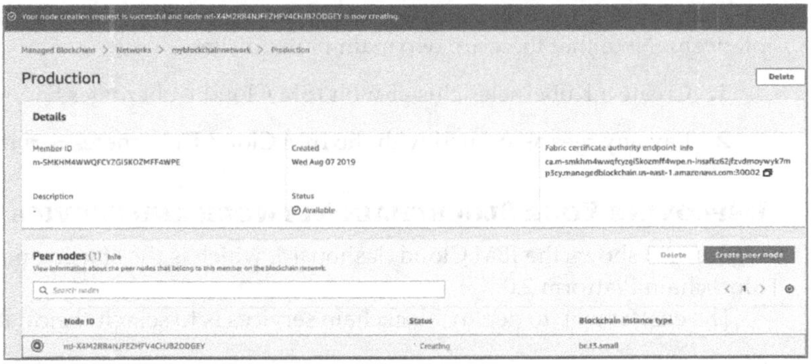

**FIGURE 7.92**
Chaincode example

**FIGURE 7.92**

# IBM Cloud Blockchain Platforms

IBM Cloud had several different blockchain deployment plans that can be used as an IBM Cloud subscriber. Blockchain Platform 1.0 is still in operation to current subscribers; however, it is closed to new subscribers. I mention IBM Blockchain Platform 1.0 only briefly because the platform was first to market and actually a pioneering, useful service for developers. IBM Blockchain was shut down effective December 31, 2019, to all customers.

**IBM Blockchain Platform 1.0**   IBM Blockchain was the first-generation platform that had two subscription models, Starter Plan and Enterprise Plan, which were true software as a service deployment models. It is important to note that existing clients can continue to add new members and create new networks until December 31, 2019.

**IBM Blockchain Platform 2.0**   IBM Blockchain Platform 2.0 is the second-generation platform and uses a pay-as-you-go model. That is, you pay only for resources used; there is no monthly fee. IBM Blockchain Platform 2.0 is the next generation of BaaS and is a flexible platform as a service (PaaS).

Both platforms deploy Hyperledger Fabric. The version of Hyperledger Fabric supported is maintained directly by IBM Cloud. Hyperledger Fabric allows components, such as consensus and membership services, to be plug-and-play for developers.

**REFERENCE**   For a quick refresher on Hyperledger Fabric, refer to Chapter 2, to the "Enterprise Permissioned Blockchains" section in Chapter 2.

## Blockchain Platform 2.0

Blockchain Platform 2.0, the second-generation platform, is vastly different from Blockchain Platform 1.0. Differences include the subscription model, user interface, deployment support, integration, and many other technical aspects. Blockchain Platform 2.0 provides an easy-to-deploy service that is deployed as a platform.

As discussed in the following sections, there are three high-level steps deploying the platform.

1. Set up Kubernetes cluster prerequisites if required. The prerequisite is to create a Kubernetes cluster if your IBM Cloud environment does not have a cluster available.

2. Link the cluster that was created.

3. Launch the Blockchain Platform 2.0 Console.

First, however, we need to select Blockchain Platform, which is the second-generation platform. Note that there are two main prerequisites.

1. Create a Kubernetes cluster with IBM Cloud Kubernetes Service in available regions.

2. Pay any fees associated with the IBM Cloud Kubernetes Service and your storage costs.

## DEPLOYING YOUR BLOCKCHAIN NETWORK AND SERVICE

Figure 7.93 shows the IBM Cloud dashboard, which is the starting point for deploying IBM Blockchain Platform 2.0.

The easiest way to deploy blockchain services is to search the catalog and select the service.

**FIGURE 7.93**
IBM Cloud dashboard

1. Select Catalog from the upper menu bar.

Figure 7.94 shows Blockchain as the only option. Blockchain shows up in the search, and the search will explain the service. To clarify for those that have not used IBM Cloud Blockchain is located under IBM Cloud as a database service.

**FIGURE 7.94**
Blockchain platform selection

2. Search for *blockchain*, and select the Blockchain service.

Figure 7.95 shows the blockchain service configuration variables for deployment. We can leave the service name, region, and resource groups at the defaults. We can also add tags to help identify resources for logging or compliance reasons, if required.

**FIGURE 7.95**
Blockchain platform
service selection

```
[ec2-user@ip-192-0-2-17 ~]$ docker exec -e "CORE_PEER_TLS_ENABLED=true" \
-e "CORE_PEER_TLS_ROOTCERT_FILE=/opt/home/managedblockchain-tls-chain.pem" \
-e "CORE_PEER_LOCALMSPID=$MSP" \
-e "CORE_PEER_MSPCONFIGPATH=$MSP_PATH" \
-e "CORE_PEER_ADDRESS=$PEER" \
cli peer chaincode install \
-n mycc -v v0 -p github.com/chaincode_example02/go
```

**3.** Click Create.

The next step is to review the blockchain platform wizard's main menu, as shown in Figure 7.96.

**FIGURE 7.96**
Welcome to the IBM
Blockchain Platform!

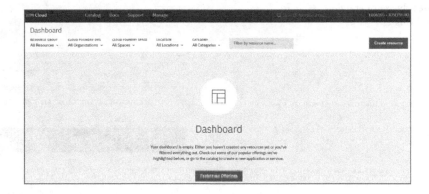

**4.** Select Continue to advance to the Create Cluster section, as shown in Figure 7.97.

We can choose to create a new cluster or use an existing cluster.

**FIGURE 7.97**
Create Cluster Optional

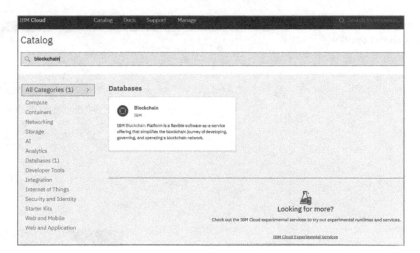

**5.** Click Create A New Cluster.

The choice in cluster deployment is quite critical for a production workload and your cloud spending. Review the following page for deployment options, especially for memory and worker nodes:

```
https://cloud.ibm.com/docs/services/blockchain?topic=blockchain-
ibp-v2-deploy-iks
```

**6.** Figure 7.98 shows the two choices for selecting a plan: Free and Standard.

**FIGURE 7.98**
Choosing to create a new free cluster or stand-ard cluster

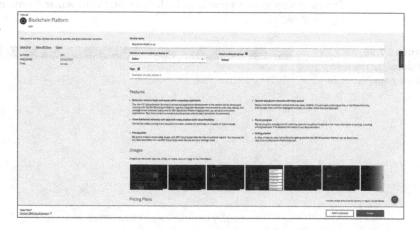

For the purpose of development, the Free option is fine; it will set up a limited deployment for testing. (If you choose the Standard option, you will be able to choose your deployment configuration, shown in Figure 7.99.)

**FIGURE 7.99**
New cluster options

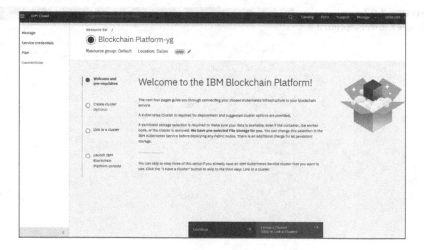

**7.** Click Free; then click Create Cluster. Figure 7.100 shows the cluster access information and is used to access the cluster and manage the cluster components. The cluster is being deployed, as shown in the top area next to mycluster. This process can take up to 20 minutes to complete.

**FIGURE 7.100**
Cluster creation progress

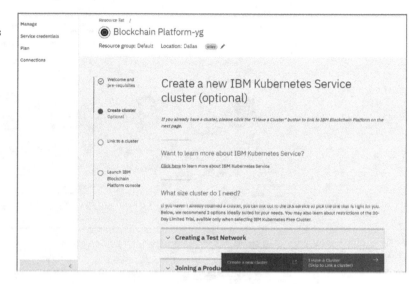

**8.** Select the Worker Nodes tab to proceed.

We can go to the overview window to see the progress of the worker nodes, as shown in Figure 7.101. The state is "Pending" for the worker nodes.

**FIGURE 7.101**
Worker node progress

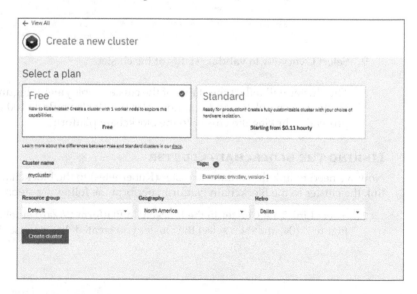

Figure 7.102 shows the Cluster Creation Overview window, which reflects 0 percent.

**FIGURE 7.102**
Cluster crea-
tion overview

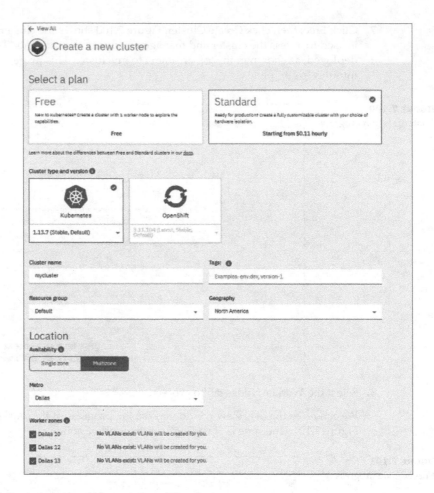

9. Select Overview to validate status of the cluster.

   The cluster will reflect the status of the cluster deployment. Figure 7.103 shows that the cluster has completed and is in normal status. It also reflects 100 percent, so we can proceed to linking the cluster to the blockchain platform.

## LINKING THE BLOCKCHAIN CLUSTER

Now we need to link the container cluster (Kubernetes) to the blockchain network services. To link the cluster to the Blockchain Platform, perform the following steps:

1. Select Link To A Cluster in the Blockchain Platform Wizard sidebar, as shown in Figure 7.104, and then select the cluster you created. In this case, it's called mycluster.

**FIGURE 7.103**
Cluster creation
completion

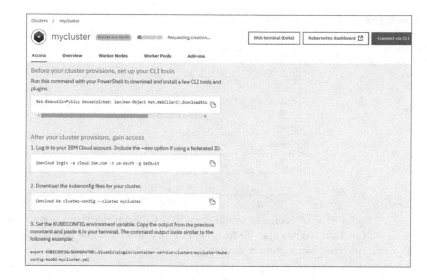

**FIGURE 7.104**
Linking to a cluster

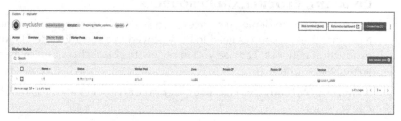

**2.** Select Deploy To Cluster at the bottom of the page.

Figure 7.105 shows that your cluster has been connected.

**FIGURE 7.105**
Cluster has
been connected

**3.** Select Launch The IBM Blockchain Platform Console. This will connect you to the console, as shown in Figure 7.106.

**FIGURE 7.106**
Welcome to the IBM
Blockchain
Platform screen

You will also receive an email from IBM Cloud welcoming you to the blockchain platform.
Now that we have set up the cluster and linked it to the blockchain network, we can move on to deploying blockchain resources.

## CREATING BLOCKCHAIN RESOURCES

The next step is to deploy resources such as peers, ordering nodes, and certificate authorities. Note that these resources need to be deployed in a specific order. Before deploying your production network, I advise you to review the blockchain deployment instructions and terminology here:

```
https://cloud.ibm.com/docs/services/blockchain?topic=blockchain-ibp-v2-
deploy-iks
```

You can get the whole platform ready in less than four to five hours if you follow the instructions for a limited deployment.

There is a really useful feature called Workflow. Workflow is similar to a wizard that provides guidance about what the next steps are in the deployment process. Select Get Started, as shown in Figure 7.107, to access the instructions and help pages.

**FIGURE 7.107**
Blockchain Platform
workflow instructions

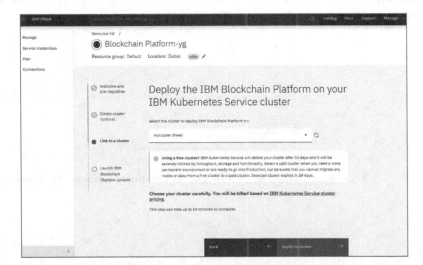

The Blockchain Platform has numerous resources, including videos and free classes. Blockchain developers should find the platform interesting and quite efficient to use once the learning curve is over.

---

**OTHER BLOCKCHAIN SERVICES**

Currently, there are more than 35 cloud-based blockchain services on the market from cloud providers and software providers. These blockchain services are generally IaaS- or PaaS-based solutions. Examples include Microsoft Azure and Google Cloud. For example, Google Cloud offers Cloud Marketplace solutions that are similar to AWS Blockchain templates.

Other providers, including Oracle, SAP, Deloitte, and Blockstream, are more niche focused.

---

## Summary

This chapter covered two of the most common blockchain as a service (BaaS) providers, AWS and IBM, as well as their blockchain deployment processes. Numerous other providers also provide services that are more niche markets, such as Azure, Oracle, or Digital Ocean, that are valid solutions for the right use case.

BaaS is a cloud services offering that allows customers to leverage cloud-based solutions to build, host, and use their own blockchain apps, smart contracts, and functions on the blockchain.

Deploying BaaS on AWS is more time consuming because you need to set up EC2 and the affiliate networking configurations. However, once your VPC, security groups, and policies are created, you can simply deploy the Hyperledger Fabric template, which is through a CloudFormation template.

Finally, IBM deploys Hyperledger Fabric on its managed blockchain service, and deploying it is simple. Blockchain Platform 2.0 is the next-generation platform that provides developers a rapid on-ramp to a managed blockchain platform.

# Chapter 8

# Enterprise Blockchain Use Cases

This chapter covers some of the potential focus areas of enterprise blockchain use cases that can provide value to not only the organization but also their suppliers, customers, and partners. I will touch on just a few of the use cases that have been announced, although new announcements are made every day.

Blockchains generally need to have both technical and business merits for an enterprise to consider the initial use case for a blockchain solution. In other words, the blockchain use case needs to address at least the technical or business merits; ideally, however, it will address both. Companies really need to have merits that make both business and technical sense and that drive value for the company.

Technical merits can be achieved in organizations that are slow to adopt new technologies. Generally, companies that are behind on initiating innovation can derive value from an innovation easier.

Business merits, on the other hand, can be more challenging to define such as how a blockchain can provide for a consistent solid return of investment (ROI) or does that new blockchain application provide a more consistent user experience. A company might realize technical benefits but not any tangible business benefits such as cost savings. However, this is becoming less of an issue as the evolution of blockchain value is properly defined, especially to organizations that are reaching end of life on some of their current legacy applications.

A slew of new use cases are being announced daily, and real-world implementations are being launched around blockchains such as Ethereum, Hyperledger, Quorum, and Corda.

Several of the more compelling areas of acceptance of blockchain technology are found in the financial, logistics, and government sectors. These sectors show no signs of slowing down in the acceptance of blockchains. Other industries are clearly showing signs of acceptance, including manufacturing, mining, and retail.

The goal of this chapter is to give you a wide view of the potential use cases for blockchain. It's evident that blockchain is more than cryptocurrency and payments. Transfer of value is not just transferring money from point A to point B. Blockchain can also be utilized to transfer real estate deeds and other assets.

**NOTE** The global blockchain business value will reach $2 trillion by 2030. —IHS Markit

## Merits of Blockchain Acceptance

As with any new technological innovation, there are challenges to the acceptance of the value of blockchain technology to the enterprise and the consumer. These challenges can revolve around the technology, costing models, and even human perception. For example, in the 1970s and 1980s, we had the war of Betamax (Sony) and VHS (JVC). Betamax was superior in many ways, and it became simpler to use with more excellent picture quality than VHS. Its tapes were smaller and easier to store. You would think that Betamax would have won the war. However, VHS was able to extend its recording time to around 4 hours. Consumers preferred recording movies, and this was a challenge with Betamax since it could record for about one hour due to the length of its tape. Sony did not innovate in time to meet the real consumer requirements and did not understand the end consumer, resulting in the end of Betamax.

The same can be said for enterprise technologies as well as other consumer technologies. Some enterprise technologies around networking and data storage have clear advantages over others. However, sometimes the better technology just does not win.

Why? It's clearly about marketing, consumer messaging and support, and costing models. Understanding your customer or enterprise requirements is critical to gain acceptance of your blockchain projects.

Some of the more common challenges to blockchain acceptance could be around technology, costing models, and human perception. These challenges are for the most part similar to what you have experienced with other technologies sales and solutions.

Common challenges include the following:

◆ Budgets and cost models

◆ Decentralization of resources

◆ End user experience of dapps

◆ Training of both executives and end users

◆ Vendor acceptance

◆ Integration of blockchain services

◆ Political environment

◆ Compliance requirements

In addition to the challenges, however, there are clearly a number of benefits that blockchain can accomplish in many different industry sectors. This section covers some of these merits.

## Technical Merits of Blockchain

The technical merits of blockchains can range from the use of cryptography to the implementation of smart contracts. These technical merits are generally accepted to be proven and effective around blockchain.

It is important to remember that blockchains are not built on new technologies. They are, for the most part, built from a molding of three existing technologies that have been around for decades. The molding of these technologies presents innovations for enterprises to create efficiencies, provide transparency, and results in numerous other benefits.

These technologies are proven and effective in their implementations from a historical perspective are as follows:

◆ Peer-to-peer networking

◆ Cryptography

◆ Computer code (smart contracts)

When we consider these technologies, we can see how simple the use cases for each technology could be applied at a high level. For example, encryption is used to ensure that your message data is sent securely from the sender to the receiver in such a manner that it cannot be read by anyone other than the receiver. Privacy, security, and confidentiality could all be achieved.

I appreciate how companies can view peer-to-peer (P2P) networking negatively and want to shut down discussions about it. Centralization is comfortable for companies since they're in the driver's seat. With decentralization, companies are effectively in the passenger seat regarding control and governance.

At its truest sense, decentralization is all about trust. Successful blockchains work in a manner of true consortium with a shared responsibility model. A shared responsibility model is where all the consortium members collaborate and contribute finances and labor.

A smart contract is nothing more than the implementation of computer logic, aka computer code. Essentially, either we receive a positive result or the smart contract (code) does not execute the proposal.

Smart contracts provide the greatest benefits when there is an intermediary process that was once a manual process that now can be removed. Smart contracts are not complex. There are containers in most blockchains with limited functions that could be executed.

Another way to describe a smart contract is as a microservice. A microservice contrasts to a traditional, monolithic application, which, from a software development perspective, is designed and built as one integrated application. An application could have 10, 20, or even hundreds of microservices. Microservices can aid in the development of an application and provide significant cost savings around manual processes. Smart contracts are microservices, and microservice, which can be combined to create a distributed application.

For more on microservices, smart contracts, and dapps, refer to Chapter 10, Chapter is now "Blockchain Development"

Removing manual processes through the implementation of smart contracts provides clear efficiencies around costing models, error rates, and the processing speed of a transaction. For example, if your bank once had transactions, such as a wire transfer, that would take hours or even a day to be executed and confirmed, this type of process would be a great target for a smart contract to provide value and, therefore, a possible use case.

Technical merits provide other benefits, such as user experience, integration, or a more efficient experience for the enterprise. However, some technical aspects—such as not being able to achieve transactions per second (TPS), latency, risk mitigation, or other significant concerns—can hinder a use case implementation.

## Business Merits of Blockchain

The most compelling use cases focus on reducing inefficiencies, providing transparency, and meeting compliance demands that companies face in this dynamic world. For example, removing inefficiencies could unlock value in areas of existing industry where trusted intermediaries were once required to record, validate, and reconcile transactions. This would be a change of a business model, which could be very disruptive to the status quo.

Generally, enterprises want to realize cost savings and create efficiencies in their current transactional processes. If you can provide cost savings in your blockchain solution, then you are well on your way to having a potential use case.

### Common Elements of Blockchain Adoption

Some common elements that can be assessed by the blockchain-focused organization are whether or not a blockchain deployment could be performant. Elements such as transparency will be realized in a public blockchain, whereas others will be realized in a permissioned or a private blockchain.

The following are some commonly realized advantages of private blockchains:

◆ Networking and collaboration benefits

◆ User experience enhancements

◆ Security and risk mitigation

◆ Privacy enhancements

◆ Transparency and performance

◆ Cost savings for the enterprise

## Financial Sector Use Cases

Blockchain is driving incredible disruption across the financial services industry. Contrary to what is being portrayed by the media, this disruption is a "clear and present" danger to parts of the financial sector. The sector has a slew of inefficiencies that are being updated by blockchain consortium or even business models that are being compacted by the loss of revenue by cryptocurrencies such as Bitcoin, Litecoin, and Monero.

On the other hand, for the banking sector, blockchain can offer a cost savings exercise when properly specified with appropriate use cases. For example, it could lower the cost for compliance reporting requirements by more than 70 percent for some dedicated financial services companies.

The financial sector is effectively being disrupted by blockchain technologies not just on one battlefront but on multiple battlefronts. The distributed ledger platforms that have defined concise leadership in the space include Ripple, Corda, and Hyperledger.

The antiquated financial sector is ripe for both disruption and innovation that clearly is required for the globalization of consumerism. The SWIFT network is more than 40 years old and relies on a network infrastructure that has not been improved upon since its inception. Companies such as Ripple have effectively challenged the status quo on cross-border payments through well-deployed infrastructure, detailed member benefits, and clearly defined efficiency opportunities for its members.

**NOTE** "Global payments are undeniably going through a sea change, led by financial institutions adopting blockchain to fix their customers' broken payments experience. Now more than 100 financial institutions are looking to Ripple as the solution to the problem. . . ." —Brad Garlinghouse, CEO of Ripple

A study released by Juniper Research states that by deploying blockchain technology, financial institutions stand to generate savings amounting to more than $27 billion on cross-border settlement transactions before the end of 2030 (`https://www.juniperresearch.com/press/press-releases/blockchain-deployments-to-save-banks-more`).

These numbers are quite impressive, and these potential savings are being discussed in the boardrooms across the world.

This section discusses the following areas around the use cases for the financial sector's significant investments into the blockchain:

◆ Cross-border payments

◆ Know your customer (KYC)

◆ Peer-to-peer (P2P) lending

◆ Security tokenization

These are just a few selected areas in the financial sector that are clearly benefiting or will likely be benefitting from blockchain. I found more than 120 different financial use cases at the time of writing.

## Cross-Border Payments

Companies that provide value by processing payments, processing cross-border payments/ transfers, and offering other financial intermediary services are typically a clear target for blockchain adoption and for that matter, initiators of blockchain innovation.

The inefficient payment protocols and payment systems of the legacy banking networks. Blockchain provides instantaneous payment solutions without payment intermediaries.

◆ The historical fragmentation of payment networks that have been in existence for more than 50 years. Blockchain is a newer and more efficient approach that is able to cross borders without fragmentation.

◆ Intentionally high costs around payments and their processing fees that are passed on to consumers. Blockchain costs are a fraction of what a traditional payment processor charges.

◆ Ever increasing and more complex compliance regulations and governance required in the banking sector. Blockchain is a peer to peer to platform that is not heavily regulated and requirements are limited as of today.

◆ The lack of transparency coupled with low consumer trust that has been inherent in the banking systems. Blockchain can be deployed in a public manner where anyone can join, send and receive funds and even view transactions. Transparency is the key benefit here.

Two examples of innovation through a consortium method are R3 and Ripple, which have effectively written the book on creating value around blockchain for their consortium members.

The concisely documented benefits—such as cost efficiencies, processing speed, and compliance adherence—are just a starting point for financial institutions. Reducing complexity, increasing efficiency, and providing value are generally the hallmarks of these leading companies.

Financial institutions typically have significant overhead in areas such as compliance, legal, and personnel. In the case of payments, there has traditionally been several challenges for organizations. Payments are considered inefficient and generally more complex than needed.

An organization that has intermediaries that effectively process, validate, and post transactions can benefit immediately from employee costs in all three of those areas.

◆ Ancillary benefits for the enterprise could be reduced fraud, elimination of chargebacks, and customer retention.

◆ Ancillary benefits for the customer base would be transparency, reduced fees, and increased efficiency of funds receipts/deposits.

Organizations traditionally have had challenges around payments, such as compliance requirements, systems that are not integrated, and costly inefficiencies. There are blockchains that can provide some significant efficiencies around cross-border payments. One such platform is Ripple.

Ripple has been increasing the acceptance of its cross-border payment technology at a rapid pace and onboarding a slew of new companies with their payment processing benefits. At the time of writing, 19 companies either have already implemented XRP for cross-border payments or are planning to, according to the latest report from Ripple Labs.

R3 recently announced that it will be providing XRP integration into its R3 Corda platform as well. R3 Corda is a consortium of some of the world's largest financial institutions. R3 Corda Consortium created an open source distributed ledger platform called Corda and has a wide acceptance in the financial industry. Its partner network has more than 60 companies. This integration of Ripple XRP integration opens the door to even more exciting and efficient opportunities with Corda.

Part of the Ripple ecosystem includes XRapid and Ripplenet. Ripplenet is the actual payment network of more than 200 banks and payment providers. XRapid is a liquidity solution that eliminates delays in global payments on Ripplenet while also dramatically lowering their cost, thus making cross-border payments instant and inexpensive.

Figure 8.1 shows how a payment transfer with Ripple works with xRapid settlement.

**FIGURE 8.1**
Ripplenet payment network

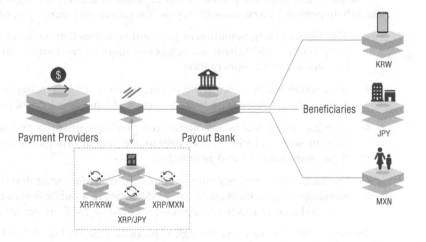

Ripple is a real-time gross settlement system (RTGS), currency exchange, and remittance network that has a well-established footprint in the financial sector.

The following are some highlights about Ripple and its underlying structure:

♦ Ripple enables global payments through its digital asset called *Ripples* or *XRP*. XRP is the native token on Ripple's blockchain.

♦ Ripplenet is the private implementation of Interledger (ILP), which is the open protocol suite for sending payments across different ledgers.

♦ xCurrent is Ripple's enterprise solution that is responsible for facilitating the instantaneous settlement and end-to-end tracking of cross-border payments between RippleNet members.

♦ The RippleNet ecosystem has two categories for participants: network members (banks and payment providers) and network users (consumers and corporations).

♦ Transactions per second (TPS) average 1,500 TPS, a substantial TPS for an enterprise blockchain.

From a technical perspective, there is a lot to consider and understand about Ripple. Ripple has clearly defined several use cases around cross-border payments and other significant aspects in the financial sector. You can find out more about Ripple at `https://www.ripple.com/`.

## Know Your Customer

Knowing your customer (KYC) is one area that blockchain shows some promise for improvements. KYC processes are commonplace within traditional businesses for many good reasons. The main reason is government compliance. Other reasons are around the goal of reducing fraud, reducing chargebacks, and reducing any liability exposure.

Financial institutions are required to participate in the KYC process with customers to comply with regulations that are routinely identified as either one or both of the following:

♦ Anti-money laundering (AML)

♦ Countering the financing of terrorism (CFT)

Organizations have challenges around KYC, most of which include the following:

♦ High validation costs

♦ Redundancy in companies with multiple lines of business

♦ Customer satisfaction

♦ Lack of complete audit trails

Figure 8.2 shows how a blockchain-based KYC solution works.

**FIGURE 8.2**
KYC blockchain solution

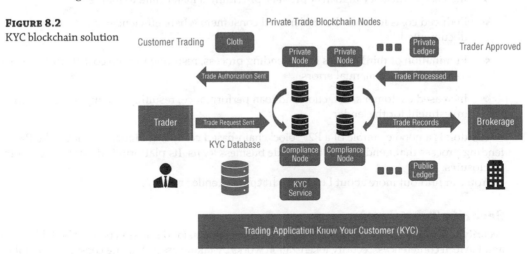

The customer typically provides KYC documents each time they require services from different organizations. This could also be true if you have tried to open a bank account one day and then an IRA a week later. They may require verification of the same documents such as your state identification, SSN number, tax ID, or even credit information.

Imagine if companies were able to share customer KYC information in a secure and easy manner while retaining the confidentiality and privacy of customer documents. This could provide some great benefits for the customer and the financial institutions. A consortium blockchain could be implemented to address this and would instantly reduce some redundancies since the consortium members would share the costs.

Blockchain will now allow for an accumulation of data from multiple authoritative service providers into one single, cryptographically secured database.

Verifications by a blockchain architecture will present the opportunity for financial institutions to provide a faster KYC solution for their customer base. This alleviates the headaches such as wait times on certain transactions after an account is opened.

The following are some benefits of a KYC blockchain:

- Increased customer satisfaction and higher retention

- Reduced operational costs while increasing efficiency

- Increased features such as audit trails, logging, and search

Blockchains can address most compliance requirements well due to their immutability—specifically, around maintaining records of customer identification, transactions, and privacy data.

## Peer-to-Peer Lending

Anyone who has ever taken out a loan knows that the process can be cumbersome and inefficient. A decentralized blockchain solution can provide clear benefits.

- Increased efficiency in loan approvals, providing a faster time to market

- Reduced costs for both the lenders and consumers where efficiencies can be clearly documented

- Elimination of third parties in the lending process, resulting in both cost efficiency as well as a reduction in manual errors

- Increased customer satisfaction and loan performance, resulting in a higher return on investment for the lender

Lendoit is a good example of a P2P blockchain-based company. Figure 8.3 shows the P2P lending process that Lendoit uses to provide business loans. Its platform is decentralized from its disclosures.

You can find out more about Lendoit at https://lendoit.com/.

## Security Tokenization

Security tokenization is one area of FinTech that is clearly a major discussion point at both blockchain and FinTech conferences. Security tokenization works by taking assets that are considered illiquid and making them liquid by "tokenization" on a blockchain-based platform. For example, a major financial trading firm could take a collateralized real estate fund that has real estate assets and essentially make fractions of a 20-story building available to noncertified investors.

**FIGURE 8.3**
P2P Blockchain lending

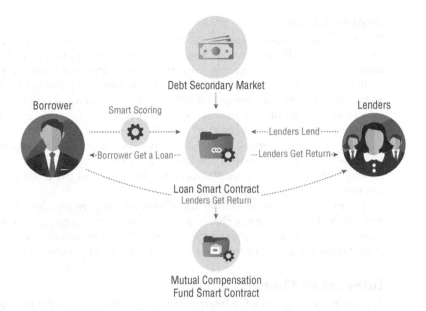

**NOTE** "It's inevitable that security tokens will transform equity just as bitcoin has transformed currency, because they afford the owner a direct, liquid economic interest and the expedited delivery of proceeds. Every type of ownership can be tokenized, which is a massive multi-trillion dollar addressable market." —Carlos Domingo, SPICE Capital

When it comes to tokenization, it is important to realize that the Security and Exchange Commission has provided two categories of tokens: security tokens and utility tokens. The main concern for providing a new blockchain project is to understand which type of token they will be releasing to the public as an investment with strict regulations.

The Howey test is used to determine whether a token is a security token or a utility token. The test was devised by the U.S. Supreme Court to determine whether certain transactions qualify as "investment contracts." For more about the Howey test, see https://consumer.findlaw.com/securities-law/what-is-the-howey-test.html.

A crypto token that passes the Howey test is historically deemed a security token. This type of token derives its value from an external, tradable asset. Because these tokens are deemed a security, they are subject to federal securities regulations. If all the regulations are properly met, then these tokens have immensely powerful use cases.

# Logistics Use Cases

Logistics is an industry segment that has hundreds of possible use cases around transport, farm to table, mining operations, and many more industry verticals. There really is not a shortage of use cases for logistics. This section covers three areas that I feel will have significant impact on the acceptance of blockchain technology.

## Supply Chain

One the more interesting use cases for blockchain is in the logistical area of supply chain management. One of the biggest challenges that enterprises might deal with is effectively managing their supply chain and handling transparency for partners, customers, and regulators.

In the use case for logistics, the use of a blockchain can provide an immutable historical record, for example, of a mining operation and for its material purchases the ability to validate when a specific lot of gold, diamonds, or other commodities were mined and from which mine. This can provide transparency as well for the consumer.

One of the more compelling logistics supply chain blockchains is called *TrustChain*. A collaboration between jewelry industry conglomerates, TrustChain enables customers to track their jewelry from source to dealer. The consortium is now past the proof-of-concept stage and expanding its membership.

The main benefit realized from TrustChain is transparency across the entire diamond, gold, and finished jewelry supply chains. Jewelry customers can be assured that their products were sourced ethically, efficiently, and transparently. Consumers will be provided with a permanent digital record of all the transactions in the diamond and jewelry value chain.

## Internet of Things

There is no question that the Internet of Things (IoT) is one of the technologies that is gaining a significant amount of interest. The convergence of blockchain and IoT has been prioritized by the blockchain industry as one of the most promising use cases for blockchain. Building smart machines that can communicate and operate via blockchain has clear advantages.

By their very nature, blockchain records are transparent; therefore, activity can be tracked and analyzed by any party authorized to connect to the network. For example, tracking, health monitoring, or fitness devices could use a decentralized ledger that would provide an immutable record of behavior.

The data collected by these devices could be stored on a ledger not only for immutability but for data standardization. For example, a blockchain platform called *IOTA* is a decentralized transactional platform on various development projects. IOTA's Tangle is a transactional data transfer and settlement system for connected devices. These connected devices could be connected and validated to a decentralized ledger.

The following are the three main benefits of blockchain for IoT according to IBM:

- Building trust

- Cost reduction

- Acceleration of transactions

From IBM's point of view, it's clear that blockchain and IoT will likely proceed into a deeper relationship in the sense of integration with other platforms.

The security and transparency provided by numerous blockchain-based platforms can empower but also enhance smart cities' use cases relying on shared information, common databases, ledger features, and other benefits.

For more information on IOTA, see `https://www.iota.org/`.

## Farm to Table

Perhaps one of the more complex use cases would be a "farm-to-table" use case in the agriculture sector. Farms are generally slow to invest and adapt to technology, and record keeping is not a consistent process. Blockchains could resolve a significant issue around recording where a product came from, where it is in the supply chain, and when it will arrive at its destination. A significant number of blockchain-focused agricultural solutions focus on improving food source traceability as well as accountability.

However, this brings into play an amazing use case of identifying challenges that can be addressed by implementing a blockchain. The challenges include provenance, traceability, transparency, and even compliance concerns around U.S.-based customs requirements.

Now more than ever, customers are demanding more accountability from their supermarkets and food suppliers. There is clearly a need for a more transparent producer-to-consumer system.

A blockchain could enable not just a food supply chain but any chain that requires traceability. This would enable a true use case of transparency for a food chain entirely verified by the consortium members. For example, if there were a concern around food safety, then all parties involved would have clear transparency, provenance, and even the ability to address other concerns through a blockchain-based implementation of a farm-to-table solution.

One of the more compelling use cases addresses the food supply chain directly. Figure 8.4 references the food supply chain with high-level details to show the number of intermediaries, sources, stakeholders and so on.

**FIGURE 8.4**

Example of Hyperledger Food Supply Chain

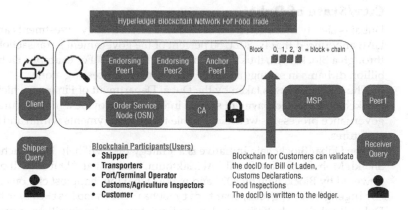

Stakeholders could be farmers, food inspectors, logistics providers, distributors, consumers, and even governments. The challenge is that the present food logistics structure is maintained at different levels by several intermediate stakeholders.

In the case of food source accountability, blockchain can provide for transparency, trust, and provenance. Enabling blockchains can provide significant advantages to stakeholders, including real-time access, trusted data, and peer-to-peer networking. When blockchain is combined with IoT, the benefits can easily be realized during the logistics processes. For example, some benefits could be that farmers are paid more quickly traceability is immediate, insurance claims could be processed faster and so on.

For more information on a farm to table blockchain solution, see https://tefoodint.com/.

# Government Use Cases

It's clear that certain government entities could benefit from blockchain implementations, which is why we are seeing a significant growth in blockchain use cases for government customers. This is counterintuitive since anyone who has worked directly with government organizations—whether federal, state, or local—knows that those "wheels" generally turn somewhat slowly.

Governments such as Dubai are the first-to-market leaders when it comes to investments in blockchain technology but also for providing real-world implementation road maps for others to follow.

The federal government of Australia recently announced a national blockchain roadmap strategy and an additional investment of AU$100,000 in further funding. That was on top of the AU$100,000,000 that was already committed.

Additionally, the Swedish land-ownership authority conducted a successful proof of concept (POC) between individuals to buy and sell properties on a blockchain.

Numerous other countries are looking at blockchain. Chile, China, Estonia, Singapore, Switzerland, Brazil, and Canada all have announced significant roadmaps, proof of concepts, or intentional direction to act on blockchain implementations.

IBM has released a survey, titled "Building Trust in Government: Exploring the Potential of Blockchains," that's worth a look. You can find it at `https://www.ibm.com/downloads/cas/WJNPLNGZ`.

## City/State of Dubai

Dubai is clearly in the forefront of blockchain technology investments and use case adoption. The UAE announced that by 2021, 50 percent of the government's transactions will be achieved through a blockchain, thus saving time and resources. For example, Dubai expects to unlock 5.5 billion dirhams in savings annually in document processing alone.

The initial leap was taken by the Dubai Department of Finance, which recently launched a blockchain-powered payment system intended to provide a more accurate and transparent governance process, as well as to enable real-time payments within and between government structures.

The Dubai Blockchain Initiative is a strategy that will help Dubai achieve the vision of H.H. Sheikh Mohammed bin Rashid Al Maktoum, who stated, "Dubai [will be] the first city fully powered by Blockchain by 2020 and make Dubai the 'happiest city on earth (`https://interestingengineering.com/smart-city-dubai-the-happiest-city-of-the-future`). The Dubai Blockchain Initiative strategy will use three strategic pillars: government efficiency, industry creation, and international leadership.

To find out more on the Dubai Blockchain Initiative, visit `https://smartdubai.ae/initiatives/blockchain`.

## Country of Georgia

The country of Georgia has an interesting use case that involved its National Agency of Public Registry (NAPR). The NAPR was an early adopter of Hyperledger and piloted a blockchain-based land-titling registry in February 2016. (Recall that Ethereum and Hyperledger were barely released in 2016.)

This proof of concept (POC) was impressive since they were the leaders in blockchain adoption for enterprises before enterprise blockchains were even in the field. The blockchain was deployed as a private blockchain, as expected with Hyperledger, and was effectively "off-chained" to the Bitcoin blockchain. They accomplished this by using a distributed digital timestamp to validate and sign a document that contained citizen information and ownership of land.

A user would log in to a web-based application and initiate a request. The backend, being the blockchain-based network, would deploy a smart contract and execute accordingly.

The country of Georgia states that the following are the most essential characteristics of their blockchain registry:

◆ Overall system transparency

◆ Fault tolerance

◆ Intelligibility for end users

Based on the articles that have been posted about this project, it appears that all these characteristics have been realized.

The main benefits are convenience and cost. More critically, however, the added level of security as a result of using hashing reduces risk and provides greater security.

To find out more about NAPR, visit `https://exonum.com/story-georgia`.

## Healthcare Use Cases

Healthcare can be complex and challenging with compliance issues such as having to meet strict privacy data requirements. Patient data is generally held across multiple different institutions which have been traditionally in a legacy application silo. This means that the health network is closed and not well integrated with open systems. The historical use of different standards poses challenges for interoperability and sharing of medical data effectively.

Another challenge is the traditionally poorly implemented IT security of the medical community in general. Blockchains can help to facilitate strict compliance requirements around data integrity and privacy and to enable standards.

Enabling encryption with a blockchain through the use of standards such as SHA 256 or ECC can facilitate compliance around a more secure approach to patient data. Companies in the United States, for example, can pay a significant cost for mishandling patient data—not just in fines but in company image.

Perhaps the most convincing example of a medical data exchange platform enabled by blockchain is Medicalchain. Medicalchain uses blockchain technology to securely store patient health records. Medicalchain maintains a single version of what is considered the medical truth, which is the original medical data. This medical truth is maintained on a blockchain ledger, and participating health organizations can request permission to access medical records.

What I find really interesting is that Medicalchain implements both Ethereum and Hyperledger Fabric. The use of a dual blockchain structure is nothing new, but Medicalchain's implementation cleverly applies both the requirements and use cases you would expect for both blockchains.

The first blockchain layer controls access to health records and is built using Hyperledger Fabric (permissioned). The second blockchain is powered by an ERC20 token on Ethereum and underlies all the applications and services for the Medicalchain platform (permissionless).

Figure 8.5 shows the object storage on the Medicalchain blockchain. A clear hashing algorithm is used to facilitate the secure storage of the medical chain information. Data is actually verified by the hashes, and these hashes must match exactly to validate against the user request.

**FIGURE 8.5**
Medicalchain data

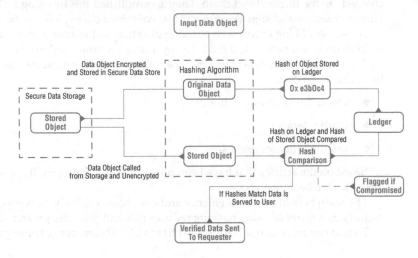

To find out more about Medicalchain, visit `https://medicalchain.com/en/`.

# Other Potential Use Cases

Blockchains are known to be a great solution for specific industry segments, but we must realize they have use cases beyond the common use cases around logistics, financial, and data exchange and can extend to other industry use cases. Some of the use cases could be for identity validation, data storage, and charity. I will cover just a few of the hundreds of use cases that have been released in the last few years.

## Zero-Knowledge Proofs

The application of zero-knowledge proofs (ZKPs) to blockchains is another area that could be utilized by numerous industries. ZKPs enable users to confirm something without revealing the actual details behind it. Essentially, a user could use the Ethereum blockchain and have a totally private transaction.

ZKPs are one area that major blockchains are taking seriously due to the demand for additional privacy-focused features. Ethereum, for example, has some interesting developments on the road map, such as the Aztec Protocol, which would enable ZKPs on the public Ethereum blockchain.

**NOTE** "Being able to answer a question of 'Does a user have enough money to send to another user' without knowing who the user is, or exactly how much they have, is one of the primary use cases for zero-knowledge proofs in blockchain." —Demiro Massessi

Even private chains have begun partnering with projects like Zcash to better understand applications for ZKPs to their blockchain solutions. Enterprise blockchains will have components or features that will support this. Hyperledger announced support of ZKPs in upcoming releases.

ZKPs provide the following benefits:

- Enable private transactions
- Reduce blockchain size
- Provide scalability
- Enable cross-asset interoperability

ZKPs are a growing area of interest, and there are a significant number of projects being announced in this area.

**NOTE**   "We're changing the world one blockchain at a time, and if we use this technology properly, we're bound to make the world a better place for everyone." —George Levy, CSBCP, CBP

## Social Impact, Charity, and Fundraising

Blockchains can provide a transparent and auditable trail for donations in order to prevent fraudulent activity. Governments could use this information to easily identity transactions and therefore give appropriate credits.

The world of social impact (or social good, as it is also known) is clearly a growing area for blockchain use cases. For example, platforms can incentivize social organizations to run projects in a transparent way and get paid for achieving their goals. The blockchain solutions can reduce the requirements for financial and legal intermediaries, which are generally costly and prone to mistakes.

One of the more interesting use cases of social impact is called Alice (`https://alice.si/`). Alice allows for complete transparency for each funding project and makes it publicly available on the Ethereum blockchain. This allows for immediate transparency but also provides actionable historical insight into what funding projects are working.

## Distributed Cloud Storage

Improvements in data security stem from a shift from a centralized means of storage to a decentralized one. Instead of going to AWS, Azure, or GCP for cloud storage, perhaps you can just use a peer-to-peer approach.

One of the more interesting cloud storage plays is called Storj. The Storj cloud platform lets users rent storage from their peers on the network. All network transactions are conducted in Storj's crypto asset, which is also called Storj and uses a token launched on the Ethereum blockchain.

According to the website, storing 1 GB on the Storj network costs $0.015 per month on average. This is far below the current cloud industry standard for cloud object storage.

For more information on the Storj storage platform, see `https://storj.io/index.html`. For more information on the Storj cryptocurrency on the Ethereum platform, see `https://www.coingecko.com/en/coins/storj`.

## Identity Management

Identity verification in the world of KYC/AML provides a new dimension to security, removing verification bottlenecks and providing more accurate results.

One interesting use case of identity management is about Civic's Secure Identity Platform (SIP). This Secure Identity Platform is designed specifically for multifactor authentication without the need for passwords or usernames. SIP relies on the user's biometric information, which is verified by the blockchain ledger.

For more information about the Civic blockchain, see `https://www.civic.com/`.

## Summary

This chapter covered several industry verticals, such as the financial, healthcare, and logistics industries. Blockchain adoption is also clearly taking on new heights in other industry verticals. One of the main thoughts before adopting any blockchain is to search for the latest blockchain use cases. IBM, Hyperledger, and Corda release updated use cases about their solutions fairly routinely. The available number of blockchain use cases is ever expanding, so I encourage you to either attend a conference or do some online research.

There are business and technical merits of blockchain technologies. The innovations around blockchain are clearly expanding the portfolio of solutions for enterprises and addressing both the technical and business challenges that enterprises have traditionally dealt with around legacy IT.

Common use cases for the financial sector include KYC, cross-border payments, and tokenization. Other possible use cases are around compliance and customs documentation.

Governments such as the City/State of Dubai are at the forefront of blockchain road maps for government. The country of Georgia was an early adopter of blockchain even before the release of enterprise blockchains such as Hyperledger and Ethereum.

There are numerous other use cases for blockchain, including identity management, zero-knowledge proofs, cloud storage, and charity.

# Chapter 9

# Blockchain Governance, Risk, and Compliance (GRC), Privacy, and Legal Concerns

Blockchains can be an ideal platform for regulatory compliance because they establish a historically trusted audit trail that can be verified in real time.

Blockchains create comprehensive log data that can be used for audits and compliance. Audit trails are critical to maintain in most compliance requirements for businesses located anywhere. Blockchains are starting to take on additional use cases and a role in the compliance world. For example, blockchains will play the following critical roles:

◆ Blockchains enable enterprises to operate lawfully in a dynamic and changing regulatory environment.

◆ Blockchains have the potential to change the way investigations and audits are completed.

◆ Blockchains can provide transparency, which can be implemented in several ways.

Compliance requirements can range from a country-based requirement, such as the Australia Privacy Amendment, to a publicly traded U.S.-based company where SOX will be required. Any enterprises that use the payment networks for credit card transactions are required to follow PCI-DSS. Some companies may choose a more voluntary compliance baseline, such as ISO.

This chapter focuses primarily on enterprise concerns for common enterprise blockchains, including the smart contracts that can be used to maintain personal data. I briefly cover some aspects around cryptocurrency, but that won't be the primary focus. I also discuss the most common compliance regulations. These regulations often address security and privacy together.

## Governance, Risk, and Compliance

Historically, compliance requirements for enterprises focused both on common concerns, such as privacy, and on more specialized concerns, such as requirements for healthcare, credit cards, and government-mandated requirements.

Blockchain technology brings new challenges but also new opportunities to enterprises around compliance. However, not all compliance requirements can be met with blockchain technology. For example, permissioned blockchains generally enable compliance, whereas permissionless blockchains generally do not enable compliance.

No matter what business you are in, chances are you will need to address compliance. Those audit logs could be kept on a blockchain. This is where there are plenty of growth opportunities in the market. Whether a blockchain solution makes sense or not is going to require more investigation on your part. The reality is that blockchain technology is not a one-size-fits-all solution and your challenges may vary.

Blockchain services can certainly have a major impact on governance, risk, and compliance (GCR) functions, which include the following key areas of the business:

◆ IT governance

◆ Corporate and IT audits

◆ Policy management and regulatory change management

◆ Risk and compliance

◆ Enterprise risk management

◆ Data protection and privacy

◆ Contracting agreements

◆ Third-party risk management

◆ Smart contracts

◆ Supply chains and logistics

◆ Proof of provenance

As a blockchain architect, you will likely run into several concerns around the General Data Protection Regulation (GDPR), the Health Insurance Portability and Accountability Act of 1996 (HIPAA), the Sarbanes-Oxley Act of 2002 (SOX), Know Your Customer, anti-money-laundering (AML) rules, and so on. For example, blockchain ledgers don't merely track compliance; they also streamline enforcement requirements, discourage fraudulent behavior, and provide valuable insight into how the platform is meeting requirements.

It's critical that an enterprise's governance structure provide directives to safeguard its IT assets and data. Because blockchains are ledgers, they maintain data that requires compliance in many situations. Blockchain applications that interface with consumers require extra caution to maintain the various facets that your company may very well be legally bound to maintain, such as GDPR.

## Compliance Benefits

Meeting compliance requirements can have some benefits for the enterprise as well as for the user base and customers. Common blockchain features that enable compliance include the following:

◆ A tamperproof record of immutable, fully auditable data

◆ Transparency to users and monitoring tools

◆ The monitoring of the reliability of services and the quality of data

## Regulatory Oversight

Blockchains such as Bitcoin, Litecoin, Ethereum, and numerous others originally did not have any regulatory requirements, at least in the United States. There has been a bit of discussion on whether a cryptocurrency is considered to be a security or a commodity in regard to how they will be regulated. Bitcoin, for example, has been treated by most countries as an asset, not an investment vehicle or security. However, this could change in most western nations in the coming years.

Determining whether a cryptocurrency is a security depends on the circumstances under which it is sold. The question is whether the Securities and Exchange Commission (SEC) maintains oversight.

### BLOCKCHAIN CHARACTERISTICS

As with any technology, there are characteristics, features, and challenges to understand, and blockchains are no different. Indeed, they can be more complex, depending on the requirements you need to meet.

Before reviewing your compliance requirements, it is important to review how blockchains are defined and the properties they generally maintain.

◆ **Transparency**—All participants can view all data recorded.

◆ **Decentralization**—Several copies of the blockchain coexist on different computers.

◆ **Immutability**—Once data is recorded, it cannot be altered or removed.

◆ **Disintermediation**—All decisions are made by consensus between the participants, without a centralized point of control or arbitrator.

When it comes to compliance for blockchains, all the properties listed could provide for mandated compliance regulations in an efficient manner.

### INITIAL COIN OFFERINGS

An initial coin offering (ICO) is where the holder of the cryptocurrency has a set of contractual interests and financial interests in the enterprise offering. An ICO is similar in some respects to an initial public offering (IPO) in the stock-trading world.

Depending on the structure of an ICO, that ICO could be under the Securities and Exchange Commission (SEC) regulations, which maintains an interest in oversight over the investment securities in the United States.

This chapter focuses on the regulatory concerns that enterprises have around compliance enterprises. I won't be getting into details of ICOs, such as funding, launching, and legal concerns. ICOs are a specialized area and generally not a concern for enterprises deploying Hyperledger, Corda, or even Ethereum applications.

### THE HOWEY TEST

The SEC's view of Ethereum's Ether token hinges on whether presales of the cryptocurrency by an initial coin offering constitutes an enterprise having a degree of influence over its value. However, the SEC has declared that Ether is not a security and doesn't fall under the agency's oversight. Essentially, Ethereum is viewed as a commodity due to how its presales are handled.

The SEC's determination is based on the precedent set by the Supreme Court's decision in *Securities and Exchange Commission v. W. J. Howey Co.*, a case that led to what has become known as the *Howey test*. By definition, ICOs are securities because they pass the Howey test.

The W. J. Howey Co. owned citrus groves in Florida, the fruits from which were considered a commodity when sold on an exchange. However, the company also leased their citrus groves, and the Supreme Court ruled that these lease contracts were considered to be a security or investment contract, not a commodity.

In a nutshell, the Howey test determines whether a financial transaction qualifies as an investment contract and thus would be a security and subject to special regulations.

For more information on the Howey test, refer to `https://consumer.findlaw.com/securities-law/what-is-the-howey-test.html`.

When deploying a blockchain, whether for a cryptocurrency or a payment gateway, it would be wise to clearly understand how the blockchain services are procured due to possible regulatory concerns.

## PERSONALLY IDENTIFYING INFORMATION (PII)

Personally identifying information (PII) is personal information that can be used to uniquely identify, contact, or locate a single person in the United States. In the European Union (EU), PII is referred to as *personal data*.

The detailed requirements between the two are slightly different. For example, in the European Union, cookies are considered personal information, but in the United States, cookies are actually considered non-PII tracking information and not subject to any PII regulations.

A more detailed explanation of PII is from the National Institute of Standards and Technology (NIST), and provides the following definition:

> *PII is any information about an individual maintained by an agency, including (1) any information that can be used to distinguish or trace an individual's identity, such as name, social security number, date and place of birth, mother's maiden name, or biometric records; and (2) any other information that is linked or linkable to an individual, such as medical, educational, financial, and employment information. (Prindle & Loos. "Information Ethics and Academic Libraries: Data Privacy in the Era of Big Data." Journal of Information Ethics 26:2, p. 22.)*

For more information on the NIST definition of PII, refer to `https://csrc.nist.gov/publications/detail/sp/800-122/final`.

When it comes to protecting personal data, the following common identifiers are generally considered to provide a crucial part in identities:

- Full name
- Home address
- Email address
- Social Security number (SSN)
- Passport number
- Driver's license number
- Date of birth (DOB)
- Telephone number
- Audit trails
- Credit and debit cards

Personal data—such as customer or employee names, addresses, dates of births, and other identifying information—may very well be located on your enterprise blockchain ledgers, so protect it accordingly.

Historically, identification of PII data was discovered through the process of an audit. When performing an audit, it is important to realize that a blockchain may contain two categories of personal identifiable data.

◆ Participants and identifier—for example, each participant/miner has a public key that identifies the issuer and receiver of a transaction

◆ Additional data contained within a transaction, such as names, addresses, phone numbers, DOB, SSN, and so on

In the United States, non-PII data is information that cannot be used on its own to trace, or even identify, a person. Examples of non-PII data include the following:

◆ Device IDs

◆ IP addresses

◆ Browser cookies

◆ Monitoring information

Blockchains are ideal for most compliance requirements and can provide a historical audit trail of PII data.

## Common Compliance Requirements

Compliance requirements vary depending on the location of your data storage, blockchain nodes, user and employee locations, and even industry verticals. This section covers the most common compliance areas that global enterprises would likely be required to consider, including how these requirements can affect a blockchain solution.

Information about common compliance requirements—such as GDPR and PCI—is readily available, so expertise should be relatively easy to locate. Other, more regionalized requirements—such as the Australia's Privacy Amendment (Notifiable Data Breaches) Act 2017, or the United Kingdom's Data Protection Act 2018—are more specialized due to the limited audience.

A best practice for compliance requirements is to discuss them with your corporate counsel. Your corporate counsel should be able to understand the ramifications of different compliance requirements and translate them in a manner that corporate risk reduces or eliminates.

Blockchains pose some new challenges not only technically but also from a business perspective. These challenges include legal concerns such as liability, legal prose structuring, resolving disputes and arbitration, jurisdiction, and data privacy, just to name a few.

### PRIVACY ACT 1988 (AUSTRALIA)

The Privacy Act 1988 (Privacy Act) was introduced to ensure the maintenance of privacy of individuals as well as to regulate how Australian government agencies handle privacy-related information.

The Privacy Act specifically includes 13 Australian Privacy Principles (APPs). These APPs apply to some private sector organizations as well as most Australian government agencies. These mandated organizations are collectively referred to as *APP entities*.

To find out more about the Privacy Act, visit https://www.oaic.gov.au/privacy/the-privacy-act/.

## BASEL II

Basel II is a global compliance requirement that is relevant for large, international banking and financially driven organizations. This regulation was actually named after where the meetings for this regulation took place in Switzerland. The Basel accords (agreements) are a series of recommendations on banking laws and regulations issued by the Basel Committee on Banking Supervision (BCBS).

The main goal of these regulations is to seek protection against financial and operational risks faced by the banking industry—specifically in terms of internal and external fraud from unauthorized activity, theft, and system security incidents, such as theft of information.

The following are the three essential features of Basel II:

◆ Mandates that capital allocations by institutional managers are more risk sensitive than previous allocations that did not assess risks

◆ Separates credit risks from operational risks and quantifies both

◆ Reduces the scope or possibility of regulatory arbitrage by attempting to align the real or economic risk precisely with regulatory assessment

The Basel III standard was announced in December 2017, and takes effect in January 2022. The new Basel III framework ensures that banks must split deposits from corporate clients into two specific buckets, which are the operating and the nonoperating buckets.

From a blockchain perspective, this Basel III compliance requirement perhaps has the least activity from what I have experienced and seen. Generally, banks are still using older technologies such as mainframes and older platforms such as SWIFT for a significant part of their data-based services. In reality, deploying enterprise blockchains will not be a one-night event or even a one-year event due to the complexity, integration, and costs associated with changes with burdensome enterprise and financial requirements.

Clearly, there are benefits of blockchain from a regulatory perspective. For example, using a blockchain would enable the regulators to oversee the processes, as all the steps are easily traceable on the blockchain ledger. Blockchains could provide the required highly structured, well-defined, and complete risk data reporting requirements of Basel II.

## DATA PROTECTION ACT 2018 (UNITED KINGDOM)

The Data Protection Act 2018 (DPA), the third generation of the act, modernizes data protection laws in the United Kingdom to ensure they are effective in the years to come. It has some similarities to GDPR but overall is far wider. The act supplements the European Union's General Data Protection Regulation but also incorporates it into UK law.

The act states that a child can provide consent for the purposes of the GDPR from the age of 13, which is used as the default age for consent.

The act also covers the intelligence services and law enforcement domains that are required to comply with data protection standards. The DPA also has provisions for data subject rights and special categories.

To find out more about the Data Protection Act, refer to http://www.legislation.gov.uk/ukpga/2018/12/contents/enacted.

## General Data Protection Regulation (European Union)

The European Union's General Data Protection Regulation (GDPR) was implemented in May 2018, and is now being fully enforced. GDPR affects all organizations and businesses anywhere in the world in the sense that if you handle EU customers as a company whether or not you're located there, you are required to specifically address the process of handling personal data of EU citizens.

GDPR was proposed and released to attempt to structurally streamline, update, and simplify the EU's data protection laws that are in effect. EU citizens theoretically have control over their data, and GDPR should simplify regulatory challenges between member states.

The main concern around privacy for citizens is the right to be forgotten (RTBF). Basically, a customer can contact you and request to be removed from your databases. This includes data types such as IP addresses, web cookies, physical addresses, genetic information, and phone numbers.

The right to be forgotten is a complex area when it comes to blockchain technology. Blockchains are not meant to be deleted or modified. They are immutable, and therefore they do not forget! For any blockchain network (permissioned or permissionless) that directly stores personal data in a block, the ability to comply with GDPR may be more challenging depending on the approach you are considering.

To address this concern appropriately, you need to identify the detailed data points that would be included in the regulatory requirements and then consider not placing those data points on the chain.

To do this, you would need to create an off-chain or a sidechain. Off-chains and sidechains are when the data is written and read from a centralized database not connected directly to the blockchain. Generally, sidechains or off-chains use centralized solutions or legacy solutions such as databases.

Figure 9.1 shows how a off-chain could be used with GDPR.

**FIGURE 9.1**
Using a side-
chain with GDPR

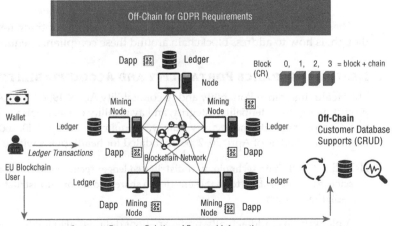

*Customer Requests Deletion of Personal Information*

GDPR is essentially another book unto itself; therefore, I am touching only on areas that I believe are important to understand for blockchain-focused engagements. At the time of writing, there are 173 recitals and more than 100 articles. Recitals list what the legislation should achieve. Each member state also has supervisory authority and maintains its own offices.

Most of the regulations are fairly straightforward, and the principles are similar to previous regulations. The main differentiator is how the member states are brought together in a standard, formatted focus. The penalties for noncompliance could be significant, so you should engage your corporate counsel on proper legal structures.

To learn more about GDPR, visit `https://eugdpr.org/`.

## Gramm-Leach-Bliley Act

The Gramm-Leach-Bliley Act (GLBA), also known as the Financial Services Modernization Act of 1999, was signed into law by President Clinton. The act seeks to protect consumers' financial privacy. Its provisions limit when a financial institution can disclose a consumer's nonpublic personal information to nonaffiliated third parties.

GLBA compliance requires financial organizations to notify customers about how they share personal information and also notify their customers about the right to request that their data remains unavailable to unaffiliated third parties.

Financial institutions must comply with the Federal Trade Commission (FTC) standards for sharing and protecting the nonpublic personal information (NPI) of your customer base.

GLBA compliance mandates the following:

◆ The Financial Privacy Rule requires financial institutions to provide particular notices and to comply with certain limitations on disclosure of nonpublic personal information.

◆ The Safeguards Rule requires companies defined under the law as "financial institutions" to ensure the security and confidentiality of this type of information. The rule also states that financial institutions must create a written information security plan describing the program to protect their customers' information.

◆ Pretexting codifies protections against the practice of obtaining personal information through false pretenses.

These regulatory requirement for the financial sector is nothing new. The new concern, though, is how to address blockchain around these compliance requirements.

## Health Insurance Portability and Accountability Act of 1996

The Health Insurance Portability and Accountability Act of 1996 (HIPAA) sets national standards for protecting the confidentiality, integrity, and availability of electronically protected health information. Compliance with the Security Rule was required as of April 20, 2005, and mandated for most health plans, and as of April 20, 2006, mandated for health plans with fewer than 1,000 members.

**NOTE**   "Blockchain technology, or distributed ledger technology, is just a way of using the modern sciences of encryption to enable entities to share a common infrastructure for database retention." —Blythe Masters

A blockchain could actually protect patient data but also facilitate privacy by default for what HIPAA refers to as *covered entities*.

These covered entities are as follows:

- Doctors, clinics, dentists, nursing homes, and even patient home services

- Organizations are defined by the law as normally the healthcare programs provided by employers, governmental agencies, and health maintenance

- Agencies that act as aggregators of information, such as clearinghouses

The HIPAA Security Rule requires appropriate administrative, physical, and technical safeguards. These safeguards are quite strict in nature and are to ensure the confidentiality, integrity, and security of protected patients' health-related information.

The HIPAA Compliance Checklist that is available online has four main requirements.

- Ensure safeguards are in place to protect patient health information.

- Provide what is stated as reasonably limited use and sharing of protected health information.

- Validate organizations' data sharing agreements that are in place with service providers that perform covered functions.

- Provide procedures to limit who can access patient health information and also training programs about how to protect patient health information.

Blockchain technology has significant potential to improve data interoperability, security, and privacy around numerous services, and healthcare is no exception, of course. Blockchains have been addressing multiple healthcare industry pain points by addressing data protection for health information exchanges, identifying varying data standards, and removing inconsistent rules and permissions.

Blockchain technology could also lower the number of HIPAA violations, which can be costly for an organization, thereby increasing privacy for patients while lowering costs for providers.

The use of blockchains in the healthcare industry is still in its infancy, although the number of platforms that support its use with HIPAA requirements is growing. That said, the level of interest is not as high as it is for logistics use cases.

## KNOW YOUR CUSTOMER COMPLIANCE

Know Your Customer (KYC) compliance in the financial sector generally involves repetitive tasks. Prior to blockchains, these tasks were performed manually and were riddled with data inconsistencies and duplicate processes. Furthermore, different banks had different systems, which added to the challenges.

According to OPUS, a KYC provider, major financial institutions report spending up to $500 million each year on KYC and customer due diligence (see `https://www.opus.com/future-of-kyc/`).

The penalties for KYC and AML noncompliance violations can be financially burdensome for some organizations. A distributed ledger, however, can provide an opportunity to act as a root of trust that is both immutable and cost efficient.

Figure 9.2 shows how a KYC solution could be used with a blockchain solution. Blockchain nodes could be used as the source for the immutable ledger and be connected to a KYC service as a compliance node to provide oversight.

**FIGURE 9.2**
KYC blockchain solution

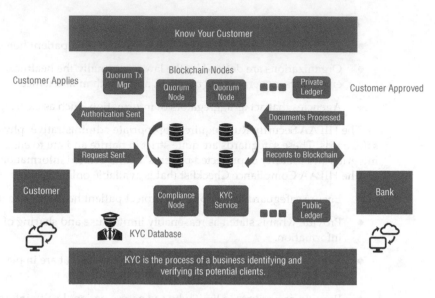

A blockchain solution, especially when implemented in a consortium approach, could clearly provide some stability, cost, and time efficiencies, as well as an increase in customer satisfaction. Imagine taking a process that took days and getting it down to seconds, removing redundancy and providing cost efficiencies.

A blockchain solution can enable regulators to oversee the start-to-finish processes of KYC due to all steps being fully traceable on the blockchain.

AML is a significant regulatory requirement that is a layer of compliance that financial institutions must both adhere to and spend large amounts of money to maintain.

For example, according to a survey by Lexis Nexus, firms with less than US$1 billion in assets averaged some US$850,000 in AML operational costs. Mid-tier firms averaged US$7.4 million, and top-tier firms with more than US$100 billion in assets spend an average of US$15.8 million on AML compliance annually. For more information, visit https://risk.lexisnexis.com/about-us/press-room/press-release/20181010-true-cost-aml.

AML compliance monitoring is used to ensure the integrity of the data and involves continuous screening of clients' personal and transaction information. Blockchain ledgers using smart contracts could provide some use cases for using blockchain technology.

Blockchains have huge potential because of their ability to prevent actions if certain predefined conditions in the smart contract are met. A blockchain deployment would identify the risks around the three defined stages in money laundering: placement, layering, and integration.

◆ *Placement* is the movement of cash from its source. This could be accomplished through any number of means such as smuggling, asset purchases, security brokers, and numerous other financial vehicles.

◆ *Layering* is the stage that money launderers use to attempt to make it more difficult to detect and uncover a money laundering activity. Layering is intentionally meant to make illegal gains and proceeds difficult for the law enforcement agencies to detect. This is when cash is converted into other forms such as stocks, bonds, cryptocurrencies, and so on.

◆ *Integration* is when the money that is laundered is now in the actual economy and looks as if it were gained through normal business means. For example, a cartel in Mexico owns a resort hotel and presents more cash than what even the highest room rates could account for. Cash is actually deposited and funneled through the banking system from a legitimate source.

A blockchain could be implemented to manage limits that could be specified, such as capital and liquidity, or to enforce restrictions. A similar blockchain structure as referenced in the KYC section could be implemented since it's common to have both KYC and AML solutions integrated at some institutions.

Figure 9.3 shows how a KYC/AML framework solution could be used with a blockchain solution. Blockchain nodes could be used as the source for the immutable ledger and be connected to a KYC service as a compliance node to provide oversight. AML services would be used to assess, analyze, and detect suspicious transactions.

**FIGURE 9.3**
KYC and
AML framework

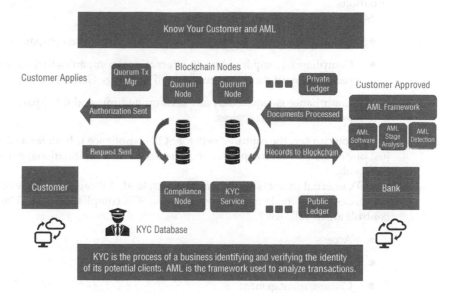

## INTERNATIONAL ORGANIZATION FOR STANDARDIZATION 27001

ISO 27001 is a highly sought-after regulation and part of the ISO/IEC 27000 family of standards. Like most security standards, its purpose is to help organizations maintain the security of their data. The 27000 family includes more than a dozen individual standards covering information security.

ISO standards differ from most other compliance requirements, in the sense that ISO is a voluntary compliance bucket. Organizations choose ISO compliance for several reasons, including the following:

◆ To avoid breaches

◆ To ensure customer acceptance and assurance

◆ To avoid fines

◆ To gain a market edge

ISO certification is quite expensive. Organizations can invest millions to be compliant.

ISO compliance requires maintenance of log files. Log files are essentially going to lead to audit trails and audits, which is where a blockchain solution could come into play to maintain ISO compliance.

## SARBANES-OXLEY ACT OF 2002

The Sarbanes-Oxley Act of 2002 (SOX) was enacted by the U.S. Senate as the "Public Company Accounting Reform and Investor Protection Act" and by the House of Representatives as the "Corporate and Auditing Accountability and Responsibility Act."

SOX was specifically designed with the goal of implementing accounting and disclosure requirements. These requirements increase transparency in corporate governance and financial reporting and formalize a system of internal checks and balances that are applicable in several situations.

SOX is applicable in the following circumstances:

◆ Compliance is required by all publicly held American companies.

◆ Compliance is required by any international companies that have registered equity or debt securities with the U.S. Securities and Exchange Commission (SEC).

◆ Compliance is required by any accounting firms and third-party organizations that provide financial services.

As you can see, the capture "net" for SOX compliance is both far and wide. SOX compliance is just one of the several compliance requirements that a multinational corporation expects to deal with.

SOX internal controls are critical to understand. A thorough review of internal controls comprises one of the largest components of a SOX compliance audit. The four SOX internal controls are as follows:

◆ Access

◆ Security

◆ Change management

◆ Backup and recovery

SOX is complex and has many moving targets around it. Your IT management should hire or train the appropriate personnel around SOX because of the significant liability around a SOX audit. Blockchain could provide some important insight into how SOX audits are handled.

## FEDERAL INFORMATION SECURITY MANAGEMENT ACT OF 2014

If you're a government contractor in the IT realm or working around government IT, whether in the military, intelligence, or civilian sectors, then you are more than likely familiar with the Federal Information Security Management Act (FISMA).

The U.S. federal government needs to maintain control. To be fair, it's clearly needed for their IT systems, as history has proven from systems being compromised. Before FISMA there were no standards in most cases even from an agency perspective with the exception of the Department of Defense (DOD).

Under FISMA, if your organization wants to deploy a new IT solution, such as a data storage array or a database server farm, it needs to go through a security authorization process for those services. The same process is true for a blockchain solution to be used in a production environment and handling live data and customers online.

FISMA requires agencies to meet stringent federal security requirements. Federal information systems must go through a complete Security Authorization (SA) process before being granted an authorization to operate (ATO), and blockchain systems are no exception.

The security authorization process uses a Risk Management Framework as defined by the National Institute of Standards and Technology (NIST), an agency under the Department of Commerce.

The NIST SP 800-37 certification and accreditation process consists of the following phases:

◆ **Initiation**—Ensures that the authorizing official and senior agency information security officer agree with the contents of the system security plan

◆ **Security certification**—Determines the extent to which the security controls in the information system are implemented correctly, operating as intended, and producing the desired outcome

◆ **Security accreditation**—Determines whether the remaining known vulnerabilities in the information system pose an acceptable level of risk to agency operations, agency assets, or individuals

◆ **Continuous monitoring**—Provides oversight and monitoring of the system controls in the information system on an ongoing basis, and informs the authorizing official when changes occur

The security authorizations reference the Risk Management Framework. It provides a process that integrates security and risk management activities into the system development lifecycle. The risk-based approach to security control selection and specification considers effectiveness, efficiency, and constraints due to applicable laws, directives, executive orders, policies, standards, or regulations.

The Risk Management Framework is outside the scope of this book. The full NIST Special Publication is available at https://csrc.nist.gov/publications/detail/sp/800-37/rev-1/final.

**NOTE** NIST's mission is to promote innovation and industrial competitiveness by advancing measurement science, standards, and technology in ways that enhance economic security and improve our quality of life.

When you are specifying a blockchain project for a federal government customer, it's important that you understand the NIST frameworks. You would want to apply a blockchain solution in the same way that you assess a new database server.

The following are some of the considerations you need to understand:

◆ Type of blockchain deployment, such as permissioned, hybrid, or permissionless

◆ Vendor support of access controls, security, audits, and so on

◆ Client applications and how authentication and authorization (AA) is applied

◆ Deployment of your enterprise nodes geographically

◆ Data storage on nodes, cloud storage, and so on

◆ Audit logging and monitoring services

◆ Off-chain services that connect to the blockchain such as compliance or currency exchange

◆ Transaction handling and monitoring

◆ Security assessments handling

◆ Code updates and smart contract updates

◆ Consistent maintenance of ledger data

◆ Managing your encryption keys

◆ Identification of security clearance classification requirements

◆ Procurement processes for blockchains

◆ Business continuity/disaster recovery

There are many other items to consider. It's not uncommon to have a detailed checklist of more than 100 areas of discovery but also presentation of blockchain design considerations around the risk management framework.

FISMA has an excellent compliance model that could be used to mitigate your federal government agency risks. Figure 9.4 shows the FISMA compliance model. FISMA is a fairly robust but also specialized area. For more information, refer to https://www.dhs.gov/cisa/federal-information-security-modernization-act.

**FIGURE 9.4**
FISMA high-level process

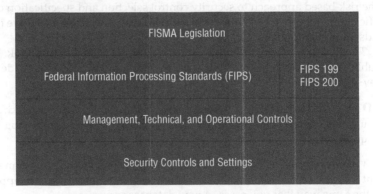

Finally, the American Council for Technology and Industry Advisory Council (ACT-IAC) has an excellent resource called the *Blockchain Playbook*, which is recommended for any government integrator or government agency. For more information, visit https://www.actiac.org/knowledge-bank.

### Payment Card Industry Data Security Standard

Transactions between two accounts at the same acquiring bank can be maintained easily due to the internal protocols being the same. The real challenge around compliance is getting the networked applications at two different banks to communicate securely and effectively. This historically is a complicated and expensive process to achieve PCI compliance between disparate systems.

Integration of blockchain technology can help with the challenge of disparate systems. By using a tailored version of blockchain, the whole process of bank-to-bank and merchant-to-bank communication can be sped up safely and securely. The benefits realized would be significantly less manual processing, enhanced data security, and effectively reduced costs to merchants.

The Payment Card Industry Data Security Standard (PCI DSS) applies to organizations of any size that accept, transmit, or store any cardholder data. Organizations can have different "levels" of compliance depending on the size of their transactions.

◆ Level 1: Merchants processing more than 6 million card transactions per year

◆ Level 2: Merchants processing 1 to 6 million transactions per year

◆ Level 3: Merchants handling 20,000 to 1 million transactions per year

◆ Level 4: Merchants handling fewer than 20,000 transactions per year

However, regardless of their compliance level, organizations need to comply with the same major requirements. PCI DSS specifies six major requirements on compliance.

◆ Build and maintain a secure network

◆ Protect cardholder data

◆ Maintain a vulnerability management program

◆ Implement strong access-control measures

◆ Regularly monitor and test networks

◆ Maintain an information security policy

The solution to this challenge can certainly rest in the consortium model where the blockchain services are maintained properly.

PCI-DSS compliance is complex, so proper planning and investments are required. Note that there is currently no direction from the PCI organization on blockchain acceptance or guidance around payment gateways—for example, where a credit card could be used to purchase cryptocurrencies.

In summary, companies that are global must be aware of major regional data privacy legislation and protect themselves accordingly. It is imperative that data security and privacy professionals assess their environments and ensure that if they do business or employ someone from the EU, GDPR will apply to their organizations.

## Smart Contract Legal Concerns

Legal concerns include jurisdiction, liability, privacy, and enforcement. Financial institutions will likely have additional concerns, such as addressing blockchain-based legal prose or interbank transfers via a consortium blockchain. Legal prose is enforced through the implementation of smart contracts.

The Uniform Commercial Code (UCC) can play a significant role in how states handle smart contract disputes and provide legal relief. Smart contract legal prose should be considered when using smart contracts.

## Smart Contract Enforcement

Smart contracts are computer code, and by definition their use may present enforceability questions using methods employed with traditional contracts. Basically, the input parameters and the execution steps for a smart contract need to be specific and direct. If "this" occurs, then execute "that" (the next step). Or if "Sally pays $100," then "ship furniture." On the other hand, if Sally does not send $100, then the smart contract does not proceed. Smart contracts act like a trigger, which in the world of web programming could be considered a webhook.

At the time of writing, there is no specific federal contract law in the United States dealing with smart contracts. Generally, the enforceability and interpretation of smart contracts are determined at the state level, which varies widely. However, when it comes to disputes, most states rely on their interpretation of the Uniform Commercial Code (UCC).

At the federal level, contracts must be in writing and additional formalities may be required, such as those under the UCC, to establish legal viability. This presents some legal challenges to understand exactly how smart contracts are applied to both state and federal contract laws. This complexity can also present challenges to which jurisdictions handle these smart contracts.

The UCC has been adopted by all 50 states, although each state has its own variations. In addition to the UCC, there may be distinct state-level fraud statutes to consider. Therefore, it would be important to consult with corporate counsel on how to address smart contract enforcement.

Currently there are no specific UCC regulations regarding blockchain smart contracts. However, this is changing slowly with federal state or local laws in the United States dealing with smart contracts. Smart contracts differ from electronic contracts in that electronic contracts have legal language clearly defined and the signers electronically sign the contract, whereas smart contracts are built in a programming language and not signed directly by participating parties.

Countries such as Switzerland, Dubai, and Germany are significantly ahead of the United States in their smart contract laws. In the United States, smart contracts should include a dispute resolution provision with clearly defined terms accepted by both parties. Your enterprise's corporate counsel really needs to be involved in smart contract law.

Traditional contracts follow what are considered by the legal community as "elements of a contract" to provide for the contract's legal enforcement and validity. Most legal scholars and prominent law firms agree that smart contracts should follow these "elements" as well to provide for relative assurance that the smart contract is "enforceable."

To determine whether a smart contract can be a legally enforceable contract, customers must consider whether each of the elements necessary for a legally binding contract is actually met through the implementation and deployment of the smart contract. According to the UCC, "To create a legally enforceable contract under US law, two or more parties must demonstrate that an offer was made and accepted through a meeting of the minds and accompanied by an exchange of consideration."

From an enterprise perspective, it is important to determine how your smart contracts will be written and how the contract elements are addressed. The common elements need to be applied and the established legal concepts and principles of contract law reviewed by your corporate counsel. In the United States, the following are common elements of a contract:

- **Offer**—An offer is "an expression by one party of his assent to certain definite terms, provided that the other party involved in the bargaining transaction will likewise express his assent to the identically same terms" (`https://quizlet.com/878323/delong-contracts-spring-09-flash-cards/`). In other words, both parties intend to follow through on the contract.

- **Acceptance**—Acceptance can be made either by a formal acceptance by the acceptor's signature or, under the right circumstances, by beginning or completing performance pursuant to the terms of the offer.

- **Consideration**—Consideration means that each party must give some form of "return or payment" to the other party. Consideration simply means a form of value must be exchanged, such as money, materials, or performance of duties.

**NOTE**   Contract law varies widely among countries. The Chamber of Digital Commerce has an insightful white paper about how smart contract viability enforcement varies between the United States and Spain: "SMART CONTRACTS: Is the Law Ready?" You can find it here:

`https://www.dlapiper.com/~/media/files/people/tank-margo/smart-contracts-is-the-law-ready web.pdf?la=cn&hash-003897A104F6A74DD9FC1C2F0FF2A4F16ADE500F`

Some states have provided legislation on smart contacts. Here are some examples:

- In 2017, the State of Arizona passed legislation that allows the specific use of blockchain smart contracts in commerce. The law prevents a contract from being denied any legal effect, validity, or enforceability solely because the contract contains a smart contract term as part of the contract.

- In 2018, the State of Vermont passed a bill that allowed limited liability companies organized for the "purpose of operating a business that utilizes blockchain technology. The law specifically states that a material portion of its business activities" must be elected to be a blockchain-based limited liability company. (BBLLC). BBBLC is a new term used for these companies.

- In 2019, the State of California has pending legislation (SB838) that would effectively allow corporations to manage the issuances and transfers of their stock using blockchain technology.

For more information on state-based blockchain laws, refer to `https://www.sagewise.io/smart-contracts-state-legislation/`.

## Smart Contract Adaptability

Smart contracts are significantly more adaptable from a legal perspective in Corda than in other blockchains because "legal prose" is natively supported. Legal prose is not supported natively in Ethereum, Hyperledger Fabric, or Quorum.

From a technical perspective, one of the main reasons Corda is adaptive is because contracts are "stateful contracts" and other platforms are "stateless." Corda smart contracts verify if a transaction is valid and therefore can be committed to the Corda ledger. Legal prose is attached to the smart contract and can be adjusted as needed and validated efficiently.

I will discuss the technical merits of smart contracts from a developer perspective in Chapter 10, "Hands-On Blockchain Development."

## Legal Jurisdiction

A blockchain can be designed to cross jurisdictional boundaries, as the nodes on a blockchain can be located anywhere in the world.

The location of your blockchain nodes could be presenting complex jurisdictional issues. The main remedy to this particular concern in an enterprise blockchain is to not use permissionless blockchains that are public. Controlling your node location is the key to avoid issues.

In situations where your services cross borders, maintain data for protected classes, or even enter new markets, you should consider consulting your corporate council and defining jurisdiction clauses.

A jurisdiction clause is commonplace in the United States for most business contract scenarios. These clauses state that involved parties have the right to settle disputes through adjudication, which is generally predetermined in typical implementations of these contracts. When a party expressly submits to the authority of a court in a specific jurisdiction, they may find it challenging to successfully argue that the court in question is not the appropriate venue for the adjudication of such disputes.

In a nutshell, a jurisdiction clause can mitigate issues in a contract whether it is a traditional contract or an electronic contract. In Corda, for example, you would simply attach a memorandum to the CordApp.

## Liability of Services

The risk to customers as a result of a systemic issue with blockchain infrastructure and its applications could be significant—for example, if a transaction is not realized or is incorrect.

Some areas of concern to focus on include the following:

◆ Designating audit responsibilities

◆ Performing duties for blockchain application administrators and users

◆ Measuring and monitoring the performance of blockchain services

◆ Handling outages and support

◆ Distinguishing services hosted in the cloud or on premises

◆ Deploying the enterprise nodes and the cloud providers' locations (multiregional)

These are just some ideas to consider. Any time legal concerns are in play, consulting your corporate counsel is paramount.

# Financial Sector Compliance

The financial technical (FinTech) sector is required to maintain compliance requirements such as SOX, Basel II, and numerous others. Other requirements, such as KYC/AML and the right to be forgotten, present other challenges. Managing your compliance requirements on the blockchain can certainly be achieved with proper planning.

Compliance requirements such as GDPR, Basel II, GLBA, and PCI DSS can be burdensome to FinTech companies. Blockchain technology can be used to reduce the burdens that companies experience with these compliance areas.

FinTech compliance is complex and specialized. Some areas of concern are handling customer data, protecting intellectual property, and auditing and logging. The complexity is a direct result of the additional compliance burden that is placed on the financial sector around these areas of concern.

## Handling Customer Data

In the financial sector, customer data is heavily regulated. Everything from privacy, maintenance of records, and removal of customer records is strictly controlled. Blockchain can both provide unique value in some areas and pose significant concerns in other areas of customer data.

Blockchains store data once, and it cannot be altered. When a customer's data is stored on a blockchain, it cannot be deleted. Complications can also arise around transparency, which is the main reason a permissionless blockchain cannot be used in the financial sector. Both transparency and privacy handling have implications around compliance, especially if there is a data breach. Privacy should be a financial-sector priority, and blockchain can provide some of these requirements.

## Intellectual Property

Intellectual property is a specialized area of law that deals with protecting the rights of those who create original works. It covers copyrights, patents, and trademarks.

Blockchains are increasingly being used to maintain immutable records of intellectual property. In the financial sector, areas such as trading algorithms, risk assessments, and stress test data may be considered intellectual property. The need to familiarize yourself with how your blockchain data maintains compliance in this area is critical.

Some areas in the financial sector where intellectual property is commonly claimed for term protection include the following:

◆ Patents are claimed for blockchain platforms, mathematical patents, and algorithms. There are different types of patents, and the term protections vary. Generally, the term protections are from seven to twenty years.

◆ Trademarks are claimed for things such as brand logos, web platform interfaces, and instructional materials. Trademark protection in the United States lasts for 20 years.

◆ Trade secrets are also claimed. They are unique in that there is no expiration date; they are indefinite.

> **NOTE** An interesting service is called Bernstein. Bernstein is a regular web app that runs in any modern browser where you create a digital trail of records of your IP using blockchain technology. The blockchain keeps a historically accurate as well as transparent record of the intellectual property you create.
>
> You can find out more about Bernstein by visiting `https://www.bernstein.io/`.

## Auditing and Logging

Blockchains have the embedded capacity to create tamper-proof system logs for use in managing access to your IT network services. Blockchains are generally considered a network resource and clearly need to be audited regularly. To mitigate risks to your blockchain, you must perform IT audits, validate audit trails, attend to auditor visits, and maintain compliance certifications.

IT server system logs and network services logs facilitate some critical functions for the enterprise. These logs can protect the enterprise against cybersecurity breaches because they provide an audit trail of who has accessed a network, application, database, or blockchain ledger, as well as identify the user's activities.

These blockchain systems and network logs essentially are audit logs and therefore allow enterprises to detect hackers and inappropriate employee behavior.

Figure 9.5 shows how a blockchain solution performs the audit log time-stamping process.

**FIGURE 9.5**
Audit logs

Audits are generally a required part of the compliance mandates your enterprise may need to comply with. Compliance audits are performed by an independent third party, referred to as the *auditor* and will reference logs that will be referencing the ledger activity on the blockchain.

Auditors need to extract the data from the blockchain and then consider whether the data is reliable. Establishing an audit trail could be tricky, especially on a permissionless blockchain. For example, a transaction recorded in a blockchain may still be

- ◆ Unauthorized, fraudulent, inappropriate, or even illegal
- ◆ Executed between related parties
- ◆ Linked to a side agreement that is processed off-chain
- ◆ Incorrect classifications made on the blockchain

There is still quite a bit of discussion in the financial sector (specifically the accounting specialization) about whether blockchains may constitute sufficient appropriate evidence for certain financial statement confirmations and whether the blockchain ledgers provide sufficient audit evidence related to the nature of the transactions that are processed.

Having as a result of multiple copies of ledger data, blockchains could provide significant benefits for ensuring consistency of audit trails. This would be as a result of removing the manually intensive, time-consuming processes involved with compliance auditing.

In a nutshell, the audit trail cannot be hacked and is immutable from several perspectives. Transparency into the blockchain ledger transactions could also be given to auditors and government regulators to view the audit logs at any time.

Blockchains are an evolving area in the compliance and legal sectors, and the baselines are still being established. Several solutions are on the market that can outsource and facilitate compliance. For example, compliance-as-a-service cloud solutions can integrate and aggregate audit trails in a compliance-as-a-service datastore that maintains compliance with GDPR and HIPAA.

A company called Log Sentinel has a blockchain-based solution called Sentinel Trails, which offers secure logging and audit trails. The solution stores evidence of every critical event on the blockchain with qualified time stamps and/or qualified electronic signatures. You can find more information at `https://logsentinel.com/sentinel-trails/`.

## Summary

This chapter covered the various aspects of data privacy, audit logs, legal concerns, and compliance. Determining whether a cryptocurrency is a security depends on the circumstances under which it is sold.

The Howey Test is the baseline that determines whether a financial transaction qualifies as an investment contract and thus is a security.

Personal identifiable information is information that can be used to uniquely identify, contact, or locate a single person in the United States. In the European Union, PII data is called personal data. There are many similarities between the two compliance requirements.

When you are considering a blockchain solution and addressing compliance requirements, a best practice is to discuss these requirements with your corporate counsel.

The location of your blockchain nodes could be presenting complex jurisdictional issues around compliance.

Compliance requirements include PCI, SOX, GDPR, and hundreds of other possible requirements. Companies that are global must be aware of major regional data privacy legislation and protect themselves accordingly. It is imperative that data security and privacy professionals assess their environments and ensure that if they do business or employ someone from the EU, GDPR will apply to their organizations.

In the financial sector, areas such as trading algorithms, risk assessments, and stress test data may be considered intellectual property, and the need to familiarize yourself with how your blockchain data maintains compliance in this area is critical.

Blockchains are generally considered a network resource and clearly need to be audited regularly.

# Chapter 10

# Blockchain Development

This chapter provides a general overview of blockchain development by offering insight into the most common development languages, development tools, and the blockchains they are used for.

I will focus mainly on the high-level aspects of development around the Ethereum, Hyperledger, Corda, and Quorum blockchains as well as the development languages they are built on. The world of blockchain development is a far and wide specialization area. Each blockchain has its own approach to development, toolsets, consensus, and dependencies, and could merit its own book on the subject of blockchain development.

Blockchain development is a growing area. The demand has never been higher due to the shortage of developers who understand blockchain. If you are developing in JavaScript, Golang, Python, or any common language, you are already on the road to being a blockchain developer.

The goal of this chapter is to give an overview of how the blockchains are built around the programming languages, data structures, and programming building blocks.

If you are looking for programming instructions, note that this chapter does not focus on developing applications or programming methods; rather, this chapter is intended as a guide for systems engineers and other nondevelopers to grasp the complexity of blockchain development.

## Common Programming Languages

Blockchain programs are computer code and are known as *smart contracts*. Developers who are programming for web apps, enterprise apps, or cloud apps are likely frontrunners to be blockchain developers.

If you're a system engineer, whether presales or postsales, you are also likely to understand some aspects of programming languages. Your customers are likely already using some of these in their development organizations, which can give your customers' organizations a head start in blockchain development.

The main point is that blockchains are about creating programs, and these programs are built on development languages you likely already use in your enterprises. The programs ultimately will solve problems, create value, or provide other tangible benefits for the company. The only significant learning curve is to know how the smart contracts interact with the blockchain network and perhaps to understand the APIs used to enable the client applications to interface with the application.

Let's run down the most common blockchain languages. This will give you a good idea of what's in demand. If you're looking for a blockchain developer, you will have a more concise requirements list to give to your recruiters.

**NOTE**   Blockchain development is not just about code; it's also about solving problems.

## Most Common Development Languages

When it comes to development languages, a few languages are clearly in high demand in blockchain development. Some languages are used on only a few blockchains. For example, Solidity is used only on Ethereum and Quorum, but it makes up well over 60 percent of the blockchain developer requirements listed on LinkedIn at the time of writing.

Note that other common development languages are also used, for example, in Bitcoin, Lisk, and EOS, as well as other newer blockchains that I do not cover in the book. The main coverage in this chapter will focus on Ethereum, Corda, Hyperledger Fabric, and Quorum.

The following are the most commonly used languages in enterprise blockchain development:

◆ Solidity

◆ Golang

◆ C++

◆ JavaScript

◆ Python

When it comes to holistic development and not just blockchain-focused development, Python is the clear winner at the time of writing. Finding Python professionals likely will not be an issue due to the wide acceptance of the Python development language.

For additional insight into which development languages are in demand and the current popularity of each language, refer to a resource compiled from Google called "PYPL Popularity of Programming Language Index," at http://pypl.github.io/PYPL.html.

### SOLIDITY

When it comes to blockchain development, Solidity is the most widely used and in-demand developer requirement at the time of writing for enterprise blockchains. A contract-oriented Turing-complete programming language, Solidity has a large base of Ethereum developers, with an estimated 250,000+ users.

Solidity is a relatively simple programming language that is used with Ethereum developers. Solidity was clearly developed specifically for the Ethereum platform.

The developers of Solidity used specific features, functions, and concepts from C++, Python, JavaScript, and Golang to assemble the new language. Solidity's main program syntax is based on JavaScript, a widely used development language. Because Solidity is built from JavaScript, it has a low barrier of entry for developers.

When you think of developing in Ethereum, you think of Solidity since it was developed exclusively for Ethereum smart contracts initially. Solidity has essentially expanded to become its own standard for other blockchain platforms to follow. At the time of writing, the most widely used languages for writing smart contracts on Ethereum are Solidity and Vyper.

Why is Solidity so popular? Solidity is a powerful and efficient toolset for developers because it allows programmers to write higher-level code, which is then compiled down into what is considered a low-level machine language. Smart contracts can be written in Solidity, Vyper, and Serpent mainly because they are high-level languages that are compiled down to bytecode. Bytecodes are essentially operation codes (opcodes) running instruction after instruction.

Blockchains that directly support smart contracts written in Solidity include Ethereum, Ethereum Classic, and Hyperledger Sawtooth (with Seth).

## GOLANG

Golang (Go) is an open source general programming language that is lightly based on the syntax of the C programming language. Golang also has some ease-of-use similarities to JavaScript, which gives Go a low barrier to entry.

Originally designed by Google engineers, Golang was released directly to the open source community in 2009. Golang has become a popular object-oriented and imperatively designed programming language. More than 800,000 developers use Golang.

Hyperledger Fabric is built from Golang. The following are some of the benefits of using Golang (Go) with Hyperledger:

♦ Provides a fast statically typed and compiled language

♦ Supports type-safety and dynamic data entry

♦ Allows the creation of flexible and modular code, and thanks to its multithreading mechanisms, enables distributed computations and simplified network interaction

♦ Provides convenient testing tools for developers on GitHub

♦ Offers efficient development processes

Ethereum's SDK protocol is actually written in Go. There are many other blockchain applications of this language. Blockchains that are written in Golang (Go) include Hyperledger Fabric and NEO.

## C++

C++ is the oldest development language used for blockchains. C++ has been around for more than 30 years and was originally known as "C with Classes." C++ features worth noting for blockchains include memory control opportunities around scalability, which is a significant problem faced by blockchains today.

C++ is considered a general-purpose programming language with an extensive user base of more than 4 million developers. It can be used for higher-level tasks and also allows programmers to program to the hardware itself. This flexibility has made C++ highly popular for uses such as embedded systems and computer graphics.

C++ offers the following benefits:

♦ Facilitates proper threading since there are many parallel operations that have to be performed simultaneously

♦ Performs move semantics, which can significantly improve performance when it comes to the value of the variables retrieved

♦ Allows compile-time polymorphism, which enables developers to use functions in different ways, thereby decreasing code volume and boosting performance

Blockchains that support C++ include Hyperledger Iroha, Bitcoin, EOS, and NEO.

## JavaScript

JavaScript is generally accepted to be the programming language of the Internet. It has been used primarily to enhance web pages to provide for a more dynamic, user-friendly experience. JavaScript is widely accepted for development use since it is good at handling asynchronous actions.

This property of asynchronous actions makes JavaScript well suited for blockchain operations that require scaling. As the number of users on your blockchain rises, JavaScript can scale with the blockchain.

JavaScript is a lower entry point to developers who are interested in programming blockchains since it's easy to learn and widely used.

Blockchains that support smart contracts in JavaScript include Hyperledger Fabric, Hyperledger Sawtooth, and Lisk.

## Python

Python is an interpreted, higher-level, and general-purpose programming language. Python was created by Guido van Rossum and was first released in 1991. Python has a design philosophy that emphasizes code readability, notably using significant whitespace.

From a development perspective, Python supports a large number of libraries. Python is also generally considered to be one of the simpler languages since it has an intuitive code structure. For example, code can be written once and run on almost any computer without needing to change the program.

NEO is an example of a blockchain that supports smart contracts in Python.

## Less Widely Used Development Languages

The following are some less commonly used but also notable development languages for enterprise blockchain development:

- ◆ C#
- ◆ Java
- ◆ Rust
- ◆ Simplicity

Although many other languages have been developed, and new languages are likely being developed as you read this, I want to focus on languages that have mainstream use.

## C#

C# tutorials claim this programming language as an option, and it can be used to create blockchains because it is object-oriented. It is a widely popular language for portability since it is somewhat easy to code in a cross-platform manner for software. It is important to note that it has a close relation to Java and would be easily understood by developers.

Blockchains that are written in C# include NEO and Stratus.

## Java

Java has been primarily used in website designs since it was simple to connect the link between blocks of information. Released in 1995 by Sun Microsystems, Java is a general-purpose programming language that is object-oriented, class-based, and concurrent.

There is also a runtime environment (JRE), which consists of the Java virtual machine and Java platform core classes and supports Java platform libraries. Java is often used for developing client-server web applications, allowing developers to run a compiled Java code on all the platforms that support Java without the need for recompilation, making it popular for running light-weight cryptocurrency applications.

Blockchains that support smart contracts in Java include NEM, NEO, and Corda.

## RUST

Rust is a system language created by Mozilla, one of the Internet pioneers. Rust has several advantages that enable rapid blockchain development, including efficient computer processing and flexibility around security.

The Rust compiler provides for risk reduction when executing code since it helps to eliminate potential problems. Rust has a very active community and a well-provisioned communication and learning system for developers.

Corda is an example of a blockchain that supports smart contracts in Rust.

## SIMPLICITY

Simplicity is a newer blockchain programming language that was designed exclusively for smart contracts. Simplicity was developed by a company called Blockstream, which had a goal to provide the flexibility and expressiveness for blockchain computations as well as verifying the safety, security, and costs of smart contracts.

Simplicity was well thought out in the sense that it was developed to ensure that the programming challenges of traditional development languages were addressed. One of the main challenges was to actually program efficiently for the role of a blockchain. The role of a blockchain should be only to verify computation. A traditional programming model would be more focused on performing computation.

For more on this exciting new blockchain development language, refer to this site:
`https://blockstream.com/2018/11/28/en-simplicity-github/`

## Summary of Blockchain Platforms

Numerous languages are used on the various platforms for cryptocurrencies and enterprise blockchains. For example, in Ethereum you have several choices, but the main language from a development perspective to focus on is Solidity.

Table 10.1 summarizes the major enterprise blockchain languages.

**TABLE 10.1:** Blockchain Platforms and Development Languages

| BLOCKCHAIN PLATFORM | PLATFORM DEVELOPMENT | SMART CONTRACT LANGUAGES |
| --- | --- | --- |
| Ethereum | Solidity | Solidity/Vyper/Bamboo/Flint |
| Hyperledger Fabric | Golang | Golang/JavaScript/Java |
| Corda | Kotlin | Kotlin and Java |
| Quorum | Solidity | Solidity |
| Ripple | Python | N/A |

When considering a blockchain platform, it is important not only to consider your organization's expertise requirements for blockchain development but also to review and document any legacy applications' requirements that may be extended to the blockchain service.

# Ethereum Development

An open source and collaborative effort, Ethereum is by far the blockchain that has the most robust development ecosystem and developer following. The main feature of Ethereum that drives this large developer following is the Turing-complete language that facilitates the development of smart contracts.

Developers should note that Ethereum is geared toward applications that automate direct interaction between peers or that facilitate group routines over the Ethereum decentralized network.

Ethereum itself is only a protocol defining how the communication should work. There are several versions of the Ethereum protocol. The two most common versions are Go-Ethereum (aka GETH), which is written in Golang, and Parity, which is written in Rust.

There is a dearth of development tools, utilities, and testnets for Ethereum. Some of the most common tools include the following:

- **IDE**: Solidity Browser, Ethereum Studio

- **Clients**: Geth, Parity, Ethereum Wallet

- **Storage**: IPFS (supported through Swarm and Storj)

- **Dapp** browsers: MetaMask, Mist

- **Testing**: Testnets, TestRPC, localhost

There are numerous other tools for testing IDE environments, frontend and backend development, and security. For more details on the robust Ethereum ecosystem, check out the ConsenSys GitHub here:

```
https://github.com/ConsenSys/ethereum-developer-tools-list#smart-contract-
languages
```

## Smart Contracts

A smart contract is computer program code capable of organizing, executing, and enforcing the negotiation or performance of an agreement using blockchain technology. From a development perspective, the blockchain is somewhat limited in the sense that the API calls that can made are minimal.

Developers are generally well versed in automating tasks, which is exactly what smart contracts perform. A smart contract is an automated process that can be considered a suitable legal contract in some scenarios.

Smart contracts define the rules of engagement and the penalties around that agreement in the same way that a traditional contract does. Developers will clearly define how to handle any violations of the smart contract from a code perspective.

In Ethereum, as in other blockchain languages, there are specific functions to deal with. Your developers should clearly understand how these functions work and how the program would come together as an application.

## SMART CONTRACT WORKFLOW

As discussed in Chapter 2, two types of functions are required in an Ethereum smart contract.

◆ Constructor function, which is called only once when you deploy the smart contract

◆ Fallback function, which is invoked when someone sends ether to the address of your smart contract

Figure 10.1 shows the smart contract workflow in Ethereum.

**FIGURE 10.1**
Smart contract workflow

Here are the steps with more information:

1. **Predefined contract:** All the smart contract participants will establish the terms and also establish the conditions for execution.

2. **Events:** These are really event "triggers" that kick off the execution of the contract. Events include initiating a transaction and receiving funds, for example.

3. **Execute transfer:** The terms of the contract specifically dictate the movement of value based on the conditions met.

4. **Settlement:** The settlement of the contract is based on the requirements being met. For example, was $100,000 received from the title company?

Smart contracts, when combined with other smart contracts, make a decentralized application (*dapp*). A dapp can be as simple as a few lines of code or as complex as possible with thousands of lines of code. Complexity can be built into the platform or could also be extended off-chain as well. Developers have myriad options during the development process to customize the dapps.

## SMART CONTRACT ENFORCEMENT

To modify a smart contract's data, a blockchain user must send requests directly to its code. That is, the request does not go through an intermediary but instead will be fully handled by the smart contract code.

The smart contract modification process that will kick off determines whether to fulfill the request and how to fulfill requests that have been sent. Effectively, the smart contract is self-enforcing the rules that are clearly defined.

Comparatively, you can think of smart contract enforcement as how a traditional database such as SQL uses what is called an *enforced stored procedure*. In SQL you can specify how the stored procedure will work by using the CREATE PROCEDURE command. The CREATE PROCEDURE command will first reference specified parameters, such as students, addresses, money, and so on. Then the stored procedure will take in the specified value and compare it to what is in the var_return value.

In SQL, all inserts have to be executed at once or none at all, which is similar to how a blockchain enforces the smart contract logic. In blockchain we would call this strict enforcement *predefined rules*. Predefined rules in a blockchain would specify whether a sender has provided the exact amount of funds. If the exact amount of funds were sent by the sender and then promptly received by the receiver, then the smart contract would execute. Simply put, smart contracts are all or nothing from a layperson's perspective.

## DAPPS

Dapps (decentralized applications) run on a P2P network of computers (such as Ethereum) and are not centralized. When developing blockchain applications with Ethereum, you have two distinct options.

◆ Use Solidity or another development language to develop smart contracts that will be deployed to the blockchain.

◆ Develop websites that interface with the Ethereum blockchain.

When it comes to developing dapps, it's important to understand how different a blockchain is from a traditional client server application. Developers are well versed in client-server applications and understand the world of the Web. Moving from Web 2.0 to the new world of Web 3.0 will take newer skillsets and application development languages. Decentralized apps will become the thing of tomorrow, and developers need to get skilled in this area.

Figure 10.2 provides a high-level comparison of Web 2.0 applications to the layers of a blockchain application Web 3.0.

**FIGURE 10.2**
Application-layer comparison

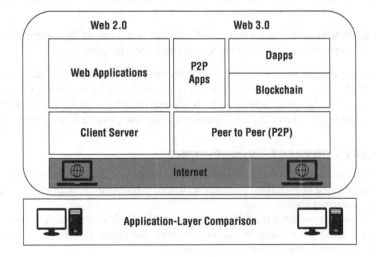

The infrastructure layer in blockchain technology is different from Web 2.0 in the sense that P2P networking is being introduced as the approach used to move from a centralized web to more of a decentralized web.

Blockchain is considered to be fully capable of providing technological benefits because of its decentralized capacity. Web 3.0 is focused on changing our application stacks from client-server to a decentralized Web. With decentralization, the risk of common security breaches could be reduced due to the decentralization of data distribution.

From an application-layer perspective, developers would need to consider dapps, business logic, application services, and even the user interfaces to integrate.

## ETHEREUM GAS

Ether, the native token of the Ethereum blockchain, is used to pay for transaction fees, miner rewards, and other services performed on the network.

To use the Ethereum network, you must pay with what is known as *gas*. Gas is a measurement roughly equivalent to computational steps for Ethereum. Every transaction is required to include a gas limit and a fee that it is willing to pay per gas. The blockchain miners have the choice of including the transaction and collecting the fee or not. Every operation has a gas expenditure on an Ethereum Virtual Machine (EVM), and that gas expenditure can be controlled from a cost perspective.

The price of gas is the amount of ether you are willing to spend on every unit of gas. This gas price is similar to an auction limit where you can determine what you get and when you get it.

Comparatively, if you are familiar with AWS EC2 virtual machines, then you may have used what are called *spot instances*. Spot instances in AWS are virtual machine instances that you can run programs on at a lower cost.

Figure 10.3 shows the main resource (ethgasstation.info) for estimating gas resource costs on the Ethereum network.

**FIGURE 10.3**
ETH gas station

Note that the more important it is to process the transaction, the higher the price. Essentially, the more gas you pay for, the faster your services execute.

One common concern around the gas model is that because it's an estimate of resources, loops should be avoided. Avoiding loops can be a challenge to estimate since if your application scales or your user base grows, then the costs could skyrocket. Loops in Ethereum are similar to an all-you-can-eat buffet and need to be avoided.

## ETHEREUM VIRTUAL MACHINE

When developing on Ethereum, it is important to understand how the EVM has been designed and enabled for the Ethereum blockchain. For example, smart contracts are written in a smart contract programming language, such as Solidity, and then compiled into what is known as *bytecode*.

Bytecode enables what an EVM can read and execute. The smart contract that is rolled out is on every node of the network, runs the EVM, and executes the same instructions.

The EVM not only provides amazing value to enterprises and their users but also enables the development of potentially thousands of different applications all on one platform.

The Ethereum blockchain is deterministic, meaning that the same input will produce the same output. This reduces the complexity of the programming involved and can remove numerous manual mistakes.

Figure 10.4 shows the development and deployment process on an Ethereum EVM at a high level. A smart contract was developed in Solidity. We would compile our program and then deploy on the EVM.

**FIGURE 10.4**
EVM development and deployment

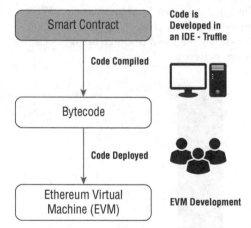

## Ethereum Ecosystem

Ethereum has a solid and well-provisioned development system.

◆ Solidity is the development language that is used to create Ethereum smart contracts.

◆ The Ethereum wallet is used for accessing Ethereum tokens, which are used to pay fees for the usage of the Ethereum resources.

- Testnets are used for the developers to deploy code on a test network away from the mainnet.

- Test ether is created to pay transaction fees on various testnets.

- Development environments are provided for the building of smart contracts.

- The Truffle framework is a widely accepted development environment, testing framework, and asset pipeline for Ethereum.

## ETHER UNITS

Ether is broken down into units or denominations. A *gwei* is a unit of Ethereum coin used to calculate transaction fees. For example, one Ethereum coin is worth 1 billion Gwei.

Table 10.2 shows the breakdown of the Ether units into the denominations.

**TABLE 10.2:**   Ether Units

| UNIT | WEI VALUE | WEI |
|---|---|---|
| Wei | 1 wei | 1 |
| Kwie (babbage) | 1e3 wei | 1,000 |
| Mwie (lovelace) | 1e6 wei | 1,000,000 |
| Gwie (shannon) | 1e9 wei | 1,000,000,000 |
| Microether (szabo) | 1e12 wei | 1,000,000,000,000 |
| Milliether (finney) | 1e15 wei | 1,000,000,000,000,000 |
| Ether | 1e18 wei | 1,000,000,000,000,000,000 |

For more information on the Ethereum denominations, visit http://ethdocs.org/en/latest/ether.html.

## METAMASK

MetaMask is an inline Internet browser bridge that facilitates significant efficiencies around development and testing. For example, developers can run Ethereum decentralized applications (dapps) right in the Internet browser (Chrome), rather than having to run a full Ethereum node locally. By using MetaMask, a developer can control both CPU utilization as well storage space requirements on their laptop, desktop, or server.

A full node would require more than 2 TB of data storage, whereas MetaMask is stored in your Internet browser. MetaMask has an ERC-20-compatible wallet and provides privacy and security tools to help prevent phishing.

Using MetaMask makes Ethereum development much more simplified around key management since it also encrypts the user's key locally and then requires the user to confirm the key. After confirming, the user signs the transactions/messages and then relays them to the Ethereum blockchain.

MetaMask includes a secure identity vault, providing a user interface to manage your identities on different sites and sign blockchain transactions. MetaMask could also be considered a "zero client." Zero clients run in the browser in JavaScript.

Use MetaMask for confirming your transaction's

- Balance
- Gas limit
- Gas price

Figure 10.5 shows the initial menu of a MetaMask browser login from Chrome. You can see contract interactions that used micro instances of gas usage. Micro gas usage is considered to be less than a gwei of gas units.

**FIGURE 10.5**
MetaMask

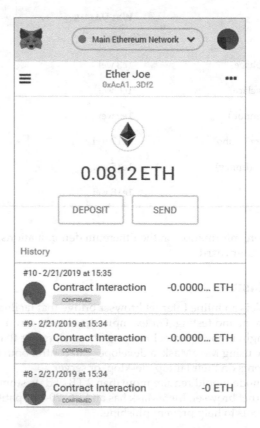

You can download MetaMask via a browser extension in Chrome or from `https://metamask.io/`. Note that you should never download MetaMask from a third-party site due to the likelihood that the version has been tampered with or is malware.

## MIST

Mist has been the browser for decentralized web apps and has recently been announced to be deprecated. However, it is still widely used, and therefore some discussion on it makes sense.

Mist is an Ethereum browser where you get a web browser with direct Web3 access. Mist is a full node, so you don't have to connect to a third-party node. This is different from MetaMask in the sense that with Mist you are downloading a full node. In MetaMask, you do not download the full blockchain to your node (full node).

A full node is where the node downloads locally the full blockchain that is the current world state. This will take up significant resources on most average personal computers, so ensure that you are not already resource challenged.

Another important note is that if you only need a wallet, then don't use Mist. Use MetaMask instead or even MyEtherWallet.

You can download Mist from `https://github.com/ethereum/mist`.

## PARITY

Parity is a lightweight browser-based wallet that gives users access to decentralized applications and currencies on Ethereum. Parity is an implementation written in Rust and is one of the most common wallet implementations used in the Ethereum network.

Parity comes with an extensive built-in Ethereum wallet and fully functional dapp environment. Parity has a Web3 dapp browser and is supported on Linux, macOS, and Windows.

## GETH ETHEREUM

Geth Ethereum is an implementation of Ethereum written in the Go programming language. To use Geth, you need to install the command-line interface and interact with a full node in Go.

Geth is supported on various platforms such as Linux, macOS, and Windows. Geth is also built to be flexible in how you install it, which can be from a package manager, containers, or even stand-alone builds. Geth allows you to take part in the Ethereum mainnet and perform a number of tasks on the Ethereum blockchain, including the following:

- Mining ether for profit
- Transferring funds between Ethereum wallet addresses
- Exploring the block history on the blockchain explorer
- Creating smart contracts and dapps

Geth is available for download at `https://github.com/ethereum/go-ethereum/wiki/Geth`.

## Ethereum Networks

In Ethereum everyone can start their own blockchain based on the Ethereum protocol. We have a mainnet, which is the production blockchain network, and we have testing or development networks, which are exactly what they sound like.

You can also deploy a private Ethereum network, or you can connect to any various networks that are available, such as Ropsten. This means the Ethereum mainnet can be replicated in a way that it behaves the same way the real mainnet does. The benefit is that it does not require any real financial resources from the developer community.

These "testnet" networks are for testing features and functions with your Ethereum smart contracts. These networks, which use a network ID, can be a moving target, so check the addresses routinely. The best resource to keep track of these Ethereum networks is the Ethereum Stack Exchange, available here:

```
https://ethereum.stackexchange.com/questions/17051/
how-to-select-a-network-id-or-is-there-a-list-of-network-ids/17101#17101
```

Note also that not every testnet is supported in the same way, and generally developers tend to stick with what they are comfortable with.

Testing your smart contracts locally with MetaMask is expected. One more area of testing your smart contracts is to extend the test to a testnet with MetaMask. For example, Developers could develop locally and test to any number of supported testnets or the mainnet.

As shown in Figure 10.6, four main testnets are supported. The default network setting is the mainnet with MetaMask. Ethereum best practices dictate to develop first locally, and then developers would want to identify which testnet we will use to test the application. The supported testnets with MetaMask include Ropsten, Kovan, Rinkeby, and Goerli. We can also create a custom remote procedure call (RPC) to test against an on-premises blockchain.

**FIGURE 10.6**
MetaMask networks

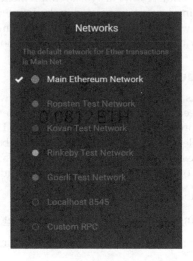

In the figure, you can see that Main Ethereum Network is the default network. When you change from the mainnet to the testnet, you need to ensure that you have test ether to perform application testing.

## ETHEREUM METAMASK FAUCET

When testing your Ethereum application on a testnet, you need to obtain what is known as test ether for the testnets. Test ether is essentially free ether to use only on the testnet to perform your application testing. To request your test Ether, you need to go to an Ethereum faucet.

An Ethereum *faucet* is an online platform that rewards users with small amounts of ether (ETH) for completing a variety of microtasks such as posting social media notices. In return, the requester receives test ether to use on the testnet.

To use the Ethereum MetaMask faucet, you need to have MetaMask installed and enabled in your browser. If you do not have MetaMask, then when you go to the Ethereum faucet, you would receive an error stating you need to have MetaMask installed and enabled.

To install MetaMask, go here:

```
https://chrome.google.com/webstore/detail/metamask/nkbihfbeogaeaoehlefnkodbef
gpgknn?hl=en
```

After installing the Chrome extension and enabling it from the extension menu in Chrome, you can go to `https://faucet.metamask.io/`.

Figure 10.7 shows the MetaMask Ether Faucet. If you want to obtain some test ether to run on the Ropsten testnet, select Request 1 Ether From Faucet.

**FIGURE 10.7**

MetaMask ether faucet

When connecting to the faucet, if your MetaMask is connected to the mainnet, then you would receive an error such as " currently on mainnet - please select the correct test network."

Figure 10.8 shows the Connect Request screen where the developer need to connect our MetaMask account. Select Connect and you are on your way to receiving test ether.

Once the task is done connecting the faucet, the developer then see test transactions under the transactions part of the faucet interface, as shown in Figure 10.9.

Figure 10.10 shows the transaction details on Etherscan. When you click the link to a transaction, you are brought to the Ropsten testnet on Etherscan (`https://ropsten.etherscan.io/tx/0x4ce3ee99e291a69f35fe00d3a84e291634ef881388adb4f77130b8bf47253017`).

## RINKEBY TEST FAUCET

The Rinkeby Ether testnet faucet (`https://faucet.rinkeby.io/`) was implemented to prevent malicious actors from utilizing all available funds. This faucet has a different approach in how to request or obtain test ether. The requests are actually done via social media. At the time of writing, a Twitter or Facebook account is used to request funds within the permitted limits.

**FIGURE 10.8**
Connect Request screen

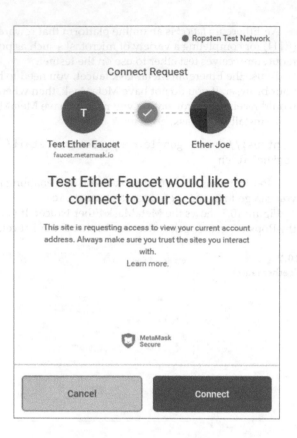

**FIGURE 10.9**
Faucet transactions

Figure 10.11 shows a tweet with my Ether address that I want to receive the Rinkeby test Ether.

On the Rinkeby site, just paste your social media link in the box and select how much ether you need (see Figure 10.12). Note that this is test ether, not something you can trade. It's that easy: just select Give Me Ether, and your account should be credited for the Rinkeby network. You can go back to MetaMask and validate the amount was deposited.

**FIGURE 10.10**
Ropsten testnet
transaction details

Transaction Details

Sponsored: 🎮 **Decentraland Game Jam** 💸 Submit your most creative interactive scenes and win! Learn more ⓘ

Overview    State Changes 🆕

[ This is a Ropsten Testnet Transaction Only ]

| ⓘ Transaction Hash: | 0x4ce3ee99e291a69f35fe00d3a84e291634ef881388adb4f77130b8bf47253017 ⎘ |
| ⓘ Status: | ✔ Success |
| ⓘ Block: | 6353267    120 Block Confirmations |
| ⓘ Timestamp: | ⏱ 27 mins ago (Sep-08-2019 07:33:06 PM +UTC) |
| ⓘ From: | 0x81b7e08f65bdf5648606c89998a9cc8164397647 ⎘ |
| ⓘ To: | 0xaca1c75d20ca47d9b0dc2c9c7f545306609c3df2 ⎘ |
| ⓘ Value: | 1 Ether   ($0.00) |
| ⓘ Transaction Fee: | 0.0000413091362 Ether ($0.000000) |

Click to see More ⬇

**FIGURE 10.11**
Requesting test ether
for Rinkeby

← **Tweet**

**Joe Holbrook** 🔒
@switchsanguru                                         ⌄

**0xAcA1C75d20CA47d9b0dC2C9c7F545306609C3Df2**

5:13 PM · Sep 8, 2019 · Twitter Web App

⫿⎮ View Tweet activity

💬          ⟲          ♡          ⬆

**FIGURE 10.12**
Rinkeby Give Me
Ether option

🛁 Rinkeby Authenticated Faucet

| https://twitter.com/switchsanguru/status/1170807420530155526 | Give me Ether ▾ |

3 Ethers / 8 hours
7.5 Ethers / 1 day
18.75 Ethers / 3 days

🌐 7 peers 🗐 5055908 blocks ♥ 9.046256971665328e+56 Ethers 🏛 31101

## Ethereum Nodes

Developers new to Ethereum should pay attention to the type of nodes deployed. One area that makes Ethereum so flexible and powerful is the different node capabilities and features.

Think of the node types as different use cases. Some are for deploying live applications, some are for development, and some are for testing your blockchain applications. Ethereum blockchain nodes that are not simulated include the following:

◆ Aleth is the new name of Cpp-ethereum, a collection of C++ libraries and tools for Ethereum blockchain. Aleth is supported on Ubuntu, macOS, and Windows.

◆ Go-Ethereum (GETH) is one of the three original implementations of the Ethereum protocol. It is written in Go, is a fully open source, and is licensed under the GNU LGPL v3. It is supported as a stand-alone client, or you can install libraries.

◆ Parity is an Ethereum client and is written in the Rust language. Parity is a full node with the following node options: Full Working Node, Light, Warp, Full Node, or Archive node.

We can use simulations as well to mimic the real blockchain for development purposes. In-memory blockchain simulations for rapid development include the following:

◆ TestRPC, which is the Ethereum blockchain simulator

◆ Ganache, which allows you to create a private blockchain for simulation and which uses the Ganache CLI, which then uses Ethereum's to simulate full client behavior

◆ Truffle Developer Console, which uses Ganache as part of the Truffle suite

Clients can gain access to the blockchain in several convenient ways.

◆ MetaMask browser plugin through Infura

◆ StatusIM Android or with iOS app through Infura

Status IM is an application that combines a messenger, a crypto wallet, and the Web3 browser. You can find information about it at `https://status.im/`.

Infura is a development suite that provides an instant, scalable API access to the Ethereum and IPFS networks. For more information, visit `https://infura.io/`.

◆ MIST dapp browser with integrated Geth

There are some simple ways to get started running a private blockchain test. For example, you are considering using Truffle there are three typical steps.

**1.** Log in and then spin up a Truffle project. The project needs to lay out the implicit structure of your project. You can run the test on the mainnet, on Ganache as a private test blockchain.

**2.** Run the deployment file. You would point your project either to use Ganache or to use the mainnet network.

**3.** Run the `truffle migrate` command. This will automatically run `truffle compile`, which will deploy the smart contracts on the network specified.

## Solidity Programming Language

Ethereum-based applications and smart contracts are written in Solidity, a language specifically designed to utilize the EVM.

Solidity, which was proposed in August 2014 by Dr. Gavin Wood, is similar to C. It is also similar to JavaScript, although it uses a whole new framework. Developers versed in JavaScript will have only a small knowledge gap to overcome. JavaScript is a universal language for the Web and is being used in a large number of applications.

Solidity is also similar to object-oriented languages like C++ and C#, whereas JavaScript is based on HTML and influenced by languages such as Self and Scheme. When it comes to handling complex data structures, Solidity is similar to Java in many respects. Solidity is designed specifically for Ethereum applications and runs only on the Ethereum blockchain.

## Ethereum APIs

Ethereum uses JSON, a lightweight data-interchange format, for its API library. It can represent numbers, strings, ordered sequences of values, and collections of name-value pairs.

Application programming interfaces (APIs) are used to interact with the blockchain network. APIs are meant to provide a rapid on-ramp for developers. They are also referred to as *endpoints*.

To talk to an Ethereum node from inside a JavaScript application, use the web3.js library, which gives a convenient interface for the RPC methods. For example, if you wanted to have your application access the Ethereum blockchain with Etherscan, you would want an API for that. The API for Etherscan is located at `https://etherscan.io/apis`.

### Remix

Remix (`https://remix.ethereum.org/`), also known as the Solidity browser, is a browser-based IDE that was built by the Ethereum development team to address ease of development. The Remix IDE is used to write, compile, and debug Solidity code.

Remix is more than just a powerful, open source development tool that enables you to write Solidity contracts straight from your browser. Remix is also an online learning solution since it enables developers to really get up to speed quickly around smart contract development. Remix supports development both locally and online.

Remix has what developers would consider modules. A module is basically a plugin that can be added to the development environment that is being used in Remix.

**FIGURE 10.13**
Remix interface

Figure 10.13 shows the Remix interface, which was recently updated at the time of writing. Remix includes a plugin for Etherscan Contract Verification. You can use the tool to verify that the code deployed with a contract is valid and to publish the code on Etherscan.

Another useful feature is that you can choose your compiler version and also correlate this version to a nightly build. You can simply compile your code with different compilers and validate how these builds work out.

Figure 10.14 shows an example of running test code in a specific version of the compiler and then receiving a green checkmark on the left sidebar indicating that the code was compiled successfully.

**FIGURE 10.14**
Compile successful

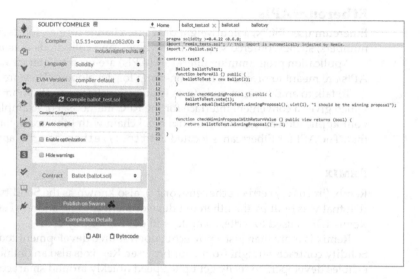

Another great feature is that you can push your code to Ethereum Swarm. Ethereum Swarm is a peer-to-peer (P2P) file storage distributed network that allows the distributed and encrypted storage of users' data.

Remix is a powerful yet complex tool since the ecosystem has grown significantly. It is the best way to learn Solidity for most developers wanting to develop in Ethereum.

## VYPER

Vyper is a contract-oriented Pythonic programming language that specifically targets the EVM. It is still an experimental programming language, but it compiles down to EVM bytecode, just as does Solidity.

Vyper is designed to be a simple-to-create and easy-to-comprehend smart contract engine that provides more transparency for all parties involved.

Vyper looks logically similar to Solidity and has some similarities to Python as well. Vyper is still in beta mode at the time of writing, so I won't cover it in detail.

## WEB3-ETH

Web3-eth is used for blockchain and smart contract development in Ethereum. The library is Web3, and I like to consider it an "on-ramp" to Ethereum development and the world of decentralized applications.

You can use Web3-eth with Ganache, for example, and create test accounts to test your smart contracts. You can specify ether to transfer from and to your accounts. There are many more features about Web3-eth that support the rapid development of decentralized applications.

The main challenge with Web3 is that if you're not careful with your development, you may actually be using a version that has some differences in how you would interact with the libraries.

After downloading the Web3 library, you would simply initialize your application node by using the following command:

```
- npm install web3
```

Before doing anything, refer to the web3 documentation at `https://web3js.readthedocs.io/en/1.0/getting-started.html`.

## Ethereum Testing

Software development generally has a flow that has been widely accepted, and this is true in the world of blockchain development as well. The main differences are that in blockchain the steps are different, and comparatively there is an additional step.

Table 10.3 compares the generally accepted steps in traditional software development to blockchain development.

**TABLE 10.3:**     Traditional vs. Blockchain Development

| TRADITIONAL SOFTWARE DEVELOPMENT PHASE | BLOCKCHAIN SOFTWARE DEVELOPMENT PHASE |
| --- | --- |
| Prototype | Prototype |
| Alpha/Beta | Framework testing |
| Production | Private chain testing |
| Update release | Testnet |
| | Mainnet |

The main point to understand is that there are software development phases in blockchain, and we must approach them differently. Blockchains deploy smart contracts and therefore, will likely be simpler to develop than typical enterprise applications. However, the main difference to be aware of is that smart contracts, once deployed to some blockchains, are immutable.

### ETHEREUM TESTNETS

Before deploying your application on the mainnet, you would want to test it on the Ethereum testnet(s). The following testnets are available directly from MetaMask:

◆ Rikeby

◆ Ropsten

◆ Kovan

The testnets, even though for testing, require the use of ether, albeit test ether, which is used to maintain the nodes. You can gain the test ether in several ways, such as by mining the testnet or by using a faucet.

## TRUFFLE SUITE

The Truffle Suite is essentially a suite of dapp solutions. The following solutions are part of the Truffle Suite:

◆ Truffle, which is the IDE

◆ Ganache, which allows developers to deploy a personal blockchain

◆ Drizzle, which contains all the needed front-end libraries

## TRUFFLE

Truffle is a developer environment, testing framework, and asset pipeline for blockchains. Truffle is essentially a JavaScript library that's based on NodeJS. Truffle is immensely popular and growing in usage monthly. Truffle was developed by Consensus.

Truffle allows developers to spin up smart contract projects at the click of a button and provides you with a project structure, files, and directories that make deployment and testing much easier (or else you would have to configure these yourself).

To install and run Truffle, you first need to install Node and the Node Package Manager (NPM). This can be found at `https://nodejs.org/en/40T`. After installing Node, you can go to any command-line interface (Terminal on Mac/Linux or PowerShell on Windows) and interact with npm.

One interesting project from the Truffle framework is Truffle Box. These are preconfigured "mini scaffolding projects" that make starting a new distributed application much more streamlined. The list of truffle boxes can be found at `http://truffleframework.com/boxes/40T`.

Use a baseline JavaScript, React, Angular, or other language to start off with a Truffle box.

You can view the number of downloads for the suite at the dashboard (`https://truffleframework.com/dashboard`).

Figure 10.15 shows the Truffle Suite Activity Dashboard.

Truffle Suite can be downloaded from `https://truffleframework.com/`.

## GANACHE

Ganache CLI is the latest version of TestRPC: a fast and customizable blockchain emulator. It allows you to make calls to the blockchain without the overhead of running an actual Ethereum node. Transactions are mined instantly.

You can think of Ganache as a personal blockchain for Ethereum development you can use to deploy contracts, develop your applications, and run tests. It is available as both a desktop application and a command-line tool.

Ganache is available for Windows, Mac, and Linux. Many developers use Ganache to test their smart contracts during development. It provides convenient tools such as advanced mining controls and a built-in block explorer.

**FIGURE 10.15**
Truffle Activity
Dashboard

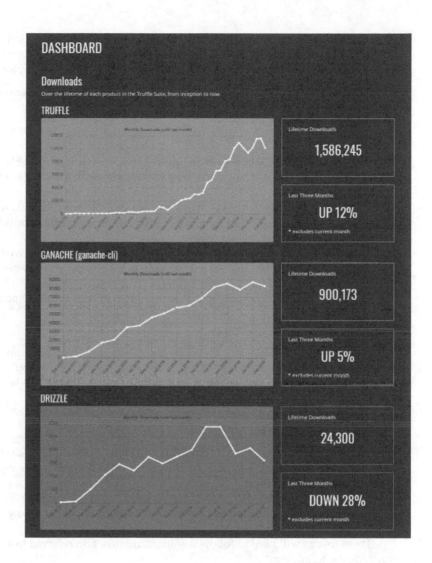

## DRIZZLE

Drizzle is a collection of front-end libraries that make writing dapp front ends simple, more efficient, and more predictable. The main core of Drizzle is based on a Redux store, and you access the development tools for Redux. The Drizzle package takes care of synchronization of your Ethereum-based services.

## TRUFFLE OR GANACHE?

Deciding when to use Truffle or Ganache can be a bit confusing because the solutions have some overlap in capabilities. Here are some tips to help you decide whether to use Truffle or Ganache:

◆ Truffle will enable you to develop, test, and deploy your dapp, and it has integration with Ganache.

◆ Ganache is part of the Truffle ecosystem, and you would use Ganache for the development of your dapps. Ganache essentially mimics a real blockchain. You could also pass on using Ganache and use Truffle to tie into a public testnet or deploy locally.

◆ Once the dapps are developed and tested, you then deploy them on an Ethereum client using Geth or Parity.

## OPEN ZEPPELIN

Open Zeppelin is a well-formatted and prevalent framework of reusable smart contracts for Ethereum and other EVM-based blockchains. Open Zeppelin is a library for secure smart contract development.

It provides implementations of standards like ERC-20 and ERC-721, which you can deploy as-is or extend to suit your needs, as well as Solidity components to build custom contracts and more complex decentralized systems.

The reusable smart contracts are useful since they have been reviewed by peers and therefore audited. Using a template that would be ready, of course, provides benefits such as shortened development time and quicker time to market.

For more information about Open Zeppelin, visit `https://openzeppelin.org/`.

## PRIVATE BLOCKCHAIN TESTING

One area of interest for developers is to be able to deploy, test, and validate an application locally and not have to connect to a VPN. Or perhaps you are developing applications and want to ensure specific variables for the networking are available. You would want to go with a private deployment such as Ganache.

## ETHEREUM TOKENS

Tokens are created to specific standards in Ethereum called the ERC-20 standards. Tokens in the Ethereum ecosystem can represent any fungible tradable item such as loyalty points, metal certificates, IOUs, coins, etc.

Tokens implement some basic features in a standard way in most cases, so this means that your token would be likely compatible with the Ethereum wallet or any other client or contract that uses the same standards.

These tokens will need to follow specific standards, also referred to as *constants*. Examples include the following:

◆ Symbol, which is your token's symbol or ticker

◆ Name, which is the name you give it

◆ Total supply, which specifies the number of tokens issued

◆ Decimals, which are the number of decimals used

The standards are listed at `Ethereum.org/token`.

### ETHEREUM REQUEST FOR COMMENTS

An Ethereum request for comments (ERC) is a glorified GitHub issue tracker. This is the main point of contact where developers can ask for comments on contracts and other issues related to Ethereum proposals. An ERC starts with #1 and increments every time a new issue is opened.

You can find ERCs at `https://eips.ethereum.org/erc`.

### ETHEREUM ERC TOKEN (ERC-20)

The ERC-20 token contract is the "standard" template to deploy fungible tokens on the Ethereum blockchain as a smart contract. The ERC token standard is basically a standard interface as well as a sample implementation of the functions necessary to create and operate an ERC-20 token.

Ethereum developers need to be very cognizant of how they develop applications. One way is to follow the ERC-20 standards. The ERC-20 standards serve several purposes, but the main purpose is focused on portability of the contracts.

### ETHEREUM IMPROVEMENT PROPOSALS

Ethereum Improvement Proposals (EIPs) have the same format as ERCs but are used to propose changes in the Ethereum protocol. EIPs serve the same purpose as Bitcoin Improvement Proposals (BIPs). BIPs are used to introduce new features or information important to Bitcoin. EIPs start with EIP #1 and increment every time a new issue is opened.

To find out more, visit `https://github.com/ethereum/EIPs`.

## Hyperledger Development

Developing applications in Hyperledger Fabric has some great benefits. The Hyperledger ecosystem is robust and well maintained for an open source project. The Hyperledger Project leaves little out for options in development and is clearly the most well-managed blockchain project.

This section provides a broad idea of what a developer in Hyperledger Fabric would need to deal with and develop around.

## Chaincode

Chaincode is a smart contract in Hyperledger Fabric and is invoked by a client application external to the blockchain network that manages access and modifications to a set of key-value pairs in the world state. The world state is the actual state of the current blockchain transactions that are recorded immutably.

Chaincode services are secured and lightweight since the environment is deployed as a locked-down, secured container. This container has a set of signed base images that contain the secure OS and chaincode language, runtime, and SDK images for Golang, Java, and Node.js.

Every chaincode must implement the chaincode interface, which is what is used to provide connections similar to an endpoint in cloud computing. The chaincode interface makes it possible for the client application to invoke a function that is called in response to the received transaction proposals. Chaincode implements the chaincode interface, in particular the Init and Invoke functions.

## INSTALLING CHAINCODE

When installing chaincode, you should ensure that you have the Go programming language installed first and then set up with the correct configuration requirements for your deployment type.

You will want to make sure that a directory is created for your chaincode application as a child directory of $GOPATH/src/.

The following command will create such a directory called `wiley:code`:

```
mkdir -p $GOPATH/src/wiley:code
```

To enter into the directory, you can use the following command:

```
cd $GOPATH/src/wiley_code
```

To create the source file for the chaincode, use the following command:

```
touch wiley_code.go
```

## WRITING CHAINCODE CONSIDERATIONS

After installing Go and setting up your environment, you then can start developing your chaincode.

Note this book will not be teaching chaincode but is organized to provide insight into the tasks developers would need to consider around Hyperledger development. Some of these tasks are different from Ethereum and worth noting for hiring managers to appreciate.

The next thing you could do is then implement the init function. The init is called during chaincode instantiation and will initialize any data as part of the chaincode. Chaincode applications will implement the two functions that would be invoked via the invoke function.

One area of confusion when setting your platform is around the database options. You may need to pay attention to the chaincode design if complex queries are based on an expected invocation sequence.

This confusion can occur because an invalid transaction may very well occur if you're not aware of the database options for the state data. The state database could be written in LevelDB or in CouchDB.

For tutorial information on getting started with chaincode, refer to the following site: https://hyperledger-fabric.readthedocs.io/en/release-1.4/chaincode.html

## BLOCKCHAIN PLATFORM EXTENSION

The IBM Blockchain Platform Extension for VSCode helps Hyperledger Fabric developers to rapidly develop, provision, and test their chaincode. This also could be used to test client applications on their local machines. The extension is currently supported on Windows 10, Linux, and macOS.

The extension works by creating a basic smart contract that locally manages an example asset in a development language of your choice.

What is really helpful is that the extension provides all the dependencies that are required to deploy your smart contract to an instance of Hyperledger Fabric directly. These features enable efficient development for your chaincode on the IBM Blockchain service.

To find out more about the VSCode extension, refer to the following site:

```
https://cloud.ibm.com/docs/services/blockchain?topic=blockchain-develop-vscode
```

## Hyperledger Fabric Consensus Options

Hyperledger Fabric has two consensus options, and it is important to understand the difference from a development perspective. You cannot just roll back once you deploy your blockchain.

◆ Solo, which is for development, is a single node with no high availability.

◆ Kafka is the production version that would be deployed on a live blockchain. Kafka is as close to a voting-based consensus as you get in Hyperledger.

As discussed in Chapter 2, consensus methods have different benefits but also cons. For example, having more nodes means more time to reach consensus. There's also a trade-off between scalability and performance that developers should be aware of. The Hyperledger Fabric white paper on consensus is the main starting point. To find out more, see the following site:

```
https://www.hyperledger.org/wp-content/uploads/2017/08/Hyperledger_Arch_WG_
Paper_1_Consensus.pdf
```

## Hyperledger Fabric Database Options

One of the important things to consider is the power of Hyperledger Fabric with the option of its state database. The ledger system in Hyperledger Fabric uses LevelDB, which allows concurrent writers to safely insert data into the database by providing internal synchronization.

State database options include LevelDB and CouchDB. LevelDB is the default key-value state database embedded in the peer process. CouchDB is an alternative external state database that supports binary data.

Table 10.4 shows the options for both the transaction logs and the state database.

**TABLE 10.4:** Transaction Log and State Database Options

|  | **TRANSACTION LOGS** | **STATE DATA (WORLD STATE)** |
| --- | --- | --- |
| **Type** | Immutable | Mutable |
| **Operations** | Create, retrieve | All CRUD |
| **DC** | LevelDB | LevelDB/CouchDB |
| **Attitude** | Embedded in peers | Key-value paired (JSON, binary) |
| **Query** | Simple | CouchDB for complex (binary) |

It's important to note that when assets are stored in the form of JSON documents, CouchDB allows you to perform complex queries for assets based on the asset state, for example. There really is no learning curve since the queries are formatted just like in CouchDB's declarative JSON querying syntax format.

## Client Applications

When developing client applications for blockchains, and specifically Hyperledger Fabric, there are some important considerations to design for depending on your specific use case. These client front-end considerations include the following:

◆ Secure the REST server via a secure protocol (HTTPS).

◆ Use authentication options such as a passport through Oath or supported platforms.

◆ Use multiuser mode for the REST API service.

◆ Understand the complete use case considerations for the blockchain applications.

◆ Use the current enterprise key management system (KMS).

◆ Use the current software development kits (SDKs) to ensure you're running the latest versions of supported components.

Figure 10.16 shows the different layers of Hyperledger blockchain development. From a development perspective, if you are developing a blockchain application that is for the end user, that is considered front-end development. In front-end development, there would be development applications, wallets, mobile applications, monitoring tools.

**FIGURE 10.16**
Front-end application
workflow

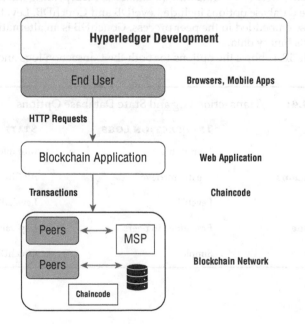

Hyperledger Fabric's business network archive (package) comprises the model file, chaincode, access control file, and static query file.

The native query language can filter results returned by using clearly defined criteria. The native query language can also be invoked in transactions to perform operations such as an update.

Blockchain queries are defined in a query file (.qry) in the parent directory of the business network definition.

Events that occur will create notifications of significant operations on the blockchain (e.g., a new block), as well as notifications related to a milestone achieved while processing a smart contract/chaincode. The client app can subscribe to this event and take appropriate business actions.

## Fabric REST Services

The REST server uses a business network card specified during startup to connect to and discover the assets, participants, and transactions within a deployed business network. This information visibility is required to generate the REST API. The business network card is known as the discovery business network card. By default, the discovery business network card is also used to handle all requests to the REST API.

Chaincode Services uses Docker to host (deploy) the chaincode without relying on any virtual machine or computer language. Docker provides a secured, lightweight method to sandbox chaincode execution. The environment is a "locked-down" and secured container, along with a set of signed base images containing secure OS and chaincode language, runtime, and SDK images for Golang.

Hyperledger includes the REST and JSON RPC APIs, events, and an SDK for applications to communicate with the network.

## Service Discovery

To execute chaincode on peers, to submit transactions to orderers, and to be updated about the status of transactions, applications connect to an API exposed by an SDK. The discovery service improves this process by having the peers compute the needed information dynamically and present it to the SDK in a consumable manner.

The application is bootstrapped knowing about a group of peers that are trusted by the application developer/administrator to provide authentic responses to discovery queries.

A good candidate peer that needs to be used by the client application is one that is in the same organization.

## Hyperledger Composer

Contributed by IBM and Oxgcains, Hyperledger Composer is an open source application development framework that was specifically built for Hyperledger. Composer simplifies the creation of Hyperledger Fabric blockchain applications and therefore brings efficiencies into the development cycle.

The Composer tool is aimed at helping users to create blockchain applications based on Hyperledger Fabric without needing to know the low-level Go programming details that are involved in blockchain networks.

If you want to build your blockchain application directly on Hyperledger Fabric, you have to write your chaincode in Go or Java, which is comparatively different from JavaScript because its composer is quite easy to code smart contract using a model file (.cto) and angular JavaScript.

Hyperledger Composer primarily uses JavaScript for chaincode development, and this has a lower barrier to entry as well.

Hyperledger Composer uses what's called *connection profiles* to define the system to connect to a connection profile, which is a JSON document that acts as part of a business network card. The connection profile describes a distinct set of components, including peers, orderers, and certificate authorities in a Hyperledger Fabric blockchain network. A connection profile is normally created by an administrator who understands the network topology.

You can use queries to get data about the state of the blockchain. Queries are defined within a business network and can include variable parameters. Queries are sent using the Composer API.

Events in Composer are defined in the business network definition in the same way as participants or assets. Events are emitted by the transaction processor function once it has been defined. An event indicates to external systems that something important has occurred on the ledger. Applications subscribe to emitted events using the Composer client API.

Developers of the business network can create a set of access controls. Access controls are rules that determine which assets participants have access to in the business network and the conditions in which they can access them.

A historian is a specialized type of registry that records successful transactions conducted on the business network.

## HYPERLEDGER COMPOSER MODELING LANGUAGE

Hyperledger Composer is an object-oriented modeling language that defines the domain model for a business.

The modeling language is saved as a .cto file. The CTO file contains the following:

◆ A single namespace, in which all resource declarations are implicit

◆ A set of resource definitions that includes assets, transactions, participants, and events

◆ The option to import resources from other namespaces

There is a system namespace that contains base definitions of the asset, event, participant, and transactions. These base definitions are abstract types that are implicitly extended by all new assets, events, participants, and transactions.

Events and transactions in the system namespace are defined by an eventID and transactionID, respectively, and a timestamp.

The system namespace also includes a historian, which is a specialized registry that records successful transactions on the blockchain, as well as the participants and identities that submit transaction requests.

## HYPERLEDGER COMPOSER RESOURCES

In Composer, resources are considered one of the following:

◆ Assets, participants, transactions, and events

◆ Enumerated types

◆ Concepts

Here is an example of `Vehicle` as a super-type and `Car` as an asset with a set of parts:

```
asset Car extends Vehicle {
o String model
--> Part[] Parts
```

In Composer, concepts are abstract classes that are not considered an asset, participant, or transaction. Concepts would need to be clearly defined because of this abstract quality. A mode of transportation could be a car, motorcycle, plane, boat, or any other mode of transport. We need to accommodate the possibility that a concept is abstract by adding strings and declaring the concepts to the code.

The following code shows how to identify New York as a string in the program. This code is extending the possibility of New York City being either a street, a city, or a state in the United States. A concept then is added to address the possibility of New York City also being a street, city, or state in Canada.

```
Address {
o String street
o String city default = "New York"
o String country default - "US"
o Integer[] counts optional
}
concept CanadaAddress extends Address {
o String zipcode
}
```

Other programming areas that Composer can address include arrays, primitives, field validators, relationships, imports, and decorators.

## HYPERLEDGER COMPOSER PLAYGROUND

Hyperledger Composer Playground, a free sandbox maintained by IBM, provides an environment that quickly models and tests a blockchain network. Composer Playground has a simple GUI to edit and test the business blockchain network. Playground simplifies what is normally a complex blockchain network for running blockchain testing.

There is both an online version and an offline version of Playground. The online playground runs the business network in browser memory, and the local playground is deployed in Hyperledger Fabric instances.

We can use Hyperledger Composer or Composer Playground to develop, test, and validate our blockchain ideas by deploying a new business network to Hyperledger Fabric. Composer is not a live blockchain and is exclusively focused on preproduction use cases.

Figure 10.17 shows the Hyperledger Composer Playground login prompt.

Composer Playground is currently available at `https://composer-playground .mybluemix.net/`.

Hyperledger Fabric v1.4+, which should feature significant improvements to the developer experience, will include a new programming model. Note that Composer Playground will likely be deprecated in the future, but no clear road map has been released at the time of writing.

**FIGURE 10.17**
Hyperledger Fabric
Playground login

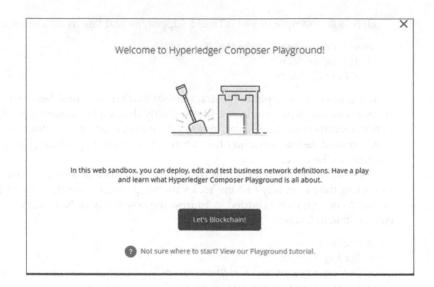

# R3 Corda Development

Corda is written in Kotlin and is compatible with any JVM language. Kotlin is an odd language to some programmers who prefer Scala, for example. Kotlin does have a better type inference, better generics with type variance, and a more modern syntax.

The two most popular languages for Corda development are Java and Kotlin. The real key is that it has great flexibility and interoperability with Java in both directions in programming perspectives.

R3 Corda is primarily focused on implementing solutions for regulated financial services. Therefore, the development of Corda solutions often involves many types of financial assets. Some of the common financial assets that are defined in Corda contracts include the following:

- Cash
- Stocks
- Bonds
- Futures
- Credit letters
- Derivatives
- Interest rate swaps

A financial transaction is an agreement between buyer and seller parties to exchange one or more asset for payment of monetary value. This is essentially the focus of the smart contracts in Corda.

When developing in Corda, there two main types of assets.

◆ Fungible assets, which are homogenous and are divisible, mergeable, and interchangeable

◆ Nonfungible assets, which are unique and represent something that is not divisible, mergeable, or interchangeable

I won't cover the business part of the house for the assets, so you may want to research more if this is of interest.

## Corda Consensus Model

Consensus in Corda is handled somewhat differently in some respects from other blockchains in that the unit of consensus in Corda is the state that can be handled in two distinct parts. In other blockchains state is considered less flexible—state meaning the current transaction view of the blockchain. Consensus in Corda is broken into two distinct parts: consensus over state validity and consensus over state uniqueness.

◆ *Consensus over state validity* is when the blockchain members reach certainty that a transaction is accepted by the contract's states and has all the required signatures.

◆ *Consensus over state uniqueness* is when the blockchain members reach certainty that the output states created in a transaction are actually unique and not previously consumed.

Corda has pluggable uniqueness services to improve privacy, scalability, legal-system compatibility, and algorithmic agility.

Pluggable uniqueness services in Corda with the use of shared cryptographic hashes ensure that restrictive viewing of transactions provide for the scalability and privacy required.

For more information on the Corda consensus model, refer to the following:

```
https://docs.corda.net/releases/release-M9.2/key-concepts-consensus-
notaries.html
```

## CorDapps

Developing applications in Corda revolves around the CorDapp (Corda distributed app) and how you define the business logic. The customer's main objective of any CorDapp is to allow participants to reach an agreement about transactions to the globally distributed ledger.

CorDapps achieve this main objective by defining flows (*workflows*) that Corda node owners must invoke via RPCs. It is important to note that the core of contracts in Corda is an executable program that authenticates changes to all state objects in Corda transactions.

CorDapps consist of the following software components:

◆ States define the facts over how an agreement will be reached.

◆ Contracts define what constitutes a valid global ledger update.

◆ Services provide the functions of the node—for example, what the node role is, such as a notary.

◆    Flows specify the entire life cycle of state changes by invoking the smart contract that is consistent and related to the current state.

◆    Service hubs maintain services and support APIs for accessing and controlling many aspects of the Corda platform from within server-side CorDapps code, not RPC client-side code.

◆    Client RPC operations are remote procedure calls.

## Corda Network and Nodes

A Corda network consists of a number of machines running nodes, including a single node operating as the network map service. These nodes communicate using persistent protocols in order to create and validate transactions.

A Corda network is a connected graph. There is no global broadcast. The network maintains point-to-point and nonpersistent connections and supports AMQP/1.0 over TLS. Corda runs on a semiprivate permissioned network.

A Corda node is a process that runs with a Java virtual machine (JVM). The Corda node's properties consist of several types of services and support custom functionality such as CorDapps.

Nodes interact with each other following the flow framework, which reflects the business logic of the proposed transaction, and the custom functionality, which is dictated by the CorDapps. After the flow framework has been verified and completed, the transaction is committed to the ledger.

To set up Corda nodes, you should use the templates provided by Corda. These templates are available in Kotlin and Java from GitHub (`https://github.com/corda`).

When you are done setting up the Corda templates, you then would need to set up the network with a number of participants (nodes) by configuring the XML file.

## Corda Service Hub

Corda nodes have something unique in the blockchain world—a service hub. The service hub maintains services and supports APIs for accessing and controlling many aspects of the Corda platform. All this is performed from within the server-side CorDapps code, not the RPC client-side code.

Think of the service hub as the starting point for most operations that are performed inside a node. The service hub also defines how nodes access services internally by three distinct service calls.

The CorDapps are what actually defines how a node owner interacts with a node. Of course, APIs are required to provide for the required operation on a Corda node. There are also a full suite of unique API calls that developer would want to review and test before deploying an application.

For more on the API categories, refer to the following:

```
https://docs.corda.net/api/kotlin/corda/net.corda.core.node/-service-hub/
index.html
```

## Corda Doorman

Corda networks are semiprivate and have a doorman service that enforces rules regarding the information that nodes must provide and the know-your-customer processes that they must complete before being admitted to the network.

A node must contact the doorman and provide the required information. The doorman will give the node a root-authority-signed TLS certificate from the network's permissioning service.

## Corda Flows

Flows are used to model business processes between parties exchanging assets. Flows are what would be called a bilateral agreement, which is between two parties. There is no way that you can invoke smart contracts directly in Corda; therefore, you must write a flow, which specifies the entire life cycle of state changes. The flow does this by invoking the smart contract that is related to the current state.

## Client RPC

A client remote procedure call is a protocol that the client's blockchain program uses to request blockchain access from a program that is located on a remote Corda node.

RPCs are used to ensure that the application can communicate without having to fully dictate or understand the blockchain network's details. An RPC is also known as a function call or a subroutine call, which uses a client-server platform. The node in Corda owner can interact with the node via a client RPC.

From a development perspective, the node owner does not have direct client-side access to Service Hub APIs. For developers to interact with a node, they need to write a client in a JVM-compatible language using the `CordaRPCClient` class. There are also a number of dependencies and permissions developers would need to address.

For more information, please refer to the following:

```
https://docs.corda.net/clientrpc.html
```

## Oracles

An oracle is a trusted external source of factual and final information. A fact can be included in a transaction as part of a command. An oracle service can be used to access or validate off-ledger data. An oracle will sign a transaction only if the included off-ledger fact is actually true from its point of view. For example, an oracle service can be used to sign the transaction to ensure the exchange rate being referenced is correct at a certain point in time.

In a nutshell, an oracle is a trusted service that can provide that capability in a controlled and deterministic manner for exchanges.

## Corda DemoBench

DemoBench is used to run a multiple-node Corda network on a local development machine. R3 Corda DemoBench is available for both Windows and macOS as a free download at the Corda download site. Developers should start by using DemoBench to get a feel of how a CorDapp would work from a user perspective and then dive into the JVM.

Figure 10.18 shows the view in DemoBench when a network is deployed.

**FIGURE 10.18**
DemoBench

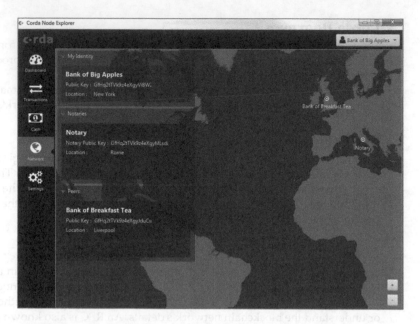

DemoBench writes a log file to the following locations:

◆ **macOS/Linux**: $HOME/DemoBench/demobench.log

◆ **Windows**: %USERPROFILE%\DemoBench\demobench.log

Figure 10.19 shows the log files in a Corda DemoBench JVM.
You can download Corda DemoBench from https://www.corda.net/download.html.

**FIGURE 10.19**
DemoBench logs

```
2018-12-04T15:12:46,545Z  [INFO   JVMConfig - Java executable: C:\Program Files\Corda DemoBench\runtime
2018-12-04T15:12:46,773Z  [INFO   ExplorerController - Explorer JAR: C:\Program Files\Corda DemoBench\a
2018-12-04T15:12:46,775Z  [INFO   WebServerController - Web Server JAR: C:\Program Files\Corda DemoBenc
2018-12-04T15:12:46,863Z  [INFO   NodeController - Base directory: C:\Users\HPE Workstation\demobench\2
2018-12-04T15:12:46,863Z  [INFO   NodeController - Corda JAR: C:\Program Files\Corda DemoBench\app\cord
2018-12-04T15:14:57,480Z  [INFO   NodeInfoFilesCopier - Now watching: C:\Users\HPE Workstation\demobenc
2018-12-04T15:14:58,002Z  [INFO   CordappController - Installed 'Finance' cordapp
2018-12-04T15:15:01,385Z  [INFO   NodeController - Launched node: O=Notary, L=Rome, C=IT
2018-12-04T15:15:08,284Z  [INFO   RPCClient - Startup took 1633 msec
2018-12-04T15:15:08,286Z  [WARN   NodeRPC - Node 'O=Notary, L=Rome, C=IT' not ready yet (Error: AMQ1190
2018-12-04T15:15:09,293Z  [INFO   RPCClient - Startup took 1006 msec
2018-12-04T15:15:09,293Z  [WARN   NodeRPC - Node 'O=Notary, L=Rome, C=IT' not ready yet (Error: AMQ1190
2018-12-04T15:15:10,293Z  [INFO   RPCClient - Startup took 999 msec
2018-12-04T15:15:10,293Z  [WARN   NodeRPC - Node 'O=Notary, L=Rome, C=IT' not ready yet (Error: AMQ1190
2018-12-04T15:15:11,297Z  [INFO   RPCClient - Startup took 1003 msec
2018-12-04T15:15:11,298Z  [WARN   NodeRPC - Node 'O=Notary, L=Rome, C=IT' not ready yet (Error: AMQ1190
2018-12-04T15:15:12,311Z  [INFO   RPCClient - Startup took 1012 msec
2018-12-04T15:15:12,311Z  [WARN   NodeRPC - Node 'O=Notary, L=Rome, C=IT' not ready yet (Error: AMQ1190
2018-12-04T15:15:14,836Z  [INFO   RPCClient - Startup took 2524 msec
2018-12-04T15:15:15,052Z  [INFO   NodeTerminalView - Node 'O=Notary, L=Rome, C=IT' is now ready.
2018-12-04T15:15:18,152Z  [INFO   NodeInfoFilesCopier - Now watching: C:\Users\HPE Workstation\demobenc
2018-12-04T15:15:18,181Z  [INFO   CordappController - Installed 'Finance' cordapp
2018-12-04T15:15:18,205Z  [INFO   CordappController - Installed 'Bank of Corda' cordapp
2018-12-04T15:15:18,265Z  [INFO   NodeController - Launched node: O=Bank of Breakfast Tea, L=New York,
2018-12-04T15:15:24,281Z  [INFO   RPCClient - Startup took 1008 msec
2018-12-04T15:15:24,282Z  [WARN   NodeRPC - Node 'O=Bank of Breakfast Tea, L=New York, C=US' not ready
2018-12-04T15:15:25,287Z  [INFO   RPCClient - Startup took 1005 msec
2018-12-04T15:15:25,287Z  [WARN   NodeRPC - Node 'O=Bank of Breakfast Tea, L=New York, C=US' not ready
2018-12-04T15:15:26,294Z  [INFO   RPCClient - Startup took 1006 msec
2018-12-04T15:15:26,294Z  [WARN   NodeRPC - Node 'O=Bank of Breakfast Tea, L=New York, C=US' not ready
2018-12-04T15:15:27,299Z  [INFO   RPCClient - Startup took 1003 msec
2018-12-04T15:15:27,299Z  [WARN   NodeRPC - Node 'O=Bank of Breakfast Tea, L=New York, C=US' not ready
2018-12-04T15:15:29,793Z  [INFO   RPCClient - Startup took 2492 msec
2018-12-04T15:15:29,934Z  [INFO   NodeTerminalView - Node 'O=Bank of Breakfast Tea, L=New York, C=US' i
2018-12-04T15:15:32,314Z  [WARN   Explorer - Failed to create symlink 'C:\Users\HPE Workstation\demoben
```

# Quorum Development

Quorum is an open source private blockchain network developed by JP Morgan directly from the Ethereum code. This blockchain is a fork of the Ethereum blockchain.

Ethereum developers will have no real significant learning curve to become proficient in the platform. Quorum development is similar to Ethereum, so I won't cover the redundant areas again for Quorum. I will focus on the similarities and major differences between Quorum and Ethereum.

Quorum's main distinguishing feature is the fact that it allows private transactions between the parties. It does this over a private deployment of Ethereum, not on the Ethereum mainnet.

Quorum introduces an interesting new consensus algorithm called Raft. Similar to proof of stake (POS), Raft does not require calculation of a hash and validates blocks/transactions in under 0.5 seconds, which is fast for a blockchain. However, this speed comes at a cost to security since it has no Byzantine fault tolerance. Basically, if this consensus is used, the security has to be provided by the entities themselves to ensure that their nodes are not accessible to an attacker.

Quorum offers more consensus mechanisms that in the long run will allow Byzantine fault tolerance, such as Quorum Chain, which is programmable through a smart contract and is intended to enable programmable consensus logic.

Quorum allows transactions to be carried out privately between network participants and allows a transaction to be visible only to a specific group of participants.

The data of the private transactions never reaches nonparticipating nodes, since instead of using blockchain communication to send the data, a point-to-point network is used, which works together with the blockchain and allows data to be sent from one node to another, called/provided by Constellation. This data is verified in the blockchain by means of its hashes, but the data is never sent via the "open" network.

## Quorum vs. Ethereum

From a development perspective, Quorum uses the same core as Ethereum. They share the same smart contract development language, Solidity.

However, there is a difference in regard to the computation pricing where the gas system is concerned. The Quorum network developer doesn't have to worry about having enough gas to interact with the contracts. Developers do not need to worry about gas because Quorum is a private blockchain and doesn't use gas. Wallets are not used in Quorum as they are in Ethereum.

However, Quorum does maintain an execution gas limit per transaction. This is to prevent someone from launching a code that could take the validators too long to process and effectively induce a vulnerability into the chain.

## Quorum Cakeshop

Cakeshop is an SDK that has APIs for creating, managing, and integrating Ethereum-like ledgers such as Quorum. It is packaged as a Java web application archive (WAR) that you can run on Docker containers. Cakeshop has an intuitive graphical user interface and is fairly intuitive to use.

Cakeshop downloads the latest version of Quorum and the boot node from Geth. This Cakeshop package includes the transaction managers, a Solidity compiler, and all the needed dependencies.

For more information on Cakeshop, visit `https://github.com/jpmorganchase/cakeshop`.

## Blockchain Performance

Blockchains are generally technologies that are distributed and decentralized, and they can be fast. For example, a blockchain could be faster than another blockchain if you removed nodes. However, when you remove nodes, you effectively mitigate security or decentralization.

It's important to note that a blockchain, like any other technology, cannot be everything at once, and therefore a compromise in the constraints must be made. This compromise is similar to how a project manager would handle project constraints. For example, in a project you could reduce the time to completion by investing more in labor, which may get your project completed earlier. The other side is that by adding more labor, you effectively increase your cost constraints.

In blockchain projects, constraints are no different from a compromise perspective, and it's a give-and-take consideration to what your blockchain application would realize from a security, speed, or decentralization perspective. Want better performance (faster transactions)? Then reduce the number of nodes but also centralize the nodes more. By improving performance, you could very well impact decentralization as well as change your security posture.

As shown in Figure 10.20, the project management triangle (aka triple constraint) comprises three constraints.

◆ Time refers to the schedule allotted to the project.

◆ Cost refers to the budget for licenses, hardware, and manpower, both internal and external.

◆ Scope refers to the amount of functionality to be delivered in the project.

**FIGURE 10.20**
Triple constraint

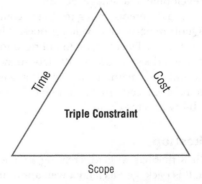

Projects need to adjust one of the three constraints to make up for another. Generally, the project sponsor will determine which two to excel at, and the third will have to be adjusted to meet the initial two constraints.

Now let's discuss blockchains. As previously mentioned, blockchains are decentralized, are secure, and can be fast relative to other blockchains. These three constraints are a choice, and the customer would need to choose.

Blockchains can effectively maintain two of three properties (constraints) where one property is effectively compromised to provide a different result for another property. These three properties (constraints) are

♦ Speed (fast)

♦ Secure

♦ Decentralized

Figure 10.21 shows the blockchain paradigm. Ideally, blockchains would meet all our expectations. However, we don't live in a perfect world, so developers need to determine what these properties really are and how they affect our blockchain implementation.

**FIGURE 10.21**
Blockchain paradigm

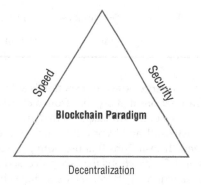

The following are the common properties developers want to measure or adjust in our blockchain performance requirements:

♦ **Speed**—The blockchain must provide for prompt processing, which should result in higher transactions per second (TPS). Speed is also referred to as how "fast" a transaction could occur. Note that "speed" or "fast" is relative only as compared to other blockchains. Comparing blockchains to client-servers is not relative here.

♦ **Security**—Generally, a certificate manager handles these encryption certificates. In most blockchain networks, X.509 certificates are commonly used to maintain these certificates. For example, in Hyperledger Fabric there is what is called a *certificate authority*. Permissions are also important to consider since they directly affect access to resources. In most permissioned blockchains, there would be permissioning, which means that there is centralized control over what users or applications have access to the blockchain resources.

♦ **Decentralization**—This is true in the permissionless blockchains, such as Ethereum. However, Hyperledger, Corda, and Ripple are centralized platforms.

To be fair, some blockchains, such as Ripple, state they can process around 1,500 TPS, and Hyperledger Fabric, in a perfect world, could process up to 3,500 TPS. However, these numbers are based on some kind of compromise.

Bitcoin's TPS is continually varying. In its current form, the network doesn't support more than 7 TPS, and Ethereum is not much better at around 14 TPS. The performance of Bitcoin and Ethereum, for example, is a direct result of the global scale, Internet reliance, and transaction workloads. More transactions increase the workload of all production blockchain nodes in Ethereum and Bitcoin, which effectively have to update their ledger for every transaction.

Table 10.5 compares some of the common blockchains and legacy services.

**TABLE 10.5:** Transactions per Second (TPS) Comparisons

|  | VISA | BTC | RIPPLE | PAYPAL | HYPERLEDGER |
|---|---|---|---|---|---|
| **TPS** | 24,000 | 4 | 1,500 | 193 | 3,500 |
| **Control** | Centralized | Decentralized | Centralized | Centralized | Centralized |
| **Notes** | Push | P2P | Hybrid | Hybrid | P2P |

The "Notes" reference how a transaction is actually processed and then ingested from the application. Transactions that are sent from a client application to the server's processor application are push transactions. Transactions that are pulled from the client application are pull transactions. Push, pull, and hybrid transactions are client-server applications, which typically are decentralized. Transactions that use both push and pull processes in the application are considered hybrid. Transactions that are processed on the blockchain nodes and processed by each node are considered P2P transactions. Blockchains that are processed in a P2P transaction platform are the native forms of blockchain transactions.

## Permission or Permissionless Performance

Perhaps the real trade-off around performance is between permissioned and permissionless blockchains. Permissioned blockchains can generally perform better since they have fewer nodes in the blockchain network, and the nodes are centralized or localized. Performance is relative to the number of nodes.

For example, it has been stated that Hyperledger Fabric could theoretically reach 3,500 TPS. Of course, this number is in a perfect world, and it is well known that Hyperledger Fabric overall does not scale well from a performance perspective. Adding mode nodes and peers will substantially drop the TPS. When you add nodes that are not localized, you can expect the network latency to also reduce your TPS.

In the case of permissionless blockchains such as Ethereum, developers know that performance should not be an expectation. Permissionless blockchains are generally widely distributed with typically hundreds of nodes as well. The user base can be dependent on sporadic behavior—for example, in the world of Bitcoin, activity can spike when there is an event in China or when the United States makes a statement about regulating cryptocurrency.

If performance is part of your use case requirements, then permissionless blockchains are out of the question.

## Performance Testing

When it comes to performance testing, the main focus is transactions per second (TPS). Another factor is the size of the transactions. For example, a larger block size may not perform as well as a smaller block size.

Performance testing is generally accomplished through what is considered to be nonfunctional testing. Nonfunctional testing is a focused area that is mainly technically driven. Some technical areas that could be tested include the following:

◆ Network latency and bottlenecks

◆ Block size adjustment

◆ Signatures removed or included

◆ Sequencing of transactions

There seems to be a limited number of performance testing tools. However, there are a few solid choices depending on your platform. Ethereum has most choices available at the time of writing.

### ETHEREUM TESTING TOOLS

There are numerous tools for Ethereum application development. It is important to note that in varying degrees when testing your Quorum blockchain applications some Ethereum tools could be made to work. At the time of writing, there are no testing tools for Quorum. From a testing perspective with Quorum you would want to ensure that you direct your tests to your localhost or a custom RPC.

The following are three common tools used in Ethereum testing:

**Ethereum Tester**  Ethereum Tester supports two distinct data formats that enable both front-end and backend testing. There is a significant installation process and some dependencies to deal with.

On GitHub, visit `https://github.com/ethereum/eth-tester`.

**Truffle**  Truffle is a battle-tested Ethereum development framework that you really have to know to develop in Ethereum. It has a great testing capacity built in as well. For example, you can write automated tests for smart contracts in JavaScript and Solidity and get your contracts developed quickly.

To find out more about Truffle Suite, visit `https://www.trufflesuite.com/`.

**Ganache**  Ganache has the most popular library for Ethereum testing. Formerly known as TestRPC, Ganache is used to test Ethereum smart contracts locally—that is, it spins up an instance on your desktop/server and simulates a live blockchain.

You can learn more about Ganache at `https://www.trufflesuite.com/ganache`.

### HYPERLEDGER FABRIC TESTING TOOLS

Hyperledger Fabric has some specific tools that can be used for testing. Hyperledger Composer currently is the most common tool used for Hyperledger development and testing. Hyperledger Composer is available for a local deployment using Docker containers, or you can use the web version called Hyperledger Composer Playground.

Hyperledger Composer is an open source development tool that contains many functions to help build blockchain applications. Some of those features also help with testing. At the time of writing, Composer supports interactive testing, automated unit testing, and automated system testing.

Composer has a command-line interface that enables you to run interactive "smoke tests" that can ensure the deployment would be successful. This also makes it easy to execute tests in a continuous integration/continuous delivery (CI/CD) pipeline.

Continuous integration (CI) is a process whereby a developer's working copies are synchronized with a shared pipeline several times a day. Continuous delivery (CD) is the next process after continuous integration and enables placing a product into production, which historically is a manually driven process. Continuous deployment, the next logical next step after continuous delivery, automatically deploys the product into production after quality assurance (QA).

## Blockchain Integration and Interoperability

Blockchains are increasingly providing much more value by either going off chain or cross-chaining. Moving value from one blockchain to another blockchain is actually somewhat of a new approach even in blockchain's short history.

Before the idea and implementation of cross chains, developers be using an off-chain approach through a cryptocurrency gateway to exchange value. The main headache with that approach was that these gateways were centralized exchanges and could pose some concerns to privacy, costing, control, and performance.

A thin client generally only presents processed data provided by an application server, which performs the bulk of any required data processing. A device using web applications is a thin client, and generally these blockchain applications can be enabled by thin clients.

To integrate the blockchain with any traditional systems or with a front end that will allow our clients to interact with it in a user-friendly way, developers must use the client libraries available for the various "traditional languages."

Generally, the blockchain technologies communicate through RPC/HTTP and a client library for NodeJS or another library. Blockchain technologies exchange payments and digital assets. The ability to transfer and exchange digital assets originating from another blockchain without trusted intermediaries can be accomplished through the use of notary schemes, relays, and hashed time locks.

Vitalik Buterin, cofounder of Ethereum, noted that there are three primary methods to achieving true interoperability for a blockchain.

◆ Notary schemes, which are an exchange of arbitrary data such as how to connect the blockchain to another blockchain. This is commonly referred to as *federation* of blockchains. An example would be a company such as Blockstream that provides a medium for transfer from one network to another network.

◆ Relays provide for the exchange of arbitrary data via what is a gateway or data exchange. Some vendors refer to relays as a relay chain. A relay or relay chain is used to provide a gateway from one blockchain to another blockchain. BTCRelay is the most widely known relay and acts as a bridge between Bitcoin and Ethereum blockchains.

◆ Hashed time lock contracts (HTLCs) provide for the exchange of digital assets via a cross-chain atomic swap. HTLCs can provide for bidirectional payment channels between digital assets on specific blockchains. The most prominent example is the Bitcoin Lightning Network.

Generally, whether a blockchain uses any one of the preceding methods is really dependent on the level of federation required, off-chain or side chain requirements, as well as any number of other factors.

## Data Exchange Methods

The terms *sidechains* and *payment gateways* are commonly used interchangeably in the blockchain industry. However, they are quite different. A sidechain is a separate blockchain that is attached to a parent blockchain using what is called a *two-way peg*. This two-way peg enables the interchangeability of assets at a predetermined rate between the parent blockchain and the sidechain. In simple terms, it's an exchange.

The original blockchain is usually referred to as the *main chain*, and all additional blockchains are referred to as *sidechains*.

Common sidechains that are in production mode include Rootstock and Liquid.

Rootstock (RSK) appears to be the most widely used and has created an open source testnet called Ginger for its sidechains. RSK has a two-way peg with the Bitcoin blockchain and rewards Bitcoin miners via merged mining. RSK's main goal is to enable the Bitcoin blockchain to have smart contract capabilities and make these integrated payments more efficient.

Liquid is a sidechain created by a blockchain startup called Blockstream. Liquid enables the instant movement of funds between cryptocurrency exchanges, and it's very efficient. There is really no waiting for the confirmation in the Bitcoin blockchain.

## Hash Timed Locks

An HTLC is a class of blockchain-based payment system that uses hash locks. Time locks require the receiver of a payment to either acknowledge receipt prior to a deadline or basically forfeit the ability to claim the payment and then return it to the payer.

HTLCs allow for cross-chain atomic swaps, which means, for example, a sender could pay in Bitcoin, but the receiver could choose Litecoin as payment. The hashed time locks are fully funded bidirectional payment channels between assets on the specified blockchain platforms.

In the case of the Lightning network, it is a decentralized micropayment solution on top of the Bitcoin blockchain.

## Relays and Gateways

A relay is effectively a way to interface a contract exchange between two different blockchains. Relays are also referred to as *gateways* or *payment gateways*.

The most prominent relay is BTC Relay, which allows Ethereum contracts to securely verify Bitcoin transactions without any intermediaries.

BTC Relay is an Ethereum contract that stores Bitcoin block headers only. It uses these block headers to build a mini version of the Bitcoin blockchain. The main benefit is that it allows Ethereum dapp users to pay with Bitcoin to use Ethereum dapps directly.

Some relays allow for a one-way exchange, and some allow for exchange both ways. For example, in BTC Relay, the exchange is one way, whereby the user can pay for Ethereum by using Bitcoin, but not the other way around.

For more on BTCRelay, refer to `http://btcrelay.org/`.

## Summary

This chapter covered various development challenges, best practices, programming models, and frameworks.

Solidity is a newer but simple programming language that is popular among Ethereum developers. Other widely used development languages include C++, Java, Golang, and Rust. Blockchain developers experienced in these languages are on their way to blockchain success.

Ethereum development requirements should be reviewed before developing on Ethereum. You learned about Truffle, Ganache, MetaMask, testnets, and several areas of development focus on Ethereum.

Hyperledger development tools include Hyperledger Composer, an object-oriented modeling language that defines the domain model for a business network definition.

Hyperledger Fabric uses LevelDB as the database for the state database, but you may want to consider the option to configure peers to store database transactions in CouchDB.

The two most popular languages for Corda development are Java and Kotlin. The real key for using these languages is their great flexibility and interoperability with Java in both directions.

Quorum is an open source private blockchain network developed by JP Morgan from the Ethereum code. Ethereum developers will have a short ramp-up time to develop on the Quorum blockchain.

There are various aspects of interoperability and integration—such as hash locks, payment gateways, and sidechains—to consider when blockchain requirements call for different blockchains.

# Chapter 11

# Blockchain Security and Threat Landscape

This chapter covers the basics of how blockchains fit into the overall picture of IT security. The chapter's main mission is to focus on blockchain security, so if you are not familiar with IT networking or IT security best practices and concepts, you may need to follow up with other resources.

I will cover many of the vulnerabilities in the threat landscape that a blockchain network could be exposed to, including DDOS attacks and 51 percent attacks. The focus will be on Ethereum, Corda, Hyperledger, and Quorum.

I will discuss how hashing, encryption, and decryption play into blockchain security. Risk assessments and risk mitigation also will be covered in detail.

I will then cover security concerns surrounding smart contracts, including legal enforcement and legal prose.

Lastly, I will dive into each enterprise blockchain security-related feature and discuss the most common aspects of the blockchains that can affect security and privacy.

## Blockchain Security Basics

A blockchain is essentially a distributed ledger that in most cases should be immutable—that is, the information (transactions) that is written to the ledger cannot be modified or deleted. This feature of a blockchain provides some distinct advantages over a traditional centralized database. For example, a centralized database could be tampered with.

A traditional database is centralized, meaning the control of data is managed by a central authority. The distributed ledger is different than the approach for deployment since it is a distributed database and not centralized. In a decentralized database, the data is not only kept in one location but generally replicated to all other nodes in the network, which could be located all over the world. For example, the Ethereum distributed ledger is on a worldwide computer network with other devices. Because it's on a shared network, it should be expected to have the potential of being exposed to network vulnerabilities and for that matter even concerns around privacy, security, and availability.

In regard to blockchain security, we need to consider the technology it has been derived from in a holistic manner. Blockchains are not built from one technology but from multiple technologies, which can expose the blockchain nodes to different threats. These threats could be malware, network attacks, data theft, and a multitude of other issues that you likely already deal with in the realm of traditional IT.

Blockchains are built from three distinct technologies.

◆ P2P networks, which can be exposed to distributed denial-of-service (DDoS) attacks wherein a node's buffer is overflowed, for example

◆ Private/public key encryption, which can be cracked through the use of reverse engineering or through flaws that affect keys generated for the RSA and OpenPGP algorithms

◆ Programs (smart contracts), which use development languages such as JavaScript, Golang, and C++, which have their own unique vulnerabilities, threats, and concerns

Because these technologies all have their own specific vulnerabilities, it's important to understand the technologies involved in order to address any possible vulnerability of the blockchain ledger and the components of the network, development languages, client applications, etc.

## Confidentiality, Integrity, and Availability

The CIA triad is a well-known staple in the world of IT security. It is one of the oldest and most popular security frameworks connected with IT security, and it certainly should be used with blockchain as well.

As shown in Figure 11.1, the CIA triad comprises three main components.

◆ **Confidentiality**—The information cannot be understood by anyone other than for whom it was unintended

◆ **Integrity**—The information cannot be altered in storage or transit between sender and intended receiver without the alteration being detected

◆ **Authentication**—The sender and receiver can confirm each other's identity and the origin/destination of the information.

**FIGURE 11.1**
The CIA triad

The CIA triad model's main goal is to help organizations to structure their security posture appropriately.

One area of concern is around consortium networks where potential competitors are participating on the same network as your company. One way to mitigate concerns around privacy or confidentiality is to enable blockchain channels between peers that are not visible to all members of a consortium network.

Data confidentiality can also be potentially hidden using cryptography or more advanced zero-knowledge proof schemes that may not be available in all blockchains. For example, if your enterprise does not use channels for privacy, then another competitor on the same blockchain network may gain insight into your transactions between other peers in the consortium blockchain. These transactions could provide your competitor insight into what your company is doing and therefore bring competitive advantages. When properly implemented on a blockchain network, channels provide confidentiality.

Implementing confidentiality is not really possible on a permissionless blockchain. However, it's more than reasonable to implement and expect privacy on Corda or Hyperledger Fabric since these platforms are membership based.

Hyperledger Fabric implements confidentiality differently by leveraging different consensus methods in its architecture through the use of an execute-order-validate consensus approach. Hyperledger Fabric also supports channels natively. These channels are private channels that provide confidentiality on a shared blockchain infrastructure such as a consortium blockchain.

## Blockchain Best Practices

As with just about anything IT related, there are best practices to consider when implementing, managing, or securing your blockchain. This section focuses on three areas: high-level best practices, software development best practices, and wallet best practices.

### HIGH-LEVEL BEST PRACTICES

Here are some common high-level best practices your enterprise should consider with your blockchain project for ensuring security, privacy, and confidentiality:

◆ Implement the blockchain vendor best practices focused on blockchain security for the development of the smart contracts. (Corda, for example, has detailed documentation.)

◆ Implement vendor best practices for crypto wallets if applicable for your enterprise environment.

◆ Prevent access to only those members that require access with close adherence to the least privilege best practice.

◆ Deny all attempts to change data or modify your client applications without a review process.

◆ Guard your encryption keys with solid security standards so they are not compromised.

◆ Document a concise membership policy with acceptable rules and a permissioning process.

◆ Implement decentralized identity as an approach to mitigate password-related concerns.

◆ Train your developers and blockchain users on best practices for IT security.

◆ Audit your blockchain applications, networks, and nodes routinely for appropriate membership but likely vulnerabilities.

◆ Read all vendor or consortium documentation before implementation and after implementation and subscribe to the appropriate security bulletins and blockchain newsletters. If your blockchain has paid support, then contact your vendor for additional help.

Ethereum, Hyperledger, Corda, and Quorum will have different recommended best practices and instructions for implementing specific services. Following the vendor or the consortium documentation should be the first step when designing a secure blockchain for your enterprise.

### SOFTWARE DEVELOPMENT BEST PRACTICES

Developing your blockchain services such as smart contracts or the client applications that use the blockchain with a development approach that follows best practices can certainly provide value. The value provided could be around reducing risk in both your development and deployment cycles.

As a previous developer who has worked in numerous enterprises, I feel you can benefit by adhering to some common best practices.

The best way to remove security threats or vulnerabilities is to actually identify them during the development process. Identifying vulnerabilities after the development process, such as in the production modes, means that your blockchain has been deployed with vulnerabilities. Results are based on whether you are proactive or are reactive in the software process, such as DevOps.

An agile DevOps-focused environment is clearly the most effective when properly invested in by the enterprise to mitigate rookie mistakes in development.

The following are the most common best practices I recommend for securing your code development resources. Also included are ways to reduce your enterprise's risk to security exploits.

◆ Use a software development lifecycle (SDLC), such as Agile, to facilitate best practice processes to design, develop, and test high-quality software programs.

◆ Implement a DevOps-based operation. In the simplest terms, DevOps represents the intersection of two large trends in software development: Agile development and Lean operational processes. Agile software development promotes the collaboration of the whole enterprise and even can involve customers as part of the processes.

◆ Audit your smart contracts effectively, as smart contracts in most blockchains are immutable and cannot be deleted or modified later. The audits should be performed on a release candidate (RC), the final stage before software is launched.

◆ Manage your smart contract releases in an effective software release lifecycle such as a release candidate (RC).

◆ Remove code churn by performing an audit on a release candidate (RC). This can be done by using a mainnet address, which is your production network, and then comparing the release candidate with your development network, which is your testnet. Code churn is a common practice to measure the performance of both the developer and the code they turn out, which can affect the value of code/program. You can use a free tool called Gitprime to obtain this insight. Gitprime offers a wealth of features to visualize the data.

◆ Validate your source code to ensure the "validated" build is uploaded from the proper repository and is a secure copy. Use a source code validator tool to verify that source code matches the bytecode at the specific address that is required for deployment and matches the compiled output from source code. One tool that is used for source code validation with Ethereum development is called the Ethereum Bytecode Verifier.

For more on blockchain development best practices, refer to Chapter 10, "Blockchain Development."

## WALLET BEST PRACTICES

Some security-related best practices revolve around how you store your private keys and how you secure your blockchain wallets. Wallets are, of course, a requirement to maintain in Ethereum development so that your developers will be able to develop, test, and integrate smart contracts into your token platforms. Protecting these wallets and the keys is critical because Ether, when stolen or lost, is not likely going to be recovered. Losing your Ether wallet private keys could also be a costly way to lose your Ether tokens.

You should consider the following best practices:

♦ Restrict unsupervised access with Ethereum wallets whether on a web-based wallet or a hardware wallet.

♦ Provide a strict acceptable user policy (AUP) that ensures strong passwords are maintained.

♦ Close all network ports that do not need to be open and maintain a strict firewall. A network assessment should identify the ports.

♦ Practice frequently changing address schemes with your Ethereum wallet transactions. A common practice is to use a different address for every transaction. This can reduce brute-force guessing attempts.

♦ Configure multiple signatures (Multi-sig) with your private keys to deter most common breach attempts.

♦ Perform audits on your Ethereum wallet balances and your user base to ensure the security procedures are followed.

Corda, Quorum, and Hyperledger Fabric implementations do not have wallets, and therefore wallets should not be a concern. However, you may have off-chain services that go to a crypto exchange as part of your enterprise application. If this is the case, then ensure that your user base has best practices implemented as well as being clearly defined for them. If your users are not trained and provided specific instructions, then the risk of security vulnerabilities could easily exist in your enterprise.

## Blockchain Security Audits

Security audits need to be performed regularly, whether that's every month or every quarter. It is not possible to audit every device on the network every time, so considering your blockchain audit schedule is really important.

From a blockchain perspective, security audits identify vulnerabilities and certify the functional correctness of your blockchain code, smart contracts, and blockchain projects.

Hiring an experienced code auditor with blockchain expertise is critical for your success.

The common security code audit processes are as follows:

♦ Static code review, also known as source code analysis, is performed during a code review. This review is focused on finding vulnerabilities.

♦ Data flow analysis is used to collect runtime information about data in the software program while it is in a static state.

♦ Code analysis can be manual or automated. In manual reviews, also known as secure code reviews or dynamic reviews, code is reviewed line by line to look at every detail. Automated reviews perform more of a scan and generally do not test every link or function.

♦ Taint analysis is an audit method that checks variables that can be modified by the user input. Some languages have this feature built in.

♦ Test coverage analysis is a focused technique that determines which test cases are going to be covering the application code. This form of testing also determines how much code is exercised when running test cases.

◆ Expert code analysis is performed by a third-party software coding expert/auditor who reviews the code to determine whether there are concerns such as vulnerabilities or fraudulent transactions. The auditor may even reverse engineer the software program as part of the audit.

I will address most of these during the chapter in various levels of detail.

## Blockchain Security Assumptions

When considering security in blockchains, you should expect the security of the cryptographic algorithms to be implemented appropriately. At least that is what is assumed in most blockchain implementations.

However, in the world of IT security, assumptions are not an option. We must identity, validate, test, and confirm again that our security functions are working as expected.

The first, most common assumption is at a basic level that we are trusting the inherently built-in security of a blockchain, such as digital signatures, affiliated hashing functions, or even membership controls.

The second assumption is that digital signatures should verify transactions and blocks. This would likely validate what is in most blockchains such as the integrity of the blockchain, for example. Other benefits such as nonrepudiation should be accomplished as well. Technically, we are assuming that it should be impossible to forge a digital signature—that is, for example, it would be mathematically impossible to take over a blockchain because of the amount of technical and financial investment required to reverse engineer the program.

A third assumption is that hash functions are used to chain blocks together in most of the enterprise blockchains as well as cryptocurrencies. Hash functions should be a one-way process and also have a state space significant enough to remove threats such as a brute-force guessing attack.

Of course, there could several other assumptions on blockchain deployments. For this chapter, I want to focus on the subject of addressing threats and maintaining security.

## Blockchain Cryptography

Blockchain platforms rely on cryptography to perform mathematical functions that are part of cryptographic algorithms. The algorithms perform critical functions for the blockchain, as they provide for or at least enable security, privacy, and trust.

Several important forms of cryptography are commonly employed for blockchain security.

◆ Hashing functions are the most basic function where an input is expected to produce a specific output all the time. Nonces, which are random numbers, can also add complementary benefits to the hashing on blockchain to enhance security.

◆ Cryptography is the study and practice of securing private messages to ensure that only the intended parties or members on the blockchain can read them.

◆ Elliptic Curve Cryptography (ECC) is a form of public key encryption (PKE) that is used to generate a public and private key that will allow two participating parties to communicate securely together.

Figure 11.2 shows the workflow of a typical cryptographic function. Plaintext is encrypted into cyphertext, which is then decrypted and converted back to plaintext so that the message can be read.

**FIGURE 11.2**
Cryptographic function workflow

Encrypting and decrypting message contents use various methods and encryption keys in different blockchains. The use of encryption keys on a blockchain provides for what is called *nonrepudiation*. Nonrepudiation ensures that the creator/sender of the information cannot deny at a later stage their intentions in the creation or transmission of the information. Furthermore, blockchains provide immutability, wherein transactions to the blockchain will not be deleted or modified.

## HASHING

Hash functions are mathematical functions that can take any input and produce an output of a fixed size. In cryptography, hash functions are typically used as a one-way function where it's easy to go forward (input to output) but computationally infeasible to go backward (output to input).

To really understand what a hash is and how it works, check out the demo at `https://anders.com/blockchain/hash.html`. Anders has put together a tool that allows you as a learner to interact with the demos.

Figure 11.3 shows data entered as "Hello readers." The data in a hash will always return the same output. Remember, the same input equals the same output.

**FIGURE 11.3**
Hash output

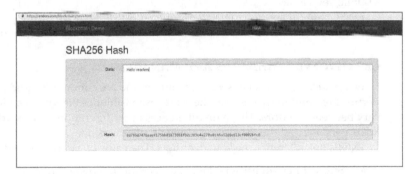

Figure 11.4 shows how a change to data will change the hash. Changing "readers" to "world" changes the output (hash).

**FIGURE 11.4**
Hash output change after input change

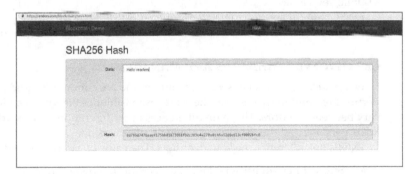

In blockchains, a node arranges the entire ledger in the form of chronologically connected blocks. To ensure that the ledger remains tamper-proof, each block is actually dependent on the previous block. That's where we get a chain of blocks, which we know as a blockchain.

Essentially, a new block will not be produced without having the hash of a previous block. In a permissionless blockchain, for example, the addition of a new block to the ledger has to be approved and verified by every node in the blockchain network.

## CERTIFICATES

An X.509 certificate is a key certificate that is under the X.509 specification standard for public key infrastructure (PKI). X.509 is a standard framework that defines the format of PKI to specifically identify users and entities over the Internet. It helps to confirm that a connection is safe.

The X.509 provides standardized formats for the following:

◆ Attribute certificates

◆ Public key certificates

◆ Certificate revocation lists

◆ Certification validation algorithms

These X.509 certificates are used to validate identities in a blockchain as well as to transmit data. Only the owners of the certificates are actually able to read them. The certificates are tied to a public key value.

DNSChain (`https://github.com/okTurtles/dnschain`) provides a scalable and decentralized replacement that does not depend on third parties—for example, on DNS services.

## CERTIFICATE STANDARDS AND MANAGEMENT

X.509 certificates also act as secure identifiers and are commonly used as digital passports. Certificates commonly perform the same responsibilities between vendors, although versions can vary between vendors. The main differences in configuration and security adherence are the X.509 versions and the extensions used with that version.

Extensions reference the key identifiers. The value of extension fields is as follows:

◆ **Subject key identifier**—Holds the certificate's owner identity.

◆ **Blockchain name**—Holds the name of the blockchain platform the certificate is used on.

◆ **CA key identifie**r is what actually holds the smart contract address of the current certificate authority (CA). For non-CA certificates, this field would be empty.

◆ **Issuer CA identifier**—The issuer holds the address of the smart contract of the CA that issued this specific certificate. This is important since it enables the validator to find a parent CA smart contract in the blockchain network. Finding the parent means it could check whether the certificate with the corresponding hash was issued and was not revoked.

◆ **Hashing algorithm**—Identifies specific information regarding the hashing algorithm that is used in the calculation of the certificate's hash.

Extensions can be a complex area to understand and generally an area for developers to master. Note that extensions can vary between certificate types as well. When reviewing your certificate management, it is important to understand the different key identifiers. It is possible to import the wrong certificates or at a minimum use a different identifier.

## CERTIFICATE AUTHORITY

In Hyperledger, the CA issues a root certificate (rootCert) to each member (organization or individual) that is authorized to join the network.

The CA also issues an enrollment certificate (eCert) to each member component, server-side applications, and end users, as needed. Each enrolled user is granted an allocation of transaction certificates (tCerts). Each tCert authorizes one network transaction.

Table 11.1 summarizes the certificates.

**TABLE 11.1:**    Certificate types

| CERTIFICATE | USE CASE |
| --- | --- |
| Root certificate (rootCert) | One issued for the organization. |
| Enrollment certificate (eCert) | One issued per member. |
| Transaction certificate (tCert) | Many issued per enrollment certificate. One certificate is needed for every transaction. |

Each type of certificate is specific to the use case. For example, just because a node (member) has an enrollment certificate (eCert) does not mean it can make transactions. The member must have another certificate, a tCert, to make a transaction. If the member needs to make 100 transactions, then the member must have 100 tCerts.

## MEMBERSHIP/PERMISSIONING

It should be clear that an enterprise blockchain should be a membership/permissioning-based blockchain in most cases. This becomes true when security and privacy are at the forefront of the enterprise's blockchain use case. Some enterprises may require an extension for off chains as well—for example, to access a stock ticker or a currency exchange.

In Hyperledger Fabric, permissioning is the concept of member enrollment certificates and transaction certificates for each member in blockchains. These two types of certificates enable an entity to be permissioned and identified while transactions are completed.

Permissioning and access management generally encompass what is known as *identity and access management* (IAM) for IT security personnel. Your enterprise needs to manage and monitor your blockchain services and the users, just like you are managing your email or Salesforce activity.

As part of most compliance requirements, you will need to validate user identities, ensure policies to process authorization, and address audit logs. Challenges can certainly abound with compliance, so having a strong IAM/membership policy is critical. Identity management is a challenging area and can encompass areas such as the following:

◆ Know your customer (KYC)

◆ Anti-money laundering (AML)

◆ Compliance requirements

◆ Reporting and auditing

For example, in Hyperledger Fabric, the Fabric CA server as well as the client store their private keys in a PEM-encoded file. A PEM-encoded file is a Privacy Enhanced Mail Certificate file. This PEM file can also be configured to store private keys in a Hardware Security Module (HSM).

### Two-Factor Authentication

Two-factor authentication (2FA) is an extra layer of security that's used to ensure that only the legitimate owner can access their accounts. Using 2FA, the user will first enter a combination of a username and password and then be required to provide other information. This other piece of information should come in the form of one of the following approaches:

◆ **Something that the user knows**—This could be information such as a password, an answer to a secret question, or maybe a personal identification number.

◆ **Something that the user has**—This method includes the second level of authentication based on card details, through smartphones, other hardware, or a software token.

◆ **Something that the user is**—This is one the most effective ways to verify the user on the second step, and this is accomplished with biometric data, for example.

# Blockchain Risks

As with other technologies, blockchains will encounter potential risks. Reviewing your enterprise risks and correlating those risks to your blockchain deployment are recommended. In reality, blockchains have no different risks from other technologies. If there is a risk, it's how compliance is handled or a lack of training that could expose vulnerabilities.

## Risk Assessment

Risk assessments are critical both before and after your blockchain implementation. Generally, IT risk assessments are the next step after performing a process called a business impact analysis (BIA). A BIA analyzes the enterprise's critical business functions and identifies the impact of a potential loss of those functions. You can then begin your IT risk assessment.

One risk is around performance. Blockchain technology will not scale to a level such as a traditional database since transactions per second (TPS) results are vastly different. For example, Ethereum is running around an average 12 TPS and Visa is running over 1600 TPS, so performance is not competitive and should not be expected. This performance risk could be eliminated with proper use case scoping.

Another concern is to ensure that enterprises specify the right solution for the right use case. Blockchain node distribution is a big concern around compliance and regulatory mandates.

Noncompliance could be costly to the enterprise. Comply with GDPR in the European Union or SOX in the United States, and then pay attention to what data center or cloud service you select. Understanding your compliance requirements will certainly help to reduce the risk of noncompliance.

A risk assessment should focus on the following areas:

◆ Assessing your risk assessment scope by determining the classes of risks to manage and identify.

◆ Identifying data privacy/permissions that will be adhered to for both the enterprise and the enterprise's customers—for example, the right to be forgotten with GDPR.

◆ Determining the liability and legal prose requirements that should be formulated from the risk assessments.

◆ Meeting compliance requirements, such as reporting, auditing, and monitoring of the blockchain applications.

◆ Specifying data management and monitoring.

◆ Analyzing performance of the enterprise blockchain's network statistics, which simply could be latency or transactions per second.

◆ Integrating enterprise applications to run on a blockchain network or extending an off-chain application to the blockchain network.

◆ Ensuring the recoverability (DR/BC) of your blockchain services if an outage or other concern occurs.

The risk assessment workflow comprises the following steps:

**1.** Perform a business impact analysis (BIA) to understand what could go wrong if a risk is not mitigated. A BIA should be sanctioned by the enterprise's leadership and funded appropriately.

**2.** Perform an IT risk assessment to identify risks, vulnerabilities, and challenges identified in the BIA. Use appropriate tools and document accordingly to gain insight into the environment.

**3.** Classify the identified risks and vulnerabilities in the assessment that need to be addressed first or in the appropriate order. For example, a weighting approach is commonly used to resolve these concerns in an ordered fashion.

**4.** Remediate the identified risks and vulnerabilities in the specified order.

Before trying to mitigate any vulnerabilities, it is important to understand what the actual risks are. Then you can assess the risk properly to perform appropriate risk mitigation techniques.

## Risk Mitigation

Risk mitigation is defined as taking steps to reduce the adverse effects of a potential risk. There are four specific types of risk mitigation strategies that hold uniquely to business continuity and disaster recovery. These risk mitigation techniques can be applied successfully to blockchain:

- *Risk avoidance* is not entering into a situation where the risk is present.

- *Risk reduction* is where you're performing responsibilities such as upgrading to the latest version of Hyperledger Fabric to avoid or reduce the likelihood of issues.

- *Transfer of risk* is relying on another organization to handle the concerns through typically insurance or a bond being purchased.

- *Risk acceptance* is where you are aware of the potential risks, impacts, and concerns and still proceed. An example would be running an operating system that cannot be upgraded or patched.

Company data should be considered an asset that is extremely valuable to the enterprise. As with any asset, it should be protected and insured and have a concise policy to restrict access. This could be an acceptable use policy (AUP), for example. The goal should be to protect the data whether it's on a blockchain or not.

When you are considering blockchain data, you need to consider the following points to address the concerns around privacy and security:

- Blockchain management and traditional IT management have some similarities, such as meeting privacy requirements, but also some differences, such as lowering performance expectations (TPS) with blockchains. The need to meet any additional requirements, such as privacy or security, will have an effect on performance because of the overhead of protocols or procedures used.

- Blockchain and distributed ledgers are immutable—the ledger cannot be deleted, modified, or destroyed.

- Blockchain data may or may not be distributed. Blockchains may not even be replicated outside a data center. No DR or BC has been planned or funded.

- Blockchains that are permissioned will have restricted access, but that does not mean everyone that is permissioned should have access to the ledger. (Channels may solve the concern around privacy.)

Blockchains may also have additional risks as compared to a traditional database. Here are some examples:

- Blockchains may not meet compliance requirements, especially if there is no redundancy or availability with DR/BC plans implemented. This lack of redundancy is common in enterprise blockchains and could be a risk to the enterprise. Generally, in a traditional database architecture, redundancy is built in or specifically addressed by replication.

- Data confidentiality may be a concern that is not addressed appropriately. Data written to blockchain is "public" data, for example, on Ethereum. Note that "private" blockchains such as Hyperledger are centrally administered and are transparent to the consortium members.

- Blockchains are combinations of newer technology (in reality, older technology melded together), so there could be a significant knowledge gap in numerous enterprises' development and production organizations.

Mitigating the identified risks to your company's blockchain data requires the following:

◆ Protecting your enterprise data in an efficient manner (replication)

◆ Enforcing a data governance policy (security, user, or acceptable use policy)

◆ Validating data (before and after entry) to minimize data corruption and data flaws (mistakes)

◆ Restricting access to permissioned membership (ensuring only authorized users)

◆ Meeting compliance requirements identified by your counsel

◆ Following IT best practices such as the principle of least privilege, which limits the permissions to the exact scope needed

Risk mitigation is a complex area and one that the enterprises need to fund. It has been well documented that most of the enterprise-based security attacks have been a result of a lack of proper risk mitigation and management. Investment in this area is critical to your enterprises blockchain application success.

## Blockchain Threat Landscape

Generally, in regard to blockchain there are some common vulnerabilities you would expect like network vulnerabilities but the other blockchain has some unique vulnerabilities where the "threat" could be a concern and must be addressed.

The following are the most common blockchain vulnerabilities that you will run into:

◆ Endpoint vulnerabilities

◆ Public and private key security

◆ Smart contract coding

◆ Lack of standards

◆ Mining issues (permissionless blockchains)

◆ 51 percent attack

◆ Phishing attacks

◆ Social media

Note that endpoints are generally focused on the blockchain network access points such as a gateway and its API.

### 51 Percent Attacks

This type of attack is almost always overhyped in the blockchain media and by security companies. It's a threat but only in specific consensus methods. The reality is that if you're an enterprise, you are likely not using proof-of-work (POW) consensus. This consensus is used in Bitcoin, Litecoin, and Ethereum.

A 51 percent attack is considered to be "selfish" mining, not rogue, in the sense that this attack happens when one single malicious miner controls more than 51 percent of the compute power on a blockchain network and can then inject false transactions into the system.

A 51 percent attack requires a miner to produce blocks in secret before posting them to the blockchain.

Finally, this attack type has been effectively rendered avoidable by a delay in transaction posting in the blockchain software.

## Phishing Attacks

Phishing attacks happen because people do not pay close attention to detail. For example, with the Bitcoin wallet Electrum, there has been an ongoing hack against its user base because users may not realize they actually used a fake wallet. As a result of this phishing attack, a malicious party was able to steal almost 250 Bitcoin (BTC), which, at the time of the attack in 2018, was $880,000.

Subsequently confirmed by Electrum itself, the attack consisted of creating a fake version of the wallet that fools users into providing password information. For more on this attack, visit `https://www.coindesk.com/electrum-wallet-attack-may-have-stolen-as-much-as-245-bitcoin`.

The lesson here is that you should pay careful attention to the domains you download your wallets or other blockchain software from. For example, if you are developing smart contracts on Ethereum and to utilize Metamask, then you need to go directly to Metamask.io. Do not go to another domain, software repository, or even `Metamask.com` or .net. These phishing attacks are generally preventable if the users pay attention to detail.

The following is the anatomy of a phishing attack:

1. The attacker registers a domain name similar to the genuine website.

2. The attacker then replicates the genuine site's content and replaces the wallet address with a rogue address.

3. The attacker uses deceptive ads to promote the copycat site, which unwitting users click.

4. The attacker intercepts the communication and then reroutes all users of the authentic site to their own site.

For more info, visit `https://resources.infosecinstitute.com/blockchain-vulnerabilities-imperfections-of-the-perfect-system/#gref`.

## DDOS Attacks

A distributed denial-of-service (DDOS) attack is an extremely common type of a network attack against a website, a network node, or even a membership service provider.

This DDOS attack is essentially initiated by many multiples (possibly thousands) of remote nodes, and then coordination is used to start their attacks. Essentially, a DDOS attack occurs when multiple systems flood a network resource with what are known as *connection requests*, messages, or other types of communication packets. The goal of this type of attack is to slow down or crash the system. The concentrated attack and subsequent shut down of the system results in a "denial of service" for legitimate users.

It's true that blockchains are "distributed ledgers," and thus being distributed can alleviate attacks. However, blockchain endpoints are certainly exposed to your corporate network and even the Internet. When connected to a network, a blockchain endpoint can be vulnerable and effectively block valid users.

**NOTE** A Kaspersky survey found that 30 percent of businesses do not take any preventive measures because they believe they are unlikely targets of DDoS attacks.

To prevent DDOS attacks, you should ensure that your networking team has the resources in place to mitigate, manage, and monitor these concerns. Load balancing is commonly used to prevent significant loss of business as a result of these attacks.

## DNS Hijacking Attacks

DNS is a domain name service that is critical to our network infrastructure. Without DNS we would not be able to access other nodes or sites. DNS hijacking is essentially a form of DDOS attack where your DNS is shut down, which can literally shut down your blockchain activity. If your members cannot access the membership service provider (MSP), for example, then your users and client applications won't be able to validate against the MSP for their authorization and certificates.

To prevent DNS hijacking attacks, you should ensure that your networking team has the resources in place to mitigate, manage, and monitor these concerns, just like in a DDOS attack.

Implement best practices such as limiting the view of DNS/bind versions and disabling DNS zone recursions and even DNS zone transfers. Some best practices around DNS take little effort and cost nothing. Lastly, consider using a provider such as Cloudflare that can help prevent DDoS and DNS attacks.

## Eclipse Attacks

Most permissionless blockchains use a peer-to-peer protocol (P2P) and are connected to each other with no centralization. However, because the blockchain network is deliberately not fully connected, this could introduce the eclipse attack.

In an eclipse attack, an attacker gains control of all of a node's connections to the network. By gaining control of the node's connections, it allows the attacker to completely control the node's view of the distributed ledger and network operations. A successful eclipse attack allows the attacker to perform a double-spending attack against the isolated node, helps the attacker perform a DoS attack, or lets the attacker use the node's computational resources for the attacker's benefit in the blockchain consensus algorithm.

These types of attacks are only successful on a permissionless chain such as Bitcoin or Ethereum. The amount of resources that are required would be substantial as well.

The ease with which an eclipse attack can occur depends on a number of factors.

♦ A network's data structure (P2P ledger versus a centralized ledger)

♦ Connection requests from client applications or other nodes

♦ Host (node) management and its IP addressing schema

To mitigate these security concerns, enterprises should be on an enterprise permissioned blockchain. If your company is using Ethereum, you may need to consider using whitelists or adjusting your connections through a concentrator such as a bastion host.

## Insider Attacks

Permissioned blockchains, even though not generally subjected to permissionless blockchain attacks, such as a replay attack or a 51 percent attack, are, by their nature, generally perceived as being more secure than permissionless blockchains such as Ethereum.

Permissioning certainly mitigates who can access your blockchain services and also helps you identify who is doing what. However, when you allow centralization of resources, history has proven that the people who believe they are not being watched or questioned will do stupid things.

An insider attack is exactly what it sounds like: an insider working in the organization has been permissioned to access your blockchain network resources and is executing an attack from the inside. That is, the attack is coming from the corporate blockchain network, not from outside the company. The inside attacker could exhibit malicious behavior by gaining control of the administrator certificate. As an administrator or admin certificate holder, the insider will have full control over the blockchain services and therefore could cause disruption, such as blocking valid transactions.

With administrative control, the attacker can add or revoke access, blacklist specific identities, and also manipulate the access a given identity has to the blockchain.

Insider attacks come in the form of the following:

◆ Account-related issues such as hidden accounts or over-privileged accounts.

◆ MSP or certificate authority hijacking where the certificate control is abused.

◆ Data manipulation of transaction logs or compliance logs occurs as a result of permissioning or exposed vulnerabilities.

To mitigate these types of issues, it is important that your enterprise considers IT security best practices such as role-based security or minimum permissions. Audits must be accomplished and routine audit log monitoring should be maintained and monitored by an IT security group member.

The one benefit of a permissioned blockchain is that your enterprises can control as much or as little as possible when it comes to permissioning, auditing, and configuration. It is recommended to be as aggressive as possible in protecting your enterprise data without interfering with your blockchain users and applications to the point where they can't work.

## Replay Attacks

A replay attack is usually a scheme that is utilized during a fork of a blockchain. For example, an attacker might copy an existing transaction and then attempt to resubmit it to the blockchain as if it were a new transaction.

A hacker may also attempt to resubmit the transaction if a hacker has your digital signature and because your original transaction was valid. If the attacker succeeds in resubmitting this rogue transaction, they would receive the wallet transactions twice.

You can easily prevent replay attacks by removing any intermingling of blockchains. For example, some blockchains such as Bitcoin Cash (BCH) have replay attack protection. This protection is accomplished by adding a special mark on the validity check that identified the transaction was for the BCH ledger and not the previous ledger from Bitcoin.

From a user perspective, to help prevent even risking this issue, you can separate your accounts by not mixing coins in the same wallets.

## Routing Attacks

A routing attack is essentially what it sounds like: traffic is hijacked and then routed somewhere it should not be routed. Basically, a routing attack relies on intercepting messages propagating through the network. While these messages are propagating through the network, the messages could be captured and tampered with.

This type of attack is generally part of a man-in-the-middle attack. This type of attack would not be successful if the hacker does not obtain full control over the blockchain network resources. The only way for the network nodes to detect tampering is when they receive a different copy of data from another node. Comparing the messages sent and received between nodes is an effective way to mitigate this vulnerability.

Perhaps the most proactive way to prevent these types of attacks requires significant monitoring of your network services and messaging traffic. Metrics should include packet round-trip times (RTT), anomaly monitoring, and even pattern matching.

## Sybil Attacks

A sybil attack is when an attacker creates multiple accounts on a blockchain in order to deceive the other blockchain participants. This behavior is similar to folks who troll on social media by creating multiple accounts to accomplish their silly behavior. A sybil attack could be quite similar to a phishing attack where an imposter pretends to be someone such as your boss asking you for your network password.

Preventing sybil attacks is considered straightforward in the sense that you need to pay attention to who your wallet funds are being sent to. These types of attacks should not be an issue on a permissioned blockchain since the members are clearly identified and wallets are not normally used.

# Smart Contract Security

In Ethereum blockchains, all modifications to a smart contract's data must be performed by its blockchain code. This means that a user cannot edit the contract directly or even delete the contract. To modify a contract's data, a blockchain user must send the request to its code, which is at a lower level. This request process kickoff will determine whether to fulfill and how to fulfill those smart contract modification requests.

For comparison purposes to Linux, we can think of a smart contract as an application that is installed on top of an operating system. We can also compare a blockchain smart contract to how a traditional database handles database modification. A traditional database uses "enforced stored procedures," or "predefined rules." In a blockchain, we append to the next block on the blockchain when a transaction is processed, as opposed to enforcing entries on a procedural basis. Security is built into the blockchain code and the smart contract platform. The enforcement of smart contracts varies widely between platforms from a technical approach.

## Smart Contract Legal Prose

Legal prose is effectively a direct method of attaching a document to a smart contract. This is done to address what the contract code may not address, such as handling disputes to help manage or mitigate issues when the contract code is not enough.

Corda supports legal prose, as mentioned earlier in the book. In Corda, addressing this as a contract class would be annotated with the @LegalProseReference annotation.

The @LegalProseReference annotation associates the smart contract with an attached document that will detail the contract's constraints imposed by the legal prose terms. Note that it is not required to attach legal prose to a Corda contract when developing one.

The main difference in Corda and other blockchains is focused on how a smart contract in Corda would attach legal prose in the smart contracts. From a privacy and compliance perspective as well as a financial perspective, the legal prose schema is quite important as well for cost savings. This is accomplished by Corda smart contracts linking the business logic and the business data to an associated legal prose structure.

When it comes to Hyperledger, Ethereum, and Quorum, there are no documented features for addressing legal prose at the time of writing.

However, if legal prose were a priority, a developer could certainly address this in a rudimentary fashion with attachments or by providing for additional steps in the smart contracts. This would enable better smart contract enforcement but won't likely address legal issues in most cases.

Your enterprise should follow up with corporate counsel to determine whether these contracts and their document attachments are legally enforceable or even valid in the jurisdictions required.

### Smart Contract Vulnerabilities

Smart contracts are essentially nothing more than logic written in computer code. The computer code is developed in specific languages, such as JavaScript, Golang, and C++, and should be vetted via software development best practices before deploying.

The software development best practices could be anything from clean code, vulnerability assessments, DevOps, and agile processes, or whatever your organization deems acceptable.

Smart contracts may introduce new vulnerability points in an enterprise permissioned blockchain such as Hyperledger or Corda. Most enterprise blockchains rely on asynchronous Byzantine fault tolerance replication protocols to establish consensus and then effectively provide their low-level trust assumptions to the smart contract applications.

The inability for smart contracts to execute on all nodes within a permissioned blockchain is a serious concern. When you consider smart contracts that do not execute properly and you have 100 nodes performing the same processes that result in blockchain failure, this could be considered a denial of service on the blockchain network.

Risks that are common around smart contracts will arise around programming oversights such as access control, return values, overflows, timestamps, and numerous other "dirty code" issues.

Chapter 10 covers smart contract coding issues in more detail.

## Blockchain-Specific Features

This section reviews the most common blockchain-specific features for Ethereum, Hyperledger, Quorum, and Corda. Each blockchain has some unique security-related functions, features, and utilities. The features discussed in this chapter are solely based on the time of the writing, so I mainly discuss features that are past the "alpha" phase of development. A slew of additional features are in incubation but won't be covered.

## Ethereum

Ethereum was the first smart contract platform that was designed to allow developers to access a Turing-complete platform on the blockchain and develop applications as smart contracts.

Because this was a first of a kind platform that was meant to be permissionless (open to the public), developers had a lack of security features to work with. Security from an enterprise development perspective in Ethereum was more of an optional feature that would be considered later in the lifecycle. The lack of security-related features was due to the use case that the Ethereum application presented to the world at the time it was deployed.

If security is truly important, then an enterprise should not deploy an application that requires privacy, security, or enterprise features on Etheruem. There are options to deploy Enterprise Etheruem, but I do not feel that Ethereum, even Enterprise Ethereum, is meant for enterprises that are concerned about security features.

Whether you deploy your own private Ethereum network or use the public network (mainnet), when assessing your security risks, you need to consider that Ethereum has four main components.

- ◆ Ethereum nodes, which are distributed worldwide and may expose corporate information

- ◆ Ethereum virtual machines, which have a copy of the ledger state, which is distributed to every Ethereum node

- ◆ Smart contracts, which are immutable and therefore once deployed are on the blockchain forever

- ◆ Dapps, which are decentralized applications and for which expecting consistent performance is not reasonable

The main security concern with Ethereum is really focused on the nodes that are deployed. A node is a device, program, or virtual machine that communicates with the Ethereum network. When an Ethereum node is deployed, that node could have numerous vulnerabilities, such as user authentication issues or lack of patching, or more common than not, the node is multitasking. That is, the node is not dedicated to running the blockchain node but is also used for other tasks, such as developing, running batch jobs, or even multimedia. Securing your Ethereum nodes is paramount for the network.

### ETHEREUM TESTNETS AND MAINNET SECURITY TESTING

Mainnet is the real data on the blockchain, including account balances and transactions, which are public. It is important to note that anyone can create a node and begin verifying transactions. Ether on mainnet has a market value and can be exchanged for other cryptocurrency or fiat currencies. Because Ether has value, we must secure our wallets and ensure we don't lose our keys.

Security testing can be done in Ethereum on any testing network. The mainnet is for production, so it's highly unadvisable to attach unsecure nodes to the mainnet for obvious reasons.

There are three main types of extended Ethereum networks that could be used for security testing.

- ◆ **Public test networks**— Developers use public test networks to perform tests on their Ethereum applications before final deployment to the main network. Ether is used for testing purposes only and actually has no value from a trading purpose. Test networks include Ropsten, Kovan, and Rinkeby.

◆ **Enterprise/private networks**—Private Ethereum networks allow parties to share data without making it publicly accessible. A private blockchain is a good choice for sharing sensitive data and scaling to handle higher read/write throughput. Quorum, for example, is a hybrid of Ethereum and a private network.

◆ **Local test networks**—Local test networks are deployed on your corporate infrastructure for your testing. Local testing can certainly provide benefits around privacy and mitigating performance issues.

The main lesson here is to identify what test network is appropriate for your situation. Perform the tests and then deploy to the mainnet only after testing is complete and the identified risks are removed.

## ETHEREUM DEVELOPMENT

From a security perspective of blockchain development, it is important to understand that there are myriad Ethereum toolsets, utilities, IDEs, and other solutions. Each of these could pose a security vulnerability to your development group but also your enterprise depending on how things are rolled out, managed, and monitored.

When designing or architecting your blockchain, there are some key areas around security to focus on, listed here:

◆ Private or public dapps that are deployed on the blockchain nodes should be processed through a proper software development framework, such as a properly implemented DevOps foundation, or at a minimum a proper change control system. Using pipelines is a best practice in the software world, so it is natural to want to extend this blockchain development to a DevOps environment.

◆ Application platform interfaces (APIs) need to be updated, validated, or deprecated based on your requirements and should be clearly documented and even maintained through an API management platform that maintains version controls.

◆ Smart contracts need to be developed, tested, audited, and secured before being deployed.

◆ Validate that the user interface to the blockchain application is secure by testing. For example, removing unneeded hot keys or function keys is a good start. However, UX testing is not all visual; the code should be inspected and tested for exploits. If cryptocurrency wallets are involved, then we must realize that integration needs to be considered as part of the user application to address wallet-specific vulnerabilities such as crypto jacking.

Each of these could certainly pose a challenge to how to mitigate potential issues such as vulnerabilities. The best place to start to remove these challenges is in the architecting phase where security concerns are identified and mitigated before the development process.

## ETHEREUM SECURITY ENHANCEMENTS

Ethereum has a limited level of integrated support for meeting enterprise privacy or security requirements. A good amount of the reasoning is that it is a permissionless blockchain with limited control over its user base. Its main security feature is the use of public keys for identity management, which give users a level of pseudo-anonymity.

Security features in Ethereum can and should be implemented appropriately in Ethereum as smart contracts or dapps.

Future development in Ethereum is planned to include support for the mathematical operations used in zero-knowledge proofs like zkSNARKS.

Organizations wanting to use Ethereum but with advanced security and privacy controls should consider looking at Quorum. Quorum is an actual fork of Ethereum and has wide support from the financial sector to deploy a private Etheruem network.

## Hyperledger Fabric

Hyperledger Fabric is a smart contract platform originally built by IBM. The Hyperledger Fabric platform is currently maintained by the Linux Foundation and is considered open source. Hyperledger Fabric was specifically designed to be an enterprise blockchain that does have some unique features around security, privacy, and other enterprise-focused requirements.

The main security feature to review is that Fabric is designed with the concept of channels. Channels are similar in some respects to tunnels in the IP networking world, which are a point-to-point network connection.

In Hyperledger Fabric, a channel is a completely distinct blockchain network with its own distributed ledger. This channel is visible only to members of the channel and provides an additional layer of privacy. This specific architecture allows multiple blockchain networks to run on the same network of nodes and provides for enhanced privacy as well as another layer of security.

As with any blockchain, vulnerabilities can exist in the blockchain smart contracts. Hyperledger Fabric refers to smart contracts as chaincode.

Hyperledger Fabric chaincode can be programmed in either Node.js or Go and will run in secure Docker containers. These chaincode programs are run by an external application interacting with the distributed ledger.

Hyperledger takes a slightly different approach to transaction validation and execution than smart contract platforms like Ethereum. Hyperledger Fabric follows an execute, order, validate control flow. It is possible in Hyperledger Fabric to have a transaction committed with a flawed smart contract due to this execution process occurring before the validation.

The best way to mitigate security vulnerabilities and ensure transactions are not committed fraudulently is to perform audits on your chaincode.

### HYPERLEDGER CHAINCODE SCANNER

There is a unique tool that is available for chaincode scanning called Chaincode Scanner by Chainsecurity. Chaincode Scanner is a static analyzer for Hyperledger Fabric–based smart contracts. It works by accepting chaincode written in Go as an input and then checks it against the input for nine specific vulnerability patterns.

Using the Chaincode Scanner will be a simple exercise for developers. The developer first uploads code to the public repository (GitHub) and then adds its path into the input field on the Chaincode Scanner website.

Developers should be proficient in performing tasks such as pathing and adapting Go packages with a go get command to use this solution. The results will be displayed as a table with detailed code review notes.

Figure 11.5 shows a snapshot of the Chaincode Scanner tool. Simply enter the URL of your application to start a scan.

**FIGURE 11.5**
Chaincode Scanner

For more information on Chainsecurity's tools, visit `https://chaincode.chainsecurity.com/`. Chapter 10 discusses chaincode in more detail.

### HYPERLEDGER FABRIC SECURITY ENHANCEMENTS

Hyperledger has a few features designed to improve its security for business use cases.

◆ Contains a pluggable identity management option that supports traditional IAM schemes such as LDAP/AD commonly used in most enterprise environments.

◆ Provides channels that are logically distinct and separate virtualized blockchains. Nodes can belong to multiple channels as designated by the admins.

◆ Allows for privacy through the exchange of data via the blockchains gossip protocol, which differs from Ethereum, for which data only goes to nodes with a need-to-know basis.

## R3 Corda Blockchain

Corda is an open source blockchain that was designed for the enterprise, including financial enterprises. Corda has some unique features and capacity around blockchain security and privacy. Note that Corda was developed with the Java environment as the virtual machine, which provides for rapid adoption by businesses.

### CORDA NOTARY SECURITY

A notary is a trusted party that guarantees that a particular state is consumed only once. In Corda, a notary is perhaps the most important node to maintain and secure. You should consider a notary more of a custodian or intermediary that acts almost like a traffic officer directing traffic (states). In Corda, each state has a specific notary, which must sign any transaction in which that state is consumed. Once a notary has done this, it must not sign another transaction for the same state. Notaries are the network's guardians of transaction uniqueness, and we cannot risk having a notary compromised.

The concept of a notary differs from most other blockchains in the sense that conventional blockchains solve this challenge by allowing every node to see every transaction, which in turn would make conflicts easy to identify and ideally reject.

There is no centralized authority in a Corda network, which differs from Hyperledger. The notary has no authority really and maintains a list of account items that have been spent. The notary is about preventing double spending—no more and no less. This is where a vulnerability could be injected into a Corda network, so we must maintain and audit our notaries.

From a security standpoint, as well as my own point of view, the fact that anyone can stand up and run a notary in a Corda network is perplexing. Basically, it's up to the parties transacting to decide who they want to act as the notary, so it's possible a rogue notary from an insider could steal information, or worse.

In a nutshell, Corda nodes see only some of a network's transactions, which means better privacy than conventional blockchains. However, the risk of a rogue notary could be introduced, and we must identify and mitigate these issues.

## CORDA SMART CONTRACTS

Contract execution and validation are performed on the Corda JVM, which is partially deterministic. *Deterministic* means the same code will produce the same output with no changes in end results. Developers can certainly make changes to ensure the JVM is fully deterministic.

The smart contract execution and validation are processed on the Corda Java virtual machine (JVM), which is locked down and quite secure. The JVM acts as a sandbox. However, the JVM is running Java, which is inherently unsecure, so you need to review Java-related vulnerabilities. These Java-based vulnerabilities could become evidently true if you are on a consortium-based blockchain with nodes that are not controlled centrally or in a secure network such as a DMZ. A DMZ is a secure partition of a corporate network and is commonplace in IT networking. If your virtual machines are in Apache MyFaces Core 2.0 with specified versions, Java can provide remote attackers the ability to read arbitrary files on your JVM.

## CORDA SECURITY ENHANCEMENTS

Corda's security is based primarily on its solid need-to-know philosophy and its unique approach to network of notaries. Since users can only see and interact with transactions in which they have a stake, the potential impact of a data leakage is reduced.

Corda also uses a point-to-point TLS-encrypted protocol. This differs from peer-to-peer broadcasts such as other blockchains.

X.509 certificates are also used in the blockchain network, and flexibility is available in this area. Security in Corda is heavily dependent on what are known as notaries, which can be considered custodians of the network. Assets and transactions in Corda can be held hostage if the assigned notary refuses to transfer or sign them. A malicious notary can allow what is considered a double-spend attack, which would ensure proper accounting of the blockchain is not achievable.

Implementing a Corda blockchain, notary trust, and security is a paramount task for the consortium members to ensure that the blockchain is secured. Corda does a good job of disclosing vulnerabilities and best practices on its website. For a concise document that describes secure coding, visit `https://docs.corda.net/secure-coding-guidelines.html`.

# Quorum

Quorum is designed to be permissioned, meaning that networks using Quorum won't be open to the Ethereum network as they are in most cases with Ethereum.

Quorum is deployed as a private permissioned blockchain (private implementation of the Ethereum protocol) that operates with extremely different expectations of trust between approved nodes than other permissionless blockchains. For some reason, there was some confusion originally on Quorum being deployed on the Etheruem public network, and this is not true. Quorum blockchain was designed for financial institutions that require a high-performing private and secure transaction platform within a permissioned group of participants that need guaranteed privacy.

Quorum directly addresses specific challenges to blockchain technology adoption within the financial industry and beyond. Most of these challenges are focused on privacy and security for financial sectors. Financial institutions are well versed in working with other institutions in a consortium manner. One example was the SWIFT network where financial transfers and related financial information were both shared but also were guaranteed levels of privacy as required between parties in the SWIFT consortium.

Quorum provides some substantial benefits around consensus and its security-related enhancements.

## QUORUM CONSENSUS

Quorum's consensus protocol, called QuorumChain, is initiated within the genesis block of the blockchain. QuorumChain is a relatively straightforward, simple majority voting consensus protocol. A certain set of nodes is relegated with voting rights, and it's possible to confer voting rights to others.

In Quorum a smart contract is used within the genesis block to specifically assign voting rights and also to track the status of all voting nodes within the network as it updates. This is actually somewhat different from other blockchains and one area where Quorum differs significantly from Ethereum.

Voting is triggered by the smart contract that pings the voting nodes. This ping is actually requesting these nodes to commit to a transaction as the correct block at a specific height in the blockchain chain. A possible vulnerability that could occur is if a mutation happens in a private transaction in Quorum. This vulnerability could easily be identified during a proper code review in most cases.

## QUORUM SECURITY AND PRIVACY ENHANCEMENTS

Quorum manages its secure message transfers through a system called Constellation. Constellation is a general-purpose mechanism that is not necessarily blockchain-specific. Think of Constellation as a message service and encryption manager all in one. It serves a similar purpose as Zookeeper and Kafka in Hyperledger Fabric. The one area that might catch developers is that Constellation is written in Haskell—not your everyday programming language. I will cover Constellation from a developer perspective in Chapter 10.

Quorum offers the following security enhancements over Ethereum:

◆ Quorum supports the implementation of both private transactions and private contracts through public/private state separation.

◆ Quorum utilizes the newer Constellation peer-to-peer encrypted message exchange for directed transfer of private data to network participants, which is fully integrated.

◆ Alternative consensus mechanisms are supported with a permissioned network with varied security features that could be enabled by your development teams.

◆ Developers with Ethereum experience will be able to develop with no real ramp-up time and with little effort to implement security features.

## Summary

This chapter covered various aspects around blockchain security that were mainly focused on best practices such as security audits and security scanning. Blockchain uses forms of cryptography to provide a secure transaction process. Many forms of vulnerabilities that blockchains can be exposed to such as an insider attack or a routing attack need to be addressed. Performing and acting on a proper risk assessment would certainly reduce or eliminate vulnerabilities. Ethereum, Hyperledger, Corda, and Quorum all offer unique security and privacy features and capacity that should be considered in your blockchain design and deployments.

# Chapter 12

# Blockchain Marketplace Outlook

This chapter covers the growing demand that has been documented by the increased use cases around blockchain technologies and the consistent documented hiring around blockchain expertise. We'll look at how blockchain got its start and where we are now in the technology investment phase.

Whether you are working for an IT vendor, integrator, or VAR, you likely have been hearing quite a bit about blockchains. Blockchains have the potential to significantly change your business as a company, especially around trust. As a sales organization or services organization, enabling your enterprise sales teams in blockchain technology would be a great step toward establishing a blockchain practice.

The goal of this chapter is to give you a factually-based approach on why blockchain demand is growing and how to justify your own enablement of blockchain-focused services.

Finally, we also cover the most common certification and training opportunities to help grow your business, knowledge base, and enablement toward blockchain.

## Technology Investments

From an enterprise standpoint, we are past the initial investment and early adopter phases of the blockchain technology cycle. We are now entering the growth phase of the blockchain cycle. Several consulting firms have identified similar patterns as well and even have detailed reports.

Both Accenture and Deloitte are examples of companies of significant industry prominence that have done a concise job of portraying blockchain as a growth area. Their blockchain-focused websites include numerous forms of collateral, such as reports, use cases, and white papers, that bring blockchain to light as a growth opportunity.

Technology investments are critical to blockchain just as in other sectors of the IT marketplace. However, these investments generally do not happen overnight. As a previous employee of several startups and a private company going public, I can attest that these phases in the technology investment cycle can take years.

Figure 12.1 shows the four phases common in the technology investment and adoption cycle. Investments in a technology are critical. This is where uses cases are proposed, and assessments, surveys, and preliminary investments are made. The early adopter phase is when a large investment bank or angel fund normally invests due to the clear benefits shown in the earlier investment phase. The growth phase is a result of investments, acceptance, and value being provided. Also, the growth phase is when an IPO may occur, bringing in additional investments. Maturity occurs when the technology reaches what is considered mainstream due to clear industry disruption.

**FIGURE 12.1**
Technology invest-
ment phases

**NOTE** The future of blockchain is looking bright. Both the demand for technical skills and the increasing number of potential use cases provide for a significantly positive outlook for blockchain use cases, implementations, and expertise.

## Investments in Blockchain

The amount of investment in blockchain technology by organizations of all sizes cannot be ignored. We are talking tens of millions of dollars in different startups annually. In addition, more than 90 percent of the major financial institutions have made investments in blockchain technology.

The organizations that invest in blockchain technology generally fall into one of three types.

◆ Financial institutions

◆ Technology companies

◆ Venture-capital funds

These types of organizations would not be pouring money into the technology unless they expected a profit. Big money tends to follow success but also creates its own form of success.

The venture-capital firms investing in blockchain are among the "who's who" of investment firms. It's hard to believe that all these companies would be investing in a technology that's not providing a return to them at some point. The following article is worth a read: https://101blockchains.com/top-blockchain-investors/.

My take is that we are witnessing another dot-come type of event in the sense of rapid investment and adoption. The question is, who will be the winners and who will be the losers? Right now, opportunities abound, so it's up to you to get in and take advantage.

## Blockchain Market Patents

One of the areas that I have never seen well documented was how patents can correlate to demand. The number of patents as well as the speed of how these patents are being applied for is mind-blowing. For example, in less than a few years, Bank of America (BofA) has more than 50 blockchain patents, including in the following areas:

◆ Cryptocurrency exchange system

◆ Wire transfers using cryptocurrency

◆ ATM as a service

◆ Blockchain-based cash handling

This begs the question: why do banks show so much interest in blockchain? The answer is the potential financial engineering opportunities that may abound with blockchain technology.

I found this patent news quite interesting since it is well documented how blockchain can be used to remove staff as well as infrastructure, considering blockchain is not just about making things easier or about the immutability of data.

Blockchain is essentially another form of "financial engineering," albeit a form that is technically driven and more challenging than cloud computing or off-shoring. Imagine that you're a bank with thousands of highly paid bankers, lawyers, investment analysts, and numerous other roles. What would you do if you saw an avenue to remove a significant target of highly paid "overhead"?

Your competitors are doing this same thing, so you essentially have to consider this as well. I have been in discussions with both insurance and financial organizations about blockchain as a cost-cutting measure. Trust me, they are working on that outcome and looking at potentially hundreds of millions in savings for the larger banks. Blockchain is another enabler for cost reductions—something a presales-focused engineer must be cognizant of.

The patents that are being applied for are indicators of potential cost efficiencies. The patent applicants and patent holders range in both size and the types of industries they serve.

**NOTE** According to BofA, which commissioned a paper, called "Bitcoin: a first assessment," compiled by its strategy team, Bitcoin has the possibility of becoming a major means of payment.

Banks are not the only types of companies flocking to blockchain patents. A significant number of other verticals—including retail, social media, technology, insurance, and transportation companies—have been procuring patents at a rapid pace. Examples include the following:

◆ Walmart

◆ IBM

◆ Facebook

◆ JPMorgan

◆ Ford Motor Company

◆ Toyota

◆ Amazon

◆ Alibaba

Amazon, for example, has two unique patents.

◆ The Signature Delegation patent, which at the time of writing is in application status, uses signatures to protect the integrity of digital signatures and encrypted communications. At first glance, this patent does not appear to have a direct application for cost efficiencies; however, when a company such as Amazon delivers more than 600 million packages per year, the potential reduction in loss, chargebacks, etc. could be significant.

◆ "Generation of Merkle Trees as a Proof of Work" (patent number US 10,291,408 B2) suggests Amazon is in the process of creating its own cryptocurrency. Amazon would be just as substantial as Facebook Libra (at least in the United States). Merkle trees historically are associated with a proof-of-work (PoW) consensus, and the only obvious use case would be to create a cryptocurrency. However, there are no statements or comments at the time of writing.

In my opinion, there is a clear and present danger in the sense that these large multinational organizations are trying to control the blockchain market. It's not just Amazon, IBM, or Walmart;

smaller cryptocurrency-focused and enterprise-focused blockchain companies are on the offensive, buying any blockchain-related patents. These patent acquisitions could also be counterproductive for the industry as a whole in some respects. For example, startups may not be able to compete on the same level and therefore, not enter the market as expected. This could limit innovation and even cost efficiencies.

To learn more, you can go to the US Patent and Trademark Office, at `http://appft.uspto` `.gov/netahtml/PTO/index.html`, and search the database for applications or patents.

## Blockchain Market Growth

The blockchain market is clearly growing—and is expected to continue to grow by just about every research firm that reports on blockchain markets. The main challenge is to decipher the market research and determine which industries would likely be the main benefactors.

An interesting report referenced in PR Newswire states the following:

> *"The global blockchain market size is expected to grow from USD 1.2 billion in 2018 to USD 23.3 billion by 2023, at a Compound Annual Growth Rate (CAGR) of 80.2%."*

To read the full article, visit:

`https://www.prnewswire.com/news-releases/the-global-blockchain-market-` `size-is-expected-to-grow-from-usd-1-2-billion-in-2018-to-usd-23-3-billion-` `by-2023--at-a-compound-annual-growth-rate-cagr-of-80-2-300762798.html`

When you compare the percentages against other technologies, it's clear that the disruption these blockchain technologies could make may be substantial.

## Complementary and Adverse Blockchain Acceptance Drivers

The main drivers that could complement the increasing acceptance of blockchain technologies include the following:

◆ Increased cost efficiency in financial, compliance, and logistics

◆ Transparency requirements especially in logistical supply chains that are consumer based

◆ Increased adoption of digital certificates for enterprises

◆ Acceptance of security tokens in the financial industries

◆ Increased capacity of blockchains mainly around transactions per second (TPS) that are more competitive with traditional applications

The main drivers that could adversely affect the blockchain market growth are commonly cited among researchers, analysts, and even vendors are as follows:

◆ Regulatory and compliance concerns

◆ Integration of enterprise ecosystems

◆ Technical expertise (developers, architects)

◆ Lack of proven implementations of blockchain technology

◆ Application performance requirements not being met by blockchain technologies such as transactions per second (TPS)

There are, of course, likely other valid explanations why blockchain technology is not yet being fully adopted. For the purposes of this book, I will not cover every aspect and even industry segment challenge. Blockchain acceptance is going to be driven by clearly defined verticals and industries.

The main benefactors of blockchain acceptance are industries that depend on intermediaries, financial institutions, logistics, and supply chains and compliance-dependent industries.

Blockchain acceptance and real-world implementations will likely grow in the double digits year over year. However, it is widely accepted that specific industries such as logistics and the financial sectors will lead the way in year-over-year growth. We know the investments are being made, and we are now transitioning into the mainstream phase of the technology lifecycle.

## Blockchain Expertise Demand

Demand in blockchain expertise is clearly being seen. At the time of writing, LinkedIn had more than 16,000 roles with "blockchain" in the job title or description just in the United States.

This is quite interesting since it would appear most employers are not looking for a full-time blockchain engineer, developer, or architect. Instead, these prospective employers are clearly showing in their job descriptions and requirements that blockchain-related knowledge is at least nice to have.

Here is a brief review of the LinkedIn demand at the time of writing:

◆ Blockchain architects are routinely in demand. Having experience in a presales capacity and postsales capacity is usually part of the required skillsets.

◆ Developers with skills in numerous languages are in demand. Programming languages that are generally in demand for blockchain developers include Java, JavaScript, Go, Simplicity, Solidity, C++, and Python.

◆ Developers should have experience in DevOps, full stack, frontend, and even backend development.

When it comes to roles, a blockchain developer is the most widely required role listed for blockchain experience.

Forbes published an article on February 28, 2019, that declared the top 15 US cities for blockchain technology jobs. The article is brief, but the list of cities is interesting. For more information, see:

```
https://www.forbes.com/sites/jeffkauflin/2018/02/26/the-top-15-
cities-for-blockchain-technology-jobs-in-america/#542098fb4ac5
```

## Blockchain Market Expertise Expansion

The market for blockchain expertise is expanding in select US cities, including New York, Atlanta, Boston, Washington DC, Austin, and the Bay Area. Overseas cities such as Toronto, Singapore, London, and Seoul are also seeing high demand. However, the majority of the demand for blockchain expertise is not just in major cities; I am seeing a significant number of startups in smaller cities as well.

The great part of searching for a blockchain role is that you may not actually need to be in a "tech hub" to get a blockchain role now. These roles may have a significant travel component or a working remotely possibility.

I can certainly vouch that developers would likely clear incomes over $200,000 in the major tech hubs in the United States. There are some interesting blockchain demand that has been documented by both the media and analyst research organizations.

To find out what the possibilities are, go to LinkedIn and perform a search. When I searched for *blockchain* in a few various cities or countries, I got the following:

United States: 4,693 results

United Kingdom: 1,416 results

Singapore: 341 results

Toronto: 115 results

Worldwide: 14,537 results

To be clear, these results are for any role that includes *blockchain* in either the job title, job description, requirements, responsibilities, or skill.

What does this mean? Well, it's basically showing that roles are requiring some knowledge of blockchain. Typically, the roles will have blockchain as a requirement for a developer but more of a nice-to-have for a marketing expert, sales engineer, or account executive.

Basically, you should be considering blockchain as a skill down the road to your areas of improvement. Get yourself enabled either through training funded by your company or through your own funding. There are numerous organizations out there to help get you enabled. Once you have completed your training, then perhaps get certified to validate your skills. Employers are always looking at certifications. I know, because they pay me to train their employees for blockchain certifications.

## Blockchain Certifications

Blockchain certifications are in high demand from both a student perspective and from an enterprise perspective. Companies are providing opportunities for employees to get enabled on blockchain technologies and for that matter spending thousands to enable their employees.

Blockchain certifications are evolving and, to be fair, in my opinion, not totally mature from a perspective of how other technologies are such as cloud computing or Linux, for example. Also, many organizations have been pumping out blockchain certifications that are poorly written and nothing more than someone overseas taking advantage of being first to market. I have taken many courses and certifications, most of which provide no real value at least from an accreditation perspective.

Training materials, exams, and objectives need to be updated routinely with a defined team that is tasked with that responsibility. Utilizing best practices such as Bloom's taxonomy, a commonly used educational industry framework, is required for a professional training organization to ensure the objectives of the training and certification are employed. When it comes to teaching or certification exams, the framework is broken down into six major categories: Knowledge, Comprehension, Application, Analysis, Synthesis, and Evaluation.

It is clear that early blockchain certifications that were first to market did not follow the Bloom taxonomy best practices due to the lack of coherent structure and proper objectives. However, I have seen great improvement from several organizations, and these are the ones I am including in this chapter. There is a dearth of blockchain certifications and training companies in the blockchain training and certification game now.

Your enterprise needs to invest in the most current and accredited training programs. The following are the certification and training leaders in blockchain technology:

◆ Blockchain Institute of Technology (BIT)

◆ Blockchain Council

◆ Blockchain Training Alliance (BTA)

The two most prominent blockchain vender certifications are from R3 Corda and the Linux Foundation.

Lastly, it is also important to note that numerous colleges now offer blockchain certificates, albeit at a much higher cost and time investment.

## Blockchain Institute of Technology

The Blockchain Institute of Technology is a training and education provider in blockchain technology and cryptocurrency. BIT partners with organizations and individuals to address their unique needs, providing training and education options that help professionals reach their goals.

The Blockchain Institute of Technology has historically been focused on training enterprises for cryptocurrency adoption and for two industry-pioneering certifications.

◆ The Certified Blockchain Professional (CBCP) certification was designed for professionals currently working in blockchain, Bitcoin, and cryptocurrency roles. The certification serves candidates who want to understand and work with blockchain technologies, level up their professional skills, and certify their level of competency and expertise.

◆ The Certified Senior Blockchain Professional (CSBCP) is the highest level of blockchain business certification offered by the Blockchain Institute of Technology. The CSBCP certification is available only to current CBCP certificate holders who have developed senior levels of blockchain knowledge and professional expertise.

For more information on the Blockchain Institute of Technology certifications, visit: https://blockchaininstituteoftechnology.com/certifications

## Blockchain Council

The Blockchain Council is an online group of blockchain experts that have put together a wide portfolio of blockchain training and certifications. With more than 1,500 members, the Blockchain Council is a private de facto organization working individually and proliferating blockchain technology globally. With more than 20 online certifications, the Blockchain Council is the most prolific content creator.

I generally recommend the Blockchain Council because of the cost of its content and exams. Most online (nonproctored) exams cost $129. The certifications do not have the same level of enterprise acceptance as the Blockchain Institute of Technology or the Blockchain Training Alliance exams because the Blockchain Council exams are taken online without proctors. However, I recommend them because they are a valuable certification route for those on a limited budget.

The Blockchain Council certifications are much more technical than the exams from Blockchain Institute of Technology or the Blockchain Training Alliance.

The following certifications have the most acceptance in the industry:

◆ A Certified Blockchain Expert (CBE) is a technical professional who understands blockchain technology. They can build blockchain-based applications for businesses and have passed exhaustive training, as well as an exam-based blockchain certification aiming to impart in-depth practical knowledge in blockchain technology.

◆ A Certified Blockchain Architect (CBA) is a technical professional who understands blockchain projects and can guide them to fruition. They can also craft the guidelines and structure of the whole blockchain system, considering the requirement of the system.

◆ A Certified Blockchain Developer (CBD) is a technical professional who understands blockchain technology and can build blockchain-based applications for businesses. The CBD undergoes exhaustive training and must pass an exam-based program for blockchain developers.

For more information on their training and certification, visit `https://www.blockchain-council.org/blockchain-certification/`

## Blockchain Training Alliance

The Blockchain Training Alliance, an organization based out of Southern California, caters primarily to enterprise organizations. The BTA has a worldwide training network of training delivery partners.

The BTA has a small portfolio of certifications—five, at the time of writing. The following are the three most important BTA certifications:

◆ Certified Blockchain Business Foundations (CBBF) is geared toward nontechnical workers to demonstrate their knowledge and skills in the blockchain. The exam focuses on the use cases, high-level terminology, and blockchain basics and why an organization should or should not use blockchain.

◆ Certified Blockchain Solution Architect (CBSA) is a route for both technical and nontechnical audiences to demonstrate their knowledge and skills in the blockchain architecture. The exam focuses on architecting blockchain solutions, working with blockchain engineers and technical leaders, and choosing appropriate blockchain solutions.

◆ Certified Blockchain Developer – Ethereum (CBDE) is a route to demonstrate your knowledge and skills in the basic development of Ethereum blockchains. Unlike the CBBF and the CBSA, the CBDE exam is designed for more of a targeted audience that includes software engineers, programmers, developers, and application architects. The exam focuses on preparing production-ready applications for the Ethereum blockchain; writing, testing, and deploying secure Solidity smart contracts; and understanding and working with Ethereum.

The BTA exams are proctored at a Pearson testing center, and each exam costs $300, with the exception of the CBBF certification, which costs $250. Each exam asks 70 questions, requires a passing score of 70 percent, and allots candidates 90 minutes to complete.

For presales professionals, I recommend the Certified Blockchain Solutions Architect from the Blockchain Training Alliance. The main reason I recommend this certification is general content scope of the exam and how the exam validates basic blockchain fundamentals and blockchain architecture that are focused on presales engineering.

Hiring managers looking for a certified developer or architect should feel confident that the candidate actually passed the exam on merit and not an open book online.

For more information on the BTA's training and certification, visit `https://blockchaintrainingalliance.com/`.

### R3 CORDA

R3 Corda has its own developer certification, called the Corda Developer Certification Exam. This technical (and difficult) exam is administered a bit differently, as it uses an open-book format.

Being Corda Certified demonstrates that you have technical expertise in developing distributed Corda applications. Developers who take the exam are expected to have extensive knowledge of the Corda-related technical features and functions, such as states, contracts, transactions, flows, Corda nodes, and Corda networks. The exam contains 70 multiple choice questions and costs $150.

For more information on Corda training and certification, visit:

`https://corda-certification.myshopify.com/products/corda-standard-certification-test`

### THE LINUX FOUNDATION

The Linux Foundation has been well known for managing open source projects. It is also well known for its content and certification exams, and blockchain is no exception. It has a great certification that is technical and is hosted and valid by these leaders in open source training and certification.

The Linux Foundation's Certified Hyperledger Fabric Administrator (CHFA) is really the "star" of the Hyperledger certifications. The CHFA is a technical certification around Hyperledger Fabric. The exam challenges candidates to demonstrate their ability to build a secure Hyperledger Fabric network for commercial deployment, including the ability to install, configure, operate, manage, and troubleshoot the nodes on that network. This exam is an online, proctored, performance-based test that consists of a set of performance-based items and is different in the sense that there are actual problems to be solved at a command line. You cannot fake your knowledge on this easily. If your prospective hire has this certification, then you know they are very technically adept at Hyperledger Fabric.

For more information on the Linux Foundation's training and certification, visit:

`https://training.linuxfoundation.org/certification/certified-hyperledger-fabric-administrator-chfa/`

## Summary

Whether you're an enterprise architect, a solutions engineer, or a marketing specialist, there are opportunities for you to update your career skills or employment situation. Obtaining blockchain knowledge is becoming a requirement for a number of roles, as shown on LinkedIn.

The roles that are being advertised are ever-increasing with expanding blockchain companies but also IT vendors, VARS, and consulting organizations. Blockchain is clearly a growing market that is providing more organizations as well as IT professionals great career opportunities.

The adoption of blockchain technologies is expanding, What was once thought unrealistic could very well be attainable from a technological perspective for emerging technologies such as Hashgraph or DAGS. The ever-increasing number of emerging technologies are also providing blockchain opportunities.

Numerous blockchain certifications are available. Obtaining a certification should provide some career recognition or even new opportunities for a sales-driven engineering professional.

I certainly hope you can take full advantage of the market and career opportunities that abound.

# Index

51 percent attacks, 335–336

## A

acceptance drivers, 352–353
ACLs (access control lists), 40–41
acyclic (DAGs), 132
administrator, 140
adoption challenges, 159
algorithms, consensus algorithm, 20
AMI (Amazon Machine Image), 200–201
AML (anti-money-laundering), 258
AMQP (Advanced Message Queuing
  Protocol), 46, 47
AP (available and partition tolerant), CAP
  theorem, 12
append, 15
application architecture
  domain, TOGAF, 82
architects, 140
  presales engineer, 140
  solutions architect, 140
attacks
  51 percent attacks, 335–336
  DDOS (distributed denial-of-service)
    attacks, 336–337
  eclipse attacks, 337
  hijacking attacks, 337
  insider attacks, 338
  phishing attacks, 336
  reply attacks, 338
  routing attacks, 339
  sybil attacks, 339
authentication
  CIA triad, 324
  two-factor, 332

authenticity, 16
availability
  CAP theorem, 12
  design for, 87
AWS (Amazon Web Services), 187. *See also*
  AWS Managed Blockchain; AWS
  Management Console
  availability zones, 189–191
  Blockchain templates (*See* Blockchain
    templates)
  CloudFormation, 190–191
  EC2 (Elastic Compute Cloud), 199–207
  Hyperledger CloudFormation
    template, 191–221
  IAM (Identity and Access
    Management), 208–216
  regions, 189–191
  security groups, 195–199
  VPC subnet, 192–194
AWS Managed Blockchain, 187
  chaincode, 230–231
  channels, 230–231
  deploying, 221–231
  network, 222–230
  templates, 188
AWS Management Console, 192–194

## B

B2B (business to business), 163
B2C (business to consumer), 163
BaaS (blockchain as a service), 6, 90, 151
  AWS and, 187–231
  overview, 183–187
Basel II, 262
best practices

funding, 166–173

fundraising, use cases, 255

# G

G2B (government to business), 163

G2C (government to consumer), 163

Ganache, 300–301

gas (Ethereum), 287–288

gateways, 321

GCR (governance, compliance, risk), 257–258

    compliance benefits, 258

    compliance requirements, 261–265

    financial sector, 271–275

    KYC compliance, 265–271

    regulatory requirements, 259 261

    smart contracts, 271–275

GDPR (Global Data Protection Regulation), 71, 89–90, 258, 263

genesis block, 79

Geth, 67, 291

Gilbert, Seth, 12

Go-Ethereum (Geth), 61, 284

governance, 257–258

government use cases

    Dubai, 252

    Georgia (country), 252–253

Gramm-Leach-Bliley Act, 264

GRC (Governance, Risk, Compliance), 71

greenhouse strategy, 32, 33

GSA (General Services Agency), 145

Guthrie, Brett, 5

# H

hash pointers, 78

hashes, 78

hashing functions, 328, 329–330

hashing lists, 78

    genesis block, 79

health care privacy, 96–97

healthcare use cases, 253–254

high-level best practices, 325

hijacking attacks, 337

HIPPA (Health Insurance Portability and Accountability Act), 96, 258, 264–265

Howey test, 249, 259–260

HSM (Hardware Security Module), 92

HTLC (hash timed locks), 321

hybrid blockchain, 26–27

hybrid cloud, 22

hybrid enterprise blockchains, 30–31

Hyperledger, 31–32, 303–310

    Blockchain Platform Extension, 304–305

    blockchains in, 34

    chaincode, 303–304

    client applications, 306–307

    CloudFormation template, 191–221

    Composer, 307–308

        modeling language, 308

        Playground, 309–310

        resources, 308–309

    frameworks, 32

    greenhouse strategy, 32, 33

    release date, 8

    service discovery, 307

Hyperledger Burrow, 35

Hyperledger Composer, 41–42

Hyperledger Fabric, 30, 34, 35, 90–91

    business networks, 40–41

    chaincode, 41

    consensus, 38, 305

    consortium for international trade scenario, 97–98

    database options, 305–306

    databases, 95–96

    definitions, 37

    design, 91

    development tools, 41–42